D0195105

KATHLEEN TURNER

············ ON ACTING ············

CONVERSATIONS ABOUT FILM, TELEVISION, AND THEATER

by

KATHLEEN TURNER
& DUSTIN MORROW

Illustrations by
KACEY MORROW

Skyhorse Publishing

Skyhorse Publishing books may be purchased in bulk at special discounts for sales promotion, corporate gifts, fund-raising, or educational purposes. Special editions can also be created to specifications. For details, contact the Special Sales Department, Skyhorse Publishing, 307 West 36th Street, 11th Floor, New York, NY 10018 or info@ skyhorsepublishing.com.

Skyhorse® and Skyhorse Publishing® are registered trademarks of Skyhorse Publishing, Inc.®, a Delaware corporation.

Visit our website at www.skyhorsepublishing.com.

10 9 8 7 6 5 4 3 2 1

Library of Congress Cataloging-in-Publication Data is available on file.

Cover design by Brian Peterson
Cover photo by Carol Rosegg

ISBN: 978-1-5107-3547-7
Ebook ISBN: 978-1-5107-3548-4

Printed in The United States of America

33614080732513

CONTENTS

FOREWORD

When you meet Kathleen Turner in person, you notice her eyes first. They are piercing and deep, deep ocean blue. Sparkling, in fact. She's far more beautiful in person than she appears on the screen, which is saying something. And it's a beauty supported by a strong sense of self and a defined, palpable confidence. She's supremely confident, in fact, but somehow her confidence isn't off-putting. It's magnetic—it draws you to her. It's the difference between cockiness and charisma.

Kathleen Turner rocketed to stardom in 1981 with the release of the classic film noir *Body Heat*, a role that inspired in the press uncountable comparisons to Lauren Bacall. That film began a decade of box office dominance for Kathleen. The success of her films made her the top-grossing actress of the decade, through such monster hits as *Prizzi's Honor, Peggy Sue Got Married, The Accidental Tourist, The War of the Roses, Who Framed Roger Rabbit,* and the blockbuster *Romancing the Stone* and its sequel, *The Jewel of the Nile.* After some time away from cinema, during which she became one of the grande dames of the American theater, she returned to roles on film and TV with the indie comedies *The Perfect Family* and *Another Kind of Wedding,* the big-budget comedy *Dumb and Dumber To,* and the acclaimed Hulu series *The Path.*

In 1985, Kathleen won the Best Actress Golden Globe for *Romancing the Stone.* One year later, she won the award again for *Prizzi's Honor,* making her one of the only actors in history to win back-to-back Golden Globes. She's also picked up a Grammy and awards from film critics' societies, and has been nominated for Drama Desk Awards, Drama League Awards, Tony Awards and an Oscar. Among her leading men have been Jack Nicholson, Steve Martin, William Hurt, Sting, Gabriel Byrne, Dennis Quaid, Christopher Reeve, Nicholas Cage, Jude Law, Bill Irwin, and her partner in three films, Michael Douglas.

Arguably the biggest cinematic sex symbol of the last three-plus decades, she has inspired songs like the Austrian pop singer Falco's "The Kiss of Kathleen Turner," and even an entire band, the legendary Toronto punk rockers Kathleen Turner Overdrive. Such cultural tributes elevated Kathleen from the status of respected actor to an enduring iconic role as a larger-than-life stage and film star on the order of Ingrid Bergman, Audrey Hepburn, and Barbara Stanwyck. In some scholarly writing, she's been examined as the last great movie star, in the classic Hollywood conception of the term.

In the Nineties, while still taking the occasional lead role in some acclaimed independent films like the cult classics *Serial Mom* and *The Virgin Suicides*, Kathleen largely turned her attention to her first love, the stage. She has played the lead in a number of the most successful and well-regarded Broadway productions of the last few decades, including Jean Cocteau's *Indiscretions*, Tennessee Williams' *Cat on a Hot Tin Roof*, and Edward Albee's *Who's Afraid of Virginia Woolf?* She originated the roles of Mrs. Robinson in the stage version of *The Graduate*, and Tallulah Bankhead in Sandra Ryan Heyward's celebrated one-woman show, *Tallulah*.

In the 2000s, Kathleen continued her great work in the theater while adding television to her resume. She's had memorable guest spots on *The Simpsons*, *King of the Hill*, *Law and Order*, *Nip/Tuck*, and in her recurring, scene-stealing roles as Chandler Bing's transvestite father on *Friends* and as the feisty, man-eating Hollywood agent Sue Collini on *Californication*.

A lifelong advocate of causes championing freedom of speech, and the rights of women and children, Kathleen generously gives her time to such organizations as People for the American Way, Planned Parenthood, Amnesty International, and Citymeals-on-Wheels, for which she has personally delivered meals to elderly people who aren't able to leave their homes. In recent years, she has become a champion of new playwrights and their work, including Margaret and Allison Engel's *Red Hot Patriot* and Matthew Lombardo's controversial play *High*, which Kathleen took to Broadway in 2011 and on a national tour in 2012.

Not content to coast on her fame or her prior successes, Kathleen is always in search of new challenges as an actor and an artist. She recently starred in her first musical, *Mother Courage and Her Children*, and is preparing her own cabaret show. She's earned her status as one of the finest actors the stage and the screen have known, and she continues with each passing year to do bold, daring, risk-taking work.

Kathleen has been interviewed thousands of times throughout her career. I did not want this book to be just another interview. I wanted it to be a conversation. I wanted to speak *with* Kathleen, not to ask Kathleen to speak *at* me. This approach stemmed from my experience as a university professor. The most rewarding courses I've taught have always been the ones where I conversed with the students, where I asked questions of them and they asked questions of me. We explored the course subjects together. I may have guided the conversations, but the students had every opportunity to inform the content and participate in the learning process. And we learned together. I will take that approach over my lecturing at a group of blank faces any day.

The conversational format of this book was also informed by what I knew of Kathleen before beginning the process of speaking with her. While she's perfectly comfortable being interviewed by the press about her plays and her films and her activism, she's less comfortable talking at length about her craft. Her approach to acting, as she stated at multiple points in our conversations, is to stop talking about it and to just do it. The name of the course she's taught at New York University is "Practical Acting: Shut Up and Do It!" So a formally structured interviewing approach would never have achieved the results that we got through having more naturally flowing, give-and-take conversations. My experience working in documentary filmmaking has taught me that a conversational approach will relax the subject in ways that formal interviewing will not. I also anticipated that Kathleen, like most actors, would be a born collaborator, and that an in-depth exploration of her craft would emerge through her collaboration with me. She needs a sounding board, someone to bounce ideas off of. She doesn't like to work in a bubble.

Thankfully, the conversational approach worked like a charm, and the depth of ideas we were able to explore during our talks was inspiring. I did not know Kathleen well before the inception of this book, but by an hour into the first conversation, she felt like an old friend. And I think that's reflected in the text, as we were able to fully plumb the depths of Kathleen's theories about her craft and its place in her life.

It may not seem like it, but this book took several years to write. I didn't anticipate that it would take so long, as it's a book built around conversation. But no one speaks like we speak in this book. Real conversation is full of sentence fragments, clumsy grammar, half-formed ideas, awkward interruptions, inquiries that lead nowhere, and lost trains of thought. If you read the transcripts for the conversations in this book, you'd see all of that. Which meant that I had to rewrite everything we said so that it made some sense and wasn't a challenge to read. I tried to retain the cadences and rhythms and choice of language inherent in the way that Kathleen speaks and the way that I speak. If I have erred on occasion, I hope Kathleen and the readers of this text can forgive me.

Near the end of this book, you will find a series of short essays that dig a little deeper into specific scenes from Kathleen's films, scenes in which I felt that Kathleen was doing particularly interesting work as an actor. The conception of these essays again came from my experience as a professor of film, running scenes over and over in classes, discussing with my students the choices made by the actors, even on the seemingly smallest levels—a gesture, a pronunciation, a single breath. These short analytical essays will give the readers of this book the opportunity to examine the craft of acting in closer detail. For each film, I've selected a single scene and noted the point in the film in which the scene begins, so that you might cue it up on your DVD, computer, or streaming service at home. I hope that, like Kathleen's discussion of her craft and her advice for young actors, these essays will be of use to students of acting and actors who are still developing their craft, and will be interesting to aficionados of theater and the performing arts.

The epic conversation that forms the bulk of the book was actually composed of a series of many separate, shorter discussions. As Kathleen told me at the beginning of the project, "I can only sit still and talk about myself for so long before I just can't do it anymore." I reworked and restructured the conversations so that they would flow together as one long cohesive piece, which I felt made for a better book. We conducted these conversations in Kathleen's apartment. Here's a fun bit of behind-the-scenes for you: because of my violent allergy to cats, I had to load up on antihistamines before going into Kathleen's place. And as they do with most people, antihistamines make me very sleepy. So I would also chug a good deal of very strong coffee. Amuse yourself for a moment with the image of your mild-mannered author sitting at a table with Kathleen Turner, simultaneously wired on caffeine and zonked out on diphenhydramine. A chemical war was waged inside my head—I could have been a science experiment. So if you find any of my comments or questions to be eccentric, well, let's just blame it on the medicine and the java.

This book will exclusively be an exploration of the craft of acting. We discuss actors' relationships with the artists with whom they most frequently collaborate, like writers and directors. And we examine the many ways in which acting and performance extend into everyday life. But the book is not a tell-all memoir, as Kathleen has already written that book. It is called *Send Yourself Roses: Thoughts on My Life, Love, and Leading Roles*. It was written by Kathleen in collaboration with Gloria Feldt. I highly recommend it.

I've been directing actors in films for many, many years. Before I began meeting with Kathleen, I thought that I basically knew what there was to know about working with actors. Was I ever wrong. In the process of writing this book, I feel I have taken an epic and intense one-on-one master class in acting from the best teacher imaginable. I hope that acting and directing students of every age, established actors and directors, filmmakers and theater pros and artists of every stripe, and Kathleen's many adoring fans will all find much to love and learn from in this book. From the first conversation to the final proof of the manuscript, it was an absolute pleasure to work on. Thank you for reading.

—**Prof. Dustin Morrow**

THE CONVERSATIONS

•••••••••••••••••••••••••

WORKING WITH THE SCRIPT

DUSTIN MORROW Let's start with where the actor's job begins.

KATHLEEN TURNER It begins the moment I accept the role. From the moment I sign the contract to do the part, I'm into it. Give me the script and let's go.

D.M. I imagine that when you first get a script, you are reading it primarily to get a sense of the narrative and you are reading it for the role for which you are being considered.

K.T. Both, and simultaneously. Obviously I am aware of and sensitive to the role that is being offered to me, but ultimately the quality of that role doesn't really matter if the plot isn't strong. Sometimes I'm offered very flashy roles, roles that could really facilitate pyrotechnical displays of acting, but the stories surrounding those roles don't hold up. If the film is no good, or the play is no good, I don't really see the point. The role has to serve the play, and the play has to serve the role.

Another thing to consider is the tone and tenor of the script. The role might be great, and the story might be strong, but there must be a sense that the story is being told in the right way. Not long ago I was reviewing a script about a family with a mother dying of cancer, and the central question of the script—whether or not to allow the mother to pass away once that became an option—was a compelling one. But the tone was all wrong, it couldn't make up its mind whether to be arch and flip, or to make this dilemma a true crisis, a true moral issue. It stayed away from both. It didn't play it lightly enough and it didn't play it heavily enough. It was too wishy-washy, which is unfortunate, because there was otherwise

1

some good writing there. But if you're going to tackle that kind of material, I think you better have a point of view.

D.M. So when you're on the fence about taking a role, what's the deciding factor for you? Is it meeting the writer and seeing whether he or she is open to experimenting with the tone of the script?

K.T. The next step would probably be meeting the writer *and* the director. On *High*, for example, the director and writer came together in the same package. They collaborated on the Tallulah Bankhead play, *Looped*, and they had a good partnership. So meeting one was meeting the other. But they're very, very different men, and I was impressed by their willingness to listen to each other, to consider each other's viewpoints, as well as their energy, their intelligence, and their commitment to the work. All of those things were decisive factors in committing to it. When I saw how they worked with each other, I knew that I could work with them, individually and together.

D.M. So once you've committed to doing a play, you begin the process of taking it apart, of breaking it down and beginning to understand it.

K.T. It all begins with the words. The words that a character uses give you an idea of the energy and the kind of mind that this person possesses. If her speech is multisyllabic, that's a cold rhythm. Short, choppy words probably indicate that the character is a fast thinker and a decisive person. If the character uses a lot of words with softer sounds, with M's or V's, as opposed to T's or D's or P's, that's also an indication of her personality. The latter is much more explosive and hard-edged than the former, and that gives me an immediate indication of the rhythm of the character.

And of course, it's a collaborative art, and immediately upon taking a role I like to start digging into the script with the director. I don't like to do a lot of work on my own, even on a one-woman show. Actors need sounding boards. I don't sit around and decide how I'm going to do something by myself. That's acting to a mirror. That's not even acting, that's pretending. So I really feel that I need the other cast members and, minimally, the director.

D.M. But there are a lot of actors that work like that, aren't there? It seems that many actors actually can get a little too internal.

K.T. Well, much of what I do comes from age and experience. Someone who is younger or less experienced might be more likely to, perhaps, try and show up off-book. They might try to have everything figured out on day one of rehearsal.

D.M. "Off-book"—meaning they have all their lines memorized on day one.

K.T. Right. And it's a mistake. Going off-book shouldn't be forced, it's something that an actor should do on her own, as part of a natural process of getting to know the character and the script. Going off-book immediately is really jumping the gun. I don't think you should be off-book until you have a sense of the play as a whole. Once you have a clear progression of the ideas and emotions in the play and your character, then the lines become extremely easy to memorize because there's a *reason* to memorize them.

You can memorize, for example, lines that demonstrate that a character is feeling disillusioned or vulnerable, but until you identify *why* that person feels disillusioned and vulnerable at that point in the development of the character, the memorization is hollow. Just sitting down and memorizing words, without knowing the "why," is possibly counter-productive. It might get in the way of really being able to allow the words and emotions and thoughts to come together cohesively.

D.M. Are you an actor that marks her script up?

K.T. One of the first things I do with a script, and this has understandably gotten me into trouble with a few playwrights, is take a black magic marker and line out all the stage directions. I prefer to find the movement in the character, so it feels real and true, rather than have my movements dictated to me by the text.

D.M. Interesting. It makes sense—too much stage direction can actually be limiting. It's like the writer is trying to direct from the page. It's definitely bad form in screenwriting.

K.T. During rehearsals for *Who's Afraid of Virginia Woolf*, Edward Albee looked over my shoulder one day and saw that I did that and boy, was he was not happy. He said, "What if I want you to do some of that stuff?" I said, "Edward, if you see something I'm doing in rehearsal that you don't like, let me know and we will go back to your original stage direction." He harrumphed—he was a master harrumpher—but he agreed and it worked out fine. He was not big on compromise, though.

D.M. So what do your scripts look like by the time the show goes up?

K.T. Pretty detailed. As we rehearse, I mark them for blocking and technical purposes. Once you get on your feet and start to move around the stage, you need notes. But I don't mark them for sound or feeling. To me, that's inherent in the line, because it isn't just a question of finding the most pleasing sound, it's also finding the sound that conveys the idea best. And that, to me, has always been very clear in a well-written script.

Having said that, I will sometimes mark my script when I'm given notes by a director. I'll mark the opposite page, usually with a keyword that represents what the director wants me to convey, so that on the subsequent pass through the script I will be reminded of what he or she wants me to try for. But I only tend to need that keyword once, if at all, before I've got it. So generally, my scripts are pretty clean.

The play is a complete story to me. The whole thing is in my head. A lot of my directors have said, when they've given me notes, "Don't you want to write this down?" And I just say, "Don't worry, I never forget a note." And I don't. I know a lot of actors need to constantly be scribbling things down, but I'm just not one of them. Again, much of that might have come from time and experience.

D.M. Are you an actor that likes a lot of language? Or would you prefer to play something with less dialogue?

K.T. Most of my work is pretty physical, really. My characters always seem to have a certain amount of physicality, no matter what they're doing. I'm not good at just sitting still.

She's not kidding. In my conversations with Kathleen, she was often moving around in her chair, or making dramatic gestures to emphasize certain points. Not fidgeting, but moving, in a sort of natural performance. To me, this is easy evidence of a true storyteller—someone for whom the capacity and the desire to tell stories is deeply ingrained, as if the story was bursting to get out of her. I saw a lot of this in my extensive work in recording oral storytelling in Ireland. The Irish have a long tradition of storytelling that comes from someplace deep inside—there's nothing anecdotal about their stories. They recognize that every story has the potential to move an audience, to frighten them or make them laugh or make them think. Having seen this onstage (evident especially in plays like High *and* Red Hot Patriot, *where she directly addresses the audience), I knew Kathleen could do this, but I didn't expect to see it in such force in a one-on-one setting. All of which is to say, the woman is a storyteller of uncommon passion.*

I have, on occasion, worked toward that stillness as a challenge. When I was doing Mrs. Robinson in *The Graduate*, I concentrated very hard on absolute minimalist movement, to have her be as still as possible. Part of the thinking there was that she is almost always a little drunk. Most of the play is set in the evening, so by the time you see her she's been drinking for several hours, and she's extremely careful about her diction and how she walks and sits, because she's scared of messing up. She's conscious of not giving herself away. So she doesn't make any sudden gestures for fear of toppling over. But most of my characters tend to end up on the floor, or thrown over something. It's fun.

D.M. With Martha, there is so much *rich* language there, but at the same time, you made her a really physical character.

Martha is Kathleen's character in Who's Afraid of Virginia Woolf, *which she played to great acclaim in a blockbuster Broadway production costarring Bill Irwin. Set in one night, the play tells the story of Martha and George, a middle-aged couple who engage in a battle of psychological warfare as their marriage disintegrates. It was authored by the legendary, Pulitzer-winning playwright Edward Albee and first staged in 1962.*

K.T. Yes, well the opportunity was always there because she's a woman who has so few restraints on herself that she doesn't really care how she moves. Her natural freedom informed her extreme behavior in terms of movement. Flinging herself around physically is completely authentic to the character, and to her willingness to fling her emotions around. She's unhinged, so why wouldn't that be reflected physically as well?

D.M. So when you do something like *Indiscretions* where the narrative prohibits you, for at least a good chunk of the play, from being able to move around, is that really frustrating for you?

K.T. Yes, in some ways. That particular play came at the time of a real acute stage of my rheumatoid arthritis. The truth was, I was in terrible, terrible pain almost all the time. And one of the reasons I thought that I could handle that play was that, as a diabetic in the 1930s, the character was largely constrained to her bed.

Kathleen has been fighting rheumatoid arthritis since the mid-1990s. RA is an chronic inflammatory autoimmune disorder that causes painful swelling in the joints.

But the thing about rheumatoid arthritis is that it's not a type of pain that can be alleviated by staying in bed. RA can't be escaped because it lives in your joints. You can't sit down and kick up your feet and expect to feel better.

And of course as soon as we started rehearsal, I couldn't help myself anyway. I found myself flinging around, falling down around the bed. And of course the whole death scene, with the thrashing about the bed, was brutal. And there was that appalling staircase in the second act that made me cry every night. Truthfully. So that didn't work out quite as I had thought. I really sort of thought, "OK, I can handle it. A woman who is in bed most of the play—how bad could it be?"

D.M. Much worse than you thought.

K.T. So much worse than I thought.

D.M. When you learn your lines, do you learn them exactly or approximately? Or does it depend on the play?

K.T. I learn the *ideas* behind the lines first. When I learn the idea behind a line then the words usually follow naturally. If, for some reason, I consistently have a problem with recalling a line, one that's just not staying with me, then it's usually because there is something wrong with the line. If the line were tracking correctly, I wouldn't stumble on it over and over again. My memory is very sharp, I have absolutely no problem learning lines. And yes, especially with a play, I try very hard to be exact with the language, but if I'm consistently making a mistake on a line, it's because the line is problematic. Playwrights understand how well an actor gets to know her character during the process of developing it, so most of them would agree to that and would revise the line accordingly.

D.M. Wasn't Albee famous for the opposite—for never adjusting a line?

K.T. Famous!? My God—try *infamous*!

D.M. "You missed a comma, Kathleen!"

K.T. Totally. He came backstage once to tell me that I left out a "Ha!" in the middle of a speech. I said, "Don't worry, it'll be there tomorrow." He's tough.

D.M. He certainly protected his words.

K.T. As he should have. Those are the rights of the writer. If he chose that word, he chose it for a reason and no one has any right to change it.

D.M. But isn't theater really the actor's medium?

K.T. The actor's and the writer's.

D.M. I've always thought of the theater belonging to the actor, television belonging to the writer, and film belonging to the director. That's why I make films, I like to direct.

K.T. Theater is a forum where the writer can have a lot of power.

D.M. I wonder if that's why a lot of writers go into playwriting.

K.T. As opposed to screenwriting?

D.M. Yeah.

K.T. Well, screenwriting is definitely looser . . .

D.M. Often, in film, the writer isn't even allowed on the set.

K.T. Not always, no. But it is understood, for one thing, that you don't have anything like the rehearsal time you have in theater. And on a film set, you're getting script changes everyday due to shooting conditions, budget problems, production politics. Even though you only shoot a couple of pages a day, you shoot it so many times, from so many angles, that if you change a word in one angle, and that's the shot the director likes, then you have to repeat that change for every other angle, because they all have to match. Even when it's a mistake, when you didn't mean to change a word, you're stuck with it.

D.M. Do you enjoy doing improvisational work? I think it's a really useful part of the rehearsal process, but I wonder if it has a place in the actual performance in theater, as it does in many cases in TV and film.

K.T. I wouldn't do it in a performance on stage, that's not really fair to the other actors. Especially if they're not ready for it, or they don't do it as well, or they don't have as much confidence in their ability to go with it. But as a rehearsal tool, absolutely. It can be a great exercise in figuring out what a scene needs, or means. It allows you the opportunity to attack it from an angle that may not be on the page. That kind of improvisation can be very useful.

D.M. Can you give me an example of how you've used it on something you've done?

K.T. With *High*, in one of the scenes where the young addict comes in and first confronts my character, he has to challenge her authority. So we tried riffing on that idea, taking it to its furthest conclusion. He tried to push me into losing my temper, just disobeying outright anything that I asked him to do. And I attempted to exert my authority over him, to put him in his place. When we returned to the scene as written, the experience of that exercise enriched the text for us.

In Matthew Lombardo's edgy drama High, *Kathleen plays the tough-talking Sister Jamison Connelly, a nun and rehab counselor who meets her match in Cody Randall, a difficult, hostile young addict. As the two face off, Sister Connelly is forced to confront her own painful history with addiction and, more importantly, her faith. The play ran briefly on Broadway and then in an extensive national tour.*

D.M. Have you worked with performers who like throwing you curve balls and surprising you in that way? Have you ever had to deal with that?

K.T. During a performance? Well, a couple of times someone might have made a mistake, or lost their line.

D.M. Which is a different kind of curveball.

K.T. Right, that's not intentional. When you see that look of panic and dread come into the other actor's eye, you think, "Oh, here we go. . . ."

D.M. "Mayday, mayday . . ."

K.T. "Mayday, we're going down!" There were a couple of times during *Virginia Woolf* where Bill Irwin had trouble with this very long, convoluted speech. He was standing behind a sofa, and I was sitting on the sofa and I could see what the audience couldn't—his eyes getting really, really big. Saucers! And so I'd just sort of turn upstage and pretend to adjust my wardrobe or something, feed him the line, and then drop back into the scene.

D.M. Oh, nice! It has to be mortifying to forget a line onstage.

K.T. It happens to every actor. If you meet one who says it never happens to her, she's lying.

D.M. What do you do?

K.T. Well, usually you're able to get it back after a moment, or another cast member can feed you a bit. Where it's problematic is in one-woman shows.

D.M. Right, there's no other actor there to help you out. Where do you turn?

K.T. Well, it happened to me a couple times when I first started out with *Tallulah*. All I could do was look to the audience and say, "Forgive me. I don't know where I am. One moment, please." And then I'd step offstage, consult with the stage manager, and come back on and continue.

> *Tallulah is a one-woman show written by Sandra Ryan Heyward, about the legendary actress Tallulah Bankhead. Bankhead was a brilliant but troubled Broadway star, considered by some critics and scholars to be the greatest actress ever to work on the American stage.*

D.M. That sounds utterly terrifying.

K.T. It was. But it's not like I had a choice, and most audiences are actually quite forgiving. They're on your side.

D.M. In a way, it's kind of endearing.

K.T. I'm only human.

D.M. But as far as improvisation in performance goes . . .

K.T. I don't usually do it. For one thing, on stage, in a play, you really wouldn't mess around with the text. It's just not done, it would be a real betrayal of the process. You have to respect the script. And in film you don't experiment that much because it's too expensive. If it costs $120,000 an hour to keep the crew on-set and working, you can't waste that time without everybody getting pretty upset.

D.M. Unless you're Will Ferrell or Jim Carrey, and you're encouraged to improvise.

K.T. And you can't help it.

D.M. Right—those guys might not be able to turn it off without a lot of concentration.

K.T. I worked with Jim Carrey on *Dumb and Dumber To*, and the directors let us do some improvising. It's not really my thing, but I enjoyed it. He's clearly very good at it, and when you do it with him it elevates your game.

D.M. Let's chat for a bit about finding subtext in a script. Stanislavski said that plays are all about subtext, and that's what actors really like to play.

> *Constantin Stanislavski was a legendary Russian actor and theater director, who created the Stanislavski System, a school of acting based on the concept of using emotional memory in performance.*

K.T. Well, certainly there is an endless interior dialogue going on with what your character is actually feeling or thinking, stemming from the decisions she's making. As an actor, you're always asking, "Why do I respond to this character in this way?" and, "Why do I use these words?" "Why do I want to be here?" or, "Why am I with this person?" "What do I want from them?" "What do I want to *give* them?"

Answering those questions, shaping the character's inner dialogue, is a huge part of the process of finding a character. It may not have anything to do with the actual words that your character is saying, because it's *behind* what the character is saying, it's all the reason and the emotion. It's what you're trying to hide and what you're trying to show. That's the endless series of choices that you make as an actor every second that you're up on the stage. Sometimes it may almost seem as though the actual words, or the concrete action of a piece, are of secondary interest. The interior dialogue, the endless exploration of what truly informs the character—the development of that never stops for as long as you play a character. That's one of the genuinely fascinating aspects of this craft.

D.M. Do you discuss that interior dialogue with the director and other actors, or do you keep that to yourself?

K.T. I'll discuss some of it with them. But much of it has to stay secret.

D.M. Why is that?

K.T. Because some things are just for you, to build the character from the inside out. And if you share that stuff with your fellow actors, you have to realize you're also sharing it with their characters. And perhaps their characters shouldn't know everything that your character is thinking. Everyone has things they keep private, and the characters I play are no exception to that.

D.M. Many actors like to compose long, fictionalized backstories for their characters.

K.T. I don't generally do that. All the information I need is usually in the script. And if it's not, then the script isn't ready to be produced yet. For example, in *High*, we learn about my character that she's a nun, a rehab counselor, she's tough and yet vulnerable, she lived on the street for three and a half years, her sister was killed because of a man that she brought home while she was under the influence, and her family felt more shame than grief in her sister's death. All of these things tell the audience enough about the character's history in order to understand the character in the context of the story, and tell me all I need to know in order to play her. So do I need to sit down and fabricate details, like what kind of house she lived in when she grew up, or who her first boyfriend was? Absolutely not.

D.M. Well, I know that some writing and acting programs have student playwrights and actors do those sorts of things as exercises.

K.T. Well whoop-de-doo.

D.M. Ha! Have you ever had a director or a writer give you that kind of information, though? Give you something that's not in the script—come up to you and say, "This character was abused as a child." And all of a sudden you have to deal with that huge piece of information.

K.T. Not that I can remember. It certainly sounds like an "acting class" kind of thing, doesn't it?

D.M. Well, it's an exercise that I will use in teaching screenwriting sometimes, having students write biographies of their characters.

K.T. Well, it's a different kind of exercise for writers. As actors, we don't use that as much in the professional world.

D.M. So if you're starting to work on a character, are there set questions that you have to ask the character, to begin to figure her out?

K.T. It depends always on the script, on the material. That is, why should the questions be set? You can't ask the same questions of different characters. I suppose the only ones that are consistent are your basic "Why's." Why does she want what she wants? Why does she go about it this way? Why does this character function this way within the context of the narrative?

Those are questions you ask in partnership with the director and the writers. Ideally the three of you must agree on what the play is fundamentally about and work toward that. Me through my character, the writer through her dialogue, the director through her staging. It's a delicate partnership that requires a delicate balance.

D.M. It sounds like a lot of questions about motivation and intent.

K.T. I think so. But not everything is. Every moment of a piece isn't always, "Why would she say this?" Once you've established the parameters of how a characters walks and talks and reacts and feels, all the little idiosyncrasies of the character become natural, almost to the point where you don't have to heavily process them as an actor, and those things color the character in fascinating ways.

But not everything in a script is equally important. Some moments are crucial and some moments are there to color the narrative, to allow the story to build to the moments that really do matter. But it's less common in screenplays, where that material is the first thing to be cut.

D.M. That's the cutting room floor stuff.

K.T. If it even makes it that far! Much of the best stuff in a screenplay is cut before shooting even starts.

D.M. It's a shame, because those colorful details are often the best parts of a screenplay.

K.T. Indeed. And a couple of times it's been quite disappointing to me. Particularly with *V.I. Warshawski*. There were some really wonderful, lovely scenes between Warshawski and the young girl that she was protecting and trying to help. Ultimately, the editing was taken over by executives at the studio, and their perspective was, "If it doesn't have action in it, out it goes." And it was such a shame because there were some really beautiful moments shared between those two characters.

> *Kathleen played the title role in* V.I. Warshawski, *a detective film based on the bestselling novels by Sara Paretsky. The film was initially intended to start a franchise, but its critical and commercial failure halted any plans for the production of a sequel.*

D.M. That must be tough. I actually like that film, but it's a film that, when you're watching it, you can easily sense that there's stuff that's not there in the final cut, almost as if massive chunks of exposition and character development had been excised.

K.T. Definitely. And the cuts really changed the tone of the movie.

D.M. Tone is an interesting question for an actor. In both your theater and your film work, you've done work not just across multiple genres, but work that has had very different and specific tones, and I wonder about how that affects your digging into a performance, from the outset.

> *While Kathleen has acted on stage in everything from broad comedies to small, personal dramas, her film work has crossed even more genres, perhaps more so than any other actor of her generation. In just a few years time, she did film noir* (Body Heat), *slapstick comedy* (The Man With Two Brains), *action-adventure* (Romancing the Stone), *erotic thriller* (Crimes of Passion), *fantasy* (Peggy Sue Got Married), *melodrama* (Julia and Julia), *animated film* (Who Framed Roger Rabbit), *black comedy* (The War of the Roses), *detective* (V.I. Warshawski), *and camp* (Serial Mom).

Can you read a script and say, "Okay, this is a melodrama, and melodramatic acting is a specific style of acting and so I need to tap into a style of acting that is consistent with that tone"?

K.T. I suppose so. The tone should be apparent in the script and my job as an actor is to align the approach of my work to that of the script.

D.M. Right. For example, a John Waters movie has a very specific tone, so you can't show up on the set of *Serial Mom* and try to give a performance rooted in realism.

> *Serial Mom is a comedy, written and directed by master of camp John Waters, in which Kathleen plays the title role of a serial-murdering and yet wholesome and traditional homemaker. Like many of Waters films, it is considered a cult classic.*

K.T. Oh God, no! On the first page of that screenplay, in the very first scene, where the family is gathered around the breakfast table, it's clear what the tone of that film was to be.

D.M. I love that scene. When your character converses with the songbird out the window, that's pretty close to the funniest thing I've ever seen in a movie.

K.T. My daughter loves that scene, too. "Who-whee, who-whee."

D.M. Easily my favorite moment in one of my favorite movies. My girlfriend and I were watching that movie recently, and I told her, "I'm going to get that 'who-whee' as my ringtone." Hint, hint.

K.T. Ha! Well, you're going to have to record it off your TV speaker, mister, because you're not getting it from me.

D.M. It was worth a shot! Part of the brilliance of that scene is the way Waters shoots it—he cuts to that tight single of you and then to the bird and then back to another tight single—it's just beyond ludicrous.

K.T. His comic timing as a screenwriter and as a filmmaker is virtually flawless.

D.M. It seems true, in most cases, that an accomplished actor knows the character better than anybody else in the process, perhaps even better than the writer who created the character.

K.T. Without question. After a couple of months I would challenge anyone to know that character better than me. And that includes the director, definitely, and that includes even the writer. I have certainly said to writers, "She just wouldn't do that, she wouldn't use that word, she just wouldn't be able to do it that way," and I say it with the authority of someone who has gotten to know the character better than anyone else in the creative process.

Film is a bit different, because things change faster, and more frequently. Even if you're shooting in a controlled environment like a studio, things change everyday. The schedule changes, the script changes, personnel changes. Whereas, ideally, in a play, you work towards setting a piece so that you can get to a point where you can say, "Okay, these are the final choices of words and actions and movement and blocking." And by that point, no one knows more about the character than me.

D.M. I hope writers and directors generally acknowledge that.

K.T. Usually they do.

D.M. But there must be some butting heads and "creative differences."

K.T. Of course there are, but not within the context of knowing the character. They simply haven't had the time with the character that I've had. You know, their focus is much wider. When I was directing *Crimes of the Heart*, I loved the idea that I could be so particular about everything—"That's the wrong color blue for that pillow"—as opposed to just focusing on my character. But I would never delve into any one of the six characters to the point that I would if I were playing them. My job as the director was to make sure that the characters and the actors complemented each other and supported each other as the story progressed.

DIRECTING YOURSELF

DUSTIN MORROW As a director who is first an actor, is that something that comes harder to you than someone who directs but has no history as an actor?

KATHLEEN TURNER That did worry me at first, years ago, when I was first directing little productions, that I would be very hard on my leading actors. And I did find myself, at first, watching their performances and literally thinking, "I would do it like this." But I got past all that and certainly by the time I directed *Crimes of the Heart*, I had four lovely women's roles and never felt tempted to act one of them, which is a relief.

D.M. How did that production come to you?

K.T. Roger Rees was the person to first pin me down and get me to commit to directing. He was the head of Williamstown at the time, and he was the one who finally locked me into doing it.

Roger Rees was the Tony-winning Welsh actor best known for his roles as Robin Concord on the series Cheers *and as Lord Marbury on* The West Wing. *He passed away in 2015 at the age of 71.*

Kathleen's production of Crimes of the Heart *received rave reviews, especially for its expert casting and nuanced performances. Many critics compared it to the 1986 film version favorably, noting the subtlety Kathleen found in the text that the film missed completely. Kathleen rarely directs, but is respected in theater circles for her capacity to bring the best out of her actors.*

D.M. It must be valuable for actors to have experience as directors.

K.T. Definitely, especially since you occasionally have to work with directors that don't know how to direct actors, in which case you have to direct yourself. Any actor who has worked as long as I have and has paid even the slightest bit of attention to what's going on around them has hopefully learned how all the elements of a working production come together. I think every good actor with a healthy track record has in them the capacity to direct. The question is whether they have the drive, the energy and tenacity to do it.

D.M. It had to have been difficult to direct yourself in the lead role in *The Killing of Sister George* because that's a demanding play.

The Killing of Sister George is a dark comedy about a cigar-chomping, hard-drinking radio actress who is nothing like the sweet character she plays on her show. It was first staged in 1965 and was adapted into a film directed by Robert Aldrich in 1968.

K.T. It was tricky. I didn't like it at all. It's a distinct challenge, wearing those two hats at the same time. To be in character and giving a performance is to be fully engaged with that character, their thoughts and motivations. So to have to be in that headspace and at the same time looking at the entire production, especially the work that the other actors are doing, is really tricky. It's almost like trying to be in two places at the same time. Some actors can do both jobs very well. I have a new respect for actors who direct themselves having now done it and felt how challenging it is.

D.M. What drew you to *The Killing of Sister George*?

K.T. I've always loved radio dramas. I've done a few of them—A Christmas Carol, a couple V.I. Warshawski mysteries, and a few other projects. And I've always been particularly drawn to the radio dramas done by the BBC. The BBC has a wonderful tradition of doing these long-running dramas that are ostensibly soap operas on the air. We haven't really had as much of that in the United States.

The Killing of Sister George is a wonderful play that is very British. The daughter of Frank Marcus, the man who wrote the play, generously allowed us to have some minor rewrites done so that the text could be structured in such a way that American audiences could understand it and relate to it.

D.M. You knew going into that production that you were going to act and direct as well.

K.T. Yes, I did. You know me—I love a challenge. I thought I could do it, I was very arrogant. It turned out to be just too big a production to have the lead actor also be the director. It definitely humbled me.

D.M. So how does that process work? How are you able to be in character and also outside the stage looking down on the entire production?

K.T. At the end of the day, you can't. That's not really how it works, not for me anyway. I truly love the process of directing and I got really caught up in it. I was working on the lights, the costumes, the set, and I got three weeks into a four-week rehearsal period and realized that I hadn't done any work on my character. So I went to my actors at the beginning of that last week and told them that the entire week had to be about Sister George. I was to do nothing but work on my character that week. The whole thing just got away from me, and the production suffered for it.

D.M. Have you worked with actors who've also directed the production before?

K.T. In film, but that's different.

D.M. Right, you worked with Danny DeVito as he directed himself in *The War of the Roses*.

K.T. Yes, but that was a different process entirely. Film is very different in that you can play the scene as an actor and then step back and view the playback as a director. It's much easier to fulfill both roles at the same time. Plus, Danny was playing a supporting role in that film.

D.M. Right, and the next time you directed yourself, in the play *Would You Still Love Me If . . .* , you played a supporting role.

K.T. Yes, although that wasn't by design. I was sort of cornered into it. I thought I was going to have a nice, easy fall by taking a smaller supporting role in a small production that I felt was worthy of my name and assistance. But of course that's not the way it worked out.

D.M. How did you end up directing?

K.T. After the first week's rehearsals it became immediately clear to everyone that the cast and the director had creative differences that were so pronounced that they would negatively impact the play. The producers asked me to step in as the director and the cast supported that decision, so I thought about it for a while and reluctantly decided to do it because I felt the play deserved to be seen.

> Would You Still Love Me If. . . , *by John S. Anastasi, is about two women whose relationship is strained by the revelation that one of them wishes to undergo gender reassignment surgery. Kathleen plays the woman's mother. The play opened off-Broadway in 2015 to mixed reviews.*

D.M. And it was the message of the play that drew you to it.

K.T. And the writing, and that my character, although a supporting one, was very interesting. This was a few years ago when very few people in American theater were mounting productions that seriously addressed issues confronting transgender people and their families. Not that there are a ton of those now, but there were particularly very few then and I felt that these issues were important that they should be addressed in the arts. I thought that the play, while not a perfect text, deserved an audience.

The play is very much about love. It's about two women in a happy and fulfilling lesbian relationship. One of the women decides that she wants to transition to the male gender, but the other woman is queer and does not want to be in a relationship with a man. The process of transitioning, the questions around it, threaten the core of their relationship. I played the mother of one of the women and the struggle my character faces as she comes to terms with this difficult idea is what attracted me to the role.

D.M. Was the process easier the second time because it was a supporting role?

K.T. There were issues with that production, so it wasn't easy as it turns out, but that aspect—acting and directing at the same time—was definitely easier.

D.M. What is the biggest challenge with directing and acting simultaneously?

K.T. The biggest issue with directing a play that you appear in is always going to be time. When you're the lead, you simply don't have the time to carry the play as an actor and steer the play as a director. I should never say never, but I suspect that I will probably never again direct a play in which I am also playing the lead role.

WORKING WITH DIRECTORS

DUSTIN MORROW The flip side of a question I asked earlier is, do you think it's valuable for directors to have some experience as actors?

KATHLEEN TURNER Well, I think that in some cases it could be dangerous, but generally I think it would be a very good thing. One semester at NYU I taught a course that was comprised of half actors and half directors, and we had the actors directing and the directors acting. And then the directors directed the actors after they had walked in their shoes, so to speak. And it was great. It was certainly humbling for the directors, because most of the actors turned out to be great directors, while the directors were all pretty crummy actors.

D.M. Interesting! Why do you think that turned out to be the case?

K.T. It just seems so often that actors don't know what the director is asking for, and they don't understand the limitations of that job, and the directors don't know what the actors need from them in order to construct a solid performance. So the actors need to understand why a director is asking for certain things or denying certain things, and directors need to understand, physically, what it is the actors are doing, that they're been given these strict blocking parameters and told to work within them. It's very valuable for directors to get a sense of the actors' needs. And it's valuable for a director to try to understand why the actor is making the choices he or she is making. Directors should talk to actors about what they did with their performances in a rehearsal or in a take before leaping to how they want to change them.

D.M. Is it better to have a director who really tightly controls your performance, or would you rather have one that gives you more leeway?

K.T. I prefer one that gives me a little more flexibility, because it allows me more room to explore. It's dangerous to have a director who has already decided how he wants a scene to play, as opposed to watching it with several different nuances and intentions and then choosing the path to follow. I want to be able to try it out many different ways before I actually have to choose one.

D.M. Where do you physically want a director to be while you're rehearsing?

K.T. Where the audience is going to be.

D.M. How about while you're shooting a film?

K.T. Back at the monitor. You don't want your attention split from the camera. There's already the cameraman, the focus puller, and some-times the cinematographer standing there, and you really don't want anybody else in your line of vision. I'd rather just have the camera to work with, when possible. I like the director back by the monitor, and all he really *has* to see, ultimately, is what that camera is seeing. So I would think that would be easier for her than watching the scene from a broader viewpoint up by the camera, where she is aware of the whole room and the conditions in which the film is being shot. But in theater, I'd rather the director just sit in the audience.

D.M. Is there an ideal place in the theater to be, though? Where do you sit when you are directing?

K.T. I sit in the center, close to the front, a couple of rows back. I want to be able to see the actors' eyes and grasp all the small nuances of their performances. That gets tougher to do the further from the stage you sit.

D.M. But that variety of perspectives in live theater seems like one of the trickiest things about it. With film, the screen is the screen—you can sit in the front row and have to crane your neck, and that can certainly color your interpretation of a film, but generally most people are going to con-sume a film the same way, with the same perspective.

K.T. It is different in theater, certainly. Some people get different angles, different viewpoints and for that reason must have slightly differ-ent interpretations of the performances. So during rehearsal the director moves around the house to be sure that everything is playing well from side to side and front to back. But I don't think it really bothers the actors, or at least it doesn't bother me, if the director is right there in front.

D.M. I know that you have worked with directors that are all technical, that know everything there is to know about lenses and cameras or staging and lights, but probably aren't able to give you much else.

K.T. Oh yeah, of course. More so in film than theater, but yeah. And because of that I would urge every actor to learn how to direct themselves. Really, truly. There were so many directors, especially young directors coming out of a certain time, in the 1980s, that emerged from Southern California film schools, that knew every lens and every technical process. And then they'd say to the actor, "Well, now you, um, you just do what you do." And you're like, *"Um, okay, thanks a lot!"* They were lost. Hopeless. There were times I was so tempted to respond, "And what exactly is it that *you'd* like me to do?" But, ultimately that wouldn't help the film, so I could never do that.

D.M. It wouldn't be real politically savvy, either.

K.T. Certainly not. But luckily, there are no politics in Hollywood. Ha! The problem with those directors, from an actor's standpoint, is that the performances in the film could be wildly uneven, because some actors have the toolkit to direct themselves and others do not. So you'll get an actor who knows exactly what he wants to do and you'll get somebody who isn't so sure. And that imbalance will come through, regardless of the storyline, and it'll end up that one actor's choices will dominate the other's.

D.M. At the other end of that spectrum, can you make use of really abstract direction?

K.T. Oh yeah, absolutely, especially if you know what you want to do. The only time that abstraction becomes an issue is if it emerges from a lack of confidence on the director's part. When you get an insecure or uncertain director, one who has trouble expressing herself to actors, then what very often happens is that the lead actor will sort of step in as director and start making suggestions to the other actors about how to play scenes. I speak from experience, I've had to do it. It's either that, or the piece suffers.

Every young, developing actor should know this—that every actor has to be able to direct herself. Hopefully, you won't have to, and you really do *need* a director as a sounding board, at the very least, but you also need to know how to resolve your own uncertainties. When you are faced with, "I don't know which choice is better, they both work, and I have to choose the one that's best for the play or the film," hopefully the director will be able to help you, but you can't always depend on it.

D.M. Speaking of abstraction, one of my actor friends once told me that a director stopped a rehearsal once to tell his actors that he wanted more "orange."

K.T. Yikes! Those are the directors you want to shoot.

D.M. Have you ever been subjected to something like that?

K.T. Not that I can remember, but then my reputation might protect me from that kind of nonsense. I'm not famous for suffering fools gladly.

D.M. That's understating it.

K.T. Ha! Well, what I have seen, and this makes me incredibly furious, are directors—and I hate to say this, but they are *always* men—who think that they can manipulate your acting on a personal level. For example, I had this director *boast* to me that he got this extraordinary performance out of this young actress because he had an affair with her and the night before the scene where her character was to be devastated by being left—he actually broke up with her! He was bragging that he got this wonderful performance out of her, this real heartbreak. I said, "Well, we won't be working together, then." How *dare* he screw with somebody's mind and heart like that, to get his so-called "perfect performance," and think that that's good directing?

D.M. Some film directors are famous for messing with their actors. Alfred Hitchcock, Werner Herzog . . .

K.T. It's appalling.

D.M. That makes me think of a story, it's nowhere near as awful as your example, obviously, but I did hear you once talk about a day that John Huston wore you out and ground you down all day on *Prizzi's Honor* and then at the end of the day, when you were practically in tears, said, "Now she's ready for the scene."

Prizzi's Honor is a dark comedy in which Kathleen and Jack Nicholson play mafia contract killers who fall in love. In the film's third act, Jack accepts a contract on his spouse, leading to Nicholson's classic lines "Do I marry her? Do I ice her? Which one of these?". The film was a huge hit and was nominated for several major Oscars, winning Best Supporting Actress for the director's daughter, Anjelica Huston. Kathleen won Best Actress at the Golden Globes.

K.T. That's entirely true. He said it to his cameramen, and he knew I heard him say it.

D.M. Very sensitive.

K.T. Yeah, it made me so angry at the time. But to his credit, I was very good in that scene. And it wasn't really personal. It wasn't the same sort of thing as the example I just gave.

We were, all of us—the actors, the crew, the hot lights and camera gear, packed into this very tiny room. It was very warm and stuffy and congested and uncomfortable. We'd do take after take after take and Huston just wasn't happy. He'd constantly reset the camera, which meant re-blocking the actors and moving all the lights, and it took all day. So, really, it was just the *frustration* of hours and hours and hours of stopping and starting on this scene, which was a huge scene for me. It was a terribly important scene, a scene that meant a lot to me. And the frustration just built and built until I was ready to snap, so to have him say what he said after I broke down in tears, it was tough for me to hear.

D.M. That kind of manipulation just seems to demonstrate a disrespect for the profession, because it implies that the actor can't do the job without the director bringing in something that's external and that has nothing to do with doing the job.

K.T. Right, I agree, in relation to the example I gave about the break-up. But the case with Huston was somewhat different, because he genuinely wasn't pleased with where the scene was, and while he may not have exercised the best judgment that day, he also pushed me as any great director might.

I did the first take on one scene and he came over to me and he said, "No, no. I need you to out-Sicilian the Sicilian." And I went, "All right, I think I can do that." And we did take two, and he came over and said, "You can do *anything*, can't you?" Yes! I thought, "I can live off that for a while."

D.M. Yeah, especially coming from him. That's the highest compliment.

K.T. Yes, it was. He was one of the greats.

D.M. I know directors who will extensively demonstrate a performance for their actors, as a way of basically saying "Do it like this."

K.T. That's pretty bad form. For one thing, most directors aren't decent actors, so they're going to sound and look pretty lame.

D.M. Can you think of a situation in which it would be permissible?

K.T. If they are demonstrating some basic blocking in the context of its relationship to the movement of the camera, then that's okay, because that's something I need to know. But to demonstrate how to play the part? No. If they could do that, they'd be actors.

D.M. It's rough—I've seen directors try to do it.

K.T. Me, too—there are directors who will act out the whole scene in front of you. But it's always just embarrassing.

D.M. Plus, it doesn't seem like it would really help an actor. What the actor needs to know is a question of motivation or action or intent, not to imitate someone else's "performance."

K.T. We need to know if we're getting there or not. Are you able to communicate what the character has to communicate? Sometimes you can't always tell that, as the actor. And *that's* what you need the director for. The director is your sounding board.

D.M. I feel that it's part of my job as a director to help an actor keep their spontanaeity in the long process of crafting a performance. It's easy, when you spend that much time with a role, to feel like it's getting a little stale.

K.T. I disagree. That's entirely up to the actor.

D.M. That's all on you?

K.T. Pretty much. Keep in mind that at a certain point the director walks away. In a play, once the production opens, their job is pretty much done. Once we're into eight shows a week, over and over again, what do they know about keeping the spontaneity? They're not even there.

And it isn't really about spontaneity, per se. It's about living in that moment. It's living *in* the moment. Which may appear spontaneous, but of course it's quite planned. Every action, every intonation, ultimately every breath is chosen. So it's about as far from spontaneous as you can get. But it appears spontaneous, because the actor is absolutely living in that second, in that moment.

D.M. Do you think that massaging an actor's ego or nurturing their confidence is a legitimate part of a director's job? Actors can be very emotional, as is the nature of their job, and the process of finding a character can make them feel vulnerable.

K.T. I think it's certainly important to avoid damaging an actor's self-esteem or to create more doubt in the actor than the actor already carries. Every good actor, starting out in a role, is going to have doubts about their performance. You can just imagine how fearful I was starting Martha in *Virginia Woolf*. This was a character that had already been famous in and of itself for decades. And it was a character I had dreamed for thirty years of one day playing. So what if I didn't live up to that role? Finding how to do it—how *I* would do it, and do it, in a sense, differently, because it's *me* doing it—it has to be different to a certain extent.

So I was a bundle of fear and nerves at the beginning of rehearsal. The director has to be very careful not to add to that. But, no, I don't think stroking somebody's ego is necessary. Although, if something is done really well, the director shouldn't withhold praise. They just shouldn't use it as a false tool. If an actor finds out you're lying to him then you've lost his trust, and a director can never lose the trust of his actors or it's over.

D.M. Not to mention that it's incredibly condescending.

K.T. It's condescending, but the loss-of-trust issues it can lead to are the most dangerous things about it.

D.M. Is that trust something that needs to be earned when you're working with somebody, or is it just there for the benefit of the doubt?

K.T. I'll give it up front. I'll trust someone unless they prove me wrong. If I'm proven wrong, if a director abuses that trust or tries to manipulate me in some way, then we're going to have to have a serious little talk. But

I'm quite willing to believe that it's all in good faith, until proven otherwise.

D.M. For me, my most important job when I'm directing, as it pertains to my collaboration with the actors, is making them feel 100% protected.

K.T. Of course. You *have* to protect them—you have to protect them from the suits, from the organization, from . . .

D.M. From the money.

K.T. Yes, the money! As the director, you have to be the one who answers to them and for them. You're the ambassador to the producers or to the institution, as it were. And your job, in part, is to protect the work of your actors. That's important.

D.M. What questions should a director have for an actor?

K.T. I would *hope* a director would have a lot of suggestions, a lot of ideas. A director should make me work hard. She should give me tools to work with, to explore my part with. When we're both generating ideas at the same time, discussing them, combining them, working them out—that's when we're firing on all cylinders and truly creative and enriching work is being done.

COLLABORATING
WITH OTHER ARTISTS

DUSTIN MORROW Part of the challenge of collaborating with other artists, even artists in the same discipline, like acting, is that everyone approaches the process slightly differently and somehow we all have to find a way to work together.

KATHLEEN TURNER You have to find a common ground. And you have to find it in the doing of the scene, if not the coming to the scene.

D.M. What do you mean?

K.T. Well, every actor needs things from the other actors during a scene, but there are also many actors who need something from you before the scene and after the scene is over. For example, there are actors who don't want to be talked to at all, or who want to be addressed only by their character name, so they're not reminded of who they really are. Whatever.

D.M. Is that tough to take?

K.T. Hey, whatever floats your boat. We all have a different way of working. For me, I'm either acting or I'm not acting. I can step onto a set and say, "So, Bob, how's the kid today? You said she skinned her knee the other day, is she all right now? What, we're ready to roll? Okay, let's do it." And ten seconds later I am in character and fully committed to the scene.

I used to drive Bill Hurt, in particular, really crazy. He lightened up a lot by the time we did *Accidental Tourist*, but on *Body Heat* he was very intense, and he didn't want to be spoken to before a scene, and he didn't want to joke around, and he didn't want to have anything going on around him until we were done for the day. Once we'd start acting, we were fine, because we both had a strong stage background and we spoke each other's language in that sense. But it used to drive him crazy that I'd go from, "How's the kid, Bob?" to stepping straight into the scene. But I've always been glad that I can get away from the acting and then come right back to it.

D.M. How about collaborating with the writer? Is there anything specific that you would want from a writer that you would work with?

K.T. Unfortunately, very often you don't have a lot of time with the writer. Either because they're just not around anymore—I've done Shakespeare, Cocteau, Tennessee Williams—or because they're on to their next project by the time you go into production. But you can consume all their works. When I did Tennessee Williams, I crawled through almost everything he wrote, and he wrote about thirty versions of everything. So I went through all the different versions and found a sort of path through his thoughts—what he was exploring, what he kept and what he rejected as he moved from one draft to the next. That gave me a lot of insight into him as a writer.

Kathleen played Maggie the Cat on Broadway in a 1990 revival of Tennessee Williams's Cat on a Hot Tin Roof. *Her co-stars included Daniel Hugh Kelly as Brick and Charles Durning as Big Daddy.*

Edward Albee, of course, was always right there, so you could ask him questions, if you were brave enough. But you wouldn't necessarily ever ask "Why?" You would sort of say, "I'm having a little trouble with this, I can't quite grasp what you wanted here." But you never took the text to him and said, "Why did you do that?" That implied criticism to Albee, and he didn't take criticism.

D.M. How about younger, less-established playwrights?

K.T. There's more room there. Working with Matthew Lombardo, who wrote *High*, was a very different relationship. That's a new play, and I was active in its development. The character is a no-bull, tough-talking nun, and a lot of Matthew's language was too flowery and proper for me at first. I just couldn't find a way to ground that language in my interpretation of the character. With his choice of words, I'd sometimes say to him, "I feel like I'm slipping into an English accent all of a sudden. 'I would never partake of that'—Wait, she doesn't say 'partake,' does she?"

So I'd insist on saying "take part of" instead of "partake" and Matthew would go, "Whatever." And ultimately, we ended up with a Turner script and a Lombardo script. The Turner script was what I actually said onstage, and his script was what he was still trying to polish as we moved through the play's development. And at the end of the process he sat down and sort of melted the two together for the published edition.

D.M. So it was probably great to have him around while you were developing the character. But was there a point where you were like, "All right, this is what it is, I've got what I needed, now please stand back"?

K.T. Ultimately there's no point to having the writer sit in on rehearsals every day. If the script is not changing and it's just exploration and polishing and fine-tuning, there's no reason for him to be there. He'd be bored, and we'd be bored with him. "So go away and come back later." Albee would come in once a week just to see how it was going.

D.M. We've mentioned your fellow actors, your writers, your director— who are the other really important collaborators for an actor besides those obvious major ones?

K.T. Your costumer is essential. Costumes are a conceptual thing that the director is ultimately responsible for, but they have to work on a very personal level for you. You have to find a way to have a dialogue with the costumer that allows them to understand your needs, while still working within a specific framework suitable to the play and the production. So it's good to have a strong rapport there.

D.M. I would imagine the makeup artist is a similar relationship.

K.T. Well, in film, makeup and hair people are an actor's close allies, but in theater it's not really an issue since you usually do your own makeup.

D.M. Do you really? Even on shows the scope and size of those that you're doing?

K.T. Yeah, always. Always. It's part of my preparation. I don't always do my own hair, because I'm not very good at doing hair. But the makeup is mine.

D.M. Is it that way because you *want* to do it, or is that just the way it's done?

K.T. I could have a makeup artist if I wanted to, but I don't want one. That's my time with myself in the mirror. I find it very, very useful. I put on some music in the dressing room, sit down with my makeup and my magnifying mirror and stare at myself for a half an hour. It's part of my process of preparation.

D.M. I thought that you just snapped into character when it was time to perform.

K.T. I do. I'm not using that time to get into character, so to speak.

D.M. What is that time for?

K.T. Just centering myself. Calming myself.

D.M. Getting ready to go to battle?

K.T. Ha! Sort of.

D.M. How about your collaboration with the cinematographer? In the golden age of cinema, under the old studio system, I know many actresses had their own cinematographers that went with them from film to film. No one else was allowed to photograph them.

K.T. Right—Marlene Dietrich had that deal, and I think Greta Garbo did, too. But those days of the stars saying, "I will only work with so-and-so" are long gone. Now the cinematographer's primary relationship is with the director, and that person's hiring is usually entirely the director's choice. But one thing I like to do, and it's fun as well as wise, I think, is to flirt with the camera crew, from the cinematographer on down to the camera operators and the focus pullers. "Okay, boys, what looks best— this? Or this? Come on now, be honest with me—aw, you flatter me, fellas." That kind of thing.

I just have a good time with them, and I know that they will protect me. They will go out of their way to make me look as good as they can. Plus, it's just fun and it's respectful. The camera crew respects the actor who demonstrates a desire to make the crew's job easier, and who demonstrates an interest in what they do. I often ask to look through the lens, so that I can really see the exact frame and the focal length, and I say to the crew, "Tell me exactly what my parameters are here, because

I don't want to step out of your frame." Or, "How would you like me to shift so that you end up with the composition you need to get?" It makes their job easier, it establishes trust, and it's a partnership that both parties benefit from.

The focal length of a lens determines the angle of view of a shot—that is, how much of what's in front of the lens will appear in the shot. A narrow-angle lens will often be used for close-ups, while a wide-angle lens is employed for shots of vistas.

D.M. When I was editing films professionally, I rarely met the actors during the editing process, which struck me as odd. I would have welcomed their insights.

K.T. I almost never met the editors. And if I did, it was not until after the production. Actors are usually not allowed in the editing room. It is very much frowned upon. I guess the assumption is that we're so vain, we'll just be looking for our most flattering shots rather than looking out for the quality of the entire film. Which I think is basically bull, but that's the way it is. More often than not the editing is also happening while you're shooting, rather than waiting until the shooting is complete, so as an actor you are consumed with the production and couldn't weigh in on the editing even if you wanted to.

D.M. It seems to me that it's the strangest bond between two people that rarely meet, because the editor has so much influence over how the actor's performance is ultimately constructed.

K.T. Absolutely. The choice of take the editor uses in each scene, or the combination of takes, can change your entire performance.

D.M. I used to be an editor before I returned full-time to academia. Sometimes I would meet the actors much later, and they would say to me, "Oh, I see you used take four in that scene." And I would always think, "Well, actually I used two lines from take four, but then I also used a line from take one and a line from take seven." The actors would speak about their performances as if they were this unified, continuous thing that they just handed to me, and I made no creative choices in putting them together. I'd always be thinking, "Well, actually, I built your performance—you gave me the raw materials, but I built the performance that the audience will see."

K.T. I think almost any actor would *love* to be more of a part of the editing process. I know I would. One thing that bothers me about film acting is that I don't get to choose the performance that the audience gets to see. I interpret a scene over a numbers of takes on the set in different ways, to give the director and the editor as many potentially useful possibilities as I can, but ultimately the choice of what takes to use is not up to me. That's completely opposite the way it works on the stage, where as an actor I take the input of my collaborators, but in the moment, during the performance, the choice is mine.

D.M. I always thought that when they give the Best Actor Oscar, they should give a smaller Oscar at the same time to the editor, and they should go up onstage together.

K.T. Interesting!

D.M. I'm kidding, obviously, but that's how much a part of building an actor's performance the film editor is.

K.T. Write to the Academy, see what you can do.

D.M. And I always felt, as an editor, that I would be better at that job if I had the opportunity to talk to the actor about the choices they were making in each scene.

K.T. It would be great, but it would slow the post-production process to a crawl so no studio would ever allow it.

D.M. That's true, but it's unfortunate.

K.T. And really, any good performance shouldn't have to be explained by the actor. It should entirely speak for itself.

IN THE BEGINNING . . .

Dustin Morrow Let's jump back to the beginning of your story for a moment.

Kathleen Turner Shall we start with *The Doctors*? I guess that was my first really big break.

D.M. No, I want to go even further back. Not to the beginning of your career, but to the beginning of your life story as an actor.

K.T. Oh boy. We're going way back then.

D.M. Way back. I'm interested in your decision to become an actor. It's a hard career, and can be a rough life, so I know that the decision to pursue acting isn't one that's made without careful consideration.

K.T. That's true. If you want to act, as a profession, you'd better *really* want to act.

D.M. Were there indications in your early life that you might grow up to be a performer?

K.T. Oh yeah, always.

D.M. They say acting starts with "acting out" as a kid.

K.T. Who says that?

D.M. Ummm . . . the mythical "they," of course.

K.T. Nonsense. Ha!

D.M. Come on, there had to be some measure of attention-seeking.

K.T. Well, I guess I did have some temper problems when I was in early adolescence. Apparently I was quite hyperactive as a child. One time, when I was ten or eleven, I came running down the stairs in our house and slammed into this porcelain duck that shattered. I remember my poor mother telling me that I was impossible to live with sometimes.

D.M. That's tough love.

K.T. Well, I could be a handful at times. I used to have this terrifying dream that I would come home from school to an empty house and would be left all on my own.

D.M. I wonder if that has something to do with wanting to be accepted, which is certainly part of any actor's DNA.

K.T. Like a fear of abandonment? Please.

D.M. Too psychoanalytic.

K.T. Indeed. You're reaching.

D.M. I could see a need for acceptance, for confirmation, possibly pushing someone toward acting.

K.T. Pffft.

D.M. What is your earliest memory of performing?

K.T. Hmm . . . I remember once when I was four years old, and we were back in Missouri around Christmas, my mom took me shopping and I decided that I was going to give a proper concert right in the middle of the department store. I climbed up on something and began warbling Christmas carols. My mom enjoys telling that story. She told me to knock it off, but I responded, "But everybody likes it!" Apparently I was under the impression I was putting on quite the show.

D.M. When did your interest in theater start?

K.T. When I was little I read voraciously, and when I read strong female characters, I imagined myself as the character. Not so much how I would play the character, but how I would act, what I would do, if I actually was the character in real life. And I began to read a lot of plays. I used to force my brothers and sisters to read them aloud with me. They didn't want to do it, but they did it to humor me.

D.M. Was that before your family moved to London?

Kathleen's father was a foreign service officer who moved his family around with his job. Growing up, Kathleen lived in Havana, Caracas, London, Washington DC, and Springfield, Missouri, before doing her last year of college in Baltimore and then moving immediately to New York City, not even waiting for her diploma—she had it sent to her mom. She's been in New York ever since.

K.T. Yes, that was in Venezuela, when I was about twelve. I began to really love drama then, through these plays I was reading, but I didn't have a sense of acting as a career one could pursue until after we moved to London.

D.M. Are you still a voracious reader?

K.T. Absolutely. I read constantly.

D.M. What do you like?

K.T. Historical drama is probably my favorite. And I love science-fiction.

D.M. That's surprising.

K.T. Why?

D.M. Because I can't think of a science-fiction play or film you've done.

K.T. That's true. I've done a lot of fantasy films, but nothing that could be categorized as explicitly science-fiction. I got into it when I was forced to move back to Missouri after my father's death. I desperately wanted to live in an alternate world, and sci-fi literature became a great escape for me.

Among Kathleen's fantasy films are Who Framed Roger Rabbit, A Simple Wish, Baby Geniuses, *and a British telefilm version of* Cinderella, *in which Kathleen played the wicked stepmother.*

D.M. So you were reading plays as a kid before you ever saw them performed?

K.T. Well, I didn't really have access to a lot of theater until we moved to London. Think about the places I was growing up: Cuba and Venezuela.

D.M. So your love of theater took root after you moved to London.

K.T. At the time that I was growing up in London, it was actually cheaper to go to the theater than the movies. So I saw everything. It was great.

D.M. What was the first play you ever went to?

K.T. I think it was *Mame*, with Angela Lansbury. I don't remember the play so much as the realization that acting was something I could actually do for a living. That it was a real profession. I knew from that night that it was a potential life for me.

D.M. So you knew that early that acting was what you wanted to do.

K.T. Absolutely. And I was lucky in that respect.

D.M. That is lucky. I knew from a young age I wanted to make and study cinema. I knew that before I was out of middle school. It was one of the lucky gifts life has bestowed on me.

K.T. I'm amazed how many people reach adulthood and still haven't figured out what they want to do. I really feel sorry for young people who haven't figured out what they want to do with their lives. Figuring that out early is one of the great gifts fate can hand you. I see young people who go to the "right schools," live in the "right neighborhoods," get the "right jobs," and they're miserable. They wait for these things to give meaning to their lives, but it doesn't work that way. You have to decide what your life means, what your work means to you. It's never going to come from someone else telling you that you'll feel great about yourself if you follow such and such a path.

I'm very lucky. At a young age I was given this conviction that this is what I have to do, and all these decades later I still feel the same way.

D.M. You started studying acting for the first time in London.

K.T. Yes, in my high school. The American School in London was a great training ground for me because our theater program was so small and tight-knit. The school itself was very experimental with its curriculum, giving the students a lot of say in what classes and programs were offered. For three years, I had six theater classmates, and we basically were the drama department. We picked the plays, directed the performances, everything. We did three to five plays a year, it was great. The school even let us take our plays to Paris, to perform at other schools. It was a wonderful experience.

The American School in London is the only nonprofit, independent American school in London. Established in 1951, it's also the oldest American school in the city. Kathleen graduated in 1972.

D.M. Was there any history of the arts in your family?

K.T. None. My siblings were all in the sciences, and they were all brilliant. All three of my siblings have doctorates. I have one too, but it's an honorary one.

D.M. In theater?

K.T. No, literature.

D.M. How do your siblings feel about a university giving you an honorary doctorate?

K.T. Actually, I called all of them before I accepted it to make sure they were cool with it, and none of them took issue with it.

D.M. Shall I call you Dr. Turner then?

K.T. Not if you want me to answer you.

D.M. It had to have been challenging to grow up in such a high-achieving family. Just in terms of the pressure put upon you to succeed.

K.T. It was, but in a good way. There's no failure in my family, and no outward, visible struggle. So when you do something, you do as well as it can be done, and you don't let anyone see how hard it is. That's a lot of pressure, but it's a useful thing to tap into when you enter such a competitive field as acting, a field where there is so much struggle.

And I was just as ambitious and strong-willed as my siblings. I remember that my eighth grade class predicted I would be the first ambassador to the moon. Who knows, maybe I still have a chance.

D.M. Your family wasn't initially supportive of your career choice, though.

K.T. My father never was supportive of it. He was a crucial part of my support system in every aspect of my life but my career choice. The thought to him that any child of his would go into such a "dubious field," as he would call it, angered him immensely. I fought a lot of disapproval. Once I went onstage and my mother came in to watch the performance while he stubbornly sat in the car in the parking lot. That really hurt my feelings. I remember it like it was yesterday. The play was *The Winners and Losers* by Brian Friel.

D.M. Did your father ever see you act?

K.T. No, never. When he died, I lost part of my support system, but I also lost the one major barrier to my becoming a professional actress. So in a way, his death freed me.

D.M. How old were you when he passed away?

K.T. I was only seventeen. And after he died, there was very little financial support for me. I was on my own to make my own way in the world. That's when we had to move to Missouri.

D.M. You studied theater there at Southwest Missouri State University. Transitioning from London to Missouri must have been eye-opening.

Southwest Missouri State University was rechristened Missouri State University in 2005. It's located in Springfield, near where Kathleen's mother lived. The Department of Theater and Dance at the university offers an annual "Kathleen Turner Performance Scholarship."

K.T. Going from London to Missouri was the greatest culture shock of my life. In London, like every other young woman, I had short stylish hair and wore miniskirts, and when I got to Missouri everyone thought I was a lesbian. Missouri could be lonely and isolating for me. I had a return ticket to England that was on my bedside for a whole year after we moved back to Missouri, but I could never bring myself to use it because doing so would have meant leaving my mother behind. So it expired.

I escaped into art, theater, and music. When I was frustrated and alone in college in Missouri, I had a recording of Tchaikovsky's first piano concerto in b-minor, and I used to listen to it and close my eyes and lie there and think, "This exists, this is out there, and the person who played this is out there, and this is extraordinary and I will get back out there into the world where this exists."

Don't get me wrong—I love Missouri. The people of the Midwest are wonderful, and my mom lived there until she passed away. It was a great school too, there were some great actors there. John Goodman and Tess Harper were in my class. It just wasn't the most creatively nurturing place for me.

Missouri wasn't easy for me, but it was ultimately a great thing for me as an actress. If my father hadn't died I would likely have remained in London, and I might have become this sort of fake British actress as opposed to a genuine American actress. So although the circumstances that resulted in my moving to Missouri were very sad, it was ultimately beneficial to the development of my craft and my career that I ended up in the Midwest during my college years.

LESSONS LEARNED FROM WORKING IN TELEVISION

DUSTIN MORROW After you finished your college degree, you moved immediately to New York City to work in theater.

KATHLEEN TURNER Yes, it was terrifying but exhilarating to move to New York. I drove there the day I finished classes. I had exactly $100 in cash. Period. I was supposed to stay with a friend that first night but she had reunited with her boyfriend. I got to New York at about 3:00 in the morning and slept in my car on the east side, up in the 80s. It was scary—Manhattan wasn't the Disney playground that it is now—but it was incredibly exciting and I was fearless.

D.M. And you were able to start working as an actor pretty quickly.

K.T. Almost immediately. I mean, I had day jobs like every other actor, but I started acting professionally very quickly. I was off-Broadway within five months, on the soap opera after nine months, and was on Broadway by eleven months.

D.M. Tell me about the soap opera.

K.T. I was a regular on *The Doctors*. Which no longer exists, for which we can all be thankful.

The Doctors *was a soap opera set in a New England hospital that ran on NBC from 1963 to 1982. Kathleen appeared on the series in 1978 and 1979. Among the many other notable alumni of the series are Alec Baldwin, Ellen Burstyn, and Ted Danson.*

D.M. No good?

K.T. Whatever. It was fine. It was just a very run-of-the-mill soap opera. My character was so incredibly dumb that at a certain point I just couldn't figure out how to justify the words that came out of her mouth, so I just asked the writers to make her a drunk.

D.M. Ha! That is crazy.

K.T. So crazy! I'll tell you the breaking point for me on *The Doctors*. I remember this like it was yesterday. I was doing a scene where I was giving birth, after a four-month pregnancy of course, and I had researched the process and learned lamaze breathing and everything. After the first take the director, who was a man of course, came up and said, "You're doing great, I can really feel what you're going through. But can you just be a little more . . . ummm . . . attractive?"

"Attractive." While giving birth. That was it for me.

D.M. Stick a fork in you.

K.T. Yessir. Done.

D.M. Actors who move back and forth between theater and cinema or theater and television always talk about the differences between stage and screen acting, so I thought that instead I would ask you to tell me about the skills that translate, especially since I know that you started in stage and then moved to TV and then to film. What were you able to carry from one step to the next?

K.T. Moving from TV to film was less of a leap for me than moving from theater to TV. That was a big transition.

D.M. How did you get the part on *The Doctors*?

K.T. Before I got the regular role on *The Doctors*, I was getting called in to do day spots on soaps because I have a near-photographic memory. I could learn scripts almost instantly. That made me pretty valuable as a soap actress.

D.M. Theater and television are wildly different forums for an actor.

K.T. Coming from the stage, I had always thought of acting as a process of rehearsal, of trial and error, of carefully fine-tuning something until it's just right. You don't have that kind of luxury, that kind of time, working in soap operas. When shooting a soap, you come in around seven or so and go through hair and makeup and wardrobe, and then you shoot until around four or so, and at five you do a light rehearsal, or sometimes just a table read, of what you are going to shoot the next day. That idea of creating a performance every single day was new to me, that idea of making choices that you had to implement on-the-spot. That was the most valuable thing that the soap opera gave me.

D.M. What did you learn from that experience about acting for the camera?

K.T. I don't think I learned a lot about camera craft because it was a soap. It was essentially these huge, hulking, awkward cameras that wheeled around in a cumbersome manner. They didn't afford a tremendous variety of camera angles. And there were several of them shooting at once, so the angle wasn't as defined or as specific as it usually is when shooting a film. And there were all these terribly artificial soap opera performance demands. I would get a script that would say, "And we slow fade on a shot of Kathleen's surprised expression." And I would have to hold this ridiculously melodramatic expression until they finished this agonizingly long fade that would take them into a commercial. It was so stupid and so unrealistic.

D.M. Well, no one watches soap operas for realism, I guess.

K.T. Isn't that the truth! But I did learn a very valuable lesson about *how* to use my personal experiences in my performances when I was doing *The Doctors*. There was a storyline in which my character's mother died, and in reading the script I had this incredible rush of feeling, remembering my father's death. It was a wave of emotion that I hadn't felt in years, as he had been dead for several years at that point. It was as though the script had torn open a scar that I thought had healed over, it was hard for me. But I went home and I just thought, "Okay, just hold it together, keep it together, don't indulge anything until the camera rolls tomorrow and then use it all."

So the next day we shot this scene in which my character spoke to her dying mother in this hospital room, and I just let it all go. And I was wracked with grief, sobbing uncontrollably almost, and when we finished the show I thought, "Well, that is one of the truest things I have ever done as an actress." And then I saw the show and it looked like the worst, hammiest acting in history!

The lesson learned was that you don't really want to be 100% real, on camera or on stage really. The performance of a real emotion is different from the actual experiencing of that emotion.

D.M. For one thing, one is controlled and the other isn't.

K.T. That's true, and you don't ever want to be out of control when you are acting. Acting isn't meant to be dangerous. We were auditioning young men for the role of the addict in the Broadway production of *High*, and one young man got so physical with me onstage that there was a genuine sense of the loss of control, and I felt for a moment that I was in real danger. He was way too rough with me. You won't get a part if you can't control your performance.

That said, I think that I have come closer to using real experiences on stage than in film because I have a lot more space to do it in. But that scene on *The Doctors* was awful, bad acting. However true it felt to me didn't matter, it wasn't about the truth.

D.M. So it's more about verisimilitude, an appearance of truth, than finding an actual truth.

K.T. It's about the truth of the scene, not the truth of the actor's personal experiences.

D.M. The compressed period of time that you were talking about, with the fast production schedule of *The Doctors*, where you have basically a day to make big performance choices—if you are coming out of a theater background where you have a luxurious rehearsal period, then that's tough to deal with. Do you just say to yourself, "It's scary but I'm going to commit to this choice I made five minutes ago and hope for the best"?

K.T. Basically. You have to. Having that experience on *The Doctors* helped me when I did move on to feature filmmaking, because I learned that on the day, on the moment when the shot was set, you had to be committed to your choices. There's no do-over if you don't like what you did on a given shoot day on a film. You can't just go reshoot something because you were unhappy with your performance, it would be prohibitively expensive.

There are times when, if I happen to catch a few minutes from one of my films on TV, I see places where I could have made better choices. But that's okay. What I am sure of is that I made the best choice I could make on that day, at that time, given the circumstances, given where we were shooting, who I was working with, and how everything had led up to that moment on that shoot day. I'm sure I said, "This is the best I can do." So I am happy with all my film performances, because they represented my best effort on the days I shot them. It does no actor any good to sit around bemoaning mistakes or missed opportunities. Move forward and be proud of what you've done.

D.M. I have heard from actor friends who've done them that soaps can provide valuable experience as an actor. If one of your students was considering going into soaps, what would you tell her?

K.T. I'd tell her to do it, but not for too long. No actor should stay on a soap for more than eighteen months. The trap that actors on soaps fall into is they lose the desire to explore because they get into the habit of thinking that the first choice is the best choice. And that's a very dangerous habit for an actor. Soaps don't foster exploration in the acting process.

D.M. Did they have teleprompters when you were doing *The Doctors*?

K.T. Ah, yes, "teleprompter acting." On *The Doctors*, they used cue cards, but it was the same basic thing. There was this guy, Bobby, who had these big white cards that he'd hold up just off-camera. I never used them, as they so obviously impede a performance.

D.M. That seems like it'd be terribly distracting.

K.T. You can always tell when an actor is using them, their eyeline is all wrong.

D.M. As a kid I can remember watching *Saturday Night Live*, which is where I first became aware of what cue card acting was, because the cast would always be looking over their co-stars' shoulders instead of into their eyes.

K.T. It doesn't work as acting, but on a broad sketch comedy show like that they can kind of get away with it. Plus, on that show the sketches are being re-written right up until the minute they are performed live, so often you just don't have time to memorize your lines.

D.M. *Saturday Night Live* must have been incredible fun.

Kathleen hosted Saturday Night Live *on January 12, 1985, and on October 21, 1989. Her musical guests were John Waite and Billy Joel, respectively. Both episodes include multiple sketches spoofing Kathleen's sex symbol image and her voice. On her 1989 episode, she performed a now-classic sketch with Phil Hartman in which Hartman played an egg and Kathleen his human wife.*

K.T. Are you kidding? Absolutely, it was great fun. The entire cast and the writers were incredibly creative and playful.

D.M. Anyone who hasn't seen you in the "Eggman" sketch with Phil Hartman should get themselves to YouTube immediately.

K.T. Ah yes, the Eggman! That was a funny sketch!

D.M. Hartman was a great loss. He was so talented.

K.T. He had a lot of charisma and range. He was the glue that held that show together for many years.

D.M. Actually, I think that was his nickname among the cast and crew, "The Glue."

K.T. I'm not surprised. His work on that show was underrated, he was easily one of the best cast members they had.

D.M. Do you find live television to be really stressful?

K.T. Not really—it's no more live than theater is live. Of course, the audience is usually much bigger. Make a mistake and rest assured that some yahoo recorded it for prosperity and that it now lives online until the end of time!

CHOOSING ROLES

Dustin Morrow After *The Doctors* came *Body Heat*, probably the biggest break of your career.

Kathleen Turner *The* biggest break of my career. Hands down.

D.M. And yet you never had any intention of becoming a film actress.

K.T. Absolutely not. After I graduated from college, I went to New York, not Hollywood. Movies happened to me, rather than my actively pursuing them. I've always thought of myself as a stage actress, and I still do, but what I hadn't realized in the early days of my stage career was that it would take me years to grow into many of the great roles that are available to women on stage. So when I found some success in film, I thought that I would spend some time in that medium while I matured into the great stage roles. Of course, I hadn't anticipated becoming so popular in film, and my career as a film actress became more high-profile than my stage career for many years.

D.M. It seems that, schedule-wise, you've managed your career exactly right.

K.T. I believe I have. The best film roles available to actresses are available to young actresses, so I did them when I was young. And now that I am a little older, I have available to me all of these wonderful stage roles for older women.

D.M. You are quite famous for having played a wide variety of roles, on both the stage and screen. It's really hard to do that and to be a lead actor. Most lead actors tend to repeat themselves quite a bit, but somehow you've escaped that path.

K.T. It took a lot of hard work and careful decision-making about the roles I took and the ones I rejected.

D.M. How quickly do you know whether you're interested in a role? On the very first read-through of the script, or do you need to think on it for awhile?

K.T. I know pretty immediately if something is going to grab me. If I'm reading a script, and by halfway through it I'm not already thinking about how I would deliver the lines and approach the character, then it's not going to happen. I have to get caught up in it right away, on the very first reading.

D.M. I've heard you say in a few different interviews that the only characters you won't play are victims. How do you define that—what is a victim?

K.T. A victim, to me, is someone who won't do anything to try and change her circumstances. So a character who fails is fine, as long as she tried to do something. But a woman who simply waits, usually for a man, to take care of her, or fix her problems, or give meaning to her life, is inherently uninteresting to me. I couldn't play a character like that even if I wanted to, because I would inevitably betray it. It would be too frustrating and limiting for me. Frankly, I find movies where male characters have to come along to save the female characters offensive.

D.M. Come to think of it, it's hard to come up with examples in your work of you being saved by men. At the end of *Romancing the Stone*, Joan Wilder has to fight off the bad guy on her own. Dennis Quaid never saves you in *Undercover Blues*, William Hurt doesn't heal you in *The Accidental Tourist*, and in *Prizzi's Honor* you end up trying to kill Nicholson as he's trying to kill you.

K.T. Yep. In movies where a male character does come to my aid, as Michael does in *Jewel of the Nile*, my character turns around and saves him right back a scene or two later.

D.M. You don't do the damsel in distress.

K.T. No, sir. Never. But what's even more important than not playing a damsel in distress, is not playing a nonessential character. So many roles for women are of the girlfriend/wife/mother variety, where they are there to provide exposition or they are there so the male protagonist has someone to explain things to. Those roles are truly degrading. I'm not a prop, I'm an actress. My character has to contribute to the narrative in a meaningful way, or I can't play her.

D.M. But what about Mrs. Robinson in *The Graduate*? Isn't that character, to some degree, a victim?

K.T. She's not a victim. She's a failure. And she knows it. She knows
she's completely let down her marriage and let down her daughter.

D.M. I'd think it would be even more draining to play a failure than a
victim.

K.T. Well, it involves a lot of self-loathing, which is not much fun to live
with day after day and week after week. And remember this is a play—so
I'm doing eight shows a week of, "God, I'm disgusting, what a piece of
crap I am." So it's not very happy. It's not a lot of fun. But, at the same
time, that character did have a sharp sense of humor, so that was a saving grace.

D.M. How do you play a character you don't like?

K.T. It doesn't happen. I always end up liking them. I'll go through a
stage, and Martha in *Virginia Woolf* and Sister Jamie in *High* spring to
mind as two prime examples of this, where I will think, "This woman is
just unforgiveable—her behavior, her selfishness, her history are inex-
cusable." But then I slowly start to find the reasons behind that behavior
and I begin to have some compassion for the woman. And once you have
compassion for someone, you can't ever hate her.

Usually, with my less outwardly likable characters, I'll go through a
stage where I don't like them at all, then I begin to understand why they
act the way they do, and then I begin to feel sorry for them, then I feel
empathetic toward them, and finally I end up totally on their side.

D.M. Can that compassion for a character change the way you're playing her if you find yourself, and maybe I'm phrasing this the wrong way,
feeling sorry for your character? Or is it always going to be a good thing,
because it's empathy?

K.T. Well, I think it's more empathy than pity—because really, you're not
that far enough outside the character to feel sorry for her, unless the
character feels sorry for herself. But self-pity as a character is a very
different thing than an actress pitying her character. I don't think, as an
actress, that I could ever objectify my character to that degree.

D.M. So you've never turned down parts because you've thought, "There's
just no way I could bring myself to empathize with this character."

K.T. Never.

D.M. So if an actor can go through the process of becoming the character, they'll always be able to find that empathy.

K.T. I've never turned down a script because I thought the character was not actable. Certainly there have been many scripts I've turned down because I felt the character wasn't worth doing, but that's usually because the play or the film isn't worth doing. I'll turn something down if the character doesn't get anywhere or learn anything or affect enough change to make it worthwhile. To really commit to developing a play, or to go away to shoot a film—you can forget dinner with friends, you can forget time off with your family, you can forget having any kind of normal life. So really, truly, it needs to be worth doing, because the sacrifice is great.

D.M. When I look at the roles you have accepted over the course of your career, it's hard to find recurring themes, and I suspect that that's because you've always made unconventional choices, and done films and plays that are dramatically different from each other by design.

K.T. It does make it tough to find threads that run through my body of work. And yes, that is by design—I never wanted to play the same character over and over again.

D.M. Of course, when you think about it, that *is* the thread in your body of film work. The thread is variety.

K.T. Which is a great thread for an actor to have, even if it does limit the degree of success you might be able to achieve.

D.M. You were the top-grossing actress of the entire decade of the eighties, how much more success could you have?

K.T. I just mean that in a place as lacking in imagination as Hollywood, if you play the same type of role over and over again, and develop a screen persona that's easy for them to understand and put a label on, then you're doing for them the work they don't want to be troubled to do, which is tell them what kind of roles you are best suited for. And as a result, you're offered all of those roles before they're offered to other actors. And you collect more frequent and larger paychecks.

D.M. But you also become pretty artistically bankrupt.

K.T. Exactly! The second you start taking roles just for the money, you're going to stop enjoying your profession and growing as an actor. That's a quick road to becoming profoundly bored with your work.

D.M. And you can see it on the screen. I won't name names, but we can all think of actors and actresses that play the same kinds of roles in the same kinds of movies over and over again, and you can just see them phoning it in. There's no spark, and you can tell they are taking no pleasure in, and have nothing invested in the work. Beyond picking up the paycheck, of course.

K.T. Yes. And that's fine for them, but I could just never do it. I took one movie for the money, and lo and behold, it was the least pleasurable filmmaking experience of my career.

D.M. That was *Switching Channels*.

K.T. It was. I did it because I wanted to work with Michael Caine, who was forced to bow out before we shot, and because they offered me an obscene amount of money. I was pregnant and knew I wouldn't be working for at least a year, so I felt I should take the money and do it. I'm not proud of it.

D.M. Although it's flawed, I think you're harder on that film than you should be. It's a little corny, but it's a respectable update of *The Front Page* and I think you have some great moments in it.

K.T. Thank you. I think it's a film that suffered as *V.I. Warshawski* suffered, in the sense that there was a lot of good material that got left on the cutting room floor. That happened later with *Monster House*, too. It hasn't happened to me too often in my career, but it has happened, and some of my films have not turned out as well as they could have.

D.M. It must be hard to go out and promote a film that hasn't turned out as well as you'd hoped.

K.T. Of course, and there are some actors and actresses who won't do it. But it's part of my responsibility to the film, whether I like it or not.

D.M. I watched an old David Letterman episode where you're promoting *Switching Channels*, and it's clear that he's trying to get you to say something negative about Burt Reynolds and about the film, but you don't bite.

K.T. Well, it wasn't a well-kept secret in the industry that Burt and I clashed on that film, so I'm sure he was in the know and was just trying to provoke me. That was Letterman for you.

D.M. He never gets you though—you say nothing but nice things about both Reynolds and the movie.

K.T. It was my professional responsibility to the studio and to all of the many people who worked very hard on the project to do everything I could to help it succeed.

D.M. I like *Switching Channels* a lot more than you do, but I can see how the rhythms of it are a bit off. For such a frantic screwball comedy, it's pretty sluggish in parts.

K.T. To say the least.

D.M. Working with Michael Caine would have been great fun.

K.T. I was so looking forward to working with Michael Caine. Before the shoot, he and I had worked out this great comedic bit where we were going to finish each others' sentences, because our characters had been married and working together for fifteen years and knew each other so well. Our comic timing on that was perfect. It might have been a better movie with Michael in it.

D.M. I think you're too hard on it.

K.T. Ah well, c'est la vie.

D.M. So beyond the variety in the roles, what else have you seen recur in your career as it's developed?

K.T. Besides a continuity in playing strong women, I can see perhaps just one, and that's a kind of . . . anger. I'd almost say rage, but rage might be too strong a word. If you break down almost every character that I've done, there is a deep anger inside them. Even a very sweet character like Peggy Sue from *Peggy Sue Got Married* is, deep down, very angry. She's so angry at what her life turned out to be, and that she allowed the senseless stupidity of her husband to destroy her life's possibilities. It's a sweet, charming film, but that undercurrent of anger runs throughout it. It's hard for me to think of a character I've done that isn't rooted in some level of frustration and anger. Maybe Joan Wilder from *Romancing the Stone*.

D.M. But Joan definitely has some self-loathing in the beginning of that movie.

K.T. Oh yeah, I suppose she does.

D.M. Like Peggy Sue, she's disappointed in where she's ended up. Despite having found commercial success, she leads a lonely and fairly unfulfilling life. I see that in a lot of your characters, that self-loathing.

K.T. Joan's definitely a big disappointment to herself. Then she realizes over the course of the film what she can really be. She comes into her true self. I agree that there's *that* in most of my characters.

D.M. It does seem to be a thread.

K.T. It almost has to be, because a character has to learn something. They have to change within the context of the story, or it's not very interesting. Otherwise, you're introduced to the character, you get to know her, and then what? That's it? That's as much as you get? No, you have to put her in a situation where she's forced to change or forced to fail. The character itself isn't intrinsically interesting, it's the character's journey that's interesting.

D.M. I grew up in a small town in the Midwest, and had a fairly sheltered childhood. I loved movies—Hitchcock and Scorsese especially, and Kathleen Turner movies. When I began working on this book, I found myself thinking back on that time and wondering why you emerged in my life as my favorite actress, beyond my passionate love for *Romancing the Stone*. That is, why Kathleen Turner and not any of the other movie stars prominent during my coming of age?

K.T. And what did you come up with, kid?

D.M. I think that the answer lies in a thread that I see in many of your characters, a thread that is most pronounced in *Romancing the Stone*. And it's that many of your films chronicle a journey of self-discovery for your characters, and your characters tend to realize a new confidence in who they are. And that kind of realization of a self-identity, of someone coming into their own, is something that I think a young person can really grab onto. I was a shy kid, and watching Joan Wilder go from a meek wallflower to a confident adventurer, a character who doesn't need anyone to save her, a character who comes to her own rescue at the end of the film, had a profound impact on me.

K.T. It's not just strength and confidence, it's the character's allowing herself to *like* herself! We don't see enough of that in contemporary film

53

and television, characters that learn to really like themselves, and accept themselves. It's a shame. And unfortunately, that's a reflection of how we teach our children.

D.M. I would imagine that's a really fun character arc to play, because it's always going up. It's a straight rise.

K.T. Yeah, it was fun to envision a character who was completely timid, physically and emotionally. All of my movements at the beginning of *Romancing the Stone* are quite hesitant and lack any kind of force or flair, and then throughout the build of the film, Joan becomes stronger, more decisive and independent and freer in her body. That's a fun plot, a great growth.

D.M. That seems like a situation where marking your script would make sense, because to play that arc out-of-sequence and under the harsh conditions of shooting in mud and rain and remote rainforests, it seems like it'd be tough to keep track of what level of confidence Joan was to be at in the narrative on any given shooting day.

K.T. For that film, a lot of that was helped by hair and makeup. I could gauge my performance based on how tattered my costume was, by how filthy I was, by how much my hair had come down. So I could say, "Okay, at this stage, I'm still in high heels and they're sticking in the mud, and I've been out here for over twenty-four hours, and my dress is falling apart . . ." And I could gauge the emergence of my self-confidence to that. That kind of thing.

It was never fair, by the way, to be bare-legged in the jungle while Michael got to wear khakis.

D.M. But he also doesn't get the flattering close-up on the legs, though, as you're hacking through the jungle with your machete.

K.T. Yeah, that's true! Good legs. I've always had good legs.

D.M. I would imagine that's a revelatory moment when working in theater as well, that first costume fitting.

K.T. Totally.

D.M. Even in a show like *High*, where the costume isn't flashy.

K.T. It still has to sit right, it has to be comfortable, it has to make sense. In *High*, she wears serviceable, institutional-looking shoes, so immediately you know she's not supposed to have much vanity. Any actress will tell you, shoes are a terribly, terribly important thing. They change everything.

D.M. You're big on the shoes?

K.T. Only as an actress. If I could I'd go barefoot all the time, I would.

D.M. Really? Not my thing.

K.T. I never wear shoes, if I can help it.

D.M. So have you ever, perhaps with shoes, selected a piece of wardrobe because it would actually make you *less* comfortable? To help you play the character?

K.T. No. Way.

D.M. You'd never say, "This character needs to be on-edge, give me the shoes that kind of hurt a little"?

K.T. Are you kidding? No, thank you. No, no, no. I can act pain *really* well. I don't actually need to suffer. No. That's why they call it acting.

D.M. It's more of a method actor thing to do, I suppose.

K.T. They can have it! No thank you.

D.M. Are there other types of characters you determinedly stay away from, besides victims?

K.T. Not really. I actually have no problem playing types of characters you've seen a million times before, so long as I think I can do something with it that you haven't seen before. Before I did *High*, how many millions of tough nun characters had there been? But there had never been a tough nun like the one I did.

D.M. I know you've played parts that you've opposed politically.

K.T. Of course. I don't believe it's my job as an actor to preach. There's a separation between my job as an actor and my job as an activist. My film and stage work is not designed to tell you what's wrong and right with your life. Sue Collini could be viewed as a feminist's worst nightmare, and I am a feminist. But it's a juicy role, great fun to play and a challenge for me, so I had no trouble accepting the part.

Sue Collini is Kathleen's character in the Showtime series California- *tion, an overly sexualized Hollywood agent and maneater. The series starred David Duchovny as a troubled New York novelist who relocated to Los Angeles to work as a screenwriter. It ran for seven seasons and won two Emmys and a Golden Globe.*

D.M. Have you consciously avoided doing parts that are too close to the real you?

K.T. Not exactly. It's okay to play characters with whom you have a lot in common, so long as there is some challenge in playing them.

D.M. A lot of actors seem to play themselves over and over.

K.T. I know, and where's the fun in that? Not only are you playing someone just like yourself, you are repeating yourself. You're typecasting yourself as yourself.

D.M. Getting typecast is an incredible danger of doing the same type of role too many times. I know it's locked up many an actor's career.

K.T. It's true that it can kill your career, but the real danger of repeating a role is boredom, and the subsequent loss of interest in a profession to which you've devoted your life. Repeating roles is just not interesting to me. The way to get me to commit to a role is to offer me something I've never done before. That's how they got me on *Friends*. They dangled in front of me something I had never even thought of doing—a woman playing a man playing a woman? Sounds like a fun challenge to me, sign me up!

On the hit NBC sitcom Friends, *Kathleen played Chandler Bing's father, a cross-dressing cabaret performer.*

D.M. Having said all that, some degree of stereotyping can actually help an actor's career. If you look at a career as the provision of steady work, if not creatively rewarding parts. Every time a certain kind of role comes available, producers will think of an actor who has done the part before, and done it well. An actor could get a lot of steady work that way.

K.T. That's far more true for men than women. Stereotypes can be so damaging to an actress. For example, the stereotypes of older women characters are the worst. When young actresses are stereotyped, it's bad—the girlfriend, the wife, the bimbo—but when an older actress is stereotyped, it's deadly—the grandmother, the bitter old lady, the senile, silly woman. Some of the parts you're offered as an older actress are just appalling.

D.M. After you debuted in *Body Heat* you were offered a million clones of that movie. Did you realize that you could be typecast because of *Body Heat* even before the offers of carbon copy roles started coming in?

K.T. I was a tomboy growing up and, before it came out, was sort of blissfully ignorant of what *Body Heat* might mean. The first time I saw it with an audience, and felt its impact in the room, I knew I could be in deep trouble. That I could be really trapped by that type of role. So even before *Body Heat* was widely released, I decided that I would spend my career doing contrasting roles, that if I did one type of role, I would try to do the opposite of it in the next film.

D.M. Do you think that you ever became a type even though you were always doing different kinds of parts?

K.T. To some degree, yes. What I became was "a strong, sexual woman with her own opinions and independent actions." It was inevitable, it was the one thing many of my roles shared.

It's always been harder for me to play vulnerability than strength. It's not in my nature to be vulnerable. For the longest time, vulnerability was something I perceived as a weakness.

D.M. So when you were doing Joan Wilder, it was tougher for you to do the earlier scenes in the film, before Joan began to exert herself.

K.T. Oh, absolutely. The mousy, insecure Joan was a stretch for me. The strong, confident Joan you see at the end of the film came naturally.

D.M. When you become a type, you are immediately identifiable to the audience, so you have more work to do as an actor to separate yourself from the part in their eyes. In theater, the roles are so much richer, and you get to do the whole role in one go, so it seems there is more of an inherent mystery in the characters. Is there more work to do in film then, where the roles are maybe shallower or less interesting?

K.T. It's not more work, but it's a different type of work. In film, characters are shallower because movies are quicker and there is less backstory and less understanding. What's the average film run now? Maybe an hour and a half? That just isn't enough time to do a lot of deep character work.

D.M. But in terms of typecasting, you don't seem to have had a problem doing characters who weren't totally strong-willed. Joan Wilder was mousy at the beginning of *Romancing the Stone*, and Joanna Crane was a very weak, troubled character in *Crimes of Passion*.

K.T. Getting out of the "strong woman" cast hasn't ever been a huge problem. My problem was always convincing Hollywood that I could do roles that an attractive, sexy woman wasn't supposed to be able to do, in their eyes. I had to prove to them, from the beginning, that a beautiful woman could also be funny. Getting *The Man With Two Brains* after being known only for *Body Heat* was not easy, and even after that film I had to audition intensely to prove I could handle the comic beats of *Romancing the Stone*. But all I need is the audition, because I am a great comedienne. *Serial Mom* is one of my greatest achievements as a film actor.

D.M. I combed through all the reviews for your films in prepping for this conversation, and your reviews on *The Man with Two Brains*, even by critics who didn't love the film, were across-the-board glowing.

K.T. Oh yeah?

D.M. You were cited in most of the reviews as one of the funniest things about the movie.

K.T. That's nice, I didn't know.

D.M. So clearly from the outset you had a lot of success proving you could do comedy.

K.T. It's a good thing too, because there are a lot of great roles in comedies. I would hate to be limited to doing only dramatic parts.

D.M. But you're okay with being typecast in these "strong, opinionated women" roles.

K.T. I have to be. But since I don't play victims, the "strong, opinionated woman" roles are the ones I gravitate toward anyway. What annoys me is that for so many playwrights and screenwriters, "strong" in a woman also means she has to be a bitch, a somewhat nefarious character. A guy can be strong and a hero, but if a woman is strong, she must be a villain.

Don't get me wrong, villains can be fun to play, and I've done a number of them, but women can be strong and good. Joan Wilder is a good person and a strong person. V.I. Warshawski is a good person and a strong person. Sister Jamie in *High* is a good person and a strong person. I hope that young women can look at the roles I have done and see a number of characters to admire. Characters that could be vulnerable, but also could be heroines.

And I mean, really, if you're going to be typecast, you couldn't do much better than "strong, opinionated woman," could you? It's not like I get all the scripts looking for wallflowers and wimps.

D.M. It's hard to imagine you as a wallflower or a wimp.

K.T. I could play them, I just wouldn't enjoy it.

D.M. Is there a downside to not really being a type?

K.T. Well, when you are a type, you get offered every role that fits that type, so you have a lot of roles to choose from. But of course, they're all the same role, so who'd want that? The biggest payoff from not allowing myself to get typecast has been longevity. I'm still working regularly, all these years later, doing great roles in great projects that I feel passionately about. If you allow yourself to be typecast, and the role you are typecast in falls out of style, then you fall out of style with it. That never happened for me because I never allowed myself to play the same type of role too often. And as a result, I'm still here while so many of the actresses I worked with in the eighties and nineties have been sort of forced into retirement. This plan, to never allow myself to be pigeonholed in one type of role, has been entirely by design, with this desired result. The plan has worked.

D.M. So you don't have a favorite type of role. Do you have a favorite genre you prefer to work in?

K.T. Well, it's always about the role and the story and the writing for me, and not the genre, but having said that, I must say that I prefer comedies. I like to laugh and I like to make people laugh. There's a great deal of truth and pathos in a laugh. Where and why one laughs can be a great lesson. It can also be a challenge—when you do most of your great dramatic roles you're working mostly with instinctive gut reactions to the material. Anger, shame, fear, pity—all these things are communicated and felt by the audience instinctively and immediately.

But when you make them laugh, you are conveying a thought. Getting a laugh from an audience is the difference between making an audience feel something versus think something. It's not hard to get an audience to feel something, because grief, rage, sorrow—those things are primal emotions—but when an audience laughs, they've acknowledged an actual idea. That means you've made them think.

When I hear somebody laugh, I know they got the idea, not just the feeling. And when you hear the laugh from the back row of the fourth level at the same time that you hear it from the front row—which is physically impossible because sound doesn't travel that way—then you know that what has happened is that the audience has become one single physical entity of its own.

That's the power of a laugh. It's an audible acknowledgement of a group of people having the same thought and the same feeling at the same time. And when it happens because of something you said or did, it's an exhilarating feeling. There's nothing like it, it's a rush.

D.M. Are there any genres you absolutely won't do?

K.T. I won't do what I call "kid jeop," films that put children in physical jeopardy as a way to generate suspense.

D.M. Those films are just cheap and offensive. Not only that, but it's also narratively lazy. Like the horror film where a woman is stalked through a house by a killer. That's just boring, lazy screenwriting. It's narratively uninteresting and tired. Try something new for once, show some imagination.

K.T. Thankfully, that type of screenplay is usually pretty easy to identify, so I don't waste my time reading the entire thing.

D.M. As a fan of the genre, what I am looking for in a good thriller or horror film are characters I can care about. Even if the story is a little tired, it's forgivable if the characters generate enough sympathy that the audience actually cares what happens to them.

K.T. Amen.

BODY HEAT

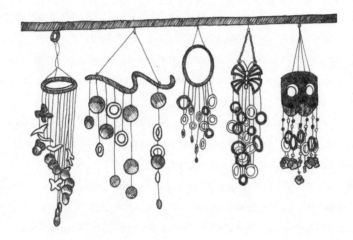

Dustin Morrow Your first film ever, amazingly, was *Body Heat*. What a film, and what a role, to debut in!

Kathleen Turner No kidding. Not only was Matty a fantastic character in a truly great film, she was at the center of the film. The whole movie rotated around her. A part like that is difficult to get as an established actress, let alone as a virtual unknown.

D.M. *Body Heat* is a really tonally specific movie, grounded in film noir, a genre that's more than half a century old. I imagine that had to have affected your performance.

Film noir is the genre of stylized Hollywood crime thrillers with dark, cynical world views. Film noir ran strong from the early 1940s to the late 1950s. Classic examples include the films The Big Sleep, Detour, Double Indemnity, *and* Gun Crazy.

K.T. Sort of. It's more important to find the tone in the rhythms and choices in the language, in the dialogue. I didn't sit down and watch a bunch of old film noir, or for a moment seek to emulate the performances of the iconic actresses in those films. If I'd done that I would have looked ridiculous.

D.M. How did you find your way into that role then?

K.T. One thing that helped us find the tone of that script was that we had a long rehearsal process. Or long by Hollywood standards, anyway. Studios don't understand why you'd want four weeks of rehearsal, although they should—if we have time to work out our choices in rehearsal, where you don't have to pay for location rentals or hundreds of crew members, they end up saving a lot of money when it comes time to shoot. They'll just never get that.

But on *Body Heat* and the other film I did with Larry Kasdan, *The Accidental Tourist*, we had tons of time to rehearse. Coppola was big on rehearsal time, too, and I think you can see that in his films and the performances he's able to get out of his actors. During the rehearsals on *Body Heat*, and sometimes on the set, Larry would play this sexy, sultry jazz music. That music created a mood that certainly helped us find the tone he was going for, the neo-noir thing. And believe me, we needed it, because there's nothing sexy or sultry about how cold we were!

D.M. Oh, that's right! You shot that in the dead of winter.

K.T. We had to keep ice cubes in our cheeks between takes to keep our breath from showing in our exhalations! It certainly would have been easier to find that sultry tone if it had actually been hot out when we shot, if our sweat didn't have to be applied artificially. We were supposed to shoot in June but there was an actors strike and we got pushed to December.

D.M. Let's talk about the most iconic scene from *Body Heat*.

K.T. Ah yes, I already know which scene you're going to ask about.

D.M. Well, it is considered by many to be the sexiest scene in the history of cinema. In the scene, your character, Matty Walker, has seduced William Hurt's character, Ned Racine, but turned him away at the door of her house. She stands inside the house, looking at him with a smoldering stare, until the passion of the moment drives him so crazy that he is compelled to send a deck chair crashing through her window to get into the house and embrace her.

K.T. It might just be the steamiest scene ever—it's always winning those polls for "Sexiest Scene in Film." It was a frustrating scene to shoot, though.

D.M. How so?

K.T. It was one of the earliest uses of the steadicam.

The steadicam is a stabilizing mount for a camera that allows the camera operator to capture fluid, smooth shots while moving over uneven surfaces. Its most famous early use was in the shot in which Sylvester Stallone runs up the steps of the Philadelphia Art Museum in Rocky.

D.M. That's a tough rig for anyone to use.

K.T. Especially back then. This was 30-odd years ago, and the steadicam then was even heavier and more cumbersome then than it is today. This poor operator was strapped into this huge rig, and the thing just kept failing. In the scene Bill is pacing back and forth outside the house, peering through the windows and the doors, while I'm in there doing my best to smolder. Then he's to take a chair off the porch and send it crashing through the glass door to get at me. Larry was intent on getting all of this in one continuous shot, tracking behind Bill with the steadicam.

But the steadicam kept failing, again and again, messing up take after take after take. It was hard for Bill and I because it was such an intense scene, and we had to stay in this heightened state of arousal and emotion for hour after hour. And Larry was freaking out because it was getting to be 5:00 in the morning and the sun was coming up, and he was going to lose the darkness he needed for the scene. When the shot finally worked, Bill smashed the window, strode in and embraced me, and Larry called cut because there was too much light in the space.

We had to pick up the scene the next night. But we had built up this incredible level of intensity and angst and sheer bloody frustration over twelve hours of trying to get the shot, so to come in the next night and have to start cold at that same place was very difficult. It was a little worrisome, but after a few minutes we found that the tension just came pouring back. It was incredible that we were able to tap so easily into that heightened state of arousal again.

D.M. So the most famous moment in that film, which lasts just seconds on the screen, was done over two separate nights.

K.T. Yep. Watch the film—there's an edit. He smashed the window and stormed in on one night, then he embraced me and we kissed about twenty-four hours later.

D.M. Crazy.

K.T. That's filmmaking for you.

D.M. As a filmmaker, I find that very frustrating, when I have to break up an emotional scene over multiple shooting days.

K.T. It hasn't happened to me that often. They try to schedule shooting so that if we have to break in the middle of a scene, it's not usually at a moment like that. But that night we had no choice. Can't stop the sun from coming up.

D.M. One of the interesting things about a lot of your characters, and this is certainly true of Matty Walker in *Body Heat*, is that they are themselves, in some way, performing or acting.

K.T. That's true.

D.M. At the beginning of that scene, Matty has invited Ned to her house under the false pretense that he's there to see her wind-chime collection, and she has to pretend that she feels really ill-at-ease that William Hurt's character has come to her house and that she has let him into her house, like she's having second thoughts about cheating on her husband. But the reality is that it's all completely premeditated on her part, and she's faking her hesitation in order to deceive him into thinking he's the aggressor in the relationship, and that it's his idea, eventually, to kill her husband, when in fact she planned it all along. I was wondering how you were thinking about that when you were doing the part, because that's true for your character for almost the entire film. It's almost like you had to give a performance within a performance.

K.T. That's exactly it. That process primarily consisted of deciding where to leave little clues as to her true nature and motivations, clues like hesitating on the choice of a word or the inflection on a phrase or the employing of backward glances. All had to be things that the audience would notice almost subliminally, or that they would notice and forget, or notice but wonder if they'd really seen what they thought they'd seen.

That way, when they get to the final reveal, and see her for who she really is, it's a shock but not outside the reality of the movie. And they can then remember those moments they questioned, those hints that I dropped, and go, "Oh yeah, I remember when she did this or she said that or she didn't seem sure about that—now that makes sense." So there was a thinking throughout the performance of leaving these little breadcrumbs, a trail leading to the real Matty Walker.

D.M. And those moments where you left those small clues were carefully calculated.

K.T. They were completely calculated and planned in advance. I knew exactly where I wanted to hesitate, where I wanted to create doubt in the minds of the audience. It was very strategic.

D.M. Was it hard to work with the stylized dialogue of *Body Heat*, which is so overcooked in the fashion of classic film noirs? Or in something like *Serial Mom*, where the dialogue is not written in a very naturalistic way?

K.T. The dialogue in *Body Heat* works because of its consistency. It's one tone, from beginning to end. So once I got into it, it wasn't an issue, because it just became the way that Matty spoke.

D.M. I think that's true for the viewer, too. It seems a bit affected when you first start watching it, but after ten minutes or so you just get wrapped up in its rhythms and you're not so aware that you are watching something very stylistically determined.

K.T. The familiarity of the structure and style of dialogue of the film noir genre is what allowed us to accomplish what we did with that movie. People were able to accept the style of the film because they recognized it as an homage to this existing genre. It's not that you have to have an encyclopedic knowledge of film noir to enjoy *Body Heat*, but if you know the genre and understand its conventions, then there's another layer of self-reflexivity there for you to enjoy.

D.M. It had to have been tough to nail those specific rhythms in the dialogue.

K.T. It took a little while to get it. But luckily, with *Body Heat* we had that luxury of the four weeks of rehearsal, which you don't get on most movies. But Larry insisted on it. And through that process we found the tone of the dialogue. As an actor and as an audience, you get used to stylized dialogue, you accept the style like you would accept the style of a novel you're reading, or you would accept the style of Shakespeare or any kind of historical press, or French comedy or farce. In the style of its shooting and music and in the structure of its plot, *Body Heat* is immediately identifiable as a film noir, and once you identify it as such, you roll with it as an audience. If you resist that, you're not going to connect with the film. The rhythms and very specific style were very helpful in *Body Heat* because they allowed you to believe that Matty might be acting, and the twist at the end was plausible because the entire film was a touch unnatural.

D.M. I suppose that's the neo-noir framing of the film, that it subscribes to the narrative conventions of the genre of film noir while seeking to slyly subvert some of its stylistic tropes. Like shooting in color, as opposed to black and white.

K.T. It's generally regarded as such, but I actually think it's an even more subversive film than it's been given credit for.

D.M. There's a moment in that scene that I always thought was interesting because I feel like it borders on comedic. As he's leaving after seeing her wind chimes, she kisses him and then she closes the door and then she hangs for a moment and looks at him provocatively through the little window in the door.

K.T. She's testing him.

D.M. I always thought that was really gutsy of Kasdan to hang on that moment, that come-hither look through the little window, because it comes so dangerously close to pushing the scene over the top, flirting even with parody.

K.T. That was entirely Larry's choice. And it's a great choice. Matty is trying to provoke him. She's taking no chances that he might not come back to the door.

D.M. Well, he isn't the smartest guy on the planet, despite his high opinion of himself. She does say when she first meets him, "You're not too smart—I like that in a man."

K.T. Yes, that come-hither look she gives him after she closes the door is like an insurance policy. She's making sure he gets the point. When she tells him earlier that he's not that smart, he reads it as flirtation, which is how she wanted him to read it. But she also really meant it, of course.

D.M. Do you think that it's important that she dupes the audience as well as Ned on a first viewing of the film?

K.T. Basically. The only issue there is that the conventions of the film noir genre are so well-known that I think a part of you expects her to betray him.

D.M. That's true, and it would almost have been a letdown if she hadn't. One of the pleasures of film noir is watching the cocky protagonist get his comeuppance. If the femme fatale doesn't engage in femme fatale behavior, well then, what's the point?

K.T. Exactly.

D.M. The great thing about *Body Heat* is precisely that it's not a conventional film noir. It tweaks the traditions of the genre just enough to keep the audience on its toes, and fulfills enough of the conventions not to disappoint die-hard fans of the genre.

K.T. It did make some bold leaps in the genre. Shooting in color for one, as you mentioned, and being explicit in ways that the older noirs weren't able to be, both in its language and its depiction of sex and nudity.

D.M. And narratively, it was different in that the villain got away. In most film noirs, the hero ended up dead or punished in some way, but the villain also ended up dead. In *Double Indemnity*, the classic film to which *Body Heat* pays the most resemblance, Fred MacMurray ends up expiring, but so does the villain, played by Barbara Stanwyck.

K.T. Matty may get away in *Body Heat*, but I don't think it's a happy ending for her. Despite the fact that she succeeds with her plan, I think she's the big loser at the end of the film. What is the use of wealth and luxury if you've lost the ability to love someone, to trust someone? What a lonely, empty life she has ahead of her at the end of that movie. In the end, she's a very sad character.

D.M. Did Kasdan reference specific movies or actors from classic film noir while you were making the film?

K.T. Never. He said we were working in an established genre, but beyond that he didn't reference specific films or actors.

D.M. Wow, really? There's so much of *Double Indemnity* in *Body Heat*.

K.T. He didn't talk about it.

D.M. So he had other methods for helping you to find that character.

K.T. He and I decided together that the key to the character of Matty was her single-mindedness. Her ability to tune out everything but what she wants, and to go after it with utter focus and steely determination.

D.M. In watching it again to prepare for this conversation, I looked closely at your performance for those hints as to Matty's true motivations. It was almost like watching *The Sixth Sense*, or any film with a jaw-dropping twist at the end, for a second time. Everything about the film plays differently. Knowing the twist at the end, knowing how Matty constructed her plan, I was able to see your performance in a completely different light, and I think I enjoyed it even more while looking at the nuances of those two layers.

K.T. I think that *Body Heat* is the rare film with a twist ending that can be just as pleasurable in repeat viewings.

D.M. Of course, again, the conventions of film noir are so widely known that it's debatable whether the twist ending is a twist at all.

K.T. That's true.

D.M. I was reading old reviews of the film and the British critic David Thompson wrote of you that you had "angry eyes" in this movie. I kind of love that.

K.T. Well, one thing that's interesting about that film is that she seduces him not by being warm and welcoming, but by being hesitant and almost a little hostile toward him. She pretends to resist him every step of the way and she presents herself to him as a woman who doesn't trust others easily or well. There is this constant challenge, this constant series of dares from her. She knew that that's what would work on him. That the only way to seduce a guy with an inflated sense of self like his would be to challenge him, to play hard-to-get. He enjoys the game as much as the reward. She read him like a book.

D.M. The other piece of critical writing I found on *Body Heat* that intrigued me came from Roger Ebert, who was a huge fan of yours throughout your career. He always wrote lovely things about you, even when he didn't like some of the films you were in. About *Body Heat*, he wrote that when the audience first begins to buy the sexual confidence in your performance, the film ceases to be a film noir. That's when he thinks it actually transcends the genre.

K.T. I can see that. As a screenwriter and a director, Larry uses genre as a base. He makes films rooted in specific genres, but he moves beyond their restrictions. And part of what Ebert may be picking up on there is that I was very young, and as I recall I was really not very knowledgeable about film noir at all. I had not been the greatest student of filmmaking. As a young actress my life had been all about theater. That was truly the extent of my expertise and my desires and my projections about myself. So although Larry directed my performance to fit within the film noir framework, that was his work. I wasn't consciously showing up on the set everyday thinking, "I am the classic femme fatale. I have to act in a film noir style."

D.M. If anything, that lack of awareness is probably one of the things that makes your performance in the film noir canon so singular.

K.T. I've always found being somewhat unaware of the work that's come before, that is very much like the work I'm doing, can actually be a good thing. This is why I will never see performances by actors in roles that I plan to do in the near future. I want to make my own choices, uninfluenced.

D.M. So the sense of all of the Lauren Bacall comparisons came much later to you, after *Body Heat*.

Bacall, with her classic femme fatale roles in The Big Sleep *and* To Have and Have Not, *her silky hair and smoky, sexy voice, was a natural comparison for about fifty million journalists and critics writing about Kathleen in her very early film career. Comparisons to Bacall were nearly omnipresent in the writing about Kathleen by the press in the early eighties.*

K.T. When people first started saying that, I had no idea what they were talking about. You would be amazed how ignorant I was and still can be sometimes.

D.M. Hey—ignorance is bliss!

K.T. In that situation, it can be!

D.M. You must have met Bacall.

K.T. Oh, many times. I think that the first time I met her, I said, "So, as you've probably heard, I'm the new you." Can you believe that? I was gutsy. That cracked her up.

D.M. Did you become friends?

K.T. Not really, but I would see her from time to time at industry functions and awards ceremonies. We used to have this great game: Everytime we would run into each other, she'd say "Ms. Turner." And I'd reply (lowers her voice) "Ms. Bacall." And then she'd go even lower: "How are you?" And then I would say, (deepens her voice again) "Well. And you?" And we'd just see who could get the lowest. It was great.

D.M. There's something to be said for you as an actor that it took you no time at all to transcend those comparisons to Bacall. It didn't take much time for people to stop referring to you as a Lauren Bacall type and start referring to other actresses as a Kathleen Turner type.

K.T. That's just career longevity, honey. I stuck around.

D.M. But I think it happened pretty early in your career.

K.T. Well, it may just have been a result of the fact that there weren't many actresses doing the kind of thing I was doing at that time.

D.M. Since it was your first film, I imagine you learned a lot from *Body Heat*.

K.T. Did I ever. *Body Heat* was an enormous education for me. I spent all my time on that set trying to learn everything I could about the film-making process, so I could give the best performance possible. I asked Larry a million questions a day. Luckily, since it was his first film as a director, he probably didn't realize that the cast wasn't supposed to pester the director to that degree. But also, since it was his first film, he had a lot to learn, and by sticking to his side, I could learn with him. And I was so lucky to have him as my first director. He's just wonderful, a great filmmaker. Utterly serious and committed to the work. He's a real writer in an industry with few real writers. He has true vision.

D.M. What was the biggest thing you took away from *Body Heat*?

K.T. A new level of courage. To take a chance, even when something seems intimidating or scary, even if you are afraid of looking foolish or ridiculous, to just do it. Take a risk. There's no reward without risk. That idea has followed me throughout my career, as I keep doing new things.

THE MAN WITH TWO BRAINS

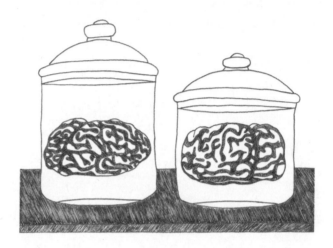

DUSTIN MORROW You followed up *Body Heat* with *The Man With Two Brains*, a profoundly silly comedy.

In Carl Reiner's film The Man with Two Brains, *Kathleen plays the not-so-subtly named Dolores Benedict, the duplicitous, scheming wife of Steve Martin's even-more-ridiculously named Michael Hfuhruhurr. Martin is a neurosurgeon who invents "cranial screw top brain surgery." It's even crazier than it sounds.*

KATHLEEN TURNER On my part, that character was a deliberate spoof of the character of Matty Walker in *Body Heat*. Just look at her name: Dolores Benedict. Classic. Even her name was ridiculous.

D.M. So it was a conscious move on your part to do a riff on the *Body Heat* character.

K.T. Oh, absolutely. I was so besieged with pressure to do a sequel to *Body Heat* or to do something exactly like *Body Heat* that I just became fed up and I decided to go the completely opposite way and intentionally spoof the role.

D.M. As we'll discuss when we get to your later roles, this wouldn't be the first time you basically flipped Hollywood the bird when it tried to pigeonhole you.

K.T. Indeed! I like that idea, giving Hollywood the metaphorical finger.

D.M. Steve Martin and Carl Reiner were known at that time primarily for *The Jerk*, one of the looniest comedies in film history. Martin wasn't yet known as an erudite playwright, novelist, and serious actor. Choosing to work with these guys at that time could not have been an obvious decision.

K.T. The screenplay simply stood out amidst all the *Body Heat* rip-offs I was being offered. Carl Reiner and Steve Martin came to me with a great opportunity to make fun of the image that Hollywood so quickly assigned to me, and I jumped on it.

D.M. You have made some broad comedies—*Baby Geniuses, Undercover Blues, Dumb and Dumber To*—but *The Man with Two Brains* is probably your goofiest movie.

K.T. I'd say so. It's a fun movie. My favorite shot is when my character is looking out the window at the Mexican gardener and he stretches and flexes his muscles and she starts panting heavily and Steve Martin walks in, surprises her, and she twirls and hits the floor. It's a great pratfall. I'm proud of that dive!

D.M. My favorite moment is when you drop-kick the cat up onto the Renoir painting.

K.T. Oh yeah, that was ridiculous!

D.M. I take that back. My favorite moment is when Steve Martin tosses you off the porch and yells, "Into the mud, scum queen!"

K.T. That's a classic line. But I'm glad that's not one of the lines I get when fans run into me on the street.

D.M. Yeah, it's a bit more aggressive than "I'm not bad, I'm just drawn that way."

K.T. Yes, that's the line I probably get the most. That or one of fifty lines from *Serial Mom*.

D.M. Your pratfall into that mud in that scene wasn't too shabby, either.

K.T. Thanks! And after *Man with Two Brains* I did *Romancing the Stone*—what was with me and the mud at that point in my career?

D.M. Good question! Maybe you were a mud wrestler in another life.

K.T. That must be it!

D.M. You've said in many interviews that one of the things that you like about film acting is how much precision there is in it, how you can be really small and detailed and deliver a lot through doing very little. So what's interesting to me about all three of the scenes from *Man with Two Brains* that we've just mentioned, and about your other broad comedies, is that there must be some fear about going that big, that expressive, on film. If film as a medium amplifies everything the actor does, it must be tough to decide how to modulate your performance so that it's just broad enough to be funny without getting so broad as to imbalance the scene. I mean, there's a moment in this movie where you turn to Steve Martin and bellow with an insane Southern accent, "I'm just gonna have to find me a new man to torture!"

K.T. "I love to see the veins in your temple throb!"

D.M. Yeah, that scene! How do you know where to pitch that note in such an unforgiving medium? You'd really have to trust your director to protect you in a scene like that.

K.T. It is very precise, it's truly very affected and the danger of overacting is ever-present in scenes like those. But if you keep it within the realm of believability, for whatever is considered believable in the context of that particular movie, and if you're ceaselessly consistent in your performance, then it will work. For as broad as Dolores Benedict is, she's a consistent, complete character, and my performance never slips or winks at the audience. That's the key.

D.M. And you were working with two comedic masters in Carl Reiner and Steve Martin.

K.T. Right, there's no way when you're acting opposite Steve Martin in a broad comedy that anyone's going to accuse you of going over the top. And directors like Carl Reiner, or John Waters, have such a precise sense of comic timing that they will never steer you wrong. I had total trust in Carl and in Steve Martin, because even though it's a very silly movie, their approach to it was deadly serious.

D.M. How do you mean?

K.T. The comedy was just very well-considered. Very deliberate. It looks effortless onscreen, but it's a result of a lot of hard work and serious discussion.

D.M. I'm a huge Steve Martin fan, and it doesn't surprise me to hear how serious he is on the set. His wonderful novels, despite their comedic touch, are actually quite melancholy.

K.T. He was very shy and very quiet on the set. Quite different from his onscreen persona. He was extremely professional and committed to the work, but not sociable on the set at all. Which is fine, if that's how he does his best work.

D.M. Dolores seems like she must have been a hoot to play.

K.T. Characters like that are fun, I just don't want to do them too often. There is a great, heightened sort of flamboyance and sense of style to a character like Dolores that is its own joy, its own fun. But I much prefer a character who thinks and feels something a little deeper.

D.M. I can see how there were definite limitations of that character, given the type of film that is.

K.T. Dolores is all surface—you really never know or care what this woman's life has been like or why she is the way she is, and you never think that she might change and become a better person. So it's a lot of fun because it's very stylized, but it's not all that dramatically satisfying. I don't know how actors who play those sorts of characters in movie after movie do it without getting bored. For me, it's an occasional treat, but I don't want to make a steady diet of that kind of part.

ROMANCING THE STONE

DUSTIN MORROW After *The Man With Two Brains* came the blockbuster hit *Romancing the Stone*. That's another film that, given your previous film work, you must not have seemed an obvious choice for.

KATHLEEN TURNER Well, I was certainly a name actress by that point. The big question that Robert Zemekis and Michael Douglas had when they considered hiring me for the role was about the earlier portion of the script, where I had to be a mousy wallflower. They knew I could be the glamorous, confident woman at the end of the film, but they weren't sold on me as a shy introvert.

Michael Douglas was both the producer of and lead actor in Romancing the Stone. *Robert Zemekis directed the film. Douglas was a seasoned producer by that point, having won an Oscar some years earlier for* One Flew Over the Cuckoo's Nest, *but was less-known as a leading man in film. Zemekis was at the time a largely untested filmmaker, having directed only two films previous, neither of which did very well at the box office.*

D.M. I guess their only reference for you was from two very glamorous parts, Matty and Dolores.

K.T. Basically. So I had to go in and show them I could do it. At the beginning of the film, Joan was so insecure and so small that I gave her this little, quiet, breathy voice, and I didn't make eye contact with anyone. When a character addressed me, I just looked away and mostly down at the floor. I kept her gestures very small, very contained, like when she picks up the book and puts it down, she does it so gingerly. Everything I did as Joan was about not drawing attention to myself. And then as the film goes on, she starts to crack open a little. It begins with a physicality that opens up in the jungle, when she finally starts to stride through the trees, leading the way and chopping the branches with the machete.

D.M. How did you approach the opening up of that physicality?

K.T. I suppose she was forced to get physical just to survive in that hostile environment.

D.M. And she was forced to get physical because he makes her carry her own weight. He makes her haul her own suitcase, and she's the first one down the mudslide, and the first one across the canyon on the rope, and when he tires of chopping with the machete, she picks it up and takes the lead to keep them moving forward.

K.T. The physicality in that role was the key to unlocking it. And not just because it was an action movie, but because so much of Joan's confidence emerged from her physicality. I've always been a very physical actress, and very physical in general—I was always an athlete as a young person—so it was easy for me to make that link.

D.M. I can see where a history in athletics would be helpful to you as an actor.

K.T. Sports give women tremendous confidence. I think it's important for young women to get involved in sports. I was always an athlete, from a very young age, and sports gave me great confidence in myself. I tapped into that to play Joan—when she starts to feel strong and more physically confident, it carries over into her personality and her own view of herself. You can see that really clearly in the film, how with every step she gains a little more confidence. So finally, during the scene at the fiesta in the village, when he pulls her onto the dance floor, she's able to pick it up and match him move-for-move, even though she doesn't really know how to dance. It was fun to plot out that physical progression for her.

D.M. So, like the slow revelation of Matty Walker's duplicitous character, that progression for Joan was very carefully pre-planned.

K.T. Absolutely.

D.M. I'd imagine that that was very complicated, not only because you were shooting out of sequence and you had to position yourself at a different "level of confidence" every day of shooting, but because it was an action movie shooting in the jungles of Mexico, and that can't have been an easy shoot.

K.T. It most certainly wasn't easy. It was especially tough on Michael since he was also producing. But it was also great fun. I got really beat up on that picture, but I had a great time all the same.

In terms of mapping the character, it all comes from the same place, regardless of what the genre is, where you're shooting, or how tough the shoot is. It's all about finding ways to color the character with small gestures, line deliveries, to propel the character arc forward. After she swings across the canyon on the vine, she lands and she's so shaken up and surprised that she's still alive that the only thing she can think to do is have a drink, so she digs into her bag for one of those tiny wine bottles she got on the airplane.

Her grabbing for that vine was unintentional, it was instinctual, so it's not like she became Tarzan all of the sudden. And yet, even though it was unintentional, she did it. She had the instinct to do it. So there was confidence to be gained from swinging over that canyon. When she nervously takes that drink, it's a comical moment because of what's just come before it, but it's also a small triumph for her.

D.M. For me, the key to her character is that she's a writer. She creates fantastical stories in her head. And like most creative types, she has a lot of self-doubt, a lot of insecurity. Of all the professions Diane Thomas could have given her, she made Joan a writer.

Diane Thomas was Romancing the Stone's *late screenwriter. She was tragically killed in an auto accident in 1985, in a Porsche that was given to her as a gift from Michael Douglas to celebrate the incredible success of* Romancing the Stone. *UCLA created the Diane Thomas Screen-writing Award in her honor.*

K.T. Specifically a writer of fantasy and adventure, that's the real key.

D.M. Exactly. Joan felt she was meant for greater things. Which, in a fairytale way, was a beautiful thing since Diane Thomas was a waitress when she wrote the screenplay, dreaming of better things for herself.

K.T. She was a wonderful person.

D.M. Her passing was tragic. To think of the stories she might have given us.

K.T. She had an incredible dignity as an artist—she was fiercely protective of her script and of the character of Joan. Even though at the time she sold it she really needed the money, she wouldn't sell that script to just anyone. It had to go to someone who would do right by that character.

D.M. It's easy to picture her like Joan, really getting into her own story at the beginning of the film. I love Joan's introduction, crying while writing her latest romance novel, with the big headphones on. It's one of the all-time great introductions to a character, in my opinion.

K.T. That's a picture of my parents on her desk in that shot.

D.M. Really? That's wonderful.

K.T. Yeah, I put them in the movie. Maybe that's why it was my mother's favorite film that I have done!

D.M. That she's crying, that she's so moved by her own writing, really resonates once she finds herself in her own real-life adventure. After she celebrates her book's completion with her cat, she stares up at a poster of one of her book covers, with the mythical hero she's created, Jesse, with such an intense longing. That moment connects with the later scene in the downed drug transport plane in the jungle, where she and Douglas's character, Jack, have camped for the night. She's giving him a hard time.

K.T. Right, she's criticizing him for not being a gentleman, not being protective, not being gallant.

D.M. He's disappointing her because she's realizing that, despite looking the part, he's not Jesse, the hero of her idealistic novels. The way you look up at him, when he first appears on the hillside, when Joan's being held up at gunpoint by the villain, it's the same look you give the Jesse on the poster at the opening of the film.

K.T. Yes, that was planned. Bob shot it so Michael looks exactly like the Jesse in the poster.

D.M. Exactly. So later, in the plane, when she starts lecturing him on what a real man is, it has everything to do with the fabricated idea of a Hero that she's created as a writer. She's written a story that can't ever be true, for no matter how swashbuckling and charming Douglas is in this movie, at the end of the film he can't save her. He can't climb the fortress wall at the end to save her, and she has to save herself from the villain.

K.T. She does. The film wouldn't have worked as well as it did if he had made it up that wall and come to her rescue. She had to do it on her own.

Joan was a wonderful character. And I like that scene in the plane very much, I think that there's great comedy in that exchange. I love when she goes face down after inhaling all the marijuana smoke. I did a great faceplant in that scene!

D.M. The way you play getting high in that scene is pretty adorable. Your eyes are very wide, you are eating olives like a squirrel, and you speak with a bit too much deliberation. Was this based on any real experiences with marijuana?

K.T. Of course not!

D.M. Hey, well, you went to college, as Joan says in the movie.

K.T. Oh please.

D.M. My closest friends in college were mostly theater majors, so I know what goes on at the parties thrown by the theater kids.

K.T. I have no idea what you are talking about, she said innocently.

D.M. Ha! I have never met anyone that doesn't really like *Romancing the Stone* when I bring it up, but in spite of its success, it's a movie that I feel hasn't gotten the credit that it really deserves.

K.T. It was written off as a lightweight action movie, not Academy Award material, not serious filmmaking. But in fact I think it's damn good. And I think it has some excellent acting.

D.M. The Golden Globes recognized that, at least, as you won the Best Actress award for it.

The film was nominated for Best Film Editing at the Oscars, and won Best Motion Picture Comedy at the Golden Globes, in addition to Kathleen's win for Best Actress. Kathleen also won Best Actress from the L.A. Film Critics Association.

K.T. I think it's really good filmmaking. If it came out now it would probably get a great deal more respect than it did then. I think it's very good work, frankly.

D.M. It's always been an inspiring and important movie for me. It's a key film in my life, and the experience of seeing it, and realizing the immersive, transporting, escapist powers of cinema, was one of the reasons that I decided to study film seriously. I can potently remember seeing it for the first time. I could probably show you the seat in the theater where I sat.

Granted, I was a very little kid at the time, not even into double digits, and I watched movies with the open-eyed enthusiasm that only kids can manage, but it was the first experience I can remember being truly entranced by a film. I was so caught up in it that by the time it ended I had literally forgotten that I was sitting in a movie theater. When it ended it felt like someone had thrown a bucket of cold water on me, it was such a sharp snapping-back into reality. I can still remember sitting in that theater as the credits started rolling and thinking, "I want this movie to go on forever. I want to stay with these characters." It was my realization of how powerful the escapism of the cinema could be—that it wasn't just a commercial thing, or a "fun" thing, that it had real capacity to move people, to affect them emotionally and to take them outside their own lives.

K.T. That's just lovely, thanks for sharing that.

D.M. For many cineastes, escapism in filmgoing doesn't just mean "relaxing" or "blowing off steam," it can be a truly transportative experience, an almost out-of-body experience.

K.T. You are lucky to be able to engage with a creative work, with art, on that level.

D.M. I am aware that it sounds a little goofy, because the notion of escapism is a sentimental one, and because *Romancing* is at its heart a popcorn movie.

K.T. Well, that's where you find escapist entertainment, in pop culture that is targeted at the masses. If it were an impenetrable little art film, you might have appreciated it in a strong way, but not been swept away by it in the way that you were. And the film's phenomenal success suggests you certainly weren't alone in the filmgoing experience that you had.

D.M. I understand that you and I have in common that Joan is our favorite role of yours.

K.T. Joan's always been my favorite film character that I've done. One of the nice things about her is that, even though she was so timid and so closed off and so insecure at the open of the film, she still had this belief that wonderful things were out there, that wonderful things would happen and that true love did exist, and that she could find it. She was an optimist. And what I think is really sort of sweet toward the end of the movie is that she learns she was right all along. She's affirmed. Wonderful things do happen, extraordinary things, if we just believe they will and work at it.

And even though the film is a romance, and she finds her Prince Charming, those things she learns about herself aren't tied to another person. She does end the film in the arms of her true love, but she doesn't need him in order to be affirmed and confident and happy. She walks the streets of New York alone with great confidence, with her head held high, before she sees him and his sailboat, come to get her and sweep her away. As you said, she saves herself at the end of the film—she's not a damsel in distress.

D.M. And at the end of the film, when Joan's publisher is finishing reading her new book about her adventure, it's revealed that she's added a happy ending where she and the Douglas character have reunited before she and Douglas actually reunite. We see her gazing dreamily out the window, and when Holland Taylor, as the publisher, says, "You're a world-class hopeless romantic, Joan," she responds, "No, a hope*ful* romantic. A *hopeful* romantic."

K.T. Right, "hopeful." It's not that she gets the guy in the end, it's that she changes, that she comes into her own.

D.M. It's such a huge change from the beginning of the film, where she seems so helpless.

K.T. *Romancing* was ahead of its time in its moving the female character to the center of the action.

D.M. That's true. Most movies up until that point, and let's face it, since that point, would never think of having the dashing male hero sliding around on the side of a fortress wall, providing comic relief, while the supposed damsel in distress is left to face, and defeat, the villain all on her own.

K.T. That was all Diane Thomas, it was a great screenplay.

D.M. The major female action hero, in the form of Sigourney Weaver in *Aliens*, and then Linda Hamilton in *Terminator 2*, was still a few years away at the time that *Romancing* came out.

K.T. The film was definitely ahead of its time in terms of the portrayal of Joan. She more than held her own. That was the point of the whole film to me.

D.M. At the time of its release, one unfair comparison that was often made about *Romancing* was to *Raiders of the Lost Ark*, with some critics going so far as to call it a knockoff. Unfair not only because Diane Thomas was working on her script well before *Raiders* came out, but also because, beyond both having some slam-bang action in a jungle setting, the two films have almost nothing in common. Karen Allen plays a spunky character in that film, but she's also consistently being rescued and dragged around by Harrison Ford through the whole film. There's not a lot of character development for her.

K.T. That's why I won't do films like that, the characters don't tend to provide a lot of room for exploration. That, and I'm not interested in being saved by a man!

D.M. Can you tell me about the casting of your good friend, Holland Taylor, as Joan's publisher? I know that her scenes were all reshoots.

K.T. Yes, originally the publisher was played by a man, and the character was very chauvinist and condescending. Diane Thomas did not like the stuff we shot, and to her credit lobbied to reshoot those scenes with the publisher played by a woman. Joan was so downtrodden and meek at the beginning of the film, it just felt like overkill to have this chauvinist pig treating her poorly on top of all that.

D.M. The few scenes you share with Holland are quite charming, you can sense that your friendship is a real one.

K.T. The scene in the bar near the beginning of the movie, where Holland is trying to urge me to find a guy to go out with, is very, very strong.

D.M. I love how Holland narrates the long line of losers at the bar in that scene. And that even though they are losers, each represents a potential opportunity for Joan to meet someone and maybe not be lonely and unfulfilled anymore, and yet she holds to her ideal, her conception of the mythical Jesse.

K.T. She's protecting herself from settling, from letting other people tell her what should make her happy. Holland's character chastises her for holding to that ideal in that scene, but Joan holds to it anyway, and demonstrates a bit of the strength that becomes fully realized by the end of the film.

D.M. Also worth mentioning about that film is your chemistry with Michael Douglas. It would be the first of three movie matchups for you, and at the time of the release of those films, some journalists and critics were calling you the new Tracy and Hepburn.

K.T. We had potent chemistry in part because it was real. I hadn't met my husband yet at the time we made *Romancing*. I was single, and Michael was separated from his wife at the time. We were a million miles from nowhere in the middle of the jungles of Mexico on this incredibly hard, rigorous film shoot, and we were flirting intensely. I really fell for him. His wife came down to the set and they began patching things up, so I stepped aside immediately and that was the end of it. Nothing really ever happened between us, but the attraction was quite real.

D.M. It's amazing that it was such a hard shoot, because the film just feels so breezy and effortless and fun.

K.T. Don't get me wrong, it was great fun. But it wasn't effortless. It rained constantly, and we fought the elements everyday. Some of those locations were so arduous and so remote that Michael had to have roads built to reach them, so we could get the crew and the equipment up to them. But it was a real adventure. I took five trips in total down that mudslide in that famous mudslide scene where Michael comes down after me and ends up between my legs. Trying to get the mud out of my ears and nose at the end of the day wasn't exactly delightful, but it was an experience I will never forget. In what other occupation are you going to be paid to go down a mudslide in a jungle in Mexico? It was great!

D.M. I know you're quite notorious for doing a lot of your own stunts.

K.T. I did most of them. That's me going down the mudslide in *Romancing*, and me hanging off the side of the train in *Jewel of the Nile*. They wouldn't let me swing over the gorge or go over the waterfall in the car. If you look closely, you can see that it's a man doubling me in that stunt over the waterfall. The poor guy—probably one of the bravest stunts of his career, and he had to do it in a dress!

The *Romancing* set was also fun for me because I'm bilingual. I grew up in part in South America, and shooting that film had something of a "good to be back home" feeling for me. I had a good time just being a translator. Many of our actors, including Manuel Ojeda, who played the lead villain, spoke next to no English, and I was able to communicate on behalf of the director and the other actors. That was a unique experience.

D.M. *Romancing* really is a very special film.

K.T. Yes, it's borderline impossible for anyone to resist. Everyone who sees it seems to really like it. I'm very proud of it and I'm glad that many people still associate me with that character. It's an ageless film, it's really stood the test of time and I hope that future generations will continue to discover it.

CRIMES OF PASSION

DUSTIN MORROW After *Romancing* you did another 180, playing a character that couldn't be more unlike Joan. Except perhaps in the way that China Blue also had little sense of self-worth.

China Blue is Kathleen's character in Crimes of Passion, *Ken Russell's controversial film about a woman who is a successful but lonely designer by day and a prostitute by night. China Blue attracts the interest of two men who want to possess her—a lonely young man (played by John McLoughlin) who falls for her and a psychotic street preacher (Anthony Perkins) who thinks he can "save" her.*

KATHLEEN TURNER No sense of self-worth! If Joan had confidence issues, then Joanna Crane had no confidence at all.
D.M. And where Joan was a very wholesome character, China Blue was—
K.T. —a prostitute! Yes, it was definitely a deliberate choice on my part to do something very different from *Romancing*. It wasn't what Hollywood wanted me to do, that's for sure.

D.M. Has your family seen this movie?

K.T. I don't think my daughter has.

D.M. Is she purposefully avoiding it?

K.T. Probably. I don't think she wants to know about it.

D.M. I imagine it would be tough for her to watch, it's a rough movie.

K.T. That film was obviously a huge risk, and nobody, and I mean *nobody*, wanted me to do it. But it's important to take risks. Isabella Rosellini once told me that she decided to do *Blue Velvet* after seeing me in *Crimes of Passion*, which was really sweet. And that's now her most iconic role. So sometimes you just have to take the risk.

> Blue Velvet *is David Lynch's surreal, nightmarish thriller about a small town riddled with corruption and murder, featuring a frightening, brilliant performance by Dennis Hopper. Rosellini's part, which involved graphic violence and nudity, was perceived as degrading by many critics, although the film itself is considered a modern classic.*

D.M. Well, it paid off in this case, because *Crimes of Passion* has some of your finest work on film.

K.T. I would agree. I'm proud of my performance in it.

D.M. Like Matty Walker, China Blue is another sort of "performance-within-a-performance." China Blue is a character enacted by Joanna Crane.

K.T. Yes, China's actually a successful designer by day, named Joanna. China Blue is the name she uses at night in her double life as a prostitute.

D.M. She's an incredibly difficult character.

K.T. *Crimes of Passion* was one of the very rare cases where I did imagine something of a detailed backstory for the character. I thought of her as having had a very destructive relationship, maybe a marriage, and that at some point the man in the relationship, because Joanna was good at her job and decisive and strong, felt threatened by her. And as so many men with fragile egos might do in that situation, he retaliated by demeaning her as a woman, by characterizing her as a ballbreaker, as not feminine or sensitive.

87

This created a sort of identity crisis for her, and she was plagued by self-doubt, and the extreme result of that became a lack of esteem for herself. She put on this platinum wig and charged fifty bucks to prostitute herself on Hollywood Boulevard. That was her way of punishing herself, of enacting this self-hatred. This guy in this relationship that predates the narrative of the film completely destroyed her. She's not walking the street for thrills, it's not because she actually enjoys it, but because she feels that she has to keep punishing herself.

D.M. It's interesting then that the scenes in this movie where her character seems the least happy are the scenes where she is Joanna Crane, not the scenes where she is China Blue.

K.T. Well, at the same time that China Blue is degrading, she's also empowering. She controls the men she's with. Joanna's playing a character, as you said.

D.M. There's only one scene in the movie where, as China Blue, she lets her guard down and reveals her true self to a customer.

K.T. Yes, the scene with the dying old man. That's my favorite scene in the film.

In this scene, China Blue has been hired by a dying old man's wife to have sex with the old man before he passes away. The old man thanks her but refuses her advances, and offers to pay her anyway. China Blue is moved by the old man's gesture, removes her platinum wig to reveal Joanna, her true self, and embraces and comforts the man.

D.M. It's a lovely moment. And it's followed by a really discomfiting scene, where this customer she's been with, this man who has taken a seemingly genuine romantic interest in her, shows up at her apartment door unannounced because he wants to "save" her from her life as a streetwalker.

K.T. When she's Joanna Crane.

D.M. Right. Your performance in that scene is very interesting, because you are conveying all your discomfort through your body language. His presence there feels so invasive.

K.T. That's it. He's invaded her personal space. She feels bullied, oppressed.

D.M. She sits down on the couch with her back to him, so he speaks down at her.

K.T. That's the key to the whole scene—she's weak, she submits to him when she's Joanna Crane. This woman hates herself. She's such a sad character.

D.M. I'm fascinated by how you play the dual identities of one character. When you are playing China Blue, are you thinking, "I'm Joanna Crane acting as this other character" or is it more of a split-personality sort of thing, where you think of China Blue as a separate character entirely?

K.T. The latter. I think that when she becomes China Blue, it's to not be Joanna Crane anymore. It's really to forcibly remove her commitments and her responsibilities to Joanna Crane. It's a time-out in a way, but in a very obviously destructive, punishing, and painful way. So it's not so much that she's "pretending" or "acting" China Blue as that she's just become China Blue in the interest of absolutely negating the existence of Joanna Crane.

D.M. There's a reaction you have in this scene where he's stormed into her apartment, when he says, "We're the same person," that is very interesting. That statement seems to hit Joanna on a gut level.

K.T. Her reaction there is a rejection. "We're the same people." She interprets that line as meaning that they are the same people in that apartment that they were in the hotel room when she was China Blue. But it was China Blue in the hotel room, and it's Joanna in her home. She can't process that they are the same person, the truth of that is more than she can handle.

D.M. For me, that conflict provides the structure of the movie. What seems to be at stake is not just whether she's going to accept the love of this guy, find herself worthy of being loved by this guy, but whether she's going to be able to accept that Joanna Crane and China Blue are facets of the same person. Her real fear is attaching Joanna Crane to China Blue, accepting them as the same person, and from that come all of the issues involving intimacy, self-esteem, and the worthiness of love.

K.T. It just seems impossible. How does it end? I can't really remember.

D.M. It goes a bit off the rails. You get kidnapped by Anthony Perkins and tied up and Ken Russell goes crazy with the symbolism and the photography and music.

K.T. Oh, that's right. And then I put on Tony's clothes and he puts mine on. That was actually my idea because Ken showed up and said that he didn't really know how to finish the film. That's why I'm vague, because the movie didn't have an ending until shortly before we shot it. So I think I suggested that Tony and I switch wardrobe and see what happened. That stuff wasn't in the script, that's why I have forgotten it.

D.M. It's totally insane, but actually a pretty great ending because the movie is very much about identity. So to swap wardrobe in that scene is to swap identity.

K.T. Yeah, so I get points for that.

D.M. And yet another movie ends with Anthony Perkins in a dress.

K.T. Right! It's *Psycho* part two!

Anthony Perkins's most iconic role was in Alfred Hitchcock's classic Psycho, *in which he played villain Norman Bates.*

D.M. That sounds like a scary prospect, having your director come to you one day and go, "Hey, do you have any ideas for an ending?"

K.T. It was terrifying, actually. That was a long, tough shoot. I got very sick. My husband jumped on a plane and flew out to L.A. and it was high drama. It turned out to be a really bad sinus infection, but they thought for a while that it was meningitis. We started shooting at six every morning, and the doctor didn't open until after eight, so of course I shot two scenes before I went to the doctor, sick as a dog. It's a crazy business. Or my work ethic is ridiculous. Or both.

D.M. It was too expensive to shut down, I suppose.

K.T. It wasn't in the budget to shut down. The budget was pretty small on that film. And Ken was a little unhinged and wasn't very healthy himself by the time we made that movie.

Ken Russell, the film's director, was a legendary British filmmaker who in his long career made a number of controversial films that explored sex and religion. Among his films were Women in Love, The Devils, The Who's Tommy, *and* Altered States. *He passed away in 2011 at the age of 84.*

D.M. A brilliant filmmaker, though. A singular voice in cinema, for sure.

K.T. Absolutely. That's one of the reasons I did the film, to work with him. He was a madman, but a genius. I really loved his film *The Music Lovers*, which came out at the beginning of the Seventies, I think.

The Music Lovers is Russell's well-regarded 1970 biopic of Tchaikovsky, Kathleen's favorite composer. Richard Chamberlain played the lead.

That's an extraordinary film, and I adored Richard Chamberlain in it, so it was great to work with him all these years later on *The Perfect Family*.

In the 2012 comedy The Perfect Family, *Kathleen played a homemaker who is up for the Catholic Woman of the Year Award, but has to hide her highly dysfunctional family in order to pursue it. Chamberlain plays her church's priest.*

D.M. Was Ken Russell tough to work with?

K.T. Well, the drinking started early in the day, so by the end of the day he was not always totally coherent. I knew about that going in, though. I'd heard that he hit the scotch starting at six in the morning. When I got to the set on the first morning, though, he was drinking wine. So I thought, well, that's an improvement, I guess!

But Ken's energy and passion for the film were so contagious that he made you want to work hard for him, and take risks. It wasn't always easy, but he was a great creative partner. My first day home after wrapping that film, I slept 22 hours straight, if that tells you anything about what it's like to do a Ken Russell film.

D.M. Did you deliberate on that a lot—that decision to work with him?

K.T. No. It was too good a part, and I wanted to play it. Ken might have been certifiable, but he was also a genius. There's a great scene in this movie that takes place in a seedy hotel room where the wallpaper is shiny and reflective. And Ken had a flashing neon light set outside the window that was meant to be the motel sign on the street. And that was the only light source in the shot, so our acting had to take place within the timing of the flashing light, which Ken regulated to interact in interesting ways with the dialogue and how we played it. The light dictated the dramatic rhythms of the scene. That's pure cinema. He was great with stuff like that, he just really understood the language of cinema in a way that few filmmakers do.

You know, shortly before he passed away, he was planning a film version of *Alice in Wonderland*, and he wanted me to play the Red Queen. Can you imagine? Ken Russell's *Alice in Wonderland*!

D.M. That would have been demented and amazing.

K.T. That would have been some film, for sure.

D.M. And how was working with Anthony Perkins?

K.T. That's another story. Ken could be a madman, but I never felt like I was in any danger around him. But Tony was more unpredictable. I never knew what he was going to do in a scene. If you see fear from me in those scenes, it's not all acting.

D.M. It works for his performance, he's very scary in the film.

K.T. Obviously everything worked out okay, he was a gifted actor and he and I have some incredible scenes together in that film, but I'd be lying if I said he was a total joy to work with.

D.M. How do you think about the film now?

K.T. I'm still glad I did it, and there weren't really any negative repercussions that came from having done it. I haven't seen it in many years, but I would imagine that it still holds up as an artistically daring film.

D.M. I think it's one of Ken Russell's signature works, and that's saying something.

K.T. He was an important part of film history, a great voice in cinema, and I'm glad I had the opportunity to work with him.

PRIZZI'S HONOR

DUSTIN MORROW Speaking of collaboration with legendary but ailing filmmakers, you also worked with John Huston when he was in failing health.

> *John Huston was the legendary director of such classic films as* The Maltese Falcon, The Treasure of the Sierra Madre, The African Queen, *and* The Misfits.

KATHLEEN TURNER Yes, *Prizzi's Honor* was his last big-budget studio film. He made one more film after *Prizzi's*, a much smaller picture based on a James Joyce story.

> *The film Huston made after* Prizzi's Honor *was the low-budget* The Dead, *starring his daughter Anjelica Huston, released in 1987. The director passed away four months before the film's release.*

D.M. Did his health hinder him as a director on that set?

K.T. Not really. He was still as feisty as ever, not mentally diminished in any way. The guy beat my pants off in backgammon so many times that I thought he was cheating. So I bought him a nice pair of silver dice for Christmas, which I knew were not weighted, and he still destroyed me.

What his health problems did result in was the actors having more freedom to work out the scenes on their own. Huston was on oxygen, and it wasn't easy for him to move around. You could actually see him counting the steps if he'd have to move across the set to say something, to decide if it was worth it. So he'd let Jack and I work out our scenes, and when we had something we liked, we would go show him and get his input then.

D.M. Huston seemed to be great with actors, with letting the camera inform the performances, and vice versa.

K.T. Oh, absolutely. There's a scene in *Prizzi's* in which Jack and I are on our first sort of unofficial date, in a restaurant, and we're sitting in a booth flirting. We keep getting closer and closer to each other, subtly shifting our posture and our weight so that we very slowly move ever closer to each other as the attraction grows. And every time we shift, even slightly, the camera tracks in a little closer. It's all done in one long shot, with no cuts.

D.M. That scene would have played differently if he'd shot it with the more traditional strategy, with a master shot and then crosscutting close-ups.

K.T. Totally. We would have had to play it differently, come up with something else to convey what that camera move conveyed. It's a great example of how an actor can have fun with the camera.

John Huston was wonderful, he really understood how to shoot a scene to pull the most out of the performances.

D.M. He was also a notorious alleged misogynist.

K.T. Well, he wasn't the greatest respecter of women, but he was a brilliant filmmaker and a very nice man.

D.M. And to his credit, his films have given us some wonderfully powerful female characters.

K.T. Indeed. He directed Hepburn in *The African Queen*, after all.

D.M. And your character in *Prizzi's Honor*, Irene Walker, falls in that line, too.

K.T. She does. She's a self-supporting, tough woman, doing a job typically assigned to male characters in film.

D.M. She's tough. In that scene where the two of you are on your first date, your character is talking about the origins of your Polish name, and Jack says, "Either way, you're sure one beautiful woman to me," and she completely ignores the compliment.

K.T. She's used to it. She uses her looks all the time. How do you think she got so far in her profession, as an assassin? People just wouldn't think that this pretty little thing could be that cold-hearted and capable of killing someone.

D.M. In that respect, is this yet another character of yours that is giving a performance within the film?

K.T. Is she acting? Sometimes.

D.M. She legitimately falls in love with Jack's character and it becomes a real relationship, though.

K.T. I believe so. In the very last scene when he pulls the knife on her and she pulls the gun on him, she misses. Now what do you think is faster, a bullet or a knife? And when does she ever miss? I think that she missed on purpose, that at the last second she just couldn't kill him. I don't know that John agreed with me, but that was my thinking as I played it.

D.M. Roger Ebert made some comment in his review that your character is so slick that he felt she could sell anything to anybody. It does seem that this is another character, like Matty Walker or China Blue, that has ulterior motives, or some semblance of a false front, a dual identity.

K.T. I don't think her original attraction to Jack's character was because he was such a heartthrob. He had a good position in the mafia, that's where the money in her business was, and she wanted in. But I do think that she does ultimately, sincerely fall for him. Of course, you find out eventually that she was married to a guy who ripped off the mob and that she has been lying through the whole film. So there is a level of performance there.

D.M. Definitely.

K.T. It's not something I've consciously thought of, to be honest, through my career. I haven't ever gone out looking for roles in which the character is herself somehow performing.

D.M. It is a through-line in much of your film and stage work though.

K.T. I suppose so. It does make for an interesting challenge for an actor, and I am always looking for roles to challenge me.

PEGGY SUE GOT MARRIED

DUSTIN MORROW Peggy Sue is a different kind of challenge.

Peggy Sue Got Married *is Francis Ford Coppola's charming time-travel comedy about a woman in her forties who is knocked in the head at her high school reunion and finds herself transported back to her days as a teenager, where she learns some valuable life lessons. Kathleen received her only Oscar nomination for Best Actress for the film.*

KATHLEEN TURNER Well, as in the earlier roles, she too is performing on some level. After she travels back in time, Peggy Sue had to pretend she didn't know what was to come in the future. She had to pretend to be oblivious.

D.M. Peggy Sue is so sweet and genuine, obviously not somebody that's calculated enough to think "I'm going to give a performance and fool all these people into thinking I'm a teenager." She just falls naturally back into the rhythms of what it was to be a teenager. Almost like a muscle memory.

K.T. She is a great character. It's a magical movie.

D.M. And another great filmmaker. You've worked with a good number of the best directors in all of film.

K.T. Francis is brilliant.

D.M. He's a very passionate filmmaker with strong opinions. Did you butt heads with him at all?

K.T. Very little. It was mostly smooth sailing. I can only remember one thing. If I recall correctly, the studio made it a stipulation of Francis's keeping final cut on the film that he had to stay strictly on schedule. And it was a tough schedule, so we often found ourselves working these epically long days. Which we were all happy to do, because Francis was such an inspiring director and we all wanted to help him fulfill his creative vision.

So we had worked one of these twenty-plus hour days, and everyone was exhausted. We were just dead on our feet. Francis asked me if I would mind if he went back to his trailer so he could relax. I said, "Well, how are you going to direct the scene?" And he told me he had a video feed from the camera piped into his trailer and he'd communicate with the Assistant Director via walkie-talkie. So I said, "No, I don't mind, you go and direct from your trailer. And I'll go to *my* trailer and give my performance there."

D.M. Ha! I'm guessing that put an end to that idea.

K.T. Indeed—he laughed and said, "Fair enough." Francis is a sweetheart and I loved working with him. He's one of the few true geniuses of cinema.

Just look at the first shot of *Peggy Sue*—he tells you everything you need to know. Peggy Sue is looking at herself in the mirror, dressed in her old prom dress, full of regret and confusion. And the camera pulls back and back, right through the mirror itself. There was no mirror there, obviously, we shot that with a body double sitting opposite me. So creative. It's just a magical opening.

D.M. And thematically it's fantastic.

K.T. That's clearly where it came from, a kind of through-the-looking-glass idea, that was definitely Francis's intention. It's a wonderful moment, pure cinema. You could not do that onstage, obviously.

D.M. The thing that everybody writes about when they write about your performance in *Peggy Sue* is the manner in which you were able to convey the attitude and mannerisms of a teenager without the aid of any makeup.

K.T. No, it was all in the voice and the body language. We didn't use any makeup tricks or anything like that to take her from forty-two to sixteen. I had to find other ways to essay that change, so for me it became entirely about Peggy Sue's loosening her grasp on the forty-two-year-old Peggy Sue and embracing the sixteen-year-old Peggy Sue. It was a letting go of all that she had learned over the years, growing up, that had not yet happened for her sixteen-year-old self.

So it was an interesting blend, for me, of both the actor and the character having to forget all this experience and try to a find a less crowded slate to work with. Peggy Sue really was a complicated character, because that's an incredibly internal thing that I had to accomplish, that I had to find some way to convey externally so that it registered with the audience.

D.M. You nailed the ways in which a teenager throws herself onto a bed, the way she holds her books, the way she flips her hair. And it's fun to watch you play those things, but what I really appreciate are the details you put in that betray Peggy Sue, that reveal her true age and life experience. She seems like a teenager pretty consistently, but she slips occasionally, and the jaded adult slips through.

K.T. A lot of the physicality of Peggy Sue followed the interior dialogue, that wrestling with being a forty-two-year-old woman in the body of a sixteen-year-old girl. As opposed to a role like Joan Wilder, where the physicality helped to create the character, this was sort of the opposite process. Peggy Sue's interior dialogue created the movement.

D.M. When she has a drink, she leans on the bookcase for a moment and all of a sudden she looks like Mrs. Robinson in *The Graduate*, she looks like she's been drinking for decades. It's such a subtle comic moment.

K.T. Those moments provided a lot of opportunity for me, those times when Peggy Sue couldn't help herself and she gave her "future self" away. For example, when she hears her grandmother's voice on the phone, the audience immediately knows from her reaction that this woman's been dead for years. That's an example of a very specific thing I used from my own life, to find a character in the moment. I was thinking of my father, who died just as I was turning eighteen, and what it would mean to me to pick up the phone and hear his voice again. That scene really resonates for me, and means a lot to me, for that reason.

D.M. There's a scene when she leaves home for her first day of school again as a teenager. Nicolas Cage's character picks her up to drive her to school. It's not played as a big scene, but it strikes me as incredibly complicated from a performance standpoint. You can argue that there are several layers of performance there.

Nicolas Cage plays Peggy Sue's husband Charlie, who as a teenager was a wild kid with a lot of ambition and grand dreams, but who grows up to be a disappointment to everyone, including himself.

K.T. Yeah. She's an adult looking at the ridiculousness of the situation, and confronting the feelings of seeing her husband looking so innocent and so young; she's putting on a front that she's an actual teenager; and she's actually beginning to slip into the natural rhythms of being a teenager. There are at least three layers to that part.

D.M. It seems like an incredibly tough part to play, especially since it's all on you, that Coppola didn't have them do any makeup magic to try to age you backwards.

K.T. It wasn't that tough, actually. It felt quite natural that she's juggling all these balls at the same time. That's what it's about. If you were to go back to your past with knowledge of the future and you don't want to betray the fact that you know what you know about what's coming, then what do you hide? What do you show? How do you react to what's happening right now?

Peggy Sue can't remember every detail of her life history, so she is hearing these words at the moment she is hearing them, but in the context of what she knows is going to happen later in her life.

D.M. It's like a constant state of déjà vu.

K.T. Not exactly. It's not that she's walking around going, "I remember this, I remember that." She's just trying to process, in the moment, everything she's encountering through the lens of knowing how things will eventually turn out.

D.M. In that scene we were just discussing, he drops her off at school, says a few things that reveal him to be the doofus he was, and you register this hilarious facial expression that says, "I can't believe I actually go on to marry this guy."

K.T. Yes, and while that's funny in the scene, and it's played for laughs, there's an undercurrent of sadness in the idea.

D.M. Right. The dark side of this story comes to a head, I think, in the scene in the basement where you really start giving him a hard time about stuff that he hasn't actually done yet, and promises he hasn't made yet, but that you know will go unfulfilled. It's a rough scene, because even though she knows he'll grow up to be a loser who takes her down with him, he hasn't done anything yet at that point. He's still just a kid, with hopes and dreams, like any other kid.

K.T. He's an innocent.

D.M. She really rakes him over the coals in that scene, but somehow Francis stages it in a way that your character doesn't lose the sympathy of the audience.

K.T. It's about where that scene comes in the film, in its narrative structure. By that point you've got to feel the frustration that she has been feeling. You, too, have to be exasperated by Charlie. What else can she do in that scene? She knows what a huge disappointment he is going to be, but what does she do with that knowledge? What can she do? It's clear by that point that she can't change him. And that's just frustrating as hell. She feels trapped, like she's going to be forced to repeat the same mistakes.

D.M. She really seems to be having the argument with herself.

K.T. And that's the key to that scene. He's so clueless that it's not really about him. It's about all those years of pent-up frustration, of broken promises and dashed dreams and pledges unfulfilled. She's being hard on him, but she's really being hard on herself.

D.M. It's a brutal, gut-wrenching scene.

K.T. Devastating.

D.M. Ebert wrote glowing things about your performance in this, even calling it a textbook study in using body language in acting.

K.T. As I said, that was all second-nature. Her state of mind, her interior dialogue informed the way she carried herself. When she hurls herself on the bed, she is sixteen. She just is. She's not thinking, "Now that I'm sixteen again, this is how a sixteen-year-old throws herself on a bed." She just does it.

And how couldn't she? How could anyone go back to being sixteen and not slip back into the true behavior that they had at that time? It would be impossible not to, because not to would mean that you'd have to be thinking about it every second, it would be a level of cognitive awareness that no one's capable of. She's literally back in her sixteen-year-old body, in her sixteen-year-old life, so she is true to the life of a sixteen-year-old. What's lovely about the role is that as the film goes on, you can see what being sixteen again does to her forty-two-year-old self. Her adult person almost slips away a little. She's renewed.

D.M. The romance of time travel, in part, is that I think people always assume that it would be the opposite of what you're saying, that if they could just go back and do it all over again, they would retain full awareness of their future selves and act accordingly.

K.T. I don't think so. She ends up with Charlie at the end of the film, after all, even knowing all the mistakes he'll make. And that's a happy ending, too. It's okay, sometimes, that history repeats itself, if we can learn from our mistakes and move forward.

D.M. In a way, Peggy Sue seems as physical a role as some of those in your action movies.

K.T. I suppose all my acting is tremendously physically oriented. The body creates emotions and creates thoughts, independent of choices, independent of your mind. If your body is feeling a certain way or in a certain state then your mind reflects the body, not just the other way around. I think the longer that Peggy Sue stayed sixteen, the more she lost her adult self. Or if not lost, then the more indistinct the teenaged Peggy Sue became from the adult Peggy Sue.

D.M. It was a role that gave you a lot to work with.

K.T. It was an incredible role. Great fun to play. Francis made a warm, wonderful film, it's one of my favorites.

THE ACCIDENTAL TOURIST

DUSTIN MORROW *The Accidental Tourist* is another favorite film of yours.

Based on a bestselling novel by Anne Tyler, Lawrence Kasdan's The Accidental Tourist *tells the story of a travel writer, played by William Hurt, who is left by his wife (Kathleen) after the death of their young son. Depressed and cut off from the world, he finds his way back into a worthy life through the friendship of an eccentric dog trainer, played by Geena Davis, in an Oscar-winning performance.*

KATHLEEN TURNER I love it. It is one of my favorite films, really. Not just that I'm in, but period. Larry's screenplay was such a rich, faithful interpretation of that book. Anne Tyler thought so too, and she's fiercely protective of her novels, so for her to endorse the film really tells you something. That film got good reviews and won some awards, but I always felt that even so, it was underappreciated.

D.M. The scene at the opening of *The Accidental Tourist*, where you tell your husband that you want a divorce, is a powerful one. It's amazing how much ground it covers very quickly, as it not only provides all of the exposition for the film, but also serves as the catalyst to send the protagonist on his journey in the story.

K.T. It was a reshoot, actually.

D.M. Really? That's surprising.

K.T. Yeah, and it was a rewrite. Larry is a great filmmaker, but his one problem is that he really overshoots. The result is that sometimes he ends up with plot holes between scenes because he has so much material that he can't get it all into the film, and in trying to cut the scenes down he loses the narrative thread. So this is one of those times when he had about three scenes that were condensed in a rewrite and reshot into this one scene.

D.M. That actually makes sense, now that I think about it, because she really cuts to the chase. She sits him down and just lays it on him. There's no softening him for the blow that's to come.

K.T. I think we had a much slower progression originally to get to the point of separation and we just had to tighten it up in the reshoot.

D.M. This scene disturbs me because of all the small things you do before you drop the bomb on him. It's like small talk, but in the way you say it, it's clear you don't really care, you don't want to hear the answer. And the way you move to make him tea, and he doesn't want the tea, is tremendously uncomfortable.

K.T. She's rehearsed the whole thing in her mind. I always thought that she sort of planned this whole thing out ahead. "He's going to come home and I'm going to do this, then I'm going to do this, then I'm going to do this, and then when he is finally comfortable then I am going to tell him."

D.M. She also seems ready for the responses that he gives.

K.T. Exactly. She knows what he's going to say. He's not a man who can change easily, we know that right from the beginning. He's predictable, she knows how he's going to react and she's ready for it.

D.M. There are several moments in this scene where you do interesting things with your breathing and where you take pauses before you say your lines, that I always read as your character telling herself, "I've got to stay strong and not waffle, because he could easily talk me out of this."

K.T. That's the difference between her rehearsing it in her head and actually having to do it. That was a tough scene. Can you imagine that, having your child shot and killed?

I was also a very early mother at the time—my daughter was less than a year old when we shot that—and you can imagine the overwhelming maternal feelings that I was having. To have to imagine that happening to my child, it was just unthinkable.

D.M. Was there ever a moment before you took this role where you thought, "I don't know whether I want to do this"?

K.T. No, that sort of came later, when we first got together and read through the script. I was about seven months pregnant.

Funny story, real quick: Bill Pullman was part of that read-through, and Larry told me later that Bill came up to him afterwards and said, "I know that you said you wanted Kathleen Turner for this role, but I think this woman is great and you really ought to consider her." I was waddling around, big as a house, and somehow he just didn't place this pregnant woman as the Kathleen Turner he'd seen on the screen. And Larry, the prankster, let him think it. He just responded something to the effect of, "Okay, I guess we'll have her back for the next read-through."

But anyway, that's when it started to sink in, the places I was going to have to go to play this part. When I took it I was just thinking of how great it would be to do an Anne Tyler character, as she's one of my favorite writers, and how much I love Larry and Bill and really wanted to work with them again. It wasn't until I actually had my daughter that I realized how horrific such an event would be, how completely life-destroying. And how hard it was going to be to have to play that level of despair.

It makes perfect sense to me that the character couldn't sustain this marriage. It surprises me that she continued to live, frankly. If that happened to my child, I don't think I could have gone on, I really don't.

D.M. She's such a sad and sympathetic character. And yet by the end of the movie you've got to want William Hurt to end up with the other woman, the Geena Davis character, for the movie to work. That's a tricky thing to have to pull off.

K.T. It's beautiful screenwriting, from a rich and wonderful novel.

D.M. And of course, the other tricky thing about that scene, for the screenwriter, is all the exposition that has to be packed into it. We have to understand by the end of that short scene that their child was killed, how he was killed, how long it's been, how each parent reacted, and how those reactions have driven them apart. That's a lot of narrative back-story to pack into a scene that also has to serve as the emotional instigating moment for the plot, the moment that sends his character in a new direction.

Exposition is backstory, the narrative context, the information an audience needs to understand the main storyline.

K.T. The tough thing is that the audience knows exposition when it hears it, whether on stage or screen. The audience is savvy to it. So you just have to find a way to do it well, and hopefully it's a compromise between the writing and the acting. It has to be written carefully, so the actor can try to play it as if it isn't a break in the action. You can almost see in many films and plays when the exposition ends, because it's like a freedom comes over the actors. As in, "Now we can get on with the meat of the story."

D.M. It can sound incredibly awkward and forced if it's done poorly.

K.T. It works so well in this scene in *The Accidental Tourist* because it's combining exposition with this great emotional action. It's not just one or the other. Sometimes you don't get to play emotional change in an expository scene, you just have to give the audience the information. But because she is taking this step to end her marriage, you're more willing to listen to her provide the exposition. That exposition backs up her decision. The audience wonders why she's doing what she's doing, so they have the impetus to listen to the exposition.

D.M. *Tourist* is a lovely film, perhaps it's due for rediscovery.

K.T. I hope so. Larry did a truly phenomenal job with it.

THE WAR OF THE ROSES

DUSTIN MORROW Like *The Accidental Tourist*, *The War of the Roses* handles its exposition by tying it to the emotional arc of the characters, only in the early parts of *Roses* they are falling in love, not coming apart.

KATHLEEN TURNER Right. And that film has a lot of exposition. It takes awhile before the two characters really go to war.

Danny DeVito's dark comedy The War of the Roses *was the third matchup between he and Kathleen and Michael Douglas. The film tells the story of Barbara and Oliver Rose, who embark on perhaps the ugliest and scariest divorce in film history. The film was acclaimed by critics and was a hit at the box office.*

D.M. The great film critic Jonathan Rosenbaum made this interesting point about *The War of the Roses*, and the roles that you and Michael Douglas played previously.

K.T. Jack and Joan?

D.M. No, not the specific parts that you played together, but the types of roles you played separately, in other films.

K.T. Go on.

D.M. You played estranged housewives in *Peggy Sue Got Married* and *The Accidental Tourist* and femme fatales in *Body Heat* and *Prizzi's Honor*, and he played master-of-the-universe types in films like *Wall Street*, and husbands of questionable character in films like *Fatal Attraction*, and if you combine your previous parts and his previous parts, you sort of have Barbara and Oliver Rose.

K.T. I can see that.

D.M. And it makes sense that *The War of the Roses* becomes about a vicious divorce. There's no way your character in *Prizzi's Honor* would put up with his character in *Fatal Attraction*, and no way his power dealer in *Wall Street* would be swindled by your character in *Body Heat*.

K.T. It's a fun theory.

D.M. The scene where you first tell Oliver how you can't stand him is one of your favorites.

K.T. Definitely. It's the scene where he's come home from the hospital after his car accident and is interrogating her about why she never came to see him.

D.M. Right. It's a great scene.

K.T. Well, it's something that anybody understands, but so few of us ever have the opportunity to voice so eloquently.

D.M. What's that?

K.T. That feeling, that you're so fed up with someone that even watching them breathe disgusts you on a gut level. The writing in that scene is so sharp. She tells him that she didn't come visit him because she was scared, and then clarifies that she was scared because she was so happy. That's just really rich dialogue.

D.M. Your matter-of-fact delivery is really chilling in that scene.

K.T. Well, that's just good comedy. To present it almost flippantly, as "I thought it was, like, worth mentioning."

D.M. How did you approach that scene, to arrive at that matter-of-fact delivery?

K.T. It all stemmed from the moment she refers to, which actually happens offscreen in the film, where she was on her way to the hospital and she pulled over and she was scared because she felt such relief and such freedom at the thought that he might be dead. She was just shocked into realizing how tremendously unhappy and dissatisfied she had become. Why would she have this wave of relief if she didn't feel some terrible burden had been lifted?

So I don't think she had actually admitted it to herself before then, she was just going through the motions, day after day. He wasn't communicative, he wasn't appreciative, he wasn't supportive, and he was completely self-involved and expected her to basically be an adjunct to his life. But I don't think that she ever realized how much she resented it and how unhappy it made her until that moment she described, when she had to pull over to the side of the road.

D.M. So your motivation in the scene where she tells him is what, to hurt him or just let him know?

K.T. Just let him know. That's why I deliver the lines in such a matter-of-fact manner. She just can't bear the thought of moving forward after that experience as if nothing has happened. She has to be sure he knows.

D.M. One thing I find interesting about this movie, that in my research on this movie I could not find that anyone had written about, is the way it subtly plays with gender role reversal. It's a film about men and women, marriage and relationships, but it's also about the roles men and women, husbands and wives, are expected to fill. And in character, at least, it flips things a bit.

K.T. Yes, he's kind of a wet noodle, not real strong in the relationship, where she has steely resolve all the way through.

D.M. Yeah, he whines a lot, plays the victim, frames himself as the weaker of the two in order to gain some kind of sympathy from her.

K.T. I think so. She's more practical. More hard-nosed. And remember, it's her decision to end the marriage. For most of the film, he wants to "work things out," by which he means of course that he wants things to go back to how they were, where she keeps her trap shut and acts the dutiful little housewife.

D.M. Were you ever worried that that would make her character come off as colder than his? It's a movie where, in a sense, you and Douglas are competing for the allegiances of the audience.

K.T. Not so much, because she is just so charming. Danny relied to some extent on my personality and my personal charisma, my capacity to charm the audience even when I was doing or saying things that made me seem cold and unfeeling. I was definitely depending on my own charisma, you bet. It's a tool for any actor, one you have to use sometimes to hook your audience.

D.M. I think you also benefitted from your previous films together, *Romancing the Stone* and *The Jewel of the Nile*. Those two films were so good-natured, and it's so clear the three of you had a ball making those films, that some of that sense of playfulness had to carry over into *The War of the Roses*. So even when Barbara and Oliver are being awful people, the audience gives them a pass because it's all in the spirit of fun that frames the movie, and the outlandish black comedy as a subgenre in film.

K.T. Yes, and that carried over on the set, too. We had a rule that at the end of every shoot day we wouldn't leave without hugging each other. Some of those scenes got pretty intense and we were quite nasty to each other, so we made sure we didn't leave without giving a hug.

D.M. That comes across in the movie.

K.T. I think so. I think it's clear that we were having a ball.

D.M. How could you not with DeVito at the helm? I met him on a corporate video shoot once—talk about personal charisma and charm!

K.T. No kidding. I love Danny. He's warped, with a genuinely sick sense of humor. And I mean that in the best possible way. He's mischievous and fun, but also very professional. And he's creatively stubborn—when he knows what he wants as a director, he'll do anything to get it. He really went to the mat to protect the ending of *War of the Roses*, and from my perspective he saved the integrity of the film in the process.

D.M. Right. Because the studio wanted the two characters to live.

K.T. They did. And it would have been anticlimactic and out-of-step with the rest of the film. They had to die, it was inevitable.

D.M. It was a controversial ending. Actually, it was a pretty controversial movie.

K.T. It definitely struck a nerve. A lot of arguments were started between couples walking out of *War of the Roses*.

D.M. Did you have any idea it was going to be so big?

K.T. We had a feeling pretty early on. The reaction to the Barbara Rose character at the press junket for *War of the Roses*, before the movie came out, was just incredible. Almost all of the men would come in and say, "What a bitch . . . how could you?" and all the women would come and say, "Well done." It split right down the middle, it was really quite incredible. The men thought she was awful and the women thought she was a hero. I loved it. By the time we finished the press junket, we knew the film really worked.

D.M. The other thing I wanted to ask you about in that scene where Barbara tells Oliver she doesn't love him was the moment where Barbara punches Oliver in the nose, after he taunts her to do it.

K.T. "Go ahead, hit me, hit me!" I hit him, alright! I scared him.

D.M. I wonder if Barbara surprises herself when she actually socks him.

K.T. No, I don't think so.

D.M. I couldn't tell. You do look down at your fist, almost as if to say, "Did I really just do that?"

K.T. Maybe she's a bit surprised, but she hasn't an ounce of regret.

D.M. The moment that follows that isn't one of pride, it didn't look like you were happy that you did it.

K.T. No, it's just satisfaction. "You want me to hit you? You don't think I'll do it? Okay, well here you go." I really startled Michael in that shot. After we shot that, he went, "God, you almost hit me!" I said, "Yeah, the important word being *almost!*"

D.M. You'd done enough stunts in your films by that point to know what you were doing there, right? He was never in any real danger.

K.T. Contrary to what he thought, no, he wasn't.

SERIAL MOM

DUSTIN MORROW Between *Prizzi's Honor, War of the Roses,* and *Serial Mom,* you've appeared in three of the best-received cinematic dark comedies.

KATHLEEN TURNER I love black comedy. I love it on film and I love it on stage.

D.M. Based on the size of its cult following, I'm guessing that *Serial Mom* is many people's favorite Kathleen Turner role. And despite the proclamations of the two detectives at the opening of the film, that Beverly Sutphin is "as normal and as American as apple pie," we can see that she's clearly loopy the moment we lay eyes on her.

John Waters's Serial Mom *tells the story of Beverly Sutphin, a* Leave It to Beaver-*like homemaker who also happens to be a psychotic serial killer. Her targets are people that don't fit her wholesome moral code, like people that don't recycle or people who don't rewind videotapes before returning them to the video store.*

K.T. Well, yeah, totally! Nobody is that wholesome, that perky and chatty. I mean, "*Cereal* anyone?!" Ridiculous. And in that opening scene, when she locks onto the housefly, anyone could see she's a killer. It's in the eyes, the Serial Mom eyes. She almost caresses that fly with her eyes. "Alright, Mr. Fly, you're mine."

D.M. And as soon as she sees the fly, when she moves to get the fly-swatter, the way she's standing becomes much more aggressive. And the dress, without sleeves, even though it's pretty conservative and whole-some, makes you look tough.

K.T. My favorite moment in that scene is when she clearly gets upset that the fly got away for a second. She stalks it around the kitchen. All you have to do is see her kill this fly and you know she is capable of any-thing. You can really see her focus because of the tight close-ups on the crazed eyes, the eyes following the fly around the room. She's like a professional killer there. She's the Terminator.

D.M. What made John Waters think of you for *Serial Mom*?

K.T. He is a big fan of *The War of the Roses*, which is no surprise because he loves really dark comedies. He also liked *Crimes of Passion*, and he felt that any major actor who would take that kind of risk would also risk working with him.

John also knows how to seduce an actress. In our first meeting he told me there wasn't another actress alive who could pull off the part. Every actress wants to hear that!

D.M. Beyond the flattery, what attracted you to the role?

K.T. What fascinated me about Beverly Sutphin was her straightness, the intense wholesomeness of the character. Even though she's a killer, she's easily the straightest character I've ever played. I also like her strict adherence to a specific set of cultural, societal rules, so strong that minor infractions of the rules result in violent death. The character taps into the rage everyone has. She gets away with doing things that all of us fleetingly fantasize about.

D.M. She also speaks to our increasingly overly reactionary times. I think it's a more prescient film today than it was when it was released.

K.T. As a New Yorker, I can tell you that that's definitely true. When people used to get bumped on the street they might be kind of annoyed, but now when someone is bumped, they are instantly enraged.

D.M. And when Beverly is bumped, she kills.

K.T. It's satire, but it's not too far off. How many minor road rage incidents end in murder every year?

D.M. It is scary that Beverly seems like an increasingly *less* extreme character.

K.T. Isn't that the truth!

D.M. The way *Serial Mom* slyly jabs at the line between famous and infamous, and the goofy nature of fame, had to have been attractive to you as well, I would imagine. You'd been famous for well over a decade by the time you did *Serial Mom.*

K.T. That was a huge appeal. *Serial Mom* isn't a satire of serial killers, it's a satire of celebrity. John has a very cynical view of celebrity. *Serial Mom* questions the idea that one can become a cult hero by murdering people. That's a sick and twisted part of our culture, and that's what that film goes after. Some audiences missed that completely—the subject of the film is fame, not serial killing.

D.M. Much of John Waters's work is obviously inspired by his fascination with the 1950's. Even his contemporary films contain a lot of Fifties iconography. I imagine you were thinking specifically about stuff like Donna Reed and *Leave it to Beaver* in creating that character.

K.T. Nope.

D.M. Not at all?

K.T. I was aware of those shows, of course, and their cultural influence and significance, but the thing you have to remember is that except for a couple of years in Washington DC when I was in first and second grade, I did not grow up in the United States. I didn't get American television, not in Venezuela, and not in London. So I never saw any of the landmark American shows, and had very little sense of that iconic American nuclear family. When I came back to the States as an adult, it took me awhile to begin to understand the cultural references to those shows. So really, Beverly Sutphin is my own imagination at work, what I think the perfect little American housewife of that period might have been like.

D.M. The whole film, for me, hinges on your sincerity in your performance. There's no winking at the camera, no self-awareness or nod to the campiness of the film.

K.T. She's completely sincere. I played Beverly Sutphin as absolutely real. Beverly believed everything she said and did—she really believed she was the perfect mother, the perfect wife, and the perfect neighbor. So when her switch got flipped, when she exhibited this *nasty*, dark, ruthless quality, it came from a place of total sincerity. She was so sincere that when the switch got flipped and she became homicidal, it wasn't for me even like flipping a switch—it just felt like a perfectly natural transition, a natural extension of the wholesome part of her life. She was such a fun character to play, I had a great time on that set.

D.M. It was a masterful stroke of Waters's to cast you in that. And to cast Sam Waterston as Beverly's clueless husband.

K.T. Sam was wonderful in the film, although he didn't quite get what we were doing, I think. He asked me one day if I thought we were glorifying serial killing. "No Sam, I don't think we're celebrating serial killers." Sheesh!

D.M. But it's precisely that "not quite getting it" that makes him work so well in that part, and it's hard to imagine John Waters didn't want that when he cast him. He had to be looking for the squareness that Waterston brought to the part.

K.T. Yes, I suppose he probably was. I don't know how he convinced Sam to do the film, but with me it was just a matter of demonstrating to me exactly how he planned to shoot it. Because sticking a poker in somebody's back and then pulling out their liver—that can be horrific, or it can be kind of funny. It wouldn't be hard to take the *Serial Mom* script and make it a B-grade horror movie, instead of the comedy that we made. But it was very obvious, when we first talked, that John and I were on the same wavelength, in terms of our sense of humor and irreverence.

D.M. Beverly's a tricky part, because if there was ever a role where an actor could kind of wink at the camera, that's the one. But to do so would let all the air out of the movie, it'd turn it into a completely different thing.

K.T. I agree. That's something I learned from John Huston. When we were shooting *Prizzi's Honor*, John said to Jack Nicholson, "You know, you're always working really hard in your films to let the audience know that you're not really your character. It would be interesting to see you *not* do that this time, to *not* let yourself off the hook." And so that was on Jack's mind throughout the shoot, that "not winking" at the audience unless it was part of the character.

D.M. I feel like, to some degree, that's one of the things that separates movie stars from great character actors—a character actor will disappear into a part, where a movie star will make sure some large part of their outside-the-film persona seeps into the character. Nicholson is a great example of that, as were John Wayne and Humphrey Bogart, and maybe more recently, someone like Will Smith or Nicolas Cage. In fact, *Peggy Sue Got Married* was one of Cage's first big roles, and you could see that even then. He didn't seem to be playing the part, he was playing Nicholas Cage playing the part.

K.T. He was definitely still finding himself as an actor then, defining his style.

D.M. Like Matty Walker and China Blue and Irene Walker and Peggy Sue, Beverly Sutphin is a character with something to hide. She lies a lot.

K.T. That's true, but even though Matty Walker and Irene Walker were both killers, Beverly is actually closer to Peggy Sue. If she performs in some way, then it's a natural extension of her personality. It's not an intentional deception, she's not trying to put anything over on anyone.

D.M. Except of course when she tortures poor Dottie Hinkle.

Dottie is the character played by John Waters regular Mink Stole. Beverly prank calls Dottie Hinkle (with a mountain of hilarious profanity) and then frames her for something she didn't do.

K.T. Ah yes, the obscene phone call.

D.M. And the scene where she breaks the Faberge egg and blames it on Dottie.

K.T. Ah, right. I stand corrected.

D.M. It's a pretty broad part, similar to *The Man with Two Brains* in some ways.

K.T. It's very similar. It's very broad, but it's shameless. It's completely shameless, which of course is why it works.

D.M. That's John Waters for you. He's fearless.

Called the King of Bad Taste, a mantle he wears proudly, Waters is known in part for the graphic moments in his campy comedies, the most infamous of which comes at the end of the notorious Pink Flamingos, *when Waters's muse, the cross-dressing actor Divine, consumes actual dog excrement onscreen. Among Waters's classic films are* Polyester, Cry Baby, *and* Hairspray, *which was turned into a phenomenally successful Broadway musical and then back into a film remake starring John Travolta, and then into a live NBC performance featuring Martin Short and Jennifer Hudson.*

K.T. Yes, and really focused and confident in the world that he's creating onscreen. There isn't a moment in *Serial Mom* that rings false, that isn't true to that world. He doesn't compromise.

D.M. I'm a huge fan of his. I think his films are hilarious, and the thing that I admire most about them is that they have such affection for their characters, no matter how deplorable they are or how badly they behave. He never mocks his characters, he never laughs *at* them or looks down on them.

K.T. John can take incredibly unattractive people and make you care for them, and that's the extraordinary talent that attracts me to him. There's no maliciousness in that man, even when he's teasing someone. Beverly Sutphin is a psychopath, but down deep she is so good-hearted. John genuinely likes her, and therefore so does the film's audience.

D.M. Seems like it must have been a fun shoot.

K.T. Are you kidding? There were days we'd laugh so hard we'd cry. John establishes a really fun and relaxed mood on his set.

D.M. I've met him twice, briefly. He's hilarious. His films actually seem less outlandish after you meet him, because he's exactly like a character from his movies. It makes the world of his films feel more real.

K.T. Well, like his characters, he's an outsider. He respects his characters and wants them to win. Serial Mom gets away in the end, after all.

D.M. I love that film, I quote it pretty frequently.

K.T. You and a million fans I run into on the street everyday!

D.M. It's a very quotable film.

K.T. Want to see something cool?

D.M. What do you have?

I follow Kathleen into her den, where she has stacked in a corner a number of framed photographs and artwork. From out of the stack she pulls the absolutely enormous framed, painted portrait of Beverly Sutphin that was used in Serial Mom. *It's easily four feet tall and maybe three feet wide. To a* Serial Mom *fan, it's a true thing of beauty.*

K.T. When I sold my house out in the Hamptons I found this in the basement. This is the original painting that was above the mantelpiece in the living room in the film. Look at those crazy eyes!

D.M. That. Is. Amazing. You should hang that up.

K.T. Yeah, right!

D.M. Or give it to your favorite co-author of Kathleen-inspired books about acting. Do you know what a rabid *Serial Mom* fan like myself would give to own that piece of memorabilia?

K.T. I'm counting on it! I think I'll sell it on eBay.

D.M. Are you serious?

K.T. Heck yeah! Maybe I'll get some good money. I mean, can you believe this thing? Look at that hair!

D.M. I'm sure people ask you all the time what your favorite role was, but has anybody ever asked you what your favorite movie haircut was?

K.T. Well, it wasn't *Serial Mom*, that's for sure! In fact, after *Serial Mom*, I instituted the rule that all of my hairdressers, whenever they tease my hair, they can't leave for the day until they've brushed it out. I was doing *Virginia Woolf*, and there is a lot of teasing in that because that's set in 1962. My hairdresser, John, would say, "Look, by the third act its completely unkempt and unbrushed anyway, so can I go home?" And I would say "Nope! You tease it, you get it out—that's the rule."

D.M. Sounds fair to me.

K.T. Me too!

D.M. As a huge Waters fan, I can say that *Serial Mom* is my favorite film by him.

K.T. Mine too. Of course, I'm biased.

D.M. I saw John Waters in a speaking engagement a few years ago say that he felt it was the best film he ever made. He also said something really funny about you.

K.T. Oh dear. What was that?

D.M. He said there's no one in the world better than Kathleen Turner to have a martini with, because when she takes the first sip, she smacks her lips, sighs big and says, "AAAAAHHH!"

K.T. If you're going to have a martini, John Waters is about the best company you could ask for!

THE VIRGIN SUICIDES

DUSTIN MORROW After *Serial Mom*, your rheumatoid arthritis really began to take hold.

KATHLEEN TURNER Right. I kept working steadily onstage and on film, but that was definitely when I began to slow down.

D.M. You did your first telefilm, called *Friends at Last*, a couple of indie film dramas, *Moonlight and Valentino* and *The Real Blonde*, and then a couple of family films, *A Simple Wish* and *Baby Geniuses*. But your next prominent big screen dramatic role was probably *The Virgin Suicides*.

K.T. That's right.

D.M. And *The Virgin Suicides* probably came to you through Francis Ford Coppola.

K.T. Yes, Francis and Sofia needed my name to help get the film financed, and I was happy to support the film and to tackle that role.

Sofia Coppola was the film's writer and director, and is Francis's daughter. Sofia Coppola previously appeared onscreen in Peggy Sue Got Married, *as Peggy Sue's little sister.*

D.M. She wrote that on spec, amazingly.

"On spec" means that she didn't have legal permission to make the film at the time that she wrote the screenplay, as she did not yet own the rights to the book that she adapted.

K.T. Yes, she wrote it with no guarantee that the author, Jeffrey Eugenides, would let her make it. As with *The Accidental Tourist, Virgin Suicides* was an example of an author fiercely protective of his book, very averse to having it turned into a movie. But Sofia's script is so delicate, so beautiful, that she sold Eugenides on it. Sofia took a huge risk in spending all that time on that script, especially since she'd never made a feature film at that point and had no track record, really, because he could have just passed. She felt that story in her bones, she was born to make that film.

D.M. It's an incredible screenplay.

K.T. Yes, the script was nearly flawless from the outset. And Francis was producing, and I wanted to work with him again. And I responded strongly to the challenge of playing that character. But that was a tough one, harder than I thought it'd be when I took the part.

D.M. She's so contained, so inert. She's quite unlike any other role you've played.

Set in a small Michigan city in the sixties, The Virgin Suicides *tells a hazy, dreamy story about the Lisbon family, which is destroyed when all five daughters commit suicide. Kathleen plays the girls' mother. Their father is played by James Woods.*

K.T. It was frustrating with a capital F. It's hard for me to play repressed. That poor, poor woman. I'll tell you why that part needed my skill set as an actor.

The girls commit suicide, and everyone's searching for a reason why, and naturally they look to the parents. But it can't be such a simple answer as that the mother was so awful or so strict or so controlling and rigid that the girls had no other option but to commit suicide. That's too easy an answer. That's scapegoating. It will always be a true mystery why a fourteen-year-old decides that there is no reason to live. That pain is unimaginable. And there are so many young suicides without any indication that the parents were in any way responsible.

We want answers to be easy, we want the assignment of blame to be easy. So for these roles of the parents in *Virgin Suicides*, it had to be an actor and an actress who could be strict, make the girls burn their albums and make them dress a certain way, but without coming across as villains. And that's something that I am very good at, taking a character that in another actor's hands would easily be unattractive, unlikeable, easily-blamed, and making the audience care about her.

D.M. It's painful to watch what your character goes through in that film.

K.T. So painful. I had this image in my head of myself as this blow-up doll with a valve in the heel. And before we would roll the camera, I would imagine pulling that plug out and letting this woman just completely deflate. I would have no energy, no intention, no awareness. Just a kind of lifeless doll, that's what this woman was to me. In my eyes, she couldn't be blamed, because she didn't have any kind of life of her own. She was so terribly sad.

And then, of course, at this time my daughter Rachel was a teenager, like the girls in the film. So I could imagine this woman's grief. If it had been my daughter, I would have been inconsolable.

D.M. Is that something you're willing to do, to imagine something like that, something that awful, like the death of a loved one, in order to inform a part?

K.T. Not usually. But sometimes it just happens whether I want it to or not. In the film, when the youngest daughter goes out the window and lands on the fence and they come out the front door and see her, lifeless and impaled, my response was very visceral, and even surprised me a bit. I had thought about it, about what I could use and how far I could go, but what then actually happened was more than I had anticipated. That came from somewhere deep inside.

D.M. Your reaction in that scene is one of the things that goes a long way toward making her a really sympathetic character and having, as you said, audiences not hold her responsible for the girls' suicides. It's because your inclination in that scene is to protect the other daughters that are on the porch and not to run out to the girl on the fence. James Woods is the only one that goes out to the fence, you stay up on the porch and turn the girls away.

K.T. Right, she shifts into full-on protection mode. Her instinct is to protect her daughters. That character, that was extremely difficult for me. That was probably one of the hardest that I've done just because I could use so little of myself, so little of my own energy, so little of my own physicality. Her face had to be almost blank all the time. I bleached my eyebrows a bit so that you would have an even blanker canvas, I just wanted all the color and life drained from my face.

D.M. As an actor, your job is to express yourself, so it must have been tough to play someone so vacant.

K.T. She is probably the furthest from myself that I have ever tried to do. Yet I knew that I needed to do it, because Sofia and Francis needed someone like me to do it.

D.M. Was it a tougher part to do than the one in *The Accidental Tourist*?

K.T. Oh yeah.

D.M. They suffered similar, horrible circumstances.

K.T. But the *Accidental Tourist* character was much younger, much less set in her ways.

D.M. She was shattered but capable of change, capable of doing something monumental like end her marriage.

K.T. Right. But the mother in *Virgin Suicides* doesn't seem to have any command of or interest in her own life. She's given up. She's just following the rules as they have been laid out for her. I'm really not good at that. At least the mother in *The Accidental Tourist* is making decisions and trying to improve her life. This woman in *Virgin Suicides* wouldn't dream of it. Poor thing.

D.M. In the scene in *The Virgin Suicides* where the high school boys come to pick up your daughters for the school dance, you have almost no lines, and you're very non-confrontational, other than asking one of the boys how long he has had his driver's license, but it looks like you are in hell. It looks like you are suppressing every urge to kick them out of the house.

K.T. I think I played that as if I was terrified of them, as I recall.

D.M. She engages them in some painfully forced small talk.

She knew they were coming, obviously, but she behaves almost as if they weren't expected, as if they have caught her off-guard. When she calls upstairs to the girls, her voice is strained, it's unnaturally high.

D.M. And you wring your hands incessantly.

K.T. Of course, the hand-wringing. She's so uncomfortable, so tense.

D.M. James Woods plays your husband with a kind of nervous over-compensation. Instead of becoming inert, as your character does, he gets too extroverted. He's too eager to try to be normal.

K.T. Yes, that dynamic really works. Jim Woods and I did not get along real well, and in a positive way that might have informed our scenes.

D.M. What was the conflict?

K.T. I should clarify—it wasn't so much that we didn't get along as we just approached the film and our performances very differently, and that might have come through in a sense.

D.M. That's unfortunate, but yeah, the marriage in this film is clearly not a healthy one, and perhaps that a little real-life tension worked in some way to your advantage.

K.T. Perhaps. Ideally you'll get along with everyone you work with, but if not, I guess it's best when it can inform the work in some way. It's happened to me so infrequently, I don't really have a strong point of reference for it. With the exception of Burt Reynolds on *Switching Channels* and Nicolas Cage on *Peggy Sue*, I've gotten along reasonably well with everyone I've worked with.

D.M. And hey, if you don't get along, at least acting isn't like most professions, where you might have to see this person year after year.

K.T. That's true. After a few months at most, they can be out of your lives forever. Until you run into them at some awards show or charity function!

D.M. And then it's awkward and uncomfortable small talk time.

K.T. I usually opt for a well-timed dirty look.

THE PERFECT FAMILY

DUSTIN MORROW After *The Virgin Suicides*, you took a long break from doing leading roles on film.

KATHLEEN TURNER Yes. It was a combination of a number of things—not liking the film roles that were being offered to me, my desire to transition into being a full-time stage actor, and the complications of my RA.

D.M. What was it about *The Perfect Family* that lured you back?

In the 2012 comedy film The Perfect Family, *Kathleen plays a homemaker who is up for the Catholic Woman of the Year Award, but has to hide her dysfunctional family in order to pursue it. The film was directed by Anne Renton, and also features Emily Deschanel, Jason Ritter, and Elizabeth Pena.*

K.T. The screenplay was lovely, and I admired the conviction of the screenwriter and the director. And Eileen Cleary is just a lovely character, the conflict in her is very interesting. She has to find a way to reconcile what the Church tells her to believe with the love and compassion she has for her family, which doesn't fit the Church's idea of an acceptable family. Her husband is a recovering alcoholic, her son is a philanderer, and her daughter is a lesbian who is pregnant and about to marry her partner. Eileen also has her own buried secrets, and winning the Catholic Woman of the Year award comes with a prayer of absolution, which would absolve her of all past sins. She sees it as something of a get-out-of-jail-free card, and she believes it will release her of the guilt from this secret she's carried for twenty-odd years.

D.M. This is another gentle satire of suburbia for you, after *Serial Mom*.

K.T. I did think of Beverly Sutphin a few times when I was doing the character of Eileen. Both women want their families to be perfect, or more importantly to appear perfect. Both are obsessed with appearances, certainly.

D.M. No one can be surprised at how likable Beverly Sutphin was, given John Waters's adoration of even the most deplorable of his misfit characters, but I'm surprised how likable Eileen Cleary is in *The Perfect Family*.

K.T. It was important to me that the film not villainize her in any way. She's stuck in her ways, but she's not unsympathetic. She's trying to make sense of her changing world, and that's relatable to anyone. Eileen's fight, of course, is not really with the Church or with anyone in her family, but with herself.

The conflict at the heart of Eileen is a universal one—we all have political beliefs, or religious beliefs, or whatever, that will on occasion crash against our experiences, our feelings. Where Eileen gets into trouble is in her unquestioning subscription to the doctrine of the Church. The Church says, "This is how you behave, these are the rules, and they're not flexible." And she just accepts it.

So the question is, if you are that kind of person, if you agree to that contract, then what do you do? How do you live? How do you get through life without constantly becoming unfair in judgment of those around you? That is what I wanted to explore with that character. And I think that we found some truth in that she fails. The contract will never work. At least, not if one hopes to lead a happy and fulfilling life. You cannot maintain that kind of rigidity *and* be true to the essence of a religion like Catholicism.

D.M. For such a gentle comedy, it really is a politically urgent film, very relevant for the U.S. right now.

K.T. It really is, it's something that a lot of Americans are being forced to address now. The great conflict of Eileen Cleary is that she tries to inhabit two roles that it is impossible to inhabit simultaneously, and that's the world of Catholic doctrine and the real world. She is not a bad person. In fact, she's a very good person. She wants to do the right thing. The family in this film, while outwardly dysfunctional, has a very real love for each other. They don't need to learn love, that's already there. They need to learn tolerance. That's the change that Eileen goes through. The film doesn't ask a miracle of Eileen—it doesn't ask her to champion issues like gay marriage, it just asks her to accept them. That's a small, important step in the right direction.

It took me a long time to begin to understand Eileen Cleary, which is I suppose why I was attracted to playing her. Her faith in organized religion is so strong it supersedes everything else in her life. That just doesn't make sense to me. That idea is so alien to me.

D.M. You weren't raised Catholic.

K.T. Not at all. In fact, when I started the project, I knew very little about it. I had to do a lot of studying before the film, to find out what the Catholic doctrine was all about.

D.M. But the point of the film isn't that it's Catholicism, it's that it's doctrine.

K.T. Exactly. It just happened to be Catholicism. It could have been any church or any organized religion that says, "This is the only way." Islam can fit that model, Judaism can fit that model—any orthodox religion can fit that model. The conflict in the film has entirely to do with trying to manage personal relationships when they conflict with the dictates of organized religion. Even though it centers on Catholicism, I think anyone raised in an orthodox religion could find it relatable.

D.M. Did you have any history with organized religion?

K.T. Not really. My great grandfather was a Methodist missionary to China, but that's probably as close a connection as I had.

D.M. Based on roles you've done in recent years, like *The Perfect Family* and *High*, I would guess you might be anti-organized religion.

K.T. Not anti-, exactly, so much as just doubtful. I don't believe in sub-scribing to someone else's doctrine. Organized religion is essentially man putting words in God's mouth. And I can't support that.

D.M. Would you describe yourself as a spiritual person?

K.T. Not really. I'm an optimist, let's say that. As Molly Ivins would say, "I'm a believer, an optimist to the point of idiocy."

Kathleen played the late, legendary Texas journalist Molly Ivins in the successful one-woman play Red Hot Patriot, *which has been staged in several cities across America.*

D.M. As a director of small independent films, I have to ask: do you like doing lower-budget indie films?

K.T. Very much so. It's like working with a new play—there's more oppor-tunity for creative input at the narrative level because there are fewer cooks in the kitchen and less financially at stake.

D.M. You went to Montreal in December to shoot another independent film. How was that?

K.T. Aside from freezing, it was great!

D.M. I can imagine.

K.T. It got to 22 below zero. We were able to move some scenes from exterior to interior, but it was really, really tough. It's so cold you can't even really breathe.

D.M. What was the film?

K.T. It's a very sweet, charming comedy called *Another Kind of Wed-ding*. It's a small film. I play a woman in a 20-year relationship with another woman, played by the great Frances Fisher. Frances's character is a photographer who has been having affairs with her talent. My char-acter finds out, totally loses it and goes off to Vietnam to live on a beach, drop out of society and recapture her. When one of our children decides to get married my character has to come back to go to the wedding and confront Frances and the rest of the family. I loved the script and all of the young actors in the film are incredibly talented, but one of the main reasons I wanted to do the film was the opportunity to work with Wally Shawn.

Wallace Shawn is a legendary actor and playwright, best known for writing and starring in the indie film classic My Dinner with Andre *and for playing the lisping, conniving Vizzini in* The Princess Bride.

D.M. Had you worked with him before?

K.T. I knew him from around the city, but we had never had the chance to work together. It was great. He plays my date for the wedding, and I spend the whole film petting him and stroking him and picking him up. He was my boy toy, basically.

D.M. Ha! Your boy toy is inarguably one of the great comic voices of his generation.

K.T. And a very sweet man and a gifted performer. A total delight to work with.

D.M. After this film and *The Perfect Family*, it sounds like you only need one more movie to fill out a trilogy of "dysfunctional family indie film comedies."

K.T. I'll have to get looking.

D.M. Do you enjoy seeing yourself onscreen?

K.T. I don't dislike it. I know a lot of actors can't stand seeing themselves on a giant movie screen, because the size and scope of that screen lays out all your flaws, but it doesn't bother me. Having said that, I don't seek out my own films. I like to see how they turn out, and how my work turned out, but that's basically it.

D.M. How often do you watch your films?

K.T. *Romancing* is the only film of mine that I have on DVD. I must confess, that when I'm feeling kind of blue, I might put that film in and watch a few minutes to cheer me up. It's the only film of mine that I might throw in on occasion. It's such a joyful film.

D.M. But you like most of your films.

K.T. Absolutely. I think *The Accidental Tourist* is an incredibly underrated film, one of the best of its decade. *Prizzi's Honor* is a lot of fun, and *Serial Mom* is hilarious. And *Peggy Sue Got Married* is a magical film, a film of uncommon grace and charm. I'm quite proud of nearly all of my film work.

D.M. Do you have any favorite lines of dialogue?

K.T. The one that's quoted back to me on the street most often is "I'm not bad, I'm just drawn that way."

D.M. From *Who Framed Roger Rabbit*.

K.T. Yes. And sometimes I get, "You're not very smart, are you? I like that in a man."

D.M. The immortal line from *Body Heat*.

K.T. Yes. That's the genius of Larry Kasdan there, the man can write some seriously wonderful dialogue. Dialogue that's just great fun to say.

D.M. And you mentioned that you get a lot of lines from *Serial Mom* quoted at you, too.

K.T. "Always rewind!" Like all of John Waters's films, that's a very quotable movie.

D.M. I like, "Chip, you know how I feel about the brown word."

K.T. And, "The only 'serial' I know anything about is Rice Krispies."

D.M. Classic.

K.T. From *Romancing the Stone*, I like, "I may be easy but I'm not cheap."

D.M. That's Douglas's line.

K.T. Right, when she asks him if he'll take American Express to escort her across the jungle to a phone.

D.M. From *Prizzi's Honor*, I like, "What kind of creep wouldn't catch a baby?"

Kathleen's character, a hired assassin, says this after a failed hit on a mobster. She tosses a fake baby to the mobster's bodyguard, in the hope that he'll be distracted by trying to catch it. He lets it drop, and the irony of her being a contract killer is lost on Kathleen's character, who deems him a creep.

K.T. That's a funny one.

D.M. And from *War of the Roses*, I love how you say to Douglas, "When I see you eat, when I see you sleep, I just want to . . . punch you."

K.T. That was a Michael Leeson screenplay, also full of great, fun dialogue.

D.M. Have you ever watched one of your films on a phone or an iPod?

K.T. Never.

D.M. Does it bother you that many of your film performances, from here on out, will be viewed on laptop computers, tablets like the iPad, and on cell phone screens the size of postage stamps?

K.T. Certainly. Cinema is cinema. It is, and always will be, best experienced communally in a movie theater on an enormous screen. Who'd want to look at the beautiful, grand jungle landscapes of *Romancing the Stone* on a one-inch phone screen?

D.M. Films comprised mostly of actors' faces definitely play better than epic adventures with sweeping vistas. *My Dinner with Andre* is an easier watch on a phone than *Lawrence of Arabia*.

K.T. But even movies with all close-ups aren't going to play that well. If you're watching *My Dinner with Andre* on a one-inch screen, are you really going to get all the performative subtlety and nuance in the close-ups on Wallace Shawn? I doubt it. Any medium that is shoehorned into a technology for which it wasn't originally intended is going to suffer artistically, to some degree.

D.M. Do you ever watch movies or TV on your computer?

K.T. I rarely watch movies at all, let alone on my computer.

D.M. I know that many actors now record their own auditions at home and upload them to agents or casting directors via the web. What do you think of this new way of auditioning?

K.T. I think it can be harmful for the actor, because they have no one to play off of, and the energy in the room in your home is not the same as the energy in a traditional audition. But I can also see some of the benefits—it doesn't cost anything because you don't have to travel to the audition, and you don't have to take the time off from work to go to the audition.

D.M. And you can do it as many times as you want, until you're happy with it, before you send it off.

K.T. That's true, but again, losing the nervous energy of a real audition, where you get one real shot at it, is not necessarily a great thing. Personally, I'm glad that way of auditioning wasn't around back when I was auditioning.

D.M. Have you ever done voice work for a video game or acted in something that can be categorized as new media?

K.T. Not that I can think of. The Screen Actors Guild has a New Media Agreement, but I'm not sure anyone has figured out exactly what is and isn't new media, so I don't know how often that contract is actually used.

D.M. I think it's great that you are so happy with your film career. I know a lot of actors who see old films they were in and just cringe.

K.T. Life's too short to have regrets like that. Those people should just move on. Love your work, live your life, and be proud of what you've done!

WORKING WITH EDGY MATERIAL

DUSTIN MORROW Is there anything in your past roles you still feel uneasy about? Like the nudity in certain roles, or the explicit sexual material in *Body Heat* and *Crimes of Passion*?

KATHLEEN TURNER Not really. The character of Sue Collini in *Californication* would make me blush on the set occasionally. It's probably for the best that I didn't actually understand a lot of Sue's sexual references. I would need people to explain them to me. At odds with this sex symbol image I've acquired over the years, I've actually always been pretty innocent. I got married young, and was married for over two decades. I never led the raucous Hollywood life that people reading the tabloids would like to think that I did.

D.M. What did your family think of Sue Collini?

K.T. Good question! I know my daughter would say on occasion, "I can't believe you said that! Do you even know what that means?" And I'd say, "No, and don't tell me!" What was the one that really got me . . . ? A "rusty trombone"?

D.M. Oh geez, Kathleen!

K.T. I *know!*

D.M. It can't have been easy for your daughter to hear her mom talk like that.

K.T. We watched the first episode I did, and she turned to me and said "Don't ever do that again." I said, "Get over it, you're twenty-two!"

D.M. I guess no matter how old you are, you always want to believe your mom is a wholesome, innocent angel.

K.T. But I am a wholesome, innocent angel!

D.M. Sue was such a fun character.

K.T. I loved Sue. She was a joy to play. I mean, she's an awful woman, but she's such a wonderful character. And she allowed me, and the show, to play with the conceptions of women in positions of executive power. Sue had great authority and decisiveness, traits that get men labeled "power players," but of course everyone said Sue was "being difficult" or "being a diva." Sue crashed the glass ceiling and laid out the double standards. There aren't many aggressive women characters on television, sexually or otherwise. Sue was a one-of-a-kind.

D.M. She really was unique in the time she was on television.

K.T. I think so.

D.M. Have you ever had to do something to prepare in some way for a part of your performance that goes beyond acting? For example, a nude scene or a sex scene on stage or in film, where there might be a heightened level of nerves? Or maybe dealing with language of the type used by Sue Collini, that you're not necessarily comfortable with?

K.T. Nudity is tough, especially when you don't really know the people you are working with yet. Larry Kasdan scheduled the nudity for *Body Heat* very early in the shooting schedule, and that was not easy. I had barely met this crew and suddenly I was disrobing in front of them. After shooting the sex scenes in that film I would go back to my trailer and cry. Not because it was degrading, but because it felt so emotionally vulnerable. It's not easy to shoot those scenes, to engage in that level of intimacy in front of dozens of people.

The problem with sex scenes isn't doing the scene itself, it's everything that happens before the director says "Action" and after he says "Cut." When I'm in the scene, it's not me, it's the character. But before and after the scene, it's me who's laying there unclothed in front of two dozen strangers. That's when I feel vulnerable and uncomfortable.

D.M. Is it even tougher onstage?

K.T. Yes and no. No, in the sense that in film, the nudity is highly choreographed and technical. It's almost like shooting a fight scene. So it makes it feel somewhat clinical, which is actually a good thing. And the crew is cut down to the bare minimum needed.

D.M. Pun intended?

K.T. Let's say yes, pun intended. The other thing about film nudity is that the camera limits the field of vision of the audience. That filter disappears in the theater.

But nudity onstage is psychologically easier in the sense that when you are nude onstage you are never out of character like you are on a film set. And I really don't think women are as uptight about the nudity as men. All the press surrounding that scene in *The Graduate* was written by male journalists. Women have a sense of humor about these things.

There's a scene in the stage version of The Graduate, *ported over from the original film, in which Mrs. Robinson surprises Benjamin by entering a room he's in and slamming the door behind her—fully nude. Kathleen famously played the scene onstage completely naked.*

When I started *The Graduate* in London and ticket sales went immediately through the roof, my friend Maggie Smith told the producer of the show she was doing at the time that she was going do a nude scene too. He didn't get that she was joking!

Maggie Smith is one of Britain's preeminent actresses, known most recently, in her ninth decade, for her roles in the TV series Downton Abbey *and the* Harry Potter *film series.*

D.M. Nudity can be a dealbreaker for a lot of actors, though.

K.T. It can, definitely. *High* has a scene in which the young addict has to take off all of his clothes. When we had the final callbacks for the role of the young addict in *High*, we did the scene where he was required to strip. I wasn't sure this was really necessary, but the writer, director, and producers felt it was, to be sure that this young man wouldn't back out, once we got into rehearsal. And it probably was a good idea to say, "Okay, can you do it or can't you?" We took every possible care of their privacy and conducted the auditions with as much respect as possible. There were no superfluous people in the room, and there was a union representative present to be sure that there was no misuse of power in any way. I have never been asked to do that at the audition stage. The only times I've actually had to do nudity was in *Body Heat* and a couple other love scenes in films, and then ultimately on stage in *The Graduate*.

D.M. I imagine that your status as a sex symbol, who did a lot of very sexy films, probably leads people to believe that you have done more nudity in your career than you actually have.

K.T. Perhaps.

D.M. Despite what you said about staying in character, *The Graduate* can't have been easy.

K.T. Believe me, it definitely was not easy. Every night I took a beat before I would drop the towel. Everyone thought it was an acting choice but it was really me summoning the courage to drop the towel, every single performance. It never really got easier.

But nobody questioned whether or not I would do it because I didn't have to prove anything. I said I'd do it, and I did it. But the director actually said to me at the beginning of the process, "If you can find any other way to have the same impact on Benjamin's character as the nudity would, then you're welcome to do it." But there wasn't. I mean, what else would work? A half-slip and bra? Nude just from the waste up? No other option carried the necessary kick, the shock value, that had to hit Benjamin, as well as the audience, that the full nudity did. Doing the full nudity moved the narrative of the play forward.

D.M. It was unfortunate that it became so famous that people were waiting for it. And so it wasn't like, "Whoa! All of a sudden she's naked!" which was the narrative intent of the scene, as much as it was, "When the heck is she going to get naked?"

K.T. I think it was all of twenty-one seconds or something. Somebody timed it.

D.M. Those twenty-one seconds sold a lot of tickets, I bet.

K.T. Heck yeah they did!

D.M. You did *The Graduate* first in London. In Europe, they have different attitudes toward sex and nudity than we do in America, so I don't imagine it was as big a deal there as it was when you brought the play to Broadway.

K.T. Oh believe me, it was a big deal. It was all the press wanted to write about. But you're right, and I was much less concerned about it in England, frankly. There is much more acceptance of and respect for actors as professionals there. I knew there would of course be some brouhaha about it, but I also knew I wouldn't be condemned for doing it. I knew it would be perceived as what it was, an acting choice.

D.M. As opposed to in the U.S....

K.T. As opposed to the United States, where I thought it would just be considered salacious or a publicity stunt or something. It wasn't that hard to do in London, but it was tougher once we brought it to Broadway. But I did it, because it was the only way to do that scene.

D.M. Well, it turned out you were right, because the U.S. media certainly treated it in a sensational fashion. Nearly every review I found commented on the nudity. But at least they all remarked at how gorgeous you looked in the buff, so that's nice.

K.T. I know, but with the caveat being that a naked forty-seven-year-old woman being attractive in the nude was some kind of miracle. Yeesh.

D.M. Hilariously, the *New York Times*, perhaps our greatest journalistic institution, actually ran a "consumer guide" to your nude scene, answering questions like "Is she really entirely naked?" "What's the lighting like?" and "Is she holding in her stomach?"

K.T. Again, yeesh.

D.M. Pretty hilarious. It says a lot.

K.T. It does. And for the record: yes, entirely; pretty dim; and definitely not, thank you very much. Ha!

There was some fun to be had with it, I must admit. The matinee crowds, which tend to skew older, would always be filled with gasps when I dropped the towel. I must confess to a slightly perverse thrill in shocking people.

D.M. Have you always had a strong sense of your sex appeal?

K.T. Heavens, no. I was an innocent, oblivious. I still am!

D.M. What about that famous quote writers are always dredging up, about how any man that doesn't look at you when you walk into a room has to be gay?

K.T. Oh brother, here we go. I've been explaining that quote forever. That quote is always taken out of context. What I actually said was, "On a night where I feel really good about myself, if I walk into a room and a man's head doesn't turn, then he's probably gay." When people quote that, they always leave out the "On a night when I feel good about myself . . ." part. And that qualifier is the whole point. I was talking about confidence, not about my sex appeal. They always take that quote out of context and it makes me sound like I'm completely full of myself, which isn't the case. The point is that anyone can feel desirable as long as you carry yourself with confidence. It doesn't matter what you look like, or what your voice sounds like, as long as you like yourself.

My looks, thankfully, have never been central to my sense of myself. I've never thought of myself as a truly beautiful woman, so much as a good-looking American woman. I'm attractive, not drop-dead gorgeous. It's been nice when other people have thought that, I really appreciate it, but it's just never factored into my sense of who I am. My daughter is a different story. She is truly beautiful in a way that I have never been and won't ever be.

D.M. False modesty.

K.T. No, I swear it isn't! Look, I always knew I had good legs, but pre-*Body Heat* I never, ever thought of myself as sexy. In fact, I was terrified right up until the day that movie came out that audiences would be howling with laughter at my attempts to appear smoldering.

D.M. Did you feel competitive with other actors and other women?

K.T. Well, it's a competitive industry, and when you don't get the part, that means that one of your competitors got it. So yes, there's always an element of competition in acting as a profession. I've never felt competitive with other women in general, and I don't think women have felt competitive with me. There was a point early in my career, when the press was labeling me as a kind of sex symbol, that I could have alienated women, but it didn't happen. I've always had a healthy female fan base. And of course, as you know, I am a huge advocate for women and women's health issues, especially in my work with Planned Parenthood. I don't buy into this idea that women are naturally competitive and backstabbing, I think that idea is a male creation. There are enough men in power, in nearly every profession and certainly in politics, who have no understanding of women whatsoever, that we ladies have to stick together.

Women my age are the first generation of financially independent women. Our mothers were not independent. Women create businesses, women work hard, women reinvent themselves. This country is underestimating the impact we're going to have in the next few years. Men don't really understand feminine confidence. They think it has to do with looks, but that's not it at all. It's about attitude and independence. Women understand this. We know better.

Women don't accept defeatism, the idea that we can't change the world. Margaret Mead once said, "Never doubt that one person can change the world because it's all that ever has." It always starts with one person, who recruits another, and another, and another.

D.M. Alec Baldwin once observed about you, "Kathleen Turner's mind is always at work. Give her a half hour and she'll solve the country's problems."

K.T. He's a smart man, he knows I'm always right. My brother is a psychologist and he told me once that he felt that three-quarters of the world grow up to feel that they will be affected by the world and one quarter grow up to know that they will affect the world. I'm in that one quarter!

ACTING IN FILM

Dustin Morrow Film acting seems to present a lot of challenges that are not present in stage acting. Not the least of which would be the constant stopping and starting. It seems completely antithetical to creating a continuity in your performance.

Kathleen Turner It absolutely is, and it's one of the most frustrating things about moviemaking. Sometimes you feel like you're just getting your creative juices flowing, and it's "Cut" and you're back to your trailer for three hours while they set up the next shot. It's maddening.

D.M. What else frustrates you about filmmaking?

K.T. Not much. I actually enjoy film acting quite a bit. It'll never be as rich and rewarding and fun as stage acting, but it's full of great challenges.

D.M. The idea of giving an actor your total attention, and supporting your fellow actor, that can be tricky in film and television, where they do close-ups hours apart and people leave the set or go to their trailers.

K.T. I've definitely heard of actors who'll head off when their close-up is done and leave the other actor hanging, but I don't think I've ever worked with anyone who walked away and let somebody else on the set read their lines.

D.M. Really? I'm surprised. Especially given the stature of the actors you've worked with.

K.T. Well, there's a reason that they're that big—they're good at their job, and that's part of the job. But I have said on occasion, at the end of a grueling sixteen-hour day, "Look, it's okay, I don't need you here. I can do this without you, so if you want to go lie down, or if you want to leave for the day, you should go ahead."

On the other hand, I've also said, "I can't do it without you, so please don't go."

D.M. It seems to me that there's also a selfish reason to stay, and not just the selfless act of helping your fellow actor, which is the idea of not wanting to surrender that aspect of your performance to somebody else because what they're doing, even if it's off-camera, is not in sync with what you're doing with your performance.

K.T. Yes, the continuity in the performance is important, and challenging to maintain because of how films are shot. One thing I've seen happen is that the performance that someone will give in a close-up is not consistent with one they'll give later in a wider shot. So, as the other actor in the scene, you need to be there to see what they're doing because you could end up looking like you had no clue what was happening. As they change their performance, you have to change your performance accordingly, or be there to help them stay on track.

D.M. Can you think of examples of actors that you've worked with that made you think, "Wow, this person is really elevating what I'm doing"?

K.T. Jack Nicholson, definitely. He was just so easy to work with, he was just so good that I never had to think about supporting him. I could just do my own work, and not worry about trying to make sure his work was also going well. As soon as I began working with him, I remember thinking, "Oh, this is such a relief. All I have to do is my job." Which is a great relief.

Whereas with a lot of other actors, you find yourself trying to, you know, help them get better, or adjust things for them, so that you're constantly thinking about what they need instead of what you need. Not having to worry about that on *Prizzi's Honor* was just a lovely luxury to have, and I'm grateful to Jack for that.

D.M. It must be tough to work with actors who have to split they're attention between roles on a set. Multitaskers, professional hyphenates. Like working with Michael Douglas on *Romancing the Stone* and *The Jewel of the Nile*, where he was not only the lead actor but the producer as well.

K.T. That was very hard on him in *Romancing*, because we had a hell of a lot of things go wrong. We shot in Mexico, where whole roads and hillsides were literally washed out with these incredibly heavy rains, and he had to have entire roads constructed just so we could get to our shooting locations. He'd have dump trucks starting at four o'clock in the morning, just dumping gravel, backing out, letting another truck in, backing out, letting another truck in. It was an endless problem. And the constant sickness, the Montezuma's revenge—the cast and crew were always getting horribly, violently ill. Michael and I were never sick, thank goodness, but most of the other people were at some point. All of that was weighing on him tremendously.

D.M. I can't imagine the stress of having to deal with that and then step in front of the camera to give a good performance, especially as a charming character like the one he played in that film.

K.T. Yeah, it was really tough on him. What he tried to do was make the acting side as easy and as worry-free as possible. Because the production side was more than enough to worry about.

And the same was true in Morocco, on *Jewel of the Nile*—it was not easy shooting in these places. I would say to him, "Michael, on the next one we are not going to shoot in a country that starts with an M, okay?"

Funnily enough, it was because we had so much trouble with the rain and the humidity in Mexico on *Romancing* that Michael decided the sequel had to be set in a dry climate. But shooting in the desert on *Jewel* ended up being as treacherous and troublesome as the jungle was during the shoot for *Romancing*.

D.M. On *War of the Roses* you were directed by, and played scenes opposite Danny DeVito. Including a very funny scene where your character tries to seduce him. As director and actor, he had to think about his performance and your performance and also think about the camera and the scene simultaneously.

K.T. His films are very visual, and what he'll do is what a lot of directors do, which is storyboard his scenes in pre-production, so that by the time we actually shoot, the camera angles and everything have already been worked out, and then he's free as a director to watch my performance, and free as an actor to think about his own performance. Also, having a reliable cinematographer that the director trusts is key to the director being able to step into the scene as an actor and not worry about what's going on behind the camera.

Storyboarding is the process, completed during the planning stage of the shoot, of drawing out all of the shots that will show up in a film. It saves time and money, particularly on big-budget films with complicated sequences, like action scenes and scenes requiring complicated or expensive special effects.

D.M. Is there any way that the stop-and-start process of shooting films can actually benefit an actor? If you have to go sit in your trailer for a couple hours between shooting each scene, is it just disruptive and rhythm-killing, or is there any manner in which it can actually work to your advantage?

K.T. That's an interesting question. Of course it is your choice to stay on set, if you wish, as nobody is going to kick you off. But in my experience, most actors, given a multi-hour break, will go to their trailers. I wouldn't say the stop-and-start way of shooting films is destructive, but it's definitely interruptive. It is a bit of a juggling act, especially since you shoot out of sequence, so after you come back from your trailer, you are not always shooting a continuation of the scene you shot before you went to your trailer. I kind of like the challenge of shooting out of continuity. I like the gamesmanship of it, to be able to flip in and out of different scenes and different places in the script and in the character. It's like my own personal little test.

But as far as sitting in the trailer goes—no, it doesn't really help in any way.

D.M. You don't find yourself rethinking choices in those periods of waiting for the crew to set up the next shot.

K.T. Never. Rethinking is really bad for acting. Imagine you shot a scene, and you are going to then shoot a scene that precedes it in the script, a scene in which you are not supposed to have a knowledge of the action of the scene you just shot. If you spent your downtime between those two shoots thinking about what you already shot, you might in the scene you are about to shoot in some way make apparent that you acquired this knowledge before the scene in which you were supposed to acquire it. And you've done that because you spent your break thinking about the scene you already shot, when you should have just forgotten it.

While you do have to give a performance with continuity and a singular vision for the whole film to work, you have to take each scene as an individual experience. It's not really a question of being self-conscious, though I suppose that that can come into it also, it's really the issue of second-guessing yourself when there are so many other factors, like the directing and the editing, that will contribute to the audience's reception of your performance but are not technically part of your job. It's hard not to rethink things sometimes. Especially if you have experience as a director, it's hard to not take on the whole thing all the time, but you have to make yourself take a little piece and do it, and then wait for the next piece.

D.M. Do you have a take that is generally your strongest take? How many takes would you like usually?

K.T. I would usually do four or five takes, but not many more. On *Prizzi's Honor* we did eighteen takes once, but that was because it was a very physically difficult scene. Jack and I were doing the love scene in bed, rolling over and over each other, and we'd hit the headboard, then we'd roll back the other direction and the camera was on a track and had a difficult time staying with us. So, that was a very clear technical thing. Jack really hated that scene because his back was hurting.

D.M. He's rolling around in bed, making out with Kathleen Turner, and he's complaining about his back!

K.T. Yeah, you should have heard him! "My back, oh my back!"

But in terms of the choices of the acting, usually four or five takes would be it for me. And yeah, I do usually say, "That's the one," or, "Don't use that one," to the director as we shoot. Just to the director as we do it, as we shoot it. Not that I ultimately have control over what take they use, but I put my two cents in.

The reality is that everyone on the set usually knows when we've got what we need and no more takes are needed. It's all about finding the correct rhythm in a scene. Every scene has a distinct rhythm. Shooting any scene is a wonderful, intricate dance between the actors, the lighting, the sound, the camera and everybody else involved in a scene. When it clicks—when the music is in tune, the lights are right and the other actors and you are in synch, and the director's direction is on point and the camera is the right place at the right time, everything comes together like this beautiful, intricate dance and you can actually feel the rhythm of the scene. It's a beautiful, elusive thing. And everyone knows it, really, when you find that rhythm. The cameraman will smile and the soundman will give the thumbs up and everything comes together and it's just perfect.

D.M. So it's a myth that actors always want another take then.

K.T. In my experience. Unless it's some egotistical twit that is just so insecure that they have to keep doing it and doing it and doing it.

D.M. I've seen many pretentious interviews with big name actors saying something on the order of, "There is always further room to explore. If I can just get just one more take, I will always take it."

K.T. Sounds like insecurity to me. Also, actors like that don't usually get that it's about the whole film, not just their performance. You're not alone out there, you know, it has to be good for everybody, it has to be good for the film. And if it's good for everyone else then unless you truly, completely blew it, then give it up. Work with your fellow cast members and your crew. Trust them.

D.M. I guess that's also just the part of the film industry that fosters self-centeredness.

K.T. Tell me about it. You could have cured cancer and walked on the moon the day before, and if you had lunch with some of these big actors, they'd want to talk about doing publicity for their new film, and they wouldn't ask you a thing.

D.M. That's Los Angeles for you.

K.T. Hell yeah.

D.M. I lived there for four years, I was bored to tears.

K.T. And what's scary is that those actors don't realize how boring they are. It'd be funny if it weren't so sad.

D.M. What about location work versus studio work? In my experience of directing actors, most of them seem to prefer the authenticity of a location over the comfort of a studio.

K.T. It depends on the film and the role. A studio is certainly always going to be more comfortable and less trouble. If the location is an exterior, if you're outside and you're subject to weather and ever-changing natural light then it can be frustrating. There's already a lot of stopping-and-waiting in filmmaking, but factor in all of the uncontrollable elements of an exterior location and it can occasionally be maddening. Holding for clouds, waiting for a wind to die down, deciding to wait out a rain or move to an interior set—it complicates the process endlessly.

If you are actually in an exotic location like a rainforest in Mexico, where we shot *Romancing*, or the Sahara desert, where we shot *Jewel of the Nile*, just surviving the elements can be a challenge, let alone shooting a film. It was an extraordinary thing when we were shooting in Morocco in the desert and we were there in June and it was over one hundred and twelve degrees with absolutely no moisture whatsoever. Your body shuts down all its natural moisture so that you drink bottles and bottles and bottles of water, yet you don't ever have to urinate and you don't sweat even though it's over a hundred degrees out. The makeup man loves it because he does your makeup in the morning and that's it, it doesn't move all day. No touch-ups. Your pores shut completely, your body's natural response to that environment is to hold on to every little bit of moisture it's got.

Things like that are quite extraordinary to deal with while also trying to shoot a major feature film. It is very frustrating sometimes. Things could be made so much easier by shooting in a studio. You can move walls around, you have a whole grid of lights above the set and you can pre-light scenes ahead of time. Nobody gets up on a ladder in between scenes and hangs lights on stage. Shoots go so much quicker. And soundstages are air-conditioned, so the cast and crew is more comfortable. The dressing rooms are nicer, and you have access to real food and bathrooms and little things that add significantly to your comfort.

Don't forget that you spend twelve to fourteen hours, minimally, on a set everyday, sometimes six or seven days a week, so little comforts go a long way. But in a studio you don't have the fun of the disasters that happen on real locations, the unpredictable things that make a shoot worth remembering. I mean, on *Romancing*, we had real, true mudslides. The one we faked in the movie had nothing on some of these mudslides, you should have seen them.

D.M. You even got caught in one.

K.T. I was! I was completely buried in thick, heavy mud, which was not fun.

D.M. I've heard you tell this story. This is the time where the crew pulled you out and they injured your legs.

K.T. Yeah! I'm yelling at them, "Don't pull on me, just dig!" But everybody panicked and they started pulling me out of the mud, and as they yanked me out, it completely tore all the skin off my lower legs. It was gruesome!

D.M. Yikes!

K.T. It was very painful. Every week, Michael used to give out these prototypes for the stone of the film's title—the big emerald—to the person who in that week suffered the worst injury. I had no trouble winning it that week.

D.M. Is that the only one you won?

K.T. No, I got two! That was a tough movie. Michael calls it my "seven-stitcher."

D.M. Because you got seven stiches?

K.T. Yep!

D.M. Yeesh. What was the other injury?

K.T. There were several. There's a scene that got cut—I think it's on the DVD in the bonus features—where Joan is bathing in this pond and Jack is kind of spying on her. They dug this pond right there in the jungle and lined it with plastic and I got in to do the scene. As I got out I realized my legs were bleeding profusely. It turns out that they had dug it partially into a trash heap and there was broken glass in there! Can you believe that?

And after we finished shooting the famous scene in the downed airplane, I was climbing out through the jagged opening they'd cut in the side of the plane and I slipped and threw my arms out to break my fall and cut my hand on a metal shard. I think that was three of the stitches. And in the fight scene from the end of the film, Manuel Ojeda, who was playing the villain, had to throw me down onto the stone rooftop of the fort, and in one of those falls I landed hard enough to earn myself several more stitches. And of course, I went down that damn mudslide five times, which looks like a hoot onscreen but was no fun at all.

D.M. Good grief, it sounds like there was as much action-adventure off-camera as there was on.

K.T. You better believe it.

D.M. Can a tough location-based experience like that be used in your performance? For example, those hardships you faced in Morocco on *Jewel*—could you say, "I'm unhappy here, but I can tap into that for my performance"?

K.T. Well, certainly Joan Wilder struggled with the desert in *Jewel* as I struggled in making that film. But that sort of environmental weather-based circumstance is an easy example. I'll give you a better one.

In Morocco there is a troubling disregard of women, and that contempt does build up, does start to get to you. I would call down to room service in the morning to get coffee and when they heard a woman's voice they'd hang up. It was so frustrating. I'd have to call Michael and have him call down to order me coffee, it was ridiculous. Danny's wife, Rhea Perlman, brought all of these foods for their new baby, but as a woman she wasn't allowed in the kitchen. So one night she and I had enough and we stormed in there and took over.

D.M. You staged a coup.

K.T. We staged a coup. They wouldn't make us what we wanted, and wouldn't prep the baby's food as Rhea directed, so we launched a revolt. They were terrified, we were a force to be reckoned with. They chased us out of the kitchen and promised us anything in the world we wanted from then on, so it worked.

While in Morocco I always observed the custom for women of wearing long sleeves and long pants, despite the overbearing heat. But one day it was so bloody hot, so insufferable, that I finally decided that if I leave the hotel, get in the car, get to the set, get out, get back in the car, you know . . . no one's going to see me, so I am wearing a sleeveless t-shirt and shorts. And of course, of all days, the car broke down that day and I could not get out of the car at the risk of being seen in a t-shirt and shorts.

And the driver had to take off to get help, we're out in the middle of the desert, and I had to sit inside this airless car in one hundred plus degree weather because I was wearing shorts and a t-shirt. So I sat there and stewed and got frustrated. And those feelings definitely came through in the performance, as Joan Wilder struggles with the same customs and attitudes in the film.

D.M. It sounds really unpleasant.

K.T. Don't get me wrong, it's a beautiful country and the Moroccan people were amazing. They were warm, beautiful people. But it was a tough experience for me. By the time we finished shooting in Morocco I was very much on edge, hardly eating, hardly sleeping. So many of our crew had gotten sick, as we found out later that at the hotel where the crew was staying there was a leak into the swimming pool from the sewer system. So many of them got dysentery. And with the relentless heat, everyone's minds were shutting down.

You know, probably the closest I've ever come to being killed happened on *Jewel*.

D.M. Yikes, what happened?

K.T. Michael and I were on a tiny plane, coming back from a remote shoot, and as we're coming into Fez to land, for some reason the runway lights went out. The pilot struggled to get control and almost overshot the runway. It was really, really close.

D.M. That sounds absolutely terrifying.

K.T. It really shook me up. And it was just one of a number of incidents that made that a very tough shoot. Michael, bless his heart, changed the schedule and let me get out a day early. I shot my last scene in Morocco and Holland Taylor and I got on a flight to the south of France, where we were going to continue shooting, and Holland told me that she hadn't seen my dimples in weeks, that my face had just become stone. And when we crossed the Mediterranean she asked me why I was crying, and I'm like, "What?" I didn't realize I was weeping, I think I was just overwhelmed with relief to be away from that shoot.

D.M. That's interesting—that frustration didn't show in your performance. And I know that you also didn't really want to do the film in the first place, that you did it because of a contractual obligation, so I'm surprised it turned out as well as it did.

K.T. Well, it's but a shadow of the original film, but it has its moments. I still don't think we ever got the script where it needed to be.

D.M. Do you think that good film acting can be learned? Do you think that any actor can learn to act on camera or do you think that there is such a thing as a "camera charisma"? Something almost indefinable, where you either have it or you don't?

K.T. I think there is, unfortunately. It would be great if every good actor could translate their talents to the screen, but it just doesn't work like that. It used to frustrate and mystify me, that abstract relationship with the camera. After I got the role of Matty in *Body Heat,* shooting was suspended because there was an actors strike. We were supposed to start in June, but we didn't start until November, and there was a lot of tension during that five-month period. We wondered whether they would continue to carry the film because we were all pretty much unknowns and for that time it was a pretty decent-sized budget.

That role was my first time ever appearing on film, period, let alone playing a lead in a big Hollywood movie. So I spent that five months during the actors strike frantically running around asking, "How do I make the camera love me?" And I would be told over and over again by anyone who seemed to be knowledgeable about it that I couldn't make it love me, that it either just would or just wouldn't. I couldn't accept this. I would say, "That's not good enough, there has to be a way to do it." But they were right. And luckily for me, the camera adored me, it worked out.

D.M. So there's no secret then?

K.T. Not that I'm aware of. I have seen wonderful actors, actors who I think have done some of the best stage work I have ever seen, actors with performances in my mind that I will never forget, that when I see them in a TV show or in a movie, I don't even recognize them. They turn into wallpaper. This one actor I saw do the most brilliant one-man play, I couldn't take my eyes off of him, I remember everything he did, every gesture, he absolutely commanded the stage. When he starred in this movie, I knew I had to see it, and it turned out to be a huge disappointment. He didn't come through at all, there was no personality, no magnetism, nothing drew my eyes to him. Some people just work better in person.

This idea isn't limited to actors. Watching Hilary Clinton in the earlier days, she came across on television as very cold, quite charmless really.

And then I met her in person and found her incredibly charming, warm, and engaging. It just does not go through the camera lens. You would be shocked at how charismatic she is in person given her on-camera history. It's like night and day. So that tells me that there is some essential quality that a camera picks up or doesn't pick up, and I don't know exactly what that is. I'm not sure anyone does.

D.M. Are there any identifiable traits then that can make one actor work better on camera than another actor?

K.T. What I would say definitely makes one actor better than another on camera, something the actor actually can control, is a sense of the spatial design of the scene—in regard to the camera, in regard to the other actors, in regard to the lights. It's a sense of being able to use and understand all of the space around you, how it functions as it reads on that camera. Some actors clearly have that more than others.

I always know, almost innately, exactly where I am in the space of a shot. I was shooting a scene with Bill Hickey on *Prizzi's Honor,* where my character is meeting his, the godfather, and we shot it from over Bill to where he takes my hand and he doesn't let it go and I sort of try to pull away but I'm afraid to. Then we turned the cameras and lights around to shoot my side, and I had to put my hand into the right place in a very tight shot so he can reach up and take it, and it can't be in front of his face, as he's lower than me as he's sitting down, and it can't fall out of frame. It has to come in, and swiftly, to an exact spot, with literally only millimeters to spare.

Time after time my hand hits the exact mark and after a bunch of takes Bill said, "What are you, a witch? How can you do that? Every time it's right, we haven't lost a single shot." I can just feel it, it's almost like a sixth sense. It is almost an athletic sense, in a way—all of my life I have been a good athlete, and part of that skill is obviously hand-eye coordination. It's an uncanny sense of space and knowing your place in it, and it takes practice. It's a skill that actors can learn. Get a camera and work on it.

D.M. Just admit it—Bill was right, it's witchcraft!

K.T. Okay, it's witchcraft. You got me!

THE STAGE VERSUS THE SCREEN

DUSTIN MORROW Here's a big question, but we can break it down if need be: how do the skillsets of the stage actor and the film actor differ?

KATHLEEN TURNER That *is* a big question.

D.M. Let's talk summarily then.

K.T. Well, making choices in acting that the camera can use as opposed to what the stage can use is the real skill. The two media are so different, they require dramatically different things. The delightful thing about the film camera and using a one-camera process, which most major films will do, is that you know exactly what that shot is, and therefore you know exactly how to fine-tune your performance for that shot. If it's a 50mm lens, which is only from the waist up maybe, it doesn't matter what your feet and legs are doing, so don't worry about them, don't bother with them. You can concentrate on your waist up. It's your arms, it's your hands, it's your head, it's your neck, it's your torso that you want to con-centrate on. Being able to be that specific and know exactly what you need to use for that shot is the joy of film work, because you have to paint a much broader canvas on stage.

On stage, from the tips of your toes to however high you can reach with your hands is your canvas, which is glorious and liberating. On the other hand, you don't get to use any of those lovely little specifics, like how many times you tap your fingers or when you blink, or if you take a breath before or after you sip wine from a glass, that you get to use in film. Those things don't tend to matter on stage, because they are too small to be seen at the back of the theater.

Having said that, I find film acting generally to be very limiting. As a theatrically trained actor, it's in my nature to project. I want to project.

For years, the sound man on my films would inevitably at some point say, "Would you please stop projecting, the microphone is right over your head." I had always equated acting with projection because of my stage background. So I really had to learn to use my voice in a smaller way, not to gesture nearly as widely or as strongly or as quickly.

Movement in particular was challenging for me, as a very physical actress, not just because movements on film register as bigger than they are, but because the technology of the film camera itself captures movement in a limited way. Especially with the old school TV cameras, you could actually be too fast—the camera couldn't resolve your movement and the image would appear blurry or out of focus. When I was doing *Julia and Julia,* which was the first feature film ever shot on high definition video, we found that with those earliest prototypes of the HD camera, any movement toward or away from the camera ghosted. It left a trail of color behind me when I moved. It simply couldn't resolve the movement. So I would have to find reasons, dramatically, when running toward the camera, to stop or to move at a slower speed, so the camera could track me. It was very limiting and didn't serve the scenes.

> *Julia and Julia is an Italian melodrama made in 1987, starring Kathleen as a woman caught between two dimensions and two lovers, played by Gabriel Byrne and Sting. Many of the supporting actors in the film were dubbed before the film's limited release in the United States.*

D.M. But it actually sort of works in that movie because it's a melodrama and those artificial beats translate.

K.T. Yes, and it helps that it's a pretty offbeat European film. We had other technical issues on that film. The Italian crew didn't do overtime, so when the end of the day came, they went home whether we had gotten everything we needed or not. One day the sound crew went home before we finished a scene, so we had to shoot it without sound and then go in during post-production and dub every line of dialogue.

D.M. Sounds like that shoot was a bit of a headache.

K.T. I suffer for my art, darling.

But nowadays, most of the time, an actor doesn't have to think about the issues surrounding technology because the equipment is advanced and you take it for granted that it can track anything you can do as an actor. But the HD was a new technology at the time we did *Julia and Julia*.

D.M. So I would assume that you recommend to young actors that want to do film and television that they should know lenses and have a basic knowledge of how the camera works.

K.T. Absolutely, it's imperative. Before every new shot, it's your responsibility to speak to the cameramen, to the cinematographer, to the director, and find out the limits of the frame. What is the depth of focus? What lens are they using? And you should know what those lenses mean. What does a 75mm look like, a 35mm, a 100mm? Such fun, the 100mm—real tight. Tight, tight, tight, tight. The bottom of the chin to the top of the eyebrow. You can get amazingly small in your performance with a shot like that.

It's important to learn lenses not just for your own performance, but as a courtesy to your collaborators. What good does it do anybody if you keep going outside of your frame, or if you move in such a way that the lens can't capture your action? What if you have a dioptric, what if you have a split lens, or a slip split focal? What if they want to pull focus during a shot to go from you to the background or to an object in front of you? You should know that they are doing it, how and when they are doing it, and how you can best assist them in getting the shot. If you are in movement when the focus puller is pulling the focus then you blew the shot. You have to be still so that he can pull the focus away from you to the object that is wanted. You should know this as an actor.

It is your job to make the shots work, not screw them up. And truthfully, a lot of camera people and a lot of cinematographers don't bother to tell the actors this stuff and then when it happens over and over again the actor has no idea why. They haven't told her, "Please don't move at this point because we are going to pull focus," and they won't, because they very often don't think of actors as full partners in the scene. They just think of them as objects in front of the camera, like any other object. So it is your job to make yourself a partner and to ask, "What are you doing with this shot and how can I help?"

D.M. As a film director, I will, with my cinematographer and camera crew, make adjustments based on the input of the actor.

K.T. That's good. That happens more with confident, accomplished directors whose egos aren't so fragile that they can be open to taking that kind of feedback from an actor. In one shot in *Peggy Sue*, I had some dialogue that Francis intended only to shoot from my back. I told him that I firmly believed the camera needed to be looking at me when I said these lines. He wasn't going to shoot it that way but I pleaded my case, and he agreed to give me two takes from the angle I wanted. And guess which shot they used in the final film.

D.M. Yours.

K.T. You betcha.

D.M. I've tried to prepare information about shots and camera movement before I get to the set and get it to the actors. Shot lists and storyboards, mainly. But to some degree it's always something that has to be figured out when we get on set.

K.T. It has to be done on set because everything on a film set changes so frequently. What if they couldn't hang a light the way they wanted to or they couldn't lay the dolly track where they wanted, or they couldn't pull that wall out or you're in a space where they had to compromise their camera position? You don't know that sort of thing generally until you arrive on set. Storyboards are all well and good and they might have a shot list that says, "We move from Kathleen's face to the blue vase in a focus pull," but you don't really know how that's actually going to happen until you are on set and everybody is doing it together.

Fortunately, most of that tedious process of figuring out the shot can happen without the actor present. They use stand-ins to light the scene and rehearse camera movement, so when the actor is called to the set, they usually have a pretty good idea what they want to do, and you just have to ask, "What do I need to know to help you get your shot?"

D.M. Of course, the challenge becomes finding a reason then in your performance to make these technical things happen, but also make them not seem like they are happening for technical reasons.

K.T. Yes, absolutely.

D.M. So when you pause as you run toward the camera in *Julia and Julia*, there has to be a dramatic reason that you are doing that and it has to make sense inside the role and the story, even though the real reason you're doing it has to do with the limitations of the camera.

K.T. You can stumble, you can catch your foot, you can hear a sound, you can do all kinds of things to make you stop, let the cameras resolve the image, and move on. It's all fine if the actor sells it. The audience won't see it.

D.M. Do you find the stage forgiving, then, in a way that film is not?

K.T. Well, for one thing, the film image is so magnified, so big, that any physical imperfections become much tougher to bury. In theater, the closest audience member to me might be eight or ten feet away, but in film, a close-up of my face might be upwards of fifty feet tall, depending on the size of the screen. Makeup and soft focus photography can do wonders, but they can't work miracles.

The stage also forgives bigger gestures and modifications in the voice. Everything has to be smaller in film. What reads as subtle on a big stage in a big theater can even play as hammy and melodramatic on film.

And of course stage acting exists only in the moment. A performance on film lasts forever.

D.M. Was there ever any fear for you, coming out of a stage background, of the permanence of a film? Is that a frightening thing for a stage actor?

K.T. Oh yeah, very. Very much so. And the flip side of that is that there are nights when you are on stage and you do a performance where you are just flying and you think, "God, how I wish that had been recorded and preserved!" But the fleeting nature of the theatrical performance is part of the joy, also. The fact that it is done and gone forever is kind of thrilling.

D.M. It is certainly part of the romance of it.

K.T. You bet. But the first time I saw *Body Heat*, because it was my first film, was terrifying. Larry arranged a screening for me, so I could see it before it hit the theaters and the critics. I sat there and I thought, "Holy cow, there is a record now. There is a record of me, forever." Which was amazing but very scary. I didn't know quite what to make of it. I was a little bothered—heck, I'm still a little bothered—by the thought that there would be this endless twenty-five-year-old version of me out there. That even as I grew and changed, as a person and an actor, this kid would still be out there for forever, representing me. That was more than thirty-five years ago, and people still talk about that movie, and that twenty-five-year-old version of me, all the time. How would you like to be asked questions about the twenty-five-year-old you for the rest of your life?

D.M. The other weird thing is that, at the time that you made *Body Heat*, if people wanted to see the film they had to go see it in the theaters, and when it was out of theaters then they missed their chance to see it until it maybe showed up on TV once every few years. So even though there is a permanence to the medium of film, it was still somewhat transient in nature—you couldn't just watch *Body Heat* whenever you wanted. But now we're even beyond home video and the brick-and-mortar video store in terms of having instant access to all films, all the time. We're always only a mouse click away from being able to watch nearly any film, any time. Today, if I have access to a computer or a streaming service on my television, I'm always just seconds away from being able to watch *Body Heat* anytime I want.

K.T. Right. At the time *Body Heat* came out, seeing it was like going to the theater. Like a play, it had a closing date, after which time you'd lost your chance to see it. And I liked that. It's one of the ways film has changed that, in my view, makes it increasingly less interesting than theater.

D.M. For what other reasons do you prefer theater?

K.T. Well, for starters, film is just less fun. The workday is less interesting. Theater is just more purely enjoyable. The day is more consistent. The film workday is acting for twenty minutes, going away for an hour, coming back and acting ten minutes, going away for two hours, coming back, acting ten more minutes, and so on. It gets tiring.

And of course, the roles in theater are far richer and more interesting. And there's more opportunity to develop new material. Doing new material is so exciting, and there's so much opportunity to do it on the stage. I enjoy working on classic texts, too, but I'm certainly not interested in remaking popular culture of the seventies and eighties, which has been the primary focus in Hollywood in the last decade. That material is stale, and those projects are about commerce, not art or drama. And with theater, I have the luxury of spending a year or more workshopping a new piece of material if I like. You just don't have that luxury of time in filmmaking.

And once you do a film, it's done. You can't change it, it's over. One of the most exciting things about theater is the constant change, the endless evolution of a performance and of a play. A change can be as small as taking a breath after a line as opposed to taking it before, or having an insight into how to change an entire scene or even an entire act of the play. Those changes, those possibilities, are without limit, and you have the entire run of the play, which can even be years long, to develop them.

Theater exhilarates and inspires me in a way that film never will. I go to the theater constantly but I get hopelessly behind with movies. I'm usually about a year behind, until Oscar season. All the Academy screeners start showing up in the mail, and I have to burn through them to catch up.

The Academy of Motion Picture Arts and Sciences, which distributes the Oscars, sends out DVD copies of the nominated films to members of the Academy for voting purposes.

D.M. I would imagine that nothing about film probably compares to the immediacy of theater, and the pressure of being in a room with a live audience, where there is no second take.

K.T. Not only is there nothing about film that compares, there's almost nothing else in life that compares to that thrill. There's so much "living in the moment" onstage. It's an adrenaline rush. It's hard to explain to non-actors.

D.M. Is there anything you can relate it to?

K.T. Well, imagine you're driving down the road, you hit some water and begin to swerve into oncoming traffic. You realize, in a millisecond, that you are about to be in a car crash and there's basically nothing you can do about it, it's unavoidable. You have just a second or two before impact. All of these things pass through your mind. Is there a passenger in my car? Is there a passenger in their car? Are there children in their car? Is the road wet or dry? Would I minimize the hit by taking it on the right or left side of the car? Am I wearing my seatbelt? Will my airbags go off? Am I about to die?

All that goes through your head in maybe one second. And that's what great stage acting is like, when you are firing on all cylinders. It's like being inside that second for the two hours you're onstage. When you are onstage you are constantly asking yourself, every second, questions like, "Do I want to take a breath before or after this word? Do I want to take this word up a note or down? Should I gesture on this sentence or not?" Living, just being, in that level or awareness, is utterly exhilarating.

D.M. Sounds exhausting.

K.T. It absolutely is, but in a good way.

D.M. Can you get that kind of awareness in film acting?

K.T. No, because you can always do another take. That level of adrenaline, of living in the moment, is only accessible in live performance. Film acting has a built-in safety net that inherently defuses the tension. That isn't to say that film acting doesn't have its own rewards, but that level of awareness and exhilaration is not one of them.

Actually, I think it's dangerous for an actor to be away from the stage for too long. You can really fall into a false sense of security when you do nothing but film. I never went more than two and a half years without going on stage, even at the height of my box office draw. I always went back, often to off-Broadway or regional theater, to keep my stage skills sharp. Many actors get afraid of the stage if they don't do it regularly. They enjoy feeling protected by getting to say "cut" or having an editor assemble their performance from the best takes. The process of doing a movie protects an actor in a way that the stage does not, and it can make an actor afraid to take risks.

Acting on the stage also exercises a set of acting muscles that don't get worked out while doing films. And they are muscles—they atrophy with disuse. So actors need to get onstage at every opportunity . . . and exercise!

ACTING IN THE THEATER

DUSTIN MORROW Most people probably think of a Broadway actress because of the high profile and success of many of the productions you've been in. But you've worked a good deal off-Broadway and in regional theater.

KATHLEEN TURNER I love it. It's certainly much less pressure than doing something on Broadway. There are a lot of demands, a lot of obstacles in doing a Broadway show that can actually impede the work.

D.M. Let me guess: the big obstacle is just good old-fashioned money.

K.T. Yep, money!

D.M. Paycheck?

K.T. Yeah, paycheck! Let's see, the first thing you notice in moving from the smaller theaters to Broadway, besides the money of course, is the caliber of the people you work with. By the time you get to Broadway, the crew you're working with is pretty elite, and those in the industry less serious about what they do have been winnowed out, so to speak. So you're dealing with a pretty high level of professionalism by that point.

But in not-for-profits, and sometimes in regional theaters and off-off-Broadway theaters, you might occasionally run into a lot of people who aren't as skilled as you might hope. Or they are less sure that they are doing with their lives what they want to do, and so their commitment to their jobs is lacking. And this will get in your way as an actor. It's unfortunate, but those theaters can't afford to pay for the highest level of talent. Once a person reaches a certain level of expertise, they tend to move up and rightly expect a higher salary and more opportunities on bigger productions.

Having said that, there is a wonderful amount of loyalty from the crews at non-profits for the theaters. And that loyalty will keep people there for a long time, and that's great. But generally it's very inconsistent, and you'll have a couple of people who are great at what they do and a couple who are incompetent.

D.M. The not-for-profit can take more creative risks than the theater that relies exclusively on profits to sustain.

K.T. Absolutely. The not-for-profit will take risks on new material, new directors, untried actors. Like Broadway shows, though, it will stabilize them to have at least one established lead actor or a name director who will put the show on the map and guarantee a certain amount of ticket sales regardless of the quality of the show itself.

It's important that we support not-for-profit theaters because that's where some of the most daring work is being done.

D.M. I imagine that, like most artists, you've been dismayed by the massive cuts in arts funding in the last twenty years.

K.T. Dismayed, depressed, angry. Arts have gone the way of civics classes because they are seen as unnecessary, as a luxury. What we have left of all the great civilizations that have come before us are the arts—the literature, the music, the architecture. These are the great legacies that that these civilizations have left behind. What will be our legacy if we don't treat it with the same respect?

D.M. I know, it's appalling how little public money goes to supporting the arts.

K.T. Why support five years' worth of great theater when you could build a single missile that will never be used?

D.M. Indeed. Getting back to Broadway—do you think its aversion to new material is purely a money issue, or is it more of a lack of genuine creativity?

K.T. Money, mostly. The issue with creative risk in a Broadway show is that there is so much financial risk involved that the producers are terrified to gamble with their investors' money. So they will shy away from creative risk and you will see yet again another revival.

D.M. It sounds like Hollywood's creative crutches—the sequel and the remake.

K.T. Exactly. It has been proven, it has been done and worked before, and it carries a reputation and name recognition. It's just a protection of the investment. And that can't include new material, new actors and new directors. Ideally, you develop a piece in a not-for-profit and you do well enough financially that a for-profit will pick it up. Which would benefit the not-for-profit too, if they have a decent agent and a decent lawyer, and they are credited with having developed the piece and paid for having done that hard work. That doesn't always happen, but not-for-profits should always try to protect themselves that way.

D.M. Broadway seems to look a little more like Hollywood every year, with the oversized productions full of spectacle and special effects.

K.T. It's a little sad, isn't it?

D.M. In the seventies, Hollywood released many more mid-budgeted, serious dramatic films. Films about people and their problems, not about ships sinking or comets heading toward Earth. Not every film had to be an action spectacular, a big-budget spectacle. But with the cost of marketing a film rising higher than the cost of actually producing the films, even the huge action films, they can no longer afford to take risks on smaller dramas. And the same thing seems to be happening on Broadway.

K.T. Yes, and *High* was a victim of that. It was a new play, a serious play, and it wasn't given a chance.

D.M. Right, because selling an intense drama about addiction takes a lot more time and work than selling a revival of a forty-year-old musical or a stage adaptation of a big Hollywood movie.

K.T. Unfortunately, that's true. And it takes a little time for a new, less-known play to find its audience and build word-of-mouth, but Broadway today, like Hollywood, needs instant hits.

D.M. Right. If a big Hollywood movie doesn't find an audience on opening weekend, it's over. It'll be out of theaters within two weeks.

K.T. It really is unfortunate. Some works just need time to find their audiences.

D.M. Another issue may be that ticket prices on Broadway have gotten so inflated that people are just less likely to spend the money on an unknown quantity. It's the same thing in film—if someone's going to spend $13 on a ticket to a movie, then they want to know exactly what they're going to see. Which is why sequels will always be viable commercial prospects. I used to edit film trailers a long time ago, and I would get notes from studios telling me to include plot twists and endings from the movies in the trailers. It was frustrating to me as a viewer, when a trailer would give away the ending of a movie, but the studios couldn't take the chance. They've done studies, I guess, where they found out that people would rather know exactly what they are getting.

K.T. That was definitely part of the problem with marketing *High*. The other problem was that the play is not just dark, but it's dark and it provides no easy answers. The play tells us that while there are things people can do to regain lost faith, and to beat addiction, neither challenge has an easy solution. Redemption is a tricky word. It's a process, not an answer. It will always be a fight, continually, for the rest of one's life. That's an honest, but admittedly bleak, way to conclude a play.

D.M. Was there ever at any point a desire to wrap things up neater at the end of that play?

K.T. No way. I'd rather do a play with a tough, somewhat ambiguous ending that is true and honest, than a play with some manufactured false happy ending, just so that people can walk out of the theater in a great mood.

D.M. What else would you like to see change about the theater industry?

K.T. We need more women writers, writing for older women. There are some actresses who have production companies and create their own material, and I truly admire that. There are a lot of great roles out there for older women, but most of them are by male playwrights. We need more roles for women, by women.

D.M. While you're working, you're doing the same play for months on end, day after day, and yet you have to maintain an excitement for it. You have to retain a level of spontaneity in the performance.

K.T. It's tough, but absolutely crucial. And it takes time to build a performance that's airtight. There's a minimum of three to four weeks of rehearsal before you go in front of an audience, and then you need a couple of months with the audience to get the performance to a place where you know that it will always be good. It's a place where, no matter how you feel that night, no matter what's going on in your private life, no matter what the weather is like, no matter what attitude people are coming into the show with, you will give a good, solid performance.

Now, given that, the variations that happen every night are the fun of the job. Once you have that base, that solid performance, then you get to play. You get to play jazz, as it were. For example, you'll think, "You know, I never really got the laugh I wanted on this line. Why? Is it the build? Is it the delivery? Is it the timing? All right, I'm going to try X, Y and Z tonight." And you start to play the variations within the base performance that you've already guaranteed. But you don't mess with that solid base performance. You just try to hone it, get it sharper and cleaner and brighter. Clearer. And that process goes on and on and on and on.

I spent eight months on Broadway with *Virginia Woolf,* six months in London, and six months of a National Tour. That's twenty months working on one text. And it really wasn't until the last couple of weeks that Bill Irwin and I felt that there wasn't anything more to learn from our characters. After over five hundred performances, we knew we'd done everything there was to do with those characters. But of course that's a great piece of material.

D.M. It seems few texts would support that level of work.

K.T. Yes. Not all pieces are going to have that level of depth, of layers to peel back and explore. With most pieces, you'll feel like you've hit the wall much sooner. And when you hit that wall, you should probably start to think about moving on. I was doing *Cat on a Hot Tin Roof,* and I agreed to eight months initially, then I agreed to an extension of another month because the show was going very well and many of the other actors didn't have subsequent jobs lined up. It just seemed like the right thing to do at the time, but about two weeks into that extension, I realized that I was really done with the part. I was going for laughs on lines that Tennessee Williams likely never intended there to be laughs on.

D.M. You were bored.

K.T. In a way. I was definitely messing around. I had to rein myself in and play the last couple of weeks while making sure I behaved.

D.M. I think that would be really tempting with a comedy, to start misbehaving.

K.T. It's part of the discipline, part of the job. To not be fresh would mean you'd be uninterested. So how do you go on stage if you're uninterested in the work that you're doing that night? That doesn't make sense to me. I have to be interested in the part, or I'm done with it. So any time I go on stage, I am in the process, examining what I'm doing in the moment and why I'm doing it. That's living the part. You're not repeating, or imitating, or recycling. It's fresh every night because you're exploring every night. You never fully know what's going to come out of your performance, or the response you'll get from the audience.

It's the same thing in film. You have to stay engaged, no matter how many takes you do. I've heard that Stanley Kubrick used to do three hundred takes on even the simplest scenes. I can't imagine how tough it would be to stay engaged in the scene, but that's what you sign up for when you worked with him. That's the job.

D.M. It sounds almost impossible.

K.T. You just have to force yourself to go through the mental process of thinking as the character and asking the right questions, about intent and motivation. What does my character want and how is she trying to get it? If you keep asking those questions in every moment of every scene, then you should automatically stay fresh because you will be fully engaged with the material.

D.M. It seems like that would be one of the toughest things about being a stage actor in a show that runs for month after month. Your life can be quite physically and mentally grueling.

K.T. Yeah, you give up pretty much everything.

D.M. In nearly all other professions, you can have down days where you can just sort of check out but still be functional in your job. Go on autopilot. But it seems like that's kind of an impossible thing to do in acting—or if you're doing it, then you're really not doing it well.

K.T. I don't think you can do that in acting, not really. Not on stage. You always have to be exploring your options in the role. That's one of the rewards of working in theater. I've always resented, working on films, the fact that I didn't have enough time to explore enough options. You really do have to choose rather quickly with film. And even if you have a director who is good enough to allow you to make exploratory variations between takes, it's still incredibly limiting. You'll be lucky to get ten takes at the most, so that's ten variations, and all in the space of just a couple hours. Whereas I'll do eight variations a week with a play, week after week. I've always sort of felt a little cut off from that exploratory process in film.

D.M. Have you ever felt like, at the end of a long run of a play, like a six or eight-month run, that you were doing a character that was pretty different from the one you started out with?

K.T. Not so much when you are doing it consistently. When you really see the difference is when you take a break from it and then you come back to it. For example, with *High,* I did it six months on the road, and then I took two months off, and then we went back into rehearsal, and we had a new actor to work with, and my thoughts about the character had changed somewhat in those two months.

But what I found in *Virginia Woolf,* where we took a break between Broadway and London and we took a break between London and the National Tour, was that every time we came back, it was clearer, it was cleaner, it was sharper. It's almost as though a lot of the fussy kind of stuff that an actor uses to make new choices has dropped away, has kind of been burnt off. You don't need the extensive prep work to get yourself to where you're going with the character, you can just go there now. And so it just becomes so clean and so clear. I love that. I absolutely love that. I look forward to revisiting roles because I *know* that they're going to be a lot clearer and cleaner than they were when I was developing them.

D.M. I've heard you describe your state of being while you are onstage performing as a kind of blissful blindness. Can you be audience-aware and simultaneously work in that state?

K.T. Absolutely. It's bringing your focus down, so narrow that everything is about what's happening in your mind, and in your body, and in your ability to portray this person, under these circumstances. That kind of focus and power is not exclusive to knowing how it's received. The necessary disconnect is just that you can be aware of how your audience may be receiving you, but you can't let that awareness influence what you're doing. For example, there have been times where I'll feel like there's this little hole of disinterest twelve rows down, four seats in. So you give a little blast of attention to that space, to say, "Hey you, perk up and pay attention."

There are obvious clues an audience will give you, too. For example, are they making noise? Are you hearing a lot of programs rustling? Do you hear a lot of coughing? Is there squirming in seats going on? It's difficult, but you can sense it, it's like you can sort of see out into the semi-darkness. These kinds of things are obvious, unfortunate, and inevitable on occasion. But on the flipside, the greatest feeling and moment of understanding is in the silences. When you stop, when you take that silent pause—do they stay with you through those beats? You can set a kind of rhythm in particular scenes, with each one being a different variation, like a different movement in a symphony. Their breath is coming more quickly because you picked up the pace and you're going for a brighter, more rapid movement. When you want to take the whole thing down a little lower, a little darker, you can slow their breath. The audience will breathe with you. It's magical. There's nothing quite like it. And when they hold their breath, it's a triumph.

I was doing the death scene in *Camille,* and I was breathing deeply and heavily. In, out, in, out. Deep inhale, deep exhale, deep inhale, deep exhale. Getting slower . . . and slower . . . and slower. And I could feel the audience breathing with me. So I died on the inhale. I stopped my breath after an inhale. And I could feel the tension in the room. Every member of that audience, because of what I did, was actually holding their breath. And when they could take it no more, you could hear the whole room release this enormous exhalation.

D.M. That must have been a trip for you, to hold an audience with that level of control.

K.T. Oh yes, it's great fun for me. But that was a special case, that scene. Generally you have to be careful not to extend those moments past the comfort level for the audience. You mustn't make them aware of their breathing, that would be counterproductive. You just want to control the pace, and by controlling the breathing, you're controlling the energy of the room.

And that's all kind of subliminal, but there is a level of awareness there. I can't say I'm constantly aware of the audience, because I can't let the audience dictate my performance.

D.M. Not at all?

K.T. They're not going to change my basic choices. I suppose I may have to make some more obvious, broader choices, if they're just not getting it, though. There are such things as brighter audiences than others. Your Saturday matinee audience is not the same as your Thursday night audience. Thursday nights are the serious theater-goers . . . the *real* theater-goers who can't wait for the weekend to see a play. They have to see it *now*. The weekend is more of a social thing or a date thing—the show is just a part of the evening, or the event. The date itself, which also involves dinner out or a coach ride through Central Park, or a drink after the show, is the real event.

D.M. Do you have a favorite audience?

K.T. I love Thursday night audiences. Thursday night is when the professional theater-goers come to the theater. And that is a smart audience. They're well-versed in the conventions and the history of theater, and they just make your job so much easier. Sometimes I feel that with a Saturday matinee crowd for a popular show, it's all tourists or all bridge-and-tunnel, as we say. You almost have to teach them how to behave at the same time that you're performing for them. I actually had someone in the audience in *High,* in the front row, start eating a hamburger and fries. He brought his lunch into the matinee! The usher actually had to say, "I'm sorry, but you *really* can't do that." It just never occurred to him.

D.M. That's mind-boggling.

K.T. He just sat there in the theater, smacking away, eating his lunch.

D.M. As a professor, it makes me crazy when a student busts out their lunch while I am trying to lecture. It's so distracting for everyone in the room. And the phone calls—it's one thing to have students text while I'm teaching, which happens more than I care to admit, but I've had students answer their phone in class.

K.T. That's crazy. I'd kick them out.

D.M. It must drive you insane when someone takes a call during your show.

K.T. Oh God, yes. "No, I can't talk now, I'm in a play. Yeah, the Kathleen Turner one. Oh, it's pretty good. I like her, you know." That's just thrilling, we actors just love that.

I was at the Drama Desk Awards years ago, and Robin Williams was there, and he'd just done his first Broadway show. He'd done his standup on Broadway, but this was his first time playing a role. And at the Awards he was telling us how he was in the middle of this huge, serious monologue where his character is speaking directly to God, and a cell phone goes off, and it's the theme music from *Deliverance*.

D.M. "Dueling Banjos!"

K.T. Right—"Dueling Banjos!" And Robin said that every atom in his body, every muscle was screaming, "Take that and shove it up that guy's ass!" But he said, "I didn't do that because it's a *play*." He stayed in character and plowed through it.

D.M. Considering his penchant for improvisational comedy, I can only imagine the material he could have done on someone having the theme from *Deliverance* as a ringtone!

K.T. No kidding! It had to be very difficult to restrain himself. Not that you ever want to hear a cell phone go off, but it's *always* at a point in the play when you're in a moment like that—a quiet scene, or an intense moment where you're talking to God or something. It's always those moments. At the very, very end of *Virginia Woolf*, we used to hear these rings, because that was a good, solid three hour show, and you know people have gone out in one of the two intermissions and they've taken a call, or they've made a call, and they didn't turn their phones off before they came back into the theater, and now it's a good three hours later, and all their friends are out of their shows that they went to, and someone is calling to say, "Are you out yet?" So it's right up to the very end of the play, and *God*, you would like to kill that guy. Because you've just given these three hours of your life some of the best work you've ever done, and then some moron takes a call. It's maddening.

D.M. So how do you respond when that happens?

K.T. I've gotten to the point where I will just pause, I'll just completely stop. And sometimes people will just think it's an intentional pause, and some people will get it. I've known actors, and I've done it myself on occasion, who will stop, turn, and look at the area of the audience where the ring is coming from. And you hear all these people going, "Shh, Shh, Shh!"

At one performance, during the second act of *Virginia Woolf*, this phone started ringing. It rang, and it rang, and it rang, and it rang, maybe ten or twelve times in total. A friend of mine who was at the show came backstage afterwards and told me that the cell phone was lying in the aisle, that somebody dropped it out of a purse or a pocket, and no one wanted to pick it up, because everyone would have thought it was theirs. So the whole audience just let it ring, because no one wanted to be blamed for it.

D.M. Maybe they should start forcing audiences to check their phones at the box office or the coat check.

K.T. In some theaters, they evidently have put in a kind of paint that can block cell signals. But by law we shouldn't do that, because if there's a doctor in the house or there's an emergency situation, those people need to be reachable. But I wish we could.

D.M. Live theater is in many ways the antithesis of being "plugged in" to your phone. When you are playing with your phone—texting, surfing the web, whatever—you are disconnected from all that is happening around you. It's giving yourself over to a virtual experience. Neurologists and psychologists tell us that cell phone use is permanently altering our ability to focus and maintain attention to something, our ability to make eye contact with people we talk to, and even our sleep cycles. But theater is immediate—it's all about being live, in the space, with the performers.

K.T. And with the audience. When you are looking down at your phone you are navel-gazing, lost in your own world. It's all about you. Theater is deliberate and communal. You are supposed to be in the moment with the entire room.

D.M. This is one of the reasons that I think theater curricula in colleges and universities is so important. I encourage my film students to take at least one course in basic acting. Not only so that they will learn how to better collaborate with actors when they begin making films, but so they can have a chance to unplug and just live in their minds and bodies, with awareness.

And back to our discussion of awareness—have you gone and seen performances or acted opposite performances where you knew the actor didn't have that awareness of the audience that we were talking about?

K.T. Oh, sure. Many times.

D.M. It just seems so against what acting is, against that immersion in a character. To have that awareness seems like a distraction, and yet it's part of the job.

K.T. It's totally part of the job.

D.M. I guess it's part of your responsibility to make sure you put on a good show, not just that you're true to a character.

K.T. That awareness can work both ways. It can lift you, it can give you more confidence when you know that you're on track and you have their full attention, or it can bring you down a little, if you feel like you've lost them. I can honestly say that's never happened to me, thank goodness. But have I worked with actors or seen actors who don't have an awareness of the audience? Absolutely.

The real problem, when you're working with an actor like that, is that it's not just about not having an audience awareness, it's that it usually extends to not having an awareness of the fellow actors. Because if you're not aware of how you're communicating with an audience, you're probably not there with the other people on stage, either. You'll jump their lines or you'll jump their timing, you'll intrude or you won't support them. It's that focus thing in theater—in film, the camera and editing will do the focusing for you, they will direct the audience's attention where it needs to be, but that doesn't happen on stage. On stage *you* have to direct the audience. And for that reason alone, if nothing else, you have to be aware of them. So that you can lead the audience over to this actor for this line, then direct them to this part of the stage for this action, and so on.

When you run into an actor who doesn't do that, who can't do that, who only steps up and takes his turn, but then does not pass the ball, then that's no good for anybody. And you know that they're not in touch with the audience either. There's an inherent agreement, an understanding that you will lead the audience through the play, and if an actor doesn't have the ability to support another actor, he is probably lacking the skill to do that, and he leaves the audience hanging, too.

D.M. That awareness must change based on the size of the house.

K.T. It can. Some houses are just too big. I've played in houses with more than two thousand seats, and just felt overwhelmed. It's like playing full football instead of touch football. By the end of a performance, you literally feel beaten up. You're trying to physically push the energy and the intention and the emotions so far, and cast such a wide net, that you come off stage feeling bruised. As opposed to a one-thousand-seat-house, which is intimate by comparison. We did *High* at The Booth, which is seven-hundred-sixty seats or so, and I'd go onstage and think, "Ah, you're just going to make this so easy for me, aren't ya?" Because I hardly had to push the awareness out past my own personal space. It felt that close.

But all theaters, despite their size, are very intimate spaces. When else do you sit so close to a total stranger? On the subway, maybe? Almost never, and certainly not for a period of several hours. So already, even before the play starts, you already have someone basically violating your personal space. Everything about the setting is designed to facilitate a communal experience, a bonding between strangers. That communal experience is the real reward of theatergoing. Communing in a theater among an audience reinforces our shared humanity. It reminds us that we find the same things funny, thrilling, infuriating and sad. It reminds us that we're not so very different after all.

D.M. The way you describe it, theatergoing can almost be a political and a moral act.

K.T. I believe it can.

D.M. Is it possible for a house to be too small, or is there no such thing as too much intimacy? Especially with a play like *High*, which is so small in its physical scope and so emotionally intimate?

K.T. Oh, yes. One of the regional theaters where we workshopped *High* had ceilings that were maybe sixteen feet, tops. With the lights hanging down, it meant the ceiling felt maybe twelve feet at most. And the audience was so close that, whether they meant to or not, they had to intrude on what was happening on stage. When someone went to get a handkerchief or a tissue out of their purse, all the movement and the sound was right there on stage with us. That was unfortunate.

D.M. In terms of your performance then, does it just become a question of modulating your performance to be as small as possible? It seems relatable to how actors have to adjust for film cameras. If you're making a film and you have a large dramatic moment, let's say, and the director has pushed the camera in too tight, then that affects the audience's perception of your performance, potentially pushing into melodrama a performance that is actually perfectly pitched, because the perspective of the camera is so close.

It seems like it would be the same in a small house. If your audience is right there, practically onstage with you, then there's a point where it starts to impede you.

K.T. I would agree in the sense that you're not going to use your full voice. You have to be aware that your square footage on stage is so much smaller than almost anywhere else. So you have to limit your personal space, as a character, in terms of gestures and the speed of your movement. If you rehearse or workshop a performance on a stage where you have fifteen feet to do something, and then you move to a stage where you have four feet for that action, that's a serious limitation. And it can affect not just that action but your whole performance, because everything has to be adjusted in proportion. That's really aggravating.

D.M. In *Virginia Woolf*, even though that character is often very big, there are also points where she's very insular and the notes you are playing are very small. But if you accept the responsibility of having to play those small moments to somebody at the back of a huge house, who feels like they're in a different zip code, then how do you work with that?

K.T. Trial and error. The director will move around the house during rehearsal and help you with that. It's just a matter of finding a happy median. You do have to make those moments a little bigger than they really should be, which is a shame sometimes. But your responsibility is to perform for the *entire* audience, not just the people in the front row.

D.M. Is your evening performance different if you have a matinee during that day?

K.T. Not by much, but yes. They're richer, deeper.

D.M. Really? I would have guessed the opposite, because it seems you'd be tired and a bit used up after already giving a full performance earlier in the day.

K.T. Well, those things are true, but there's a way of looking at them as a positive and not a negative. I tell friends to come to the Wednesday night or the Saturday night show precisely because I have matinees on those days. I think once you've done it in an afternoon, even though you have a couple hours to recover before the evening performance, you've used up your edge in a way. Obviously you don't have the same strength, but also, your barriers have been lowered, the barriers you use to protect yourself.

D.M. What do you mean by barriers?

K.T. Both because you're a little tired and because you've done it already that day, you don't have that instinctive lack of protectiveness, that edge, that you do when you start out fresh for the first time on a given day. So to me the second show gets deeper because I am less self-aware and more vulnerable. And very interesting things begin to happen, because I'm not protecting myself the same way that I was at the earlier show.

And I like that vulnerability. *Virginia Woolf* was a long, grueling show, but I would always tell people to come to the Saturday night performance. The company never talked about it as a second show—we referred to it as Acts IV, V, and VI. Because there was so little time in between shows that we didn't really feel like we were ever off stage. So count that as basically a solid nine hours of performance.

D.M. I don't see how you do that and not just collapse. It would be exhausting, mentally and physically.

K.T. I rarely get tired when I'm onstage. Just after the show ends, I'm wiped, but during the show I'm not often weary.

D.M. I don't know how you did the two back-to-back shows with *Virginia Woolf*, because you've said that that play leaves you so spent at the end of it. I think you've been quoted as saying that Martha "used up everything I had as an actress." I can't imagine how you could turn around and start it over after just finishing it.

K.T. It wasn't easy, that's for sure. But I loved those second shows of *Virginia Woolf*. Yeah, I was damned tired and I was really used up in a lot of ways, but because of that I was forced to dig deeper. I went darker sometimes, too. On some nights I would be so exhausted I wouldn't know where to look for the drive to keep going, but I had to pull it up from somewhere, and sometimes that was when I found the most rich and textured performance.

D.M. Did you even have a matinee cast?

K.T. No. I had an understudy, in case I got sick, but I'm the only Martha to ever not have a matinee cast. Both Uta Hagen and Colleen Dewhurst had matinee casts. So they did six shows a week. I was offered one, but I said, "No, I just can't allow it." And I'm so glad I did. I just didn't want anyone else to do it. I would have been sitting at home while the matinee was going on, tearing myself apart, knowing that the show wasn't as good as it could be because I wasn't there. I couldn't live with that. I couldn't live with the thought of people buying tickets to my show and not seeing my performance.

D.M. Did you ever have to cancel a performance?

K.T. Unfortunately, yes. When I got sick before the last performance of *Virginia Woolf* during our Boston run, I cried and cried because I couldn't bear not doing the show.

I really hate cancelling a performance, or using an understudy. Hate it. When I do a role, it's my role. When I injured my knee while doing *The Third Story*, I got a cane and a knee brace and soldiered on.

The Third Story is a comedy written by and starring Charles Busch, which tells the 1940s-set story of a testy collaboration between mother-and-son screenwriters. Kathleen starred with Busch in the off-Broadway play in 2009.

D.M. The show must go on.

K.T. Indeed. Even if it means the character has an unexplained knee brace and cane.

D.M. Theater feels primarily like an evening activity. Theater doesn't really work in the same way when the sun is out, for some weird reason.

K.T. Well, I don't like shows at ten o'clock in the morning, that's for sure. Sometimes, when you're in regional theaters or smaller houses, the theater will agree to do a performance, if it's appropriate, for a school or something. So you've got a morning performance, and you find yourself just after breakfast putting on makeup and thinking, "Wait a minute, I just woke up, why am putting on giant false eyelashes?!" That just feels wrong.

D.M. For me, when I go to a matinee, I just feel like I'm not getting as much out of the experience as I could be. Even if I'm not doing anything else when I go out in the evening to see a show, like not going out to eat before or after, there's still something about it that feels more substantial at night. It shouldn't be any different, because there are no windows in a theater, there's no direct awareness of the environment outside, but there's just something about going into a matinee that feels . . . incomplete. I always wondered if performers felt that way.

K.T. For us, the big difference is that the matinees cater to a much older crowd. They're the ones who aren't working, or they're retired, or whatever. I've heard them referred to as "the cauliflower crowd," because you look out from the stage and see all these little white, fuzzy heads. I shouldn't say that, but it's true.

Anyway, you will think, "Okay, they're not going to get this cultural reference, or they're probably going to take offense to this piece of dialogue." Those kinds of considerations. Not that you change the text for them, but it might affect how you deliver certain lines. But the biggest difference between the matinees and the evening shows is the energy level. Matinees just feel more low-key, more low-energy.

D.M. Maybe that's what I'm sensing.

K.T. That's probably it. Part of that is the age of the audience, and part of it, like you said, is that theater is more exciting as an evening activity because it's more of an event.

THE INTIMACY OF THE THEATER

DUSTIN MORROW When you are onstage, what are you looking for from your fellow actors?

KATHLEEN TURNER Most importantly, complete and total attention. You should be watching every single thing that other actor is doing, at every single moment that you are in contact with them. Your focus may shift from one character to another, but when you are in a dialogue, or in a relationship with another character, they must have your complete and full attention. Anything less is disrespectful and probably not very effective.

Beyond that, you should just be generally supportive, and realize that you're all in it together, working toward a common good, which is to put up the best show possible. That support could come in a hundred different ways. I might say to someone, "You know, I've got to reach this extreme state by this line of dialogue, so I need a tighter, harder build and I need you to assist me in getting there."

Work together to find the rises and falls within a scene, within the characters' interactions. And of course there are basic rules, like not stealing another actor's scene, and not placing yourself upstage, physically, of a person that you're in a scene with. I call that "ass-acting."

D.M. "Ass-acting!?" Is that a real term or is that a Kathleen Turner term?

K.T. That might be a Kathleen Turner term.

D.M. A "Kathleen Term." Term—a "Termer."

K.T. You got it. "Kathleen Termer" could be a Kathleen term.

D.M. Just don't forget that I coined it.

K.T. I will give credit where it's due. Actually, I think I prefer "Turnerism."

D.M. Yeah, that's cleaner. Let's go with "Turnerism."

K.T. In all seriousness though, there is a form of ass-acting that drives me crazy. Sometimes it's very effective to have your back to the audience at certain moments, or even on certain lines. But that's because you choose to do it, not because another actor has forced you into that position, because you're more polite than they are. Oh, that makes me mad. When I see actors doing that I call them on it.

D.M. Ass-acting also seems like it would misdirect the audience's attention.

K.T. It totally does. That awareness of the audience that we were discussing—you don't have that if you're doing a lot of ass-acting.

D.M. But theater audiences have a lot of control in where they look.

K.T. Less than they think they do. Obviously, they have more control than in film, where the camera dictates what they can and can't see. But the actors and the director in theater are in control of the audience, even if the audience doesn't realize it. And that's a great example of the beauty of the subliminal work of theater.

Even though they can't necessarily see some of the fine details or have the ease of being directed by editing, as they are in cinema, audiences see a bigger picture in theater that is very rewarding. And maybe they're not always sure where to look, or they might miss something that's happening depending on how it's staged and what the actors are doing, but there is this incredible subliminal understanding of the emotion of the work.

D.M. Part of that has to be just being in the same room as the actors. Feeling connected to a real, living being before you, not an image on a screen.

K.T. And the communal experience of live theater is unrivaled. I was doing a play in London some time ago where we had four tiers of seats in the theater. We had the orchestra, the mezzanine, the balcony and then the gods up at the top. We call it that because you are so close to God up there. Now we know that sound travels more slowly than light, and most of the time in a theater that big you can actually feel the wave of recognition of a moment on stage across the theater, from front to back. For a big gag, the people in front will laugh a split-second faster than the people in the gods.

But it is possible, when everything is moving wonderfully, when the actors are really flying, that you will have a laugh at the same exact instant from the gods as you will have from the orchestra, which should not actually physically be possible, because of the sound lag. But what happens in that theater is a sort of magical communal understanding. There's that old story about the hundred monkeys, that when ninety-nine monkeys learn something the hundredth will somehow just know it. This is the kind of thing that can happen in a theater, where there is this extraordinary understanding that is passed through the audience without conscious thought, without decision, but everyone starts to laugh at the same time, hold their breath at the same time, tense up at the same time, or relax at the same time.

It shouldn't be possible that everyone in a huge theater has the facility to feel something at exactly the same moment. But what happens is that there is a great understanding happening because of the act of communal sharing. When you go to the theater, you don't just experience the play, you experience the audience, the collective act of being with that audience. This is why theater is invaluable and should be sacred and was once considered sacred in so many cultures. When people walk out of a theater, if it's gone well, if the play was worthy and the production has held them and moved them, then they have been part of something larger than themselves as individuals, and larger than the play itself. And that is a gift, and that is why I love the theater.

D.M. Is there a dramatically different challenge when working in a theater in the round as opposed to a traditional proscenium theater?

K.T. They are tremendously different. Proscenium is terribly different from thrust. When doing play on the road, I will often have to work in thrust theaters, which are theaters where the stage extends out significantly beyond the proscenium, and you have the audience on your sides as well as in front of you. So what that means for the actor is that most of your movement, most of your actions must be on a diagonal line so that you can have two-thirds of the audience seeing as much of you as possible at any given moment. But inevitably there must be moments where half the audience is going to get your back.

D.M. Ass-acting.

K.T. It's not that, because the stage forces you into that position, so you have to plan it carefully in rehearsal. Now that can be a great choice sometimes. You can actually make wonderful choices as to when to turn your back to the audience and use that denial of your face effectively. But where it's always a choice when working in proscenium, it is not often a choice in the thrust or in the round, where you have the audience all around you.

So you find yourself trying to present two-thirds of your face at any given time to two-thirds of the audience and you have to make your choices as an actor based on that limitation. When we brought *High* back to Broadway, after having done it in thrust stages on the road, we were in a proscenium house and all the staging had to change. Now suddenly we're moving front-to-back or side-to-side, and there is no point in moving on diagonals because it doesn't change what the audience can really see. It necessitated a complete re-blocking of the play.

And one thing that made *High* tricky on those thrust stages was that my character frequently broke the fourth wall. I had to speak directly to the audience. If you have to do that, and you have the audience all around you, where do you look?

D.M. You've had to break the fourth wall in several of your plays. *Red Hot Patriot* had you speaking directly to the audience pretty much for its entire running time.

Red Hot Patriot *is a fiery one-woman play, a monologue by Kathleen in the role of the late, legendary Texas political journalist Molly Ivins.*

Is that a hard thing to reconcile when most plays have been designed where you pretend the audience isn't there?

K.T. Actually, I always find it rather amusing, deep down inside, that we all pretend this imaginary wall is there when we go to the theater. You pretend it as the audience and I pretend it as the actor. Hundreds of people are staring at me and I'm not supposed to know I'm being looked at. That conceit kind of makes me giggle, it's part of the fun of theater.

Anyway, in *High*, one of the things that I loved about it was the back-and-forth. I took the monologues through that fourth wall so that I was deliberately and directly engaged with the audience, but then I stepped back into the scenes with the other actor as if the audience was no longer there. Sliding between those two modes of address was interesting.

D.M. Is that the best way to directly address the audience, through the breaking of the fourth wall?

K.T. Well, if you position an actor between me and the audience, so I am turned toward that actor and therefore toward the audience, I can almost directly address the audience.

D.M. Hmm. It's almost like editing in film, choosing where to cut between shots. Only you are using blocking to direct the audience's attention and to align their sympathies and identification with specific characters.

K.T. Exactly. And in proscenium theaters, because the fourth wall is so clearly defined—it's always that front edge of the stage—you can be really specific with your choices. It gets trickier with thrust theaters and theaters in the round.

D.M. Do you prefer one kind of theater to the other?

K.T. It depends on the play, doesn't it? The proscenium is more powerful in a lot of ways because you can be so specific in your choices. Within the round or thrust, you can't always highlight things that clearly because so much of it is out of the field of vision of the audience. Another problem with a thrust stage is that the audience really becomes a part of the whole theatrical experience in a way that they don't with proscenium stages. They become part of the scenery. They're part of the set, essentially, because if you are sitting on one side of a thrust, looking across the stage, you see the audience on the other side of the thrust.

So I guess, ultimately, in my heart, I prefer the specificity of the proscenium. Theater in the round is tough, it's just really hard. When we did *Midsummer Nights Dream* in the round, that was a tough production.

D.M. That was right after *Body Heat* came out.

K.T. Yes. I played Titania and Hippolyta, and Avery Brooks was Oberon and Theseus. He was absolutely marvelous. We had a wonderful cast and crew, but a director who was perhaps not ready to stage a production that complicated in that type of theater.

Avery Brooks is an accomplished stage and television actor, probably best known for his TV roles as Hawk on the Robert Urich detective series Spencer for Hire *and as Captain Sisko on* Star Trek: Deep Space Nine.

D.M. What made the production so complicated?

K.T. Yeesh, it would be easier to tell you what didn't make it complicated.

D.M. It's such a magnificent play, so open to interpretation. Incredibly challenging.

K.T. So challenging. For starters, the set was very intricate. We had a sunken pool and the fairies and I were in the water a lot, and then we had the forests and this thing built to enable characters to be in the sky, a sort of plexiglass corridor built high above the stage. That was the idea, that they would all represent the major elements. It was very difficult because we found that in order to have the best audience sightlines for the pool we could only sink it about four feet into the stage. And then we had to escape from the pool under a lip in its side, where you would swim under the stage, climb out of the tank under the lip, race upstairs, throw on your wig and wardrobe and dash back out wearing this sort of scuba suit.

I was wearing this kind of wet suit, it was too damn cold not to. The problem with the four-foot pool, especially if you are a 5'8" actor like myself, is that it becomes a very shallow dive, with very little space to dive in. So if you are going to dive, you've got the break that dive immediately once you hit the water, or it will carry you right into the wall of the pool. So of course we devise a whole complicated series of dives for my character—I did back flips, I did handstands, all kinds of stuff, because straight diving just took me too hard against the side of the tank. So I got real good at doing handstands and flips into this pool. But there were other characters with costumes more complicated than mine, that couldn't move underwater, where the actors would actually have to put their costumes on underwater. It was just a big mess.

And then the problem became that when you came out of the pool and you're running around the stage, trying to be all whimsical and charming, you would slip and fall because you're soaking wet. So they had the great idea to cover the stage with a paint that had sand in it, so we wouldn't break our necks. But that was really hard on the lovers because they went down on their knees to play scenes, and the floor would tear up their legs.

And that plexiglass contraption above the stage was frightening. Avery was running around on that thing in half-darkness. I kept expecting him to fall off and break his leg, it was incredible what he did up there.

D.M. That sounds like the craziest production ever.

K.T. It was insane. The play opened in darkness with the sound of a quarterstaff fight between Avery and myself. All the audience would hear would be the ringing of the iron staffs hitting each other. We rehearsed this to death, and I was a tremendous athlete at that time, but Avery is a very big, very strong man. So I would have to change my iron staff every two weeks because it would start to bend from where he would be beating it in. We rehearsed this fight blindfolded and with our eyes closed—first position, second position, third position, fourth position—so that in the darkness, even though we couldn't see, we would never miss the hit because we knew the fight so well. If he'd missed a hit, I would be looking at a broken skull or a broken shoulder.

Amazingly, nobody got seriously hurt on that production. A couple of my fairies got a little hurt during the dives. They didn't pull up fast enough and they hit the edge of the pool. One of the fairies quit because she was so scared. But nobody got seriously hurt, which was frankly amazing because the whole show was so on the edge. It was a spectacular looking production, and beautifully acted, but in hindsight the whole endeavor was rather foolish.

D.M. In *Red Hot Patriot* you go beyond breaking the fourth wall—there's a couple of scenes where you sit right on the edge of the stage to speak to the audience.

K.T. I know. Wasn't that fun?

D.M. It really works because Molly Ivins is such a folksy character, sometimes called the Mark Twain of her era, so that choice to sit so casually on the edge of the stage seems a natural one.

K.T. It was. I figured that one out early. Molly would not have wanted to be removed from the audience. She would never allow the separation. That's so inherent in her character, it seemed to me that sitting on the edge of the stage was the way to go. Molly also liked to get in people's faces, she wasn't afraid of confrontation, so that was part of that decision too. I'm sure that she would want to take as much of the dignity and the sort of social protocol away from any theatrical thing as she could. It made sense to me.

D.M. When you break the fourth wall like that, especially in that play, where you are literally sitting just a few feet from the audience, you can probably feel a change in the energy of the audience, like a perking-up or a snapping-to-attention.

K.T. Definitely, but you have to be careful with that. There's snapping to attention, and there's making them uncomfortable. It can make a lot of the audience very uncomfortable because they think they are safe in their role of just sitting there and watching the action, and suddenly when you bring it to them, especially the way Molly would do, where she'd get right in their faces, you have to be careful. They can get uneasy because they are not sure what their job is then, what their role is, how they are supposed to be behaving. Are they still passive viewers? Do they look her in the eye or not? Do they look away?

Playing Molly, it's not hard to put them at ease, which is why I am able to get so intimate in breaking the fourth wall in that play. Molly was very charming, a real co-conspirator. I turn on the charm, tell a joke, whisper something to them, get them on my side. Wake them up, get them to smile, make them feel okay.

D.M. But you couldn't use that charm in a play like *High*, where you are playing a tougher, harder character and the content of the play is so disturbing.

K.T. That's true. Even though I broke the fourth wall in that play, I didn't directly address anyone in the audience, I didn't look anybody in the face. Or if I inadvertently did, there was still a certain distance with the design of the lighting and the staging. Dangerously, breaking the fourth wall can sometimes invite feedback from the audience. That was okay in *Red Hot Patriot*—I could even answer as Molly—but I didn't want that in *High*. In some ways, *Red Hot Patriot* was more like a lecture hall than traditional theater, while *High* was very theatrical.

D.M. Feedback from the audience—that sounds like a nightmare.

K.T. It can be, yes!

CAMILLE

DUSTIN MORROW Let's talk about some of your theatrical roles and the acting moments in them that really stick in your memory as particularly challenging.

KATHLEEN TURNER Okay, let's start with *Camille* and the death scene.

Camille *is a classic love story by Alexandre Dumas, about a courtisane who falls in love with a man above her station, but whose love is doomed by the interference of the man's family and the tuberculosis which ultimately takes her life. The play was the basis for the classic Verdi opera* La Traviata.

D.M. You mentioned this scene earlier in passing, what's the whole story?

K.T. It was basically my trying to find a new way to die on stage. I mean, how many millions of death scenes had been done over centuries of theater? Finding a way to die on stage that isn't over-the-top and melodramatic or the opposite, totally forgettable, is really tough.

D.M. So your solution was to make it all about the breathing.

K.T. Yes, specifically the rhythm of the breathing. The challenge in that scene wasn't just that it was yet another theatrical death scene, but it was a death scene everyone knew was coming. *Camille* is so well-known that most theatergoers were aware that she was going to die of tuberculosis at the end of the play. I had to find a way past that, to still hook them, to work some suspense into a scene where the outcome was a forgone conclusion.

I started with wardrobe, changing from a ball gown into a night-gown, and I slapped on a ton of white powder, to pale her, pale her, pale her even more. There's a sort of daybed, a reclining couch, on the stage, and I drift out in total silence, alone. There's no other sound, there's nothing else happening, there's no dialogue, there's nothing. All you hear is my breath, which is incredibly painful, incredibly difficult, incredibly labored. I breathe in and then there is this horrible exhalation and the fight to breathe back in is tremendous. I do this three times, four times, five times, to the point where the audience has to start wondering what's going to happen. They begin to wonder, "Is there going to be a scene here? Is somebody else going to come in? Is she going to speak?"

So I take it to maybe five or six inhalations, which are absolutely desperate, and by now I have set a rhythm. And on the last one, I inhale deeply, but there is no exhalation. But the rhythm has been set firmly by that point. There is no exhalation, and the audience waits and waits and waits and then they exhale together. It was audible in the theater. You could hear the audience collectively exhale. They were holding their breath and they just couldn't hold it anymore. The whole room was breathing with me, I was controlling their very breath. I brought them together as one unit, one single entity. Over a hundred people, breathing together, it was amazing.

D.M. That really is a great example of the communal experience of theatergoing. Where you cease to be a group of individual audience members and become one thing, an audience.

K.T. Indeed, it's magical. And I always knew when I had them. Some nights it only took four breaths, some nights it took six. But I could feel it on the stage, and I knew when I could stop breathing, when I could die on the inhale.

And it was very moving, initially very unexpected in a lot of ways. It taught me a great lesson about what I share with the audience, what tools I could use to bring them on stage with me, into my character's experience. And it was just great fun for me, of course. There were nights when I would sit there and I'd be dead and I would hear that gasping exhalation from the audience, and inside I'd go, "Oh yeah, I got 'em!" Inside I was grinning like a fool.

D.M. Was that something you decided to do during rehearsal or did you find that in the performances with the audience there?

K.T. It was certainly a concept in rehearsal, it was something that I wanted to try, but I didn't know if it would work until I started doing it in front of an audience.

D.M. It's a great example of how important rhythm is in live theater.

K.T. Indeed.

D.M. Did the critics mention that moment in their reviews? It sounds like a showstopper.

K.T. To tell you the truth, I can't remember. The reviews were good, but I can't recall the details.

D.M. You've had a number of other death scenes, both in film and on stage.

K.T. It's not like I seek out roles in which the character dies at the end, but those scenes do often provide for a nice acting moment. And nobody does a death scene like me, babe.

D.M. Not a dry eye in the house?

K.T. You better believe it!

READING REVIEWS

DUSTIN MORROW Do you always read your reviews?

KATHLEEN TURNER Always. I always read my reviews. Any actor who says they don't is probably lying. If you don't read them somebody's going to quote them to you anyway. And I'm thin-skinned—bad reviews sting. But I have a mutual respect with critics, after thirty-odd years having them evaluate my work.

D.M. Do you remember your first review?

K.T. I can't remember my first stage review, but I sure remember my first film review. She really ripped me. It was quite an introduction to reading one's reviews.

D.M. What was that?

K.T. Janet Maslin, for *The New York Times*.

D.M. Reviewing *Body Heat*?

K.T. Yes.

D.M. Do you still remember what she wrote?

K.T. I don't remember the exact wording , but it was something to the effect of, "Mr. Kasdan demonstrates enough talent to breathe life into certain sections of the movie, particularly those parts that don't involve Miss Turner."

D.M. Ouch.

K.T. All of the other reviews were great, so it was fine, but it just so happened that the only really negative one was the first one I read. For a brief moment, I thought it was all over.

D.M. That had to be demoralizing.

K.T. No kidding. For about five minutes I thought my film career was done. But no art is universal. Any kind of art is going to be very personal, and its reception will always be subjective. You're never going to appeal to everyone.

D.M. Do you find that your performances are ever affected by critics? Is there anything positive you can do with a review?

K.T. Not usually. But not because I'm one of those actors who is stridently anti-critic. It's just that the reviews tend to be too general. Rare is the review that will pick out a specific moment in a play and provide feedback detailed enough to be useful. And it's probably good that they are so general. Even praise, if it's hyper-specific, can be problematic. It makes me a little crazy when someone says, "You know, I loved exactly how you said that one line tonight." Because you find yourself in that spot in the show the next night, and you're distracted into thinking, "Wait, how did I do it last night?" It takes you out of the moment. So don't give me a specific compliment, because I might get hung up on that place for days.

D.M. This is probably a tough question for you to answer, because you got so famous so quickly, at such a young age, but do you think critics have gotten easier on you as you've grown professionally in stature, or is it maybe the other way around?

K.T. Well, I don't exactly think I get a pass, but I've certainly reached a point in my career where most people will assume that I will be able to perform well with any role I take. When I came back to Broadway after doing a lot of big film roles, to do *Cat on a Hot Tin Roof*, there was an element of, "Oh yeah, Ms. Big Movie Star, you think you can still handle Broadway?" But I proved myself, got good reviews and good box office, and it was quickly not an issue.

But there are a lot of famous film actors who seem to assume that if they can be successful on film, they can be successful on stage, and that's not necessarily true. In fact, we have had many examples in the last few years alone where that was demonstrated. Film acting and stage acting are not the same thing, and most actors can't slide back and forth effortlessly between the two. I was recently telling a very famous film actress, who has never done anything on stage, about my upcoming stage work, and she said something to the effect of, "Oh yes, I think it might be time for me to try that. Do you think I should just go do

Broadway, Kathleen?" So ridiculous. As if Broadway were something you "just go do." As if you don't spend years, *decades* even, building and honing your skills as a stage actor. It's amazing how delusional some actors can be about that.

D.M. I know young actors in particular will take criticism very hard sometimes. I think they forget that Theater Critic and Film Critic are very weird professions, with their own agendas and politics that have nothing to do with the production being reviewed.

K.T. Of course. A critic has to represent the publication he's writing for, and write specifically for that publication's audience if he hopes to keep his job. For example, the reviewer of the *New York Post* is not going to write the same kind of review or focus on the same kind of issues as the critic for the *New York Times*, even though they may have the exact same personal opinion of the show they review. The *Post* will look for something sensationalistic, language that will be catchy and pithy, and it's in his favor to find fault in the production and point it out. As opposed to the *New York Times* review, which might look closer at the play, and the words, and the *intention* of the piece and whether or not that comes across. A critic writes for the organization they are employed by. Period. So all reviews have to be read from that perspective, and never taken personally.

D.M. What's it like to win awards for your acting? You received back-to-back Golden Globes—just a few actors in history have achieved that.

K.T. Awards are nice, but not necessary and, deep down, kind of silly. I wanted the Tony nomination for *Virginia Woolf*, because I really felt that was some of the best work of my life and I felt the nomination would be a lovely validation of that beyond the reviews and the box office, which were all great. Beyond that, it's all just been icing on the cake. The Oscar nomination was wonderful, because *Peggy Sue* is a very special film. And winning back-to-back Golden Globes was also a great honor.

But look, the nature of the awards system is ridiculous. If you nominate five actors for an award, you are singling them out, celebrating them, because they managed to stand out. Because they were unique. But how do you judge someone's uniqueness against someone else's uniqueness? It doesn't make any sense. If something is unique, it can't be any more or less unique than something else. By definition. Even the nomination process is a bit goofy, when you think about it, because there are certainly way more than five actors in any given year doing work worthy of that level of recognition.

D.M. So there really is truth in the old saying, "It was an honor just to be nominated."

K.T. Of course. That's what awards are—recognition. Just to be recognized at all is enough. To then sort of falsely compete with four other actors to decide who is most unique is silly. That's not about the actors, that's about TV ratings and box office returns.

D.M. Can you think of any reviews that you felt were really unfair?

K.T. Not really. Because again, the critic is writing for their very specific audience, so that critic is not interested in being fair to the production they are reviewing but to the readership they are reviewing it for.

D.M. That's true. There are many film-based websites out there now which focus on a specific genre, and some of their reviews are hilarious because they will rave about the most awful movies, but they understand their audience. The websites focusing on horror films have to understand that what might be absolute dreck to 99% of the filmgoing audience might be *Citizen Kane* to their readership.

K.T. Right. It's the same in all professional criticism, regardless of the medium or the publication.

D.M. But even accounting for that qualification, occasionally some reviews must really annoy you.

K.T. Of course. I thought critics were generally unfair to *The Graduate*, for instance.

D.M. Well, at least you got good reviews. Although the critics were harder on the play itself, you got universally rave reviews for your performance. Critical consensus seemed to be that you played a tougher and more coldly calculating Mrs. Robinson than Anne Bancroft, but also a sadder and more deeply felt character.

K.T. I thought the critics were a bit too tough on the production overall, but I appreciate that they said nice things about my work.

D.M. Didn't you take out an ad in the *Times* after the show failed to get any Tony nominations?

K.T. Yes, it was to congratulate the cast and crew on producing one of the biggest Broadway hits in years, and to thumb the proverbial nose at the Tony's nominating committee. They messed up!

D.M. A big splashy ad in the *Times*. That's just so . . . Kathleen Turner.

K.T. I've got style!

THE GRADUATE

DUSTIN MORROW Mrs. Robinson is a heck of a part. The list of actresses that went on to play the role onstage after you originated it is quite impressive—Lorraine Bracco, Anne Archer, and Patricia Richardson, to name just three.

KATHLEEN TURNER She's an incredible character, full of depth and possibility.

D.M. Besides the nudity we discussed earlier, what were the other challenges of playing Mrs. Robinson?

K.T. I am a very physical person and I'm usually throwing myself all over the set. Even when the rheumatoid arthritis was killing me, I was still throwing myself around the set, but I found in creating Mrs. Robinson that I had to be incredibly still. I needed to move minimally, to be almost completely still. As I developed her in rehearsals I found myself cutting away and cutting away and cutting away all gestures and movements. I cut any unnecessary crosses, any unnecessary rises or seatings or anything. Once she sat down she stayed down, once she stood up she stayed up, she crossed in, she crossed out, there was no extraneous movement at all. In making that choice, I actually rather surprised myself because that's just not the way I usually develop a role.

D.M. What was the thinking in making her so still?

K.T. Mrs. Robinson simply would not move more than she absolutely had to because she was always precariously on the brink of being fall-down drunk. She had always just possibly drank enough to make a foolish move, to stumble or to slip or to embarrass herself. Her stillness was a measure of compensation, of self-protection.

D.M. Did you like Mrs. Robinson?

K.T. That came to me, as usual, over spending time with her. I started out intrigued and wanting to explore her, then I started to dislike her intensely and then I started to think, "What a bitch," or "What an idiot," or "What is wrong with this woman, why doesn't she get her act together?" But then through working on her I began to unearth answers to those questions and I started to explain her and then I started to care about her and then of course I eventually thought she was totally right, whatever she said or did.

D.M. Your Mrs. Robinson seemed much harder than Anne Bancroft's. Hers was more fragile, more delicate, but your Mrs. Robinson was tough.

K.T. Well, I've always been accused of that, haven't I?

D.M. Being tough?

K.T. Yes. It's my rep, for better or worse.

D.M. I wouldn't tangle with you.

K.T. Oh now, I'm sweet.

D.M. You are, I'm just kidding. I wouldn't say you're tough, I'd say you don't suffer fools, and you have a very keen B.S.-detector.

K.T. Now that *is* true.

D.M. Many of your most famous roles, both on stage and on screen, are quite funny, but the humor is wrapped around a core of discontent and uneasiness.

K.T. Damage.

D.M. Yeah, damage.

K.T. I'm good at that. I like damage. Damage is interesting. Rich.

D.M. Mrs. Robinson has some great one-liners, and the comic timing required to play her is really precise, but she's also a profoundly sad character.

K.T. Oh, she's miserable. She's very sad.

D.M. She played by the rules, doing everything that it seemed life demanded of her, and it led to a world of disappointment basically.

K.T. She's a hollow woman, ultimately. A waste of a great intellect and a great wit. I do seem to have played a lot of women who are rather underused and angry. Frustrated. Sadly, I think those characters are a reflection of our time in some ways, politically. But I won't go into that now.

D.M. That mix of humor and pathos is attractive in a character.

K.T. Of course, what actor wouldn't want that?

D.M. Mrs. Robinson seems to have a lot in common with Martha in *Who's Afraid of Virginia Woolf.* She was kind of a dry run for that character, in retrospect.

K.T. Funny you should mention that—she was, but not in the way you are thinking. It was more about the size of the production. I needed to be sure of my own power, my ability to command an audience on a stage that size. *The Graduate*, like *Virginia Woolf*, was a huge play, and I was at the center of it. Mrs. Robinson was a great test. I knew I could command a production of that magnitude after I did it. *The Graduate* gave me the confidence to tackle *Virginia Woolf.*

CAT ON A HOT TIN ROOF

DUSTIN MORROW *Cat on A Hot Tin Roof* is one of the great plays in the American Theater.

> Cat on a Hot Tin Roof *is Tennessee Williams's personal favorite of all his plays. The winner of the Pulitzer Prize for Drama in 1955, it tells the story of a wealthy, troubled family on a plantation in Mississippi. The play is centered around the birthday of Big Daddy Pollitt, a wealthy cotton tycoon, and his relationships with his duplicitous daughter-in-law Maggie the Cat, and his son Brick, an aging football hero.*

KATHLEEN TURNER That was great fun. And our approach to it was very focused.

D.M. And that was to rediscover the comedy in it.

K.T. Yes. That's a very funny play, but over the years the comedy had been lost. Elia Kazan had a negative influence on that play.

Kazan is the filmmaker (On the Waterfront, A Streetcar Named Desire) *who directed the original 1955 stage version of the play, starring Barbara Bel Geddes as Maggie the Cat and Burl Ives as Big Daddy. Kazan was an undeniably gifted filmmaker but will always be a figure of controversy due to his cooperation with the House Committee on Un-American Activities at the time of the Hollywood Blacklist.*

D.M. How so?

K.T. Through all the changes he made to the text, both small and large, he stripped the humor out of it. At the time we revived it, it wasn't thought of as a particularly humorous play. But when you look at the original text, Williams had laced a ton of humor into it. So the first thing we did was go back to the original text.

D.M. Did that involve any significant narrative changes, or was it more a change in tone?

K.T. From the version developed by Kazan?

D.M. Yes.

K.T. Well, the biggest narrative change was that it cut Big Daddy out of the third act. When Kazan did it, Burl Ives agreed to play Big Daddy, but he was very displeased that he dropped out of the play after the second act. In the original play, Big Daddy appears only in the second act, he does not come back in the third act, and the third act is essentially Big Momma's. So Kazan agreed to bring Burl Ives back in the third act. What that did was that when Maggie comes out and says, "I am with child," Big Daddy is there to say, "I see that you are, I know you are." Big Daddy gives his approval, he gives Maggie a sort of permission to go on.

In the original text, which is the version that we did, Big Daddy does not come back in the third act, so when Maggie says, "I am with child," she instead looks to Brick and Brick chooses to keep his mouth shut, allowing her to float this lie, and it is Brick's choice, not Big Daddy's, to allow this lie to be accepted. And taking Big Daddy out of the picture in the third act also allows Big Momma to slip into control of the family in a way that she really never could when Big Daddy was around, and that really changes her character. And there was a lot of humor to be mined in making those two major changes.

So once we got past the battle to allow us to do the original play, the original third act, then that opened up a lot of doors, in terms of exploring humor in the play. I cannot help but look for the humor in everything. I think that it is the best part of life, finding ways to laugh at it.

D.M. That's a very wordy play, too, full of subtle laughs in all of that dialogue.

K.T. Believe me, I know it's wordy. Maggie doesn't shut up in the first act. I was really looking forward to all of that rich Williams language in the first act, and then we started rehearsal, and holy cow, it's forty-seven minutes of me talking nonstop! Be careful what you wish for!

It was such a burden, and Maggie's not drinking so my throat would completely dry up. And so I would have to have little glasses of water around the set and find excuses to take a swig and go on. It was terrible! There was this one bit, right on the edge of the stage, where she is putting on her mascara, and in those days they just had a cake and a brush, so she had to spit into the mascara to make it soft. And I had no saliva!

The other challenge of having all the dialogue in the first act is that I had the responsibility not just for doing my character, but for setting the tone for the entire production. I set the accent, I set the rhythms of the dialogue. I established early that it was okay for the audience to laugh. I set the level of intensity in the narrative. Maggie basically vanishes in Act II, but her presence needs to carry through that act even if she's not immediately a part of the story, and that means that I had a lot of work to do in the first act.

D.M. Williams isn't the easiest writer, either, in terms of his use of language.

K.T. He sure isn't. He writes in a very poetic style. It's beautiful, but sometimes tough to find a way to deliver. He experiments with the placement of his verbs quite a lot. A line like, "That more than likely explains why their usual summer migrations to the coolness of the great Smokies was passed up this summer," which Maggie has to say in that play, is a real challenge because the verb is clear at the end of the sentence. It's beautiful to listen to, but tough to deliver. It's not a natural rhythm.

D.M. In your interpretation of the character, do you think she really loved Brick?

K.T. Ultimately I think she did. That's how I played her. It took me awhile to come to that conclusion in my performance though. When we worked on the play in Wilmington, pre-Broadway, I wasn't sure of that, and as a result the Maggie I did there was much angrier, much less vulnerable. But by the time I got to Broadway, I think I had decided that she really, truly loved Brick.

D.M. How did that change come about?

K.T. Slowly, through really small decisions. For example, there's a moment where Big Mama says, "Do you make my son happy in bed?" Maggie's response is, "Why don't you ask if he makes me happy? It works both ways." At first I played that response really defensively. But as I worked on the part, I decided to say "It works both ways" with less anger and more sadness. It made all the difference. Suddenly, with the softer, slower delivery of that line, you could see the pain beneath Maggie's tough exterior. It's a seemingly minor change, just affecting the delivery of one line, but it makes a world of difference in finding the character.

D.M. You also got hurt doing that play.

K.T. Did I ever! One night we were doing a pre-Broadway show in Pittsburgh, and there's a scene where Brick loses his temper and he grabs this crutch at its base and swings it around over his head to try to knock Maggie's head off. We choreographed it so that in his swing around he would hit this lamp and that would slow it enough that I would have time to get out of the way. So this one night he misses the lamp, and there was nothing slowing this flying crutch, so I threw my hand out because, well, better my hand than my head. I knew immediately that something really bad had just happened. I got through the rest of the first act with my arm behind my back.

So I had a friend who was a young intern, an orthopedic surgeon, there in Pittsburgh, and he came to the show that night. They brought him backstage to look at my hand, which was destroyed. My fingers had swollen into big sausages and turned jet black. He splinted them, wrapped them up, and I finished the show.

D.M. The show must go on.

K.T. Indeed! And the funny thing is, all these years later, he's still one of my doctors. He's my knee surgeon!

But anyway, as far as the humor in the play goes, I think that people sometimes forget that Williams wrote *Cat* when he was still fresh, before he fell on hard times. He wrote it before his sister got terribly ill, and before drugs and alcohol really overtook his life. During that period there was still a little devil in him, a sly sense of humor that was delightful. Plus, we had a cast that thrived on playing comedy. Charles Durning, who played Big Daddy and who I totally adored, had the most marvelous sense of humor. We enjoyed finding the humor, that was the pleasure in the play for us.

D.M. In addition to the comedy, it's also a pretty sexy play.

K.T. Daniel Hugh Kelly and I enjoyed spicing up the play's sexual moments. We steamed up the stage. We choreographed the end in a way that I don't think had ever been done until then. Toward the end of the play Maggie starts to seduce Brick, and they're sitting on the edge of the bed and she begins to undress him. It gets very quiet and the whole stage comes down to this one spotlight, and she starts to unbutton his pajama top and she takes his head and gives him this deep, deep passionate kiss. And she takes the shirt off of his shoulders and the lights go out. And you just know that she is going to get pregnant.

D.M. Sounds like steamy stuff!

K.T. Oh yeah! It was pretty hot. The audience was sweating, I can assure you!

INDISCRETIONS

DUSTIN MORROW Your next really significant stage role was probably *Indiscretions*.

> Indiscretions, *also known by its French title* Les Parents Terribles, *is a 1938 satire of Parisian bourgeoisie by Jean Cocteau, about a dysfunctional family led by Yvonne, a bed-bound woman who has an unhealthy obsession with her grown son.*

KATHLEEN TURNER Yes. Yvonne in *Indiscretions* was the rare role that got under my skin and followed me offstage. That character was so helpless, so dependent and self-pitying, and some of that, unfortunately, carried over into my private life. I was in such agonizing pain from the RA at the time that I really spent a lot of time, onstage and off, wallowing in self-pity.

D.M. Why did you take the role if you were in such pain?

K.T. I hadn't been onstage in awhile and I needed to work, I was going out of my mind. That role I took in part precisely because the rheumatoid arthritis was at its peak, in terms of the pain it was causing me, because I spent most of that play in a bed. But I also loved the role and the play. Cocteau actually wrote this piece in twenty days. He locks himself in a room, completely high on his drugs, probably out of his mind, and blazes through the writing of the entire *Les Parents Terribles*. I don't really think it is a reflection of his own life, I don't think anybody really thinks that, but it certainly draws on his life.

D.M. He once said that he didn't believe there was any such thing as excess. He said, "You *are* excess." So in a way, there is probably no such thing as going over-the-top when doing Cocteau. His writing gave you that privilege, which I would imagine be really freeing for an actor.

K.T. I loved my character—the character of the mother. I think many people believe her to be consciously manipulative, but that's not how I played her. I just think that's the way she was, naturally. She was ill, she couldn't do absolutely anything for herself, she relied on others for everything. A life lived that way would mess anyone up, at least a little.

She was a scary but rewarding character to take on. It was interesting to look into the behavior of that period and that place—Paris in the Thirties—and to think about that disease and what it might do to someone. She felt so helpless, but also so blameless. She couldn't do anything about this disease, this thing that controlled all of her family's lives, and I was rather in that same position myself with the R.A., which was affecting my husband and my daughter and the people I worked with or worked for me. There were days when I felt I could do anything and days when I could do nothing. It was maddening.

D.M. I know that that was still a physical performance for you because you were throwing yourself all over that bed, but you were still confined to a bed in the end. That seems like it would be really limiting for a physical actor.

K.T. Of course. But again, that limitation was part of the reason I took it. I thought I could get through it with a minimum of pain. Of course, it didn't quite work out that way. I had to wear shoes in the second act, which was terrible. At that time I couldn't even bear to have a sheet or a blanket on my feet at night because it was so painful, anything and everything was excruciatingly painful. And of course, there was the climb up the staircase in the second act, which was torture.

D.M. How long had you been a mom when you did that show?

K.T. It was in 1995 or thereabouts, so my daughter would have been seven or eight years old.

D.M. Yvonne has such a bizarre relationship with her child in that play.

K.T. It's definitely twisted, there's nothing normal about it. She's a lover to him in every sense but sexually.

D.M. And Jude Law played your son.

K.T. Yes.

D.M. That was probably his first prominent role.

K.T. He had done the role in London and yes, he was just making a name for himself. He was virtually unknown, certainly to America.

D.M. It seems a calculated decision to cast somebody so good-looking, to make the nature of that relationship all the more discomfiting.

K.T. I imagine so. That was the decision of Sean Matthias, the director. Jude was the only actor he brought over from the original production in London. All the rest of us, Roger and Ivy and myself and Cynthia, were new to the production in New York.

Roger Rees, legendary stage actress Dame Eileen Atkins, Cynthia Nixon (of Sex and the City*), and Law were Kathleen's co-stars in the production.*

I was always incredibly impressed by Jude's discipline. At that time he was, what, twenty-two? And he was tremendous. He didn't have any of the rubbish and uncertainty of many twenty-two-year-old actors who can't focus, make decisions and stick to them.

D.M. I was never a huge fan of his but then I saw his *Hamlet* in London and was very impressed with it.

K.T. I never did. How was it?

D.M. He did a very big, physical Hamlet. Unruly, a bit undisciplined, but in a good way.

K.T. Reckless, you mean.

D.M. Yeah, that's a good word. In cinematic reference, because I'm a film nerd and I put everything in cinematic reference—he was more the Mel Gibson Hamlet than the Kenneth Branagh Hamlet.

K.T. Gotcha. I can see how that'd work for him.

D.M. I'll ask you about the RA and its effect on your acting later, but I'm guessing that because of it your memories of *Indiscretions* are not, on the whole, very positive.

K.T. Sadly, no. It was a very tough production for me because of the pain, which bordered on the unbearable. And even more so because I was keeping my RA a secret. So I know that I was occasionally unpleasant to be around during that production, and my fellow actors didn't know why.

But my experience on that production was in no way reflective of the people I worked with, all of whom were wonderful, nor is it a reflection of the material. It's a fantastic play and a great part, and even though it was very, very hard for me, I'm deeply grateful that I had the opportunity to play that role.

WHO'S AFRAID OF VIRGINIA WOOLF

DUSTIN MORROW On to your all-time favorite role.
KATHLEEN TURNER Martha.
D.M. Martha.

In Who's Afraid of Virginia Woolf, *Kathleen played Martha to Tony-winner Bill Irwin's George. The two are a professor and his wife, the daughter to the college's president. Late one night, after a party, they invite a young professor and his wife back to their house for cocktails, where they torment each other, and their guests, with a series of increasingly abusive mind games.*

K.T. I've certainly thought more about that character than any other I have ever done. I have a lot to say about her, I could talk for hours about her. By the end of its run, I had done well over five hundred performances as Martha. By that point, Bill and I were like a machine—every breath, every tone, every accented syllable had been carefully chosen.

That play changed me, artistically and professionally. Heck, it even changed me physically, because thanks to the rheumatoid arthritis I had to have my knee replaced to do it.

D.M. Really?

K.T. There was no way I was going to be able to do it otherwise. It's a three-hour play.

D.M. And it changed you artistically and professionally.

K.T. It brought me to a new level of challenge in what it demanded of me. That play used everything I had as an actress. By the end of every performance I had almost nothing left. It's rare that you find a piece of material that gives you the privilege of leaving *everything* on the stage.

And while I think that I proved myself with *Cat on a Hot Tin Roof* and the plays I did subsequent to it, it wasn't until *Virginia Woolf* that I felt I had the full, legitimate respect of the Broadway community. After *Virginia Woolf*, no one could ever accuse me of being a movie star doing the stage. Since that play, I have been a respected stage actress who occasionally does movies, not the other way around.

D.M. I know that you've said that you knew you wanted to play the part from the time you were an undergrad in Missouri.

K.T. Yes, I discovered the play when I was very young and vowed that one day, decades from then, I would do it. I just had to wait until I was old enough to do it. Then I went after it.

D.M. Albee had said that you had the part before the end of the very first reading. He had read at least half a dozen hugely famous actresses before casting you.

K.T. I knew I had it, too, and I told him so. It was cocky of me, I know, but I just nailed that part. It was *mine*, there was no way anyone was going to take it from me.

D.M. So what was the obsession for you?

K.T. It's *the* great play about the American Dream. Everything there is to say about the American Dream, about all our hopes and dreams and disappointments and struggles, is said at some point in that play. Even the characters' names—you know where Albee got them?

D.M. George and Martha Washington?

K.T. You got it.

D.M. They are two genuinely amazing characters. There's a lot to love about Martha.

K.T. What's not to love about Martha? For starters, her appalling lack of manners just makes her immense fun to play. She's just one of the all-time great roles for women. The level of challenge in playing that part well is almost indescribable. And Albee's language is incredible, he wrote with such fierce intelligence. His word choices were absolutely precise. And by the time of our production, he had forty-seven years with this play and he knew what he wanted. You don't often get the opportunity to work with a playwright who's had five decades to think about his play.

D.M. It's a shockingly raw text, even all these decades later. I find parts of it almost unbearable.

K.T. Part of the genius of Albee was that he didn't seek to protect his characters in any way. He laid them bare. And because he did that, made them completely and utterly vulnerable, people could see themselves in his characters. And for many people, that's a tough thing. Most art doesn't do that.

D.M. I know he was a legendarily grumpy personality, but working with Albee, actually collaborating with him one-on-one, must have been an incredible education.

K.T. It was one of the high points of my professional life. On the closing night of the show on Broadway, I got back to my dressing room and there was a note from Edward that said, "You are the reason I am a playwright." That note means a lot to me. I keep it in a very safe place.

D.M. Just as you'd done earlier with *Cat on a Hot Tin Roof*, I think your production of the play changed a lot of people's conceptions of it.

K.T. Oh, it absolutely did. Before our production of *Virginia Woolf*, all people knew about it for the longest time was the film. But that film is not the play. At all. Watching the movie, it's easy to see why people only thought of *Virginia Woolf* as a play about a couple of drunks screaming at each other for three hours. We showed audiences that there's so much more to that brilliant play. We showed them all of the humor and the pathos and the love in it.

The 1966 film adaptation was directed by Mike Nichols (The Graduate, Carnal Knowledge, Working Girl) and starred Elizabeth Taylor and Richard Burton. While its reputation as a great film has waned dramatically in the decades since it came out, it was very well-received at the time of its release. It was nominated in every eligible category at the Academy Awards, the only film in history to hold that honor. It won five, including Best Actress for Taylor.

D.M. The humor, especially, is missing from the shrill treatment the film gives the material.

K.T. As a play, Virginia Woolf would be impossible to get through without the humor. It'd be too heavy. Laughter in a theater is so important as a tension breaker. In a play with as much tension as Virginia Woolf, the drama wouldn't be endurable if it weren't frequently relieved by laughter. The laughs physically deflate the audience, and give you the opportunity as an actor to begin to build them back up again. Those ups and downs, highs and lows, that's the ride on which you take the audience over the course of the play.

D.M. What was the central conflict of Martha for you?

K.T. In 1962, there were few women professors with tenure, and no women university presidents. That's the world Martha lived in. So she lived through her father, who looked down on her, and her husband, who had none of her ambition. The anger and restlessness in her character resonated with me. When something is wrong, and there's nothing I can do about it, as was the case with my R.A. for so many years, that frustration drives me up the wall. And Martha just encapsulated all of that. Some of the best and the worst aspects of my own personality found release through Martha.

People need to know that they can do something really well, that they got a chance to do that thing, that they weren't trapped. Martha didn't get that—she was trapped. Martha spent her entire life kicking against walls that would never come down. Thankfully I've been more fortunate in my life, because a lot of the walls I've kicked have gone down.

D.M. And yet the audience sympathizes with Martha, despite her often-atrocious behavior.

K.T. By the end, I think they do. She's obviously a deeply sad, self-hating woman, and she clearly loves George, despite all the abuse she heaps on him. And at the end, his vengeance is far more devastating than anything she's said or done to him.

D.M. It's an epically long play. Is there one scene that sticks with you above all others?

K.T. It's at the top of the third act. It's essentially a monologue. Nick comes in and is her audience, but she's really speaking to herself, and to the audience of course. I love that the third act, until George comes back in, is basically Martha's monologue.

And there's so much to play in that monologue, it's so rich. At the top of the third act Martha comes down the stairs, she is not really drunk anymore, the booze has all but worn off. And she's had quite a humiliating little session in the bedroom with Nick, where he couldn't get it up, and the failure embarrassed them both. She begins to realize how incredibly stupid and sordid the whole thing is, what a mess she's created, how pathetic she is. And having had my own experiences with drinking too much, and my own regrets, I had much to draw on there. It was pure remorse. It was the "I can't believe I did that" feeling, the "How could I be so stupid? How could I be so senseless?"

She's pulled on one of George's shirts, whatever was hanging on the chair next to the bed, as I imagine she wanted to get the hell out of that bedroom as fast as she could. Full of self-loathing, she comes down the stairs to an empty room, not knowing if George is there or not, dreading it, and her whole body is just defeated. She feels sick, she drank too much, so her head and her stomach are aching. And she is physically aching because she tried to pull off these pyrotechnics in the bedroom that she failed miserably at. She is a woman in late middle age, and when she sees that the door is a little open, she wonders if George has finally left her forever, and she doesn't know whether to feel happy or sad about that. Has she finally driven him to the point where they are so disgusted and fed up with each other that he has finally walked out and that's it? She is scared as hell, she hates herself, and yet she still has a bit of fight left in her. "Screw you all, if you don't like me, tough." All of those wonderful contradictory emotions, those are so wonderful to play.

D.M. I wondered if that "fight" she has was just protective, a measure of self-preservation, or if that was genuine. Did you always play that feeling as genuine or was that just Martha trying to steel herself against having to accept something she didn't want to accept?

K.T. It was both. Yes, it is a defensive posture to think, "Well, screw you if you don't like me," but at the same time there is at the core of Martha—a strength of self. She knows who she is. And that contradiction is fun to play. She's such a gorgeous mixture of a lack of energy, slumped shoulders, slight dizziness, with an anger and a sort of defiance toward George and toward herself and toward Daddy.

There is just a great physicality at the top of the third act, where she doesn't have anything near the energy or the spring in her step that she had in the second act, and she slumps on that ottoman and really just physically feels beaten up. It's just great to play.

D.M. Was there anything you had to do in between those acts, to start that third act in that mindset? I know you talk sometimes about how quickly you can snap into character, almost like throwing a switch, but is that true when the moment you have to open with is so heavy?

K.T. At first, it wasn't easy at all. But once you do something enough, then it becomes much, much easier to move in and out of character. But at the same time perhaps in some ways Martha was more personal to me than a lot of roles because of some of the mistakes I made in the past. I never performed irresponsibly or under the influence or anything like that, but I have certainly behaved badly at home and in private circles as a result of drinking too much. I knew well that shameful feeling of waking up and thinking, "Oh God, I can't believe I did that last night." And no matter how many times I played that role, its evocation of those very real feelings for me never really got any easier.

And I would certainly never suggest to any actor that they should have those kind of experiences in real life in order to play that type of role. But having done so, it was easy enough to evoke those feelings, to use them. Not a recommended procedure, but having had it, I used it.

D.M. Not that it is a silver lining or anything, but at least you were able to use those terrible experiences positively in some way. Most people don't work in a profession where they can find any positive outcome from something like that.

K.T. That's true, and at least I had the distance from it to be able to use it constructively. To not have had that distance would have been self-destructive. Every so often you meet these actors who think they have to go out and experience something firsthand in order to play that thing on stage or onscreen. What a self-destructive thing to do. I played a prostitute in *Crimes of Passion* but that didn't mean I had to walk Hollywood Boulevard looking to sell myself. It's called acting. Act it, don't live it!

D.M. Sounds like solid advice for any actor.

K.T. Yes—act it, don't live it!

HIGH

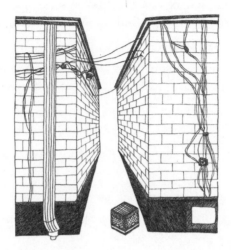

Dustin Morrow Your play *High* dealt directly with addiction, and your personal experience with alcohol must have become a part of the Sister Jamie character.

Kathleen Turner Oh, definitely. That's part of what made her interesting to me, my own experience of having wrestled with alcohol abuse. But it's important to note that I was an abuser of alcohol, but was never actually an addict. They're two different things.

D.M. Right. And unlike you, Sister Jamie hasn't quite defeated it.

K.T. She hasn't, and coming to that realization is part of what makes her character arc compelling. She is a deeply damaged woman herself whose job is to help damaged people.

D.M. I would imagine the play was a tough watch for many audiences, since so many people have to deal with addiction, or with an addict, at some point in their lives.

K.T. We worked on the play first in Hartford and the response from the audience was polarizing from the get-go. We knew immediately that we were on to something. During talkbacks after the show we got confessional after confessional from audiences. It was amazing to hear people get up and pour their hearts out. The play touches something very deep in people who've fought with, or known someone who has fought with, the horrors of addiction.

D.M. You've fought your own battle with addiction.

K.T. When I was abusing alcohol, the physical side effects were certainly terrifying, but truly the most frightening thing was the utter lack of control that I felt. I don't want to give any control of my life over to anything. Certainly not to a substance like alcohol. And not even to other people, or institutions, or the concept of faith. It's faith that Sister Jamison in *High* and Eileen Cleary in *The Perfect Family* are really dealing with.

D.M. It's interesting that you played those two roles almost back-to-back.

K.T. I called it my year of Catholicism.

D.M. The character in *High* is very complex, even beyond her fight with combating addiction.

K.T. I knew the playwright before he wrote *High*, and he wrote the play with me in mind. *High* plays to my strengths, and the great journey that the character goes on over the course of the play was very appealing to me. Sister Jamie is tough but conflicted. She's a character who's made huge mistakes. Whether she succeeds or not, she can't just let something be, and I share this with her. She's driven, determined, stubborn even. And she's an unpredictable character. You never know which way she's going to go, and that's what makes her interesting.

I was also interested in working on a new play, as opposed to reviving something. I wanted an active voice in the development of the script. That's a fun process, leading up to taking the play to Broadway.

Working on a play during a pre-Broadway tour is very exciting, because the material is still constantly evolving. While doing *High* in Cincinnati, we would rehearse a new scene in the afternoon and have it in the play that night. That's nerve-wracking but exhilarating at the same time.

D.M. I know we talked about this a little earlier, in reference to the tough economics of successfully launching a show on Broadway, but do you think the subject matter of *High* turned people off?

K.T. Of course. It's a challenging play. It's not escapist entertainment. It's not a big sunny musical, which is about the only kind of surefire winner on Broadway these days. The language is tough, the topic is tough. Often what happens with new plays is that they get softened during the period leading up to Broadway. Producers will take the rough edges off so as to not offend the greatest number of people and attract the largest possible demographic. But we protected the script of *High* because it's a great script. We refused to let the Broadway system Disney-fy it. We protected its integrity, and we went to Broadway with a very tough play that forced people to engage with hard truths. *High* isn't a passive viewing experience for an audience. The play confronts you. It's not an easy watch.

D.M. But it's not without humor and light.

K.T. Absolutely, it does have a lot of humor in it. It's not a cold play. The monologues that my character delivers directly to the audience, and the great humor of the character help the audience get through the difficult material. But the play provides no easy answers, and I think that bothers some people. It's one of the things I love about it, though. How could it possibly offer easy answers and retain its integrity? Everything about faith and addiction is an endless searching, testing, trying, uncertainty and conflict.

D.M. I think much of the public had a misconception of what the play is really about. The concepts of addiction and faith were at the center of the play, but what the play is really about, to me, is the capacity for people to change whatever it is in their life, be it addiction or faith or family or work or self-doubt, that is holding them back. It's about breaking free of whatever it is that is preventing you from engaging with the world around you in a positive way.

K.T. Absolutely. No matter what's happened to you, no matter how bad things have gotten, you always have the ability to change. That's the positive message of this admittedly dark play. Everyone has the capacity for change. We can have faith in the capacity of people to change.

D.M. That's the real faith at the heart of the play.

K.T. And the play is not just about the addict changing. There are three characters in this play—the addict, the enabler, and the counselor—and all three must change over the course of the play. It's not just the addict. The ending kind of pulls the rug out from beneath all three characters. Ulterior motives are revealed and change has to happen.

D.M. It must be fun to do plays with so few characters.

K.T. Of course. For one thing, it means you get more stage time and more of the text. And it strengthens the relationships between the actors. And I was lucky on *High* to have great actors to work with.

Kathleen's co-stars in High *were Evan Jonigkeit and Michael Berresse. Berresse's role was played by Stephen Kunken for the Broadway production.*

D.M. It's a play with something to say, it's unfortunate that it didn't find an audience on Broadway.

K.T. It is too bad, it's a play that is worth supporting and considering. I have zero regrets about doing it, it was a rewarding and challenging piece of work and I'm proud of it.

RED HOT PATRIOT

DUSTIN MORROW In *High*, you only had two co-stars, and in the play you did after it, *Red Hot Patriot*, you had no co-stars at all.

KATHLEEN TURNER Are you looking for a pattern?

D.M. Maybe the next step is an empty stage and we just hear your voice over the speaker system from backstage.

K.T. Ha! Sounds a little too avant-garde to me.

D.M. I can see many reasons why *Red Hot Patriot* must have appealed to you.

K.T. Well, it *was* a one-woman show, which is fun for its own reasons.

D.M. You played the spunky, outspoken Texas political journalist Molly Ivins.

K.T. Right. Molly Ivins was an American treasure. She was my generation's Mark Twain. It was a great honor to have the opportunity to play her. Beyond that, what attracted me, as with any project, started with the script. It was a great script, and the playwrights were wonderfully collaborative. It was richly rewarding for me to have a hand in developing the text.

Red Hot Patriot was written by journalists and twin sisters Margaret and Allison Engel.

D.M. How did that work for this play?

K.T. We started, obviously, with all of her writing. That was a great challenge, because she wrote so much. We combed through her books and her columns, whittling them down in a way that allowed us to get a grasp of her as a character. All of the early structure for the play began with that process of digging through her writing.

I also liked the challenge of doing a one-woman show, which I hadn't done since *Tallulah*. And I just love Molly Ivins as a character. She's fun, just a genuine pleasure to play.

D.M. And you met her.

K.T. Sure, a few times. Our activism brought us together. Like myself, Molly was a staunch defender of the first amendment and of the rights of women. We weren't close friends or anything, but we got along well.

Molly and I share many of the same values and some personality traits. We're certainly both strong, sometimes outspoken women. Neither of us suffer any BS from anyone. We were pretty politically aligned. And we shared some similar family history, especially in that we both dealt with conflict with our fathers when we were young. Molly's father was an old-school oil and gas Texan, and they definitely butted heads.

D.M. Having met her, did you find your personal experience of knowing her affecting how you played her?

K.T. Not really, except in the sense that I sought to capture her spirit. I act Molly, I don't imitate her. I have no interest in ever doing an impersonation of anyone as part of a performance. That I got to know her was a great gift, but at the end of the day, for the play to work, I had to approach her as a character, and think of her just as I would any fictional character.

D.M. How did you find her character then? Did you go back and watch interviews with her?

K.T. Minimally. We didn't want to do a docudrama. Although we use a lot of Molly's language and expressions, like the way she used to call George W. Bush "Shrub," the play is mostly fictionalized.

I found Molly in some ways as I subtly transformed myself physically. When I dyed my hair the same shade of red as Molly's, that was really motivating. That, and the cowboy boots. When I got those boots on, the way I walked changed dramatically. I developed a swagger and a bravado in my stride that really informed the character. Whenever I got up from sitting in my play, I'd have a specific way of kicking out my feet with confidence and flair. It's a small, subtle thing, but it demonstrates self-possession and purpose. Little touches like that—in hair, makeup and wardrobe—can be very helpful in finding a character.

D.M. Based on what I have seen and read of Molly, your version of her seemed really true-to-life.

K.T. I think we nailed it. Her brother came backstage after the show and was crying and hugged me and said, "Thank you for keeping her alive." We definitely captured her wit and her spirit and her passion.

D.M. You must have responded strongly to the politics of the play, as you and Molly were I imagine pretty similar in your views of the Bush administration.

K.T. Yes, neither of us was a fan of Shrub. I definitely responded to the politics of the play. It's a fun play, full of one-liners, but it's got something to say. Molly did not let politicians off the hook when other writers did. She was fierce and determined in calling them on their BS. That's definitely something she and I have in common.

D.M. It cost her professionally, that's for sure.

K.T. Oh heavens, yes! She paid a price for her integrity. Her goal in going into journalism was to expose the intolerances and prejudices that she saw in American politics. And that goal cost her, personally and professionally. She was obviously a brilliant writer, and she could have made much more money in other, "safer" arenas of writing. And she could have likely had a family of her own if she hadn't been so doggedly committed to her mission of seeking and telling the truth.

For me, *Red Hot Patriot* is really about empowering Americans as citizens. It's about our rights and responsibilities as American citizens. That's why we took the production to Washington to do it just before the last presidential election. It's a reminder, a wake-up call, to get involved.

Molly loved Americans. Loved them. She was a profoundly committed American patriot. Ultimately, I believe her greatest hope and desire was for us to do the right thing, to always act in a way that was deserving of this great nation that we are all so fortunate to live in.

D.M. Is that what you hope people take away from the play?

K.T. Yes, that and a renewal of the idea that we're all in this together. We are *one country*. Molly started most of her writing, even the heavily critical writing, by addressing her readers as "My beloveds." I love that. "My beloveds." She wrapped her arms, warmly and respectfully, around her audience. She loved Americans, sincerely, with a huge heart. That's what I take from her. That's the great gift that she gave to me.

D.M. Your father was in the U.S. foreign service, you must have thought of him once or twice while doing this play.

K.T. I did. My father called himself a public servant in the best sense of the word, he's really the one that taught me a sense of civic responsibility. It was from my father that I learned to have a presentational front, which has actually helped me handle stardom and the public life. It comes from being told by my dad at age ten that everything I did reflected on my country. That's a lot to think about for a ten year old!

D.M. What do you mean by a "presentational front?"

K.T. Just a sense of how I was being perceived. When you move around a lot at a formative age, it makes you learn to present yourself when you walk into a new school, a new country, a new language and a new culture. You have to make a statement, in a way. You have to act yourself a little bit.

D.M. As a mechanism of survival.

K.T. As a mechanism to gain a sense of self, of confidence. That's really what I learned from my dad—confidence. I had great confidence that I could be safe anywhere in the world, because I knew if I could get to a phone or an embassy anywhere I could reach my dad and he would protect me. That confidence stretched into every aspect of my life, and freed me to take risks and to challenge myself even after he passed away.

We would all be better off—this would be a better country—if we were engaged civically in the way that Molly was, and if we challenged ourselves in the ways that Molly challenged herself and those around her. Molly was an antidote to political apathy.

D.M. Doing a one-woman show seems as though it would be more wearying than a show in which you have other actors to play off of.

K.T. It's not as a rule, it depends on the play and the role. But there is certainly some truth to the idea that having other leads to help you shoulder the carrying of the narrative can be a relief. Ultimately, though, regardless of whether you have no actors to play off of or a dozen, you have to be fully engaged with your character the entire time you're onstage. While you shouldn't feel tired onstage, because of the performance energy, every show should leave you weary when it's over. If you come offstage feeling a little wiped out, then you've done your job.

MOTHER COURAGE AND HER CHILDREN

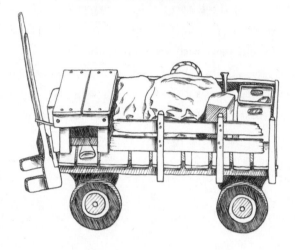

Dustin Morrow I know from reading interviews with you that you've never been a huge fan of musicals.

Kathleen Turner Well, I like going to see them, I just haven't ever really had an interest in doing one.

D.M. Until *Mother Courage and Her Children*, several full decades into your career.

K.T. *Mother Courage* is a play with music, not a musical.

D.M. I see.

K.T. I have nothing against them, but musicals just aren't my thing. I did *Sweet Charity* as my very first production at Missouri State and couldn't get over how stupid I felt. "Hey big spender, spend a little time with me!" Not for me.

D.M. I can't imagine that when you were young there was much demand for a voice like yours in musical theater anyway.

K.T. That's certainly true. I may have looked like an ingénue when I was starting out, but I didn't sound like one. I couldn't sing soprano then, and

I never will. And the female roles in musical theater are nearly always sopranos.

As an actress, I just don't find the narratives in musicals that interesting. Dramatically, the material isn't usually as good as it is in a play. One Broadway producer in particular has been after me to do a traditional musical for years, he's been very persistent. He keeps saying, "Even Bacall did it, so what's your problem?"

D.M. Do you enjoy singing in general?

K.T. I love it! I didn't use to have any affinity for it until recently.

D.M. What changed?

K.T. It was the process of working with the vocal coach, Andy Gale, with whom I worked on *Mother Courage*. While we were prepping the songs for that play, he kept telling me that I should sing professionally and stage a cabaret show. I hemmed and hawed and put it off, but the more I worked with him the better my singing got and the more I started to think seriously about the idea. It helped that I began to really enjoy the process and the ways in which singing allows me to express myself.

D.M. So you are going to do a cabaret?

K.T. Hopefully, that's the plan. My cabaret show will be an autobiographical mix of singing and storytelling. I am trying to choose songs that tell a story. Although I must say that there will be a few songs that I will introduce by saying, "You know, I just love this song and that's why I'm singing it."

D.M. I could certainly hear smoky jazz coming from your voice.

K.T. There will be some of that but that's not it. People keep asking me what period the songs will come from, in what style and around what theme. But there is no one style, period, theme or genre. I'm just finding my voice. All I can say is that it will be songs I like to sing.

D.M. So no showtunes?

K.T. Defintiely no showtunes!

D.M. In fact, you've played a cabaret singer in the past, when you played Chandler's dad on *Friends*.

K.T. But that was for comedic effect, of course.

D.M. Do you find yourself drawing on your experience as an actor when you sing? Did your long career as an actor in any way prepare you to be a singer?

K.T. It certainly put me ahead of the game in terms of issues like pitch and the placement of the voice. I already know those things. And now I certainly understand why many musical theater actors claim that it is easier to sing a full production than it is to speak through a production. In many ways, singing is actually easier on the voice.

D.M. Has the singing had any effect on your acting?

K.T. I don't think I've been doing it long enough to know. But I like what singing does for my voice in general. My speaking voice is so much more limber and melodious after a singing session. That's been a wonderful bonus.

D.M. Do you remember singing a duet with Paul Young for one of his albums in the early nineties?

K.T. Wow, you did your homework!

D.M. I'm a professor. We research, it's in our DNA.

K.T. Yes, I did a song with him, it was a favor.

D.M. It was called "Down in Chinatown." Have you heard it recently?

K.T. Ha! Umm, no.

D.M. Would you like to? I can pull it up on YouTube.

K.T. Don't you dare.

D.M. Had you ever taken singing lessons before *Mother Courage*?

K.T. Maybe some required stuff in college, but never any serious musical training.

D.M. So what finally convinced you to make the leap to doing a "play with music" with *Mother Courage*?

K.T. It was a number of things. For starters, it's one of the great roles in the theater for an actress of a certain age. Although I will have you know that I'm a little young to play Mother Courage, thank you very much.

Mother Courage and Her Children, *by German poet and playwright Bertolt Brecht, is generally considered to be the greatest anti-war play of all time. Written in 1939 as a critique of the rise of Nazism and fascism, it tells the story of a woman who amorally attempts to profit from a war that ultimately ends up taking her children from her.*

And with the role came the music, so I just had to do it. I started working with Andy months before going down to Washington to start rehearsals on the play, because I thought that if I could have the songs down before rehearsal started, I'd be well ahead of the game.

D.M. Looked at through the frame of our modern age, it's a remarkably prescient play.

K.T. Absolutely. *Mother Courage*, despite having been written clear back in 1939, is a stunningly relevant play. Brecht wrote a profound work of anti-war sentiment. As a nation, there's rarely been a time in the last century that the U.S. hasn't been at war. And with the current division between the haves and the have-nots in contemporary society, it's a play that I think we need right now.

I also very much liked the translation done by David Hare—despite the fact that it's a very dark play, he worked a lot of wry humor into it. Which I made even broader in my performance, because I thought it worked for the production, and because I love to make people laugh, of course.

And I was seduced by the prospect of working with the Arena Stage and the director Molly Smith again. I did *Red Hot Patriot* there and it was an incredible experience. The Arena Stage is just marvelous, one of the best in the nation.

D.M. For such a dark play, your production of *Mother Courage* was full of humor and good spirit.

K.T. Right, which surprised a lot of people. People hear "Brecht" and "Anti-war" and they assume it's going to be this big, heavy, oppressive, humorless thing. But there's a great deal of humor in it. Many past productions haven't seen that, but we made it an important part of our version. Much like I did with *Cat on a Hot Tin Roof,* I worked to look at the text on the page and find where its innate humor could be emphasized.

D.M. She's certainly spirited, but Mother Courage is not the nicest character.

K.T. I disagree. She makes mistakes, big mistakes for which she pays dearly, but I rather like her. She does what she has to do in the position that she is in. She's not a landowner or a businesswoman, so she turns to marketeering and black market sales, and she prospers by reading the political and financial landscapes around her.

D.M. The play earned you some of the best reviews of your career. They loved your singing. I think the *Washington Post* called you "an actress of epic force."

K.T. It was a wonderful production, beautifully staged. I loved how so much of the music was created by the cast right on the stage. All of the musicians played multiple instruments and were all so incredibly gifted. We staged it in the round and the set was basically a big bombed-out shell. We had all of these wonderful supporting players who would play the different armies and the villagers. They were constantly slipping off the stage to make lightning-quick costume changes so they could play many different roles. And the actors were marching around the stage playing instruments throughout. It was just wonderful, one of the best productions I've done in recent years.

D.M. Did you actually enjoy the singing, or was it just something you had to get through because you wanted to do the role?

K.T. Well, the singing was not the most attractive element of the part to me—it's a deeply earthy dramatic role, a true classic—but I was surprised to find how much I enjoyed it in this case. The music in *Mother Courage* provides the character with another avenue through which to express her emotional interior, so it was useful to me in that way.

D.M. And it was obviously tailored by the director and the musical director to fit your very particular and recognizable voice.

K.T. It had to be, yes. They are not easy songs. The songs in *Mother Courage* are very challenging and can really tire out your voice because they are war songs. For the most part, they're not nice lyrical ballads. They are songs you have to shout. It was a physically challenging role.

D.M. Just because of the singing, or in other ways too?

K.T. In many ways. For starters, it was a three-hour production and I was only offstage for four minutes in the whole thing. And I was dragging around this big wagon throughout the show. There was one scene that was particularly problematic because of my RA: my last living daughter climbs up this enormous ramp and is shot, and she slides slowly down this ramp into my arms. I'm meant to cradle her as she reaches the ground, but the ramp only comes to eighteen inches above the ground, so for that last foot and a half I have to lift her and bring her to the ground. That was tough on nights when my RA was flaring up.

D.M. That's a powerful scene though.

K.T. One of my favorites, because after I take her to the ground, I cradle her in my arms and sing this beautiful, delicate, profoundly sad song. Every night the audience would be dead silent, you could hear a pin drop except but for my voice. All you could really hear was this quiet breathing and sobbing emanating from the audience. And I thought, "Okay, I get it, this is what I could do with a song as an actor."

THE YEAR OF MAGICAL THINKING

DUSTIN MORROW I know that you have worked with a number of woman directors in recent years. Is that by design?

KATHLEEN TURNER Oh yes, absolutely. In fact, on *The Year of Magical Thinking* I was determined to have a woman director. Not only did I want a woman director, but I wanted a mature woman—a woman of a certain age with a significant amount of life experience.

> The Year of Magical Thinking *is a play by Joan Didion, based on her 2005 book about the year following the death of her husband and the serious illness of her daughter. The play premiered on Broadway in 2007 in a production starring Vanessa Redgrave.*

D.M. How did you come to select Gaye Taylor Upchurch as your director?

K.T. She understood the material better than anyone else I interviewed. She has worked her way up through the ranks in a long, impressive career and she had the experience to take on a play this challenging. She and I worked well together—she was supportive of me but also unafraid to stand up to me.

D.M. Is that something you want, a director who will stand up to you?

K.T. Well, you don't want a director who will impede your process, but yeah, it's important to have a director who won't be afraid to speak her opinion. Especially on a one-woman show. One of the women I interviewed for *The Year of Magical Thinking* was quite brilliant, but really just too young. She was still in her thirties and I was thinking as I interviewed her, "You know, you're wonderful and very smart but I am just going to run roughshod over you." I need someone who can stand up to me or the production is just not going to work.

D.M. Do you find that the process is different with a woman director?

K.T. The major difference I've noticed is simply that a woman director is often more thoughtful and reflective and less immediately judgmental of what they're seeing and hearing. The *Times* recently ran a story about this craze that's going around where men are taking testosterone supplements because many of them have lower testosterone levels than they would like. Which is crazy because studies have shown that higher levels of testosterone result in faster decision-making with less information. Which is very interesting if not at all surprising.

I find that women directors are less overly result-oriented, which sounds like a negative but is actually a positive. I'll give you an example. If I'm working on a character and I am in the midst of my process trying to figure out who that character is, I don't need a director to say to me over and over again, "Where are you going with this character?" Because I don't know yet.

D.M. So the woman director has more respect for the process?

K.T. Not necessarily respect, but patience. In my experience the male director says "where are you trying to get" while the female director says "how can I help you with the process." I'm speaking in generalities, of course—not every male director interferes with the process of his actors, but I will say this after a four-decade career of working with both male and female directors: I have found, *generally*, that female directors actually interfere with my process far less often than male directors.

D.M. Were you familiar with Joan Didion's writing before you decided to do *The Year of Magical Thinking?*

K.T. I was a huge admirer. I wanted to meet her while I was working on the play but she was not feeling well at the time and was not up to meeting any new people, which I could certainly respect.

D.M. Did your decision to do a play about grief felt from the loss of a loved one have anything to do with -

K.T. -the loss of my mom? Absolutely. Doing *The Year of Magical Thinking* was an emotional and therapeutic process in some ways.

I was in a run of *Red Hot Patriot* at Berkeley when my brother and his wife, who now live in Santa Rosa, California, went back to Missouri to pull my mom out of Assisted Living, where she was very unhappy, and brought her back to Santa Rosa. They made many changes to their home—they put railings on the wall so she could get around and they moved everything she might need down to the first level so she would not have to climb stairs. As soon as my run at Berkeley ended I jetted back to New York to gather my suitcases and my cat and I headed to Santa Rosa to help out. I did the shopping and the cooking and basically relieved my brother and his wife so they could go back to work and get back to their lives. I had about ten days with my mother where it was really just me and her and it was really good. Until the last day or so her mind was really sharp—at lunch we were discussing things like the refugee crisis in the Mediterranean!

My brother Andy and I were there holding her when she passed away. My mother and I were very close. Despite outward appearances, she and I were alike in many ways. And luckily, since after I left college we never again lived in the same city, our relationship was never really based on proximity. We always wrote letters and spoke to each other as much as we could.

After her passing, I would find myself thinking of her a hundred times a day and those memories were triggered by the smallest things. Like, I'd read something in the paper and think, "oh, my mom would really love this—I should tell her about it when I talk to her on Sunday." I was still going through this process when *The Year of Magical Thinking* came across my desk and it just resonated with me.

D.M. It's a tough play.

K.T. It's an incredibly intense, brilliant piece of writing. It's a single monologue and it runs almost an hour and forty minutes. I'm not sure I realized how grueling it was going to be when I started it—just the sheer duration of it. It was nearly twice as long as *Red Hot Patriot*, the one-woman show I was doing at the time. And Joan Didion's language is so precise and so specific that you really cannot paraphrase even a little bit.

D.M. One hundred minutes onstage, with no breaks, by yourself. Wow.

K.T. Yeah! I must say I was very impressed with my mind. If I ever need an exercise to battle dementia, this is it.

D.M. Did you read the book from which the play comes?

K.T. Yes, and it's wonderful, but its relationship to the play is a little problematic. The criticism that has haunted the play has always been that Joan Didion's language is so specific and so precise that it comes across as sort of cold and almost clinical. I don't know for sure, but I suspect that perhaps one of the reasons Joan adapted the book into a play was precisely for that reason. What reads as cold and somewhat unfeeling on the page becomes relatable and warm and empathetic when you see an actual woman, in the room with you, delivering the lines. You see an actual flesh-and-blood person suffering and feeling in front of you.

D.M. That's an interesting disparity.

K.T. When you read a book you are very much alone with the text. When you see a play you are having a communal experience not just with the actors but with the audience and it really changes the way you receive the material. It was a wonderful play and a wonderful production, but it was very hard because of the nature of the material. Delivering a monologue that raw, with that much emotion, night after night alone on that stage was a real challenge.

D.M. It sounds emotionally exhausting.

K.T. My daughter came to see the play and came backstage afterwards and said "Oh mother!"—and I know when she uses the word mother that I'm in trouble—"Oh mother, I always wear waterproof mascara when I go to your plays, but for some reason I forgot to tonight and now look at me!"

D.M. Whoops!

K.T. That's not all! She also said, "And mother, could I request please that for once perhaps you could choose to do a piece of material in which your child does not die!"

D.M. She's got you there!

K.T. Yes, okay, so there was *Mother Courage*—I lost three there, and *Virginia Woolf*, but that child was imaginary.

D.M. Don't forget about the movies—you lost one in *The Accidental Tourist* and, like, four or five in *The Virgin Suicides*—

K.T. —yes, yes, okay, okay!

D.M. Did you make any significant changes in the play from earlier productions?

K.T. We didn't touch a word of the text, but we certainly changed the staging. The only other really famous actress to do it on a large scale was Vanessa Redgrave. I didn't see her production, but I have heard that she performed most of the monologue from a desk, staying mostly seated. I couldn't do that if I wanted to, I'm just too reliant on my physicality as an actress.

Our production was staged in a very interesting way. The stage was an open frame, like three sides of a rectangle. The set was a sort of combination office-and-living room. We had a sofa and chair on one side of the stage and a desk where she would do her writing at the other side. We had a very gifted sound designer on the production who layered the play with soft background sounds of things like the ocean when the character speaks about California. At the end of the play those sound effects would come up very slowly and the stage itself began to almost imperceptibly recede so it was backing up and backing up and leaving me standing there alone. It was a haunting way to end the play. And it was done so subtly that many people in the audience didn't even perceive that the set had moved until after the lights came up at the end. It was very elegant.

D.M. Given how dense Didion's language is, and how much of it you had to deliver in those one hundred minutes, how did you approach learning the text.

K.T. It wasn't easy. It wasn't just that the text was so precise, but that it was a one-woman show. When you are doing a play with other actors, they are constantly feeding you lines which prompt your next lines. But when you are doing a monologue you don't have other actors to play off of, so you have to find other ways to prompt your lines. That's another reason I wanted to put movement and physicality into the play. I found passages in the text that I attached to movements and to locations around the set. So for example, if I'm at the desk for a second time then I need to be saying such-and-such a line. If I am walking behind the chair for the fourth time then I need to be saying such-and-such a line.

D.M. Wow, that's incredible discipline.

K.T. That, and I just had to drill the lines over and over. At the end of the day, there's just no shortcut—you just have to learn the lines. Before rehearsal everyday I would run lines with the assistant stage manager for two hours, then we would have the full day's rehearsal, and at the end of the day I would run lines with her for an additional one to two hours. So in addition to rehearsing all day I was doing at least four hours of nothing but drilling on the lines, trying to commit them to memory.

D.M. Sounds fun.

K.T. Yeah, it's not a good time. It's an enormous challenge not to have other actors to work with, a challenge I welcome when I do these one-woman shows. But as much as I like to challenge myself, I will say that it's far more fun to do a play with other actors and to have other actors to work off of.

D.M. Were there any other challenges in that play that you hadn't encountered before?

K.T. Just one, really. The run of that play was during the election so I was using Mondays—my days off—to fly around the country and open new clinics for Planned Parenthood and canvas and help Hillary in any way I could. The production added a matinee for the day after the election so I went to bed early on the night of the election because I needed a lot of rest in order to do two of these emotionally grueling performances in one day. So I woke up at five the morning after the election to feed my cat and I flip on the television to CNN and I see "President-elect

THE LIFE OF AN ACTOR

DUSTIN MORROW I've heard you say doing theater is like being an Olympic athlete.

KATHLEEN TURNER Heck, yeah. Eight shows a week, that's hard on anyone, I don't care what kind of shape you're in.

D.M. That's something a lot of people aren't aware of, I think. The physical discipline required of a stage actor.

K.T. No, they don't see that. And it's incredible. For me, it's been made more difficult by my rheumatoid arthritis. I have to do a certain amount of movement and working out. I do yoga, I do Pilates, I work out in the gym at least five days a week.

D.M. It seems there have been many instances in your career where you've had to face significant physical obstacles to your performances.

K.T. Well, I've certainly given performances while very sick, where I barely even have a voice, and I've been injured pretty significantly on some of the action movies I have done, but really nothing compares to the R.A. Dealing with that disease has been one of the great challenges of my personal and professional lives.

D.M. The pain of that terrible disease must border on unbearable.

K.T. Well, the medication has advanced light years in the time since I first started really suffering from the R.A. That has helped me tremendously. Beyond that—swimming, massage, physical therapy, acupuncture, and above all else, Pilates. Pilates saved me.

D.M. You hid the R.A. for awhile.

K.T. Well, it took forever to correctly diagnose, so for a long time even I didn't know what it was. But yes, I kept the arthritis a secret because

I wanted to work. People knew I was drinking heavily, but no one knew about the R.A. And that's because drinking has always been a disease that show business understands and tolerates. Hollywood and Broadway will hire drunks, but they won't hire actors with diseases they don't understand. That's sad but true.

D.M. There was a lot of unfortunate discussion of the weight you gained from the steroids, when no one knew you were actually being treated for R.A.

K.T. I couldn't move without the steroids. I literally couldn't walk across a room without them. The big problem with the steroids wasn't the weight gain, though. Don't get me wrong—I'm an actor and I have vanity and the weight gain was tough, but the problem with steroids is how angry they make you. They generate pure rage. That was tough, trying not to act out that rage at friends, family, and coworkers.

D.M. How much of you has been replaced? Are you the Bionic Woman?

K.T. Close! Put it this way, you don't want to go to the airport with me. I always set off the TSA machine, and then they have to pat me down. Actually, it's pretty funny, because they want to talk about my films while they're giving me a full pat down. Imagine, being asked for an autograph by someone while they're groping your ass. It's delightful!

D.M. "Hold your arms out to your side and spread your legs please, and what's Michael Douglas really like?"

K.T. That's pretty much it!

D.M. *Indiscretions* was the worst production for you, it seems.

K.T. Yeah, *Indiscretions* was probably the worst, because the pain from the rheumatoid arthritis was just so acute then.

D.M. I don't know how you blocked that out to the degree to which it enabled you to give a real performance.

K.T. Looking back, I don't know how I did it either. Maybe the pain actually helped the performance. Perhaps my pain became the character's pain. I don't know.

D.M. Was it ever a relief, in a sense, to escape into a role for a couple hours?

K.T. How do you mean?

D.M. In the sense that when you are onstage in *Indiscretions* you are playing a woman who does not have R.A., and that's the headspace you had to get into as an actor.

K.T. Possibly. So much of the experience of doing that play was so centered on coping with pain that I think in some way I have tried to block out the memory of it. What I will always remember about *Indiscretions*, which is unfortunate because it's a great play and a great role, is from the second act, and that was what I called "the mountain."

D.M. The staircase?

K.T. Yes. It may as well have been a mountain as far as I was concerned. The excruciating pain of climbing that staircase every night in the second act, it bordered on unbearable. I had to keep makeup at the top of the staircase so I could deal with the tears streaming down my face after I got to the top. The relief of going into the third act, getting back into my nightgown and slippers, back into my bedroom set, I can remember that potently.

It was a huge challenge just getting past that second act. In some ways I could use the discomfort and the pain in the performance, because this was a woman who hadn't been outside her bedroom or her home for years, so dressing up and going outside the home was terrifying and painful to her in many ways. So it worked in that regard. Not that I think I couldn't have acted it without that, but I was stuck with it so I might as well use what I could.

D.M. In both of the Joan Wilder films, on a much smaller scale obviously, you had to deal with discomfort too.

K.T. I didn't have R.A. yet then.

D.M. Right, but there was a lot of discomfort involved with the making of those movies.

K.T. And it absolutely worked to my advantage, because Joan Wilder was very out of her element in those environs. Actually, the toughest thing about shooting in that locale for me wasn't the physical stuff, because I was very young and very physical as a person at that time, but having to fake a bad Spanish accent. Having grown up in part in Venezuela, I am bilingual and my accent is flawless. But Joan couldn't speak

Spanish, and she certainly couldn't do an accent, so I had to come up with this intentionally bad accent. I actually thought of this Spanish teacher I had in junior high school, who came from Texas and had the worst accent I had ever heard. I would just crack myself up every time I tried to use that accent, it was so ridiculous.

D.M. That's funny. Actors are always working to perfect accents, not the other way around.

K.T. Exactly! It's much harder to do a bad accent intentionally than to do a good accent.

D.M. Let's see Meryl Streep do the bad accent!

K.T. I'm sure she'd nail it!

D.M. I always thought that when actors get to give intentionally bad performances, like in the films *Soapdish* or *Waiting For Guffman*, that that must be just about the most fun that an actor can have.

K.T. Yeah, working on those movies must have been hysterical, it must have been the best fun.

D.M. But it seems like it would be tough at the same time, because you would have to go against everything you'd learned in training as an actor, and against all of your natural talent.

K.T. Well, in the end, it's still a performance, and you have to find your way into it just as you would any other role.

D.M. What are some of the physical demands an actor has to consider while they are in the run of a show?

K.T. Umm, how about everything you do, and all day long.

D.M. How about some specifics?

K.T. How much sleep do you get and how good is that sleep? Do you need tea, do you need a valium? At what hours are you sleeping? How long after or before you go onstage? How much do you work out? When do you work out? How much recovery do you need from your workout? When do you eat and what do you eat? I like to be empty at eight o'clock. I like to feel very, very light before I go onstage. So I eat around three o'clock in the afternoon. And I only do that in order to generate the energy that I need to get me through that eight o'clock show. I want to be digested but I still want to have fuel, so that usually means a certain level of carbohydrates. For example, maybe a pasta and something to give me enough protein that'll burn slow enough to carry me through that performance.

D.M. I do a lot of public speaking, at conferences and film festivals and other events, and I also like to speak on a pretty empty stomach. Eating beforehand kind of saps my energy.

K.T. Exactly. You have to think of this stuff. How much do you talk each day? How much do you talk on the phone? Talking on the phone requires a different use of your voice than just talking in person to someone. It's very subtle, but it's different.

D.M. How would you describe that? I'm just curious.

K.T. When you're on the phone, you tend to place your voice differently, because there's no space around you. You're just talking straight into this instrument. And so you keep it further down in your throat because you don't have the need to fill the space. It's almost subliminal, but it's there.

Another question, then, is how much voice rest you give yourself. I will turn off the phone from at least four to five every day that I have to perform. So that I rest, and I don't talk, for at least that hour. Without fail. Anybody who knows me, if they try and call me during that hour, they'll say, "Oh, it's four o'clock. Forget it, she's not picking up." Voice rest can mean going completely without talking. I'll carry a little notebook sometimes, and the first page says, "I am on voice rest so I'm not talking, but you can." And I have to include that "and you can" because it's very funny how people will react—it's like, as soon as they see that I'm not talking, they think that they can't talk either. They'll start whispering. It's goofy.

Anyway, the point is that everything you do, all day long, should be about preparing you for that eight o'clock show. Taking care of yourself that way erases any doubt you might have going into the performance. You won't be offstage, ready to go on, thinking "If I hadn't done that today I'd be giving a better show tonight." It's like an insurance policy. But it takes discipline and control.

Another thing it does is that it guarantees that when you are off in your performance, or really on, that it's not a result of something you did or did not do earlier in the day. It's just all about the work, the performance. There are nights when you just take off and you're flying and you have no idea why, you just know it's so good it's like music. And oh, if you only knew what triggered that! But you don't. You just don't, you can't. Some nights it's as though everything is effortless and every note that comes out of your mouth is in perfect pitch. And then there are other nights where you simply struggle to make each note correct.

And the difference has nothing to do with when you slept or what you ate, because you were disciplined in being ready for the show. You have to be so prepared that you don't have anything to regret. You didn't do anything that day that would possibly compromise your work that night. Your performance, whether it's on or off or somewhere in the middle, is truly your own.

D.M. What about your intake of other arts? If you're doing a play, do you have any problem with reading other plays, or with reading certain kinds of books or seeing certain kinds of films? I know that when I am in the thick of working on a film, it can be tough for me to engage with other people's work, whether that's a book or a show or a movie or whatever.

K.T. If someone sends me a script, I'll just say, "I can't work on this until I'm well into the play I'm doing now." During rehearsal, I'm not going to work on another script because all my attention must go to the one I'm working on. And even once I open, it'll be another few weeks before I feel solid enough to say "Okay, now I can work on this other piece" or "I can make a decision about that." All the focus must go toward the piece that I'm currently creating. But that's just me. I'm sure other people can multi-task better than me. I will read tons of books, though. That's not a problem.

D.M. You have to choose what you're reading carefully while you are working.

K.T. Yes. They're usually books I don't have to think about too much. Escapist stuff. Once I'm in rehearsal, I read a lot of science fiction and mysteries. Books that have familiar rhythms. For TV, it's basically stuff like *Law and Order*.

D.M. Comfort food.

K.T. Yeah, comfort food.

D.M. Do you ever find it difficult to come down after the high of performing a show?

K.T. Occasionally, but not often. It's easy to turn off performance energy because by the end of a show you've used it up anyway. *Virginia Woolf* was sometimes the exception, just because it was such a marathon, such a long play, that by the end you're on such an exhilarating high that there has to be a cool-down period. Some nights, when I got home, I would actually run my stairs for a little while to bring myself down.

D.M. Martha is such a consuming character, I can't imagine how you didn't bring her home with you some nights.

K.T. Some nights. Some evenings I would get home and my daughter would look at me sideways and ask, "Is it *you*?" Most nights Kathleen showed up, but sometimes it was Martha.

D.M. Speaking of being consumed, occasionally when I am writing and researching, I will have the strange experience of dreaming *as* a character.

K.T. I don't really dream as my characters, but I will sometimes dream *about* them. *Virgin Suicides* hit my dreams. And during *Peggy Sue*, when we did the scene where Peggy Sue speaks to her grandmother on the phone—that came into my dreams. I had several dreams about picking up the phone and hearing my father's voice.

D.M. Well, dreams lie in the subconscious, which is where much of acting comes from.

K.T. I suppose that's true, there could be a tie there.

D.M. Is it difficult to flush a character out of your system after you finish a production?

K.T. I know it is for some actors, but for me it's never been that tough. There have been a few exceptions—I had trouble shaking *Indiscretions* after it was over, and *Virginia Woolf* followed me home on occasion—but when I finish the run of a production, the character is almost instantly gone. Ten days after I finish a character I won't be able to remember the lines, even if it's a character I've done for years.

D.M. Wow, really? That's wild.

K.T. Yes, and that's a good thing. It's good to be able to compartmentalize your work like that, to be able to let something go when it's over. I don't want to carry my past characters around with me for the rest of my career. I will carry the lessons I've learned from doing them, but not the characters themselves.

D.M. I suppose holding onto a character would get in the way of approaching the next one.

K.T. That's right. I need a clean slate.

D.M. Has there ever been a case where you have actually wanted to carry one character over to another?

K.T. Not that I can think of. Even when there are similarities—for example, Martha and Mrs. Robinson are both unhappy drunks—they are drunks for different reasons, so it doesn't do me any good to think about Mrs. Robinson's circumstances in trying to render Martha. Each new character is a new adventure.

D.M. Your daily schedule while doing a role, while rigorous, also sounds comforting in its regularity.

K.T. It is. It takes discipline and it can be hard, but at the same time it can center you and be very relaxing.

D.M. I could see a danger in getting too relaxed before going on stage. I'd think you would want a certain level of tension and nerves.

K.T. You want a great level of focus, but not necessarily nerves. Focus doesn't necessarily mean tension, but it certainly doesn't mean relaxation. That's why I go to the theater at six for the eight o' clock curtain. I will spend at least twenty to thirty minutes doing yoga, stretching, opening up all the parts of the body. I like to take a mat and my blocks down to the stage because at 6:20, when I usually get down to the stage, the stagehands don't need the stage yet. And from 6:15 or 6:20 to 6:45ish, I will do yoga right on the stage, and at the same time I will do my vocal warm-ups and breathing exercises.

At 6:45 I go back upstairs and start my makeup. And by 7:30 I am ready to go, so I go see the other actors in their dressing rooms, just to see how they're doing, how their day was, what frame of mind they are they in. Some actors don't want to see their co-stars until they get onstage, but I don't believe in that. I think it's a courtesy to everyone to have a little time together before you go on stage. But I don't take any phone calls or talk to anyone outside of the cast or crew. From 6:00, when I arrive at the theater, until that curtain goes up, nothing else comes into my world.

When I hit the stage, I'm physically warmed up, I'm vocally warmed up, I'm mentally ready, I've gone over any snags in my mind with regard to what happened the night before, I've spoken to the other actors, and I've cleared my mind of everything but the play and the performance ahead of me. It doesn't mean that I'm relaxed, it just means that I'm settled, prepared, and focused. I've had to rush into the theater once or twice, and I hated it. Once my daughter took a bad fall right before I was to leave for the theater and I rushed her to the plastic surgeon. She had a terrible cut gushing blood everywhere, she had fallen off of her bike and split her chin.

So I'm at the plastic surgeon with her until at least 7:15, I get her home and put her in bed, I'm calling the theater to tell them to hold the curtain, that I was indeed coming, and I got to the theater at about five until eight and I was on stage by ten after. Fifteen minutes, from walking into the building to being at full performance mode on the stage. I wouldn't wish that on anybody. It's just no way to go into the night's work, it only adds to any anxiety you might already have about the work. I'd much rather get to the theater early and have time to kill than have to rush around and not feel centered before going on stage.

D.M. It also seems like you would be in a terrible mood going into the performance.

K.T. That's true, but my mood doesn't ever affect my performance.

D.M. Really? How do you do that?

K.T. My job as an actor is to reveal the character's intention, not to let the audience see how I "feel" on a specific day. So regardless of what mood I am in when I come into the theater, the performance remains the thing I honed over months of rehearsal and prep. It's a chosen pattern of behavior that has nothing to do with my personal mindset. And as a pattern of behavior, it is in a sense separate from me. It is a thing that I render as an actor, but it isn't me.

D.M. So, in the way that a painting is a painter's work, but the painting is not the painter, the performance is not the actor.

K.T. Yes. The performance is something that the actor, the artist, creates. It's harder to separate a performance from an actor than it is a painting from a painter, because a performance is not a concrete thing that you can hold in your hand or hang on a wall. It's a bit clearer in cinema, where an actor's performance is recorded, and can be replayed and studied, than in a play, where the performance kind of vanishes into the ether.

D.M. That separation also gets at something that is murky about stardom and celebrity. As a young person, I always loved your performance in *Romancing the Stone*, and I loved the character that Diane Thomas and you created. But it was the performance I loved.

K.T. Right. You loved the painting, not the painter.

D.M. I guess so. And yet my love of your work in that film extended to your other performances in some way. It's impossible for me to say for sure because I can't un-see *Romancing*. But it's hard for me to imagine that I would have loved your work in, say, *Peggy Sue*, quite as much if I had not seen *Romancing*. *Peggy Sue* is not a film that speaks to kids, really, but I loved it as a kid just because I love watching you work.

K.T. Well, that's true in all of the arts—you carry some residual goodwill for the artist from project to project.

D.M. And it's also, I imagine, why an audience can feel betrayed. If you love a band, and you relish their first three albums, but then they change their sound on their fourth, you can feel utterly betrayed. Almost personally affronted. And yet they didn't owe you anything, shouldn't be expected as artists to make the same kind of music for their entire career, and the new album doesn't change the fact that you still have the first three, which you can continue to love.

K.T. People develop intense relationships with art, and that can lead to the imagination of some kind of contract with the audience. It can feel like you owe them something.

D.M. That's what George Lucas has been dealing with for most of his career.

K.T. How so?

D.M. His constant reworking and re-releasing of the *Star Wars* movies has driven his fans nuts, and I think that's because, culturally, those movies have become so big that we feel that we all sort of own them. Fan and critic reaction to his alterations of the films has been almost universally negative, and Lucas knows this, but he keeps tweaking the movies anyway. His argument, of course, is that they're his films to tweak, and he wants them the way he wants them. Which, to me, brings up an interesting question about the ownership of the moviegoing experience—in changing the movies, is Lucas somehow disrespecting the fans who love them? Are the *Star Wars* movies so popular, so embedded in our cultural consciousness, that they are now the property of the fans?

K.T. *Star Wars* is a special case, though, because it's ascended to something higher than just another media work.

D.M. That's true, but there have been plenty of similar cases. Steven Spielberg has publicly admitted regret over having made awkward digital changes to *E.T.* for its re-release in 2002, stating that he should have left it alone because "every movie is a signpost of its time."

K.T. What did he do?

D.M. Well, the one I really remember is that there's a scene where the kids are on their bikes with E.T., near the end of the movie, fleeing the government agents. The agents were holding guns and Spielberg had the guns digitally erased and replaced with walkie-talkies.

K.T. Interesting.

D.M. As a part of viewers feeling nostalgic for a specific time in their lives, especially their youth, I think they feel protective of those memories, and the films and books and plays and TV series from that period that entertained and shaped them. That's perhaps why people get really upset when they find out that Hollywood is remaking a film they loved from their youth. In theory, the remake doesn't replace the original—it's not like you no longer have access to the original because there's now going to be a remake out there. No one is focing you to see the remake. But for many fans, it feels weirdly like a personal betrayal. For many, Lucas's digital reworking of the *Star Wars* films is like someone photoshopping their old family photos.

K.T. Well, let's all feel sorry for George Lucas.

D.M. Right, the poor billionaire.

K.T. I see what you're driving at, though. There can be a real sense among fans of actors that the actors somehow owe them something. If you've entertained them in a specific genre of film, you should keep making films in that genre.

D.M. That must have been particularly difficult for you, since you have never liked to do the same kind of role more than once.

K.T. It has been. I'm sure I had a lot of fans after *Body Heat* that, just like the studios, would have been happy to see me do nothing but variations on that movie for the rest of my career. Or fans of *Romancing* and *Jewel* that would have been thrilled to see me churn out sequels to those films forever.

D.M. Ahem.

K.T. Yeah, like you!

D.M. I'm just kidding. It would have saddened me if you'd kept doing increasingly lower-quality sequels about my favorite movie characters. I liked *Jewel* well enough, but one sequel was more than enough.

K.T. One too many.

D.M. The studio filed suit against you to get you to do *Jewel*.

K.T. They did. But the script wasn't ready. My objection wasn't to doing the film necessarily, it was to the underdeveloped screenplay.

D.M. So you said no.

K.T. I said no. The ability to say no is one of the only powers an actor has in Hollywood. You can become as known for what you say no to as for what you say yes to. I'm too intelligent to starve, so I can turn down big paydays and I can say no to projects I don't believe in.

D.M. Did you ever feel a lot of pressure then to go against your natural instincts to different kinds of movies, not for the financial reasons the studios wanted, but as an obligation to your fans?

K.T. I never really did, because if I had done those sequels or those variations on *Body Heat*, they would not have been good and I would not have been good in them. Even if the scripts had been great, and I can tell you with assurance that they weren't, my heart wouldn't have been in them and my work would have suffered for it. And that would have been the true disservice to my fans. What I owe my fans isn't a specific kind of play or film or role—what I owe them is good work about which I feel passionate. I owe them interesting characters, solid stories, and a total commitment to and investment in any role I'm playing.

FAME, AGING AND VANITY

Dustin Morrow Did you feel more pressure working in films than working in the theater industry?

Kathleen Turner Certainly. The pressure to repeat the same kind of role exists in the theater industry, but it's nothing like it is in Hollywood. Hollywood can be a very poisonous place in that regard.

D.M. One thing that always bothered me when I was living in Los Angeles and working in the film industry were those two levels of conversation that were always happening simultaneously. You're at lunch or a party or whatever, and you're talking about something totally innocuous and innocent, but underneath that, there's this subtextual conversation centered on, "What can I get from you, and what can you get from me?"

And everybody just seems to be okay with it, like it's no big deal. It's just expected that they're going to use each other, and when the level of professional use they have for each other dries up or becomes imbalanced, their personal relationship will drift away. I don't know, maybe it bothered me because I grew up in a small town in the Midwest, where people are genuine and generally say what they mean.

K.T. Tell me about it, I've spent my entire adult life in New York. Talk about "saying what you mean." There's no one more honest, brutally sometimes, than your average New Yorker.

That game you're talking about is one reason I could never live in L.A. A lot of people think that, because I've achieved a high level of success in this industry, that I am really savvy to the Hollywood game, but I am not. I just can't play that game, I don't have it in me. Life's too short.

D.M. But I imagine you are forced to sometimes, just to work.

K.T. Unfortunately. More often, the game is being played around me without my realizing it.

D.M. How do you mean?

K.T. I'll give you a recent example. I knew this one woman with an organization that I really do care for and support, who said to me, "Can you come on the twenty-sixth for this fund-raising event? Just come for the opening and give a welcome, you'll be in and out in less than an hour." I was very busy working at the time, but because I had an hour of time I could devote to it, I said yes. But then I get there and I realize there's this whole long press line, there are all these cameras for TV and print and everything, and she wants me to go through the entire press line. And then she wants me to sit next to this guy who swears he'll give the organization a ton of money if I'll sit next to him. I was there the whole night.

It becomes a game for these people, they get me there and then work to see how long they can keep me there before I finally get fed up and leave. That kind of misdirection drives me crazy.

D.M. It's very disrespectful.

K.T. It is. But I try not to complain about it, because it's one small downside if it means I can also use my celebrity to do good in the world.

D.M. Has dealing with fame gotten easier as you've gotten older?

K.T. Of course. As with anything, there's a learning curve. And it's something I've been dealing with most of my adult life. The important thing is not to let it overtake your work as an actor.

D.M. How do you mean?

K.T. Well, that's what the one-woman show *Tallulah* was about, to some degree. Tallulah Bankhead was obsessed with being recognized as a serious actress, but her public persona was so larger-than-life that it overtook her roles. Which is a shame, because she had talent.

D.M. I can only imagine some of the insane encounters you've had with fans over the years.

K.T. Oh geez, there've been many. Fame makes people do crazy things. People following me, coming up to me and spilling their guts, begging for photos. It's crazy. At the height of the *Body Heat* madness, I had on multiple occasions guys actually lie down in front of my car. Isn't that insane? "Get up, you fools!"

D.M. Do those sorts of things still happen?

K.T. Not as often since I stopped regularly doing leads in movies, but occasionally. I was at the Provincetown Film Festival for a screening of *The Perfect Family* a couple years ago, and I decided to go for a bike ride through town. I was mobbed! People were actually physically pulling me off the bike to try to get a picture with me. It was crazy, and scary and threatening. I had to hide in a shop and call my hotel to come pick me up because I wasn't going to be able to ride back.

I don't get that in New York, thank god, because New Yorkers are totally jaded by celebrity and too busy to have time for that kind of nonsense, so sometimes my celebrity sneaks up on me when I go to other cities.

D.M. One odd thing about fame is that those people could theoretically have watched *Body Heat* that day, and for them that period of thirty-five years has not passed. They see you on the street, and even though you look different than you did in that film, to them you're still Kathleen-Turner-from-*Body Heat*.

K.T. That's the permanence of film, I guess.

D.M. It's sort of a scary thought.

K.T. It is very bizarre. I didn't need to think about that, thank you!

D.M. Sorry, I just think it's fascinating.

K.T. It is fascinating, I hadn't really thought about it before, but I suppose that's it. That's a real serious disconnect.

D.M. And of course, many people have trouble distinguishing between an actor and a role. If someone runs into you on the street, they might see Serial Mom, not Kathleen Turner.

K.T. Ha! Well, I hope they're not seeing that character!

D.M. It seems like it could be charming in the case of children, who don't know better, who might know you from *Baby Geniuses* or *A Simple Wish* or even as Jessica Rabbit.

K.T. It is cute, it's great when kids recognize me from one of the children's films I have done.

D.M. I'll confess to it myself—having discovered and fallen in love so deeply with *Romancing the Stone* as a child, I think that some part of me would have been really disappointed if you had been completely un-Joan Wilder-ish, as it were.

K.T. Well, luckily for you, of all the parts I've played, that one is probably the closest to the real me.

D.M. When people approach you, what are they most likely going to say?

K.T. Usually it's just something along the lines of "I'm a fan" or "I like your work." Some want to know what I've been up to. One that kills me is when people come up to me and say, "Oh, you still look good." As if they're surprised. How am I supposed to look? One time this woman in L.A. said that to me and I responded, "You know, I wish I had met you before so I could say the same to you."

D.M. Burn!

K.T. Not my finest moment, perhaps, but I was just so tired of hearing it.

D.M. Again, that's that idea that they can't separate you from your characters. We don't want our movie stars to get R.A. or to age, we want them to always look the same way they did in our favorite movies.

K.T. Which explains the pressure that so many actors feel to get cosmetic surgery as they age.

D.M. I understand that impulse. But ultimately, I suspect it's more harmful than helpful, both professionally and personally. For one thing, most of the plastic surgery in Hollywood doesn't look particularly good. I mean, some of these actors, who do they think they're kidding?

K.T. You're right. And it's not like they're actually getting cast in these roles as younger women when they're competing with actual younger women, and when everyone in the world knows how long they've been around.

D.M. And on a personal level, I'd think it would not boost one's confidence if one got plastic surgery and it looked like plastic surgery. And it didn't really result in any professional advancement. Wouldn't you just feel worse about yourself than you did before you got the surgery?

K.T. Beyond that, it's just dishonest, and it does a disservice to young women. It makes them fear aging. It reinforces this BS, media-driven link between youth and beauty.

I want to look my age. I want to be attractive, and I want to look my age. And frankly, I wouldn't want to look thirty if I could, because the stage roles for women my age are so much more interesting than the roles available to women that age.

D.M. You've said that your supporting part in the *Dumb and Dumber* sequel was in some way a comment on feedback you've gotten from the public over the years about your appearance changing as you've aged.

K.T. That was absolutely it. That's why I did it. So much of modern cinematic comedy is mean-spirited, it's about putting people down, but the Farrelly Brothers movies are really sweet. Don't get me wrong—they're ferociously dumb, but they're also really sweet. And in that context—a well-meaning comedy—that role gave me an opportunity to have a little fun with that conceit that Hollywood actresses should always look the same as they get older. I play a woman that Jeff Daniels's character had decades before had an affair with, and when he and Jim Carrey's character track me down all these years later, they can't believe how much my appearance has changed. It was a chance for me to say, in character and as Kathleen Turner, "This is how I look now, I've aged. I actually look my age. Now get over it!"

D.M. I hope that you realize that you've been an inspiration to many women in your positive embracing of the aging process.

K.T. I get some lovely letters from time to time.

D.M. Well, I know you don't do the social media thing, and you're not looking at comment threads on discussion boards or on YouTube videos, but there are a lot of really lovely things written about you in those arenas.

K.T. Like what?

D.M. Just some lovely, affirmative comments about how you've dealt with aging and with the R.A. Many people suffering from arthritis and from other debilitating, pain-inflicting diseases have drawn inspiration from you. And you've been applauded for rejecting plastic surgery in an industry that embraces it, for retaining your confidence while—just imagine the thought—actually looking your age.

K.T. That's really nice.

D.M. Can I read you something?

K.T. What's that?

D.M. I printed out this comment that was on a clip from one of your films online, from a YouTube user named Laurie Uebbing. I thought it was nice and demonstrative of all of the support that's out there for you.

K.T. Oh geez, are you going to embarrass me here?

D.M. Not at all! I just think this is really nice and I wanted you to hear it. "I remember like it was yesterday, when she won the Hasty Pudding Award at Harvard. I was standing right behind the car she was riding in. God, she has a great pair of gorgeous blue eyes. I like her self-confidence, she has gone through so much and come out like a phoenix rising through the ashes."

K.T. "Like a phoenix!" I like that. That's just lovely.

D.M. Isn't that nice?

K.T. Indeed. You know, aging has never really been tough for me. Like I said, I see aging as opportunity. As I age, I get better at my craft, richer roles come my way, and outside of acting, I become a happier and more interesting person. It was the RA that was always the tough part for me. I find confidence in aging, but the arthritis took a lot of that confidence away. Because so much of myself, and so much of my craft, was in my physicality. When I was told by doctors that I would spend the rest of my life in a wheelchair, you can't imagine what that did to my confidence. Obviously I proved them wrong, but the limits on my physicality have always continued to be the toughest part of this disease.

D.M. And yet you've fought your way through it and triumphed over it.

K.T. Well, I don't know if I've triumphed exactly, but the RA and I have found a way to live together. And while I no longer let it impede me, the RA doesn't exactly do my vanity any favors.

D.M. You don't strike me as vain, in life or in your choice of roles.

K.T. That's definitely true about the roles. I mean, in everyday life, I can be as vain as the next person. I like to look good, just like everyone else wants to look good. It gives one confidence. I took this role on *The Path* because it was a great part, and it was necessary that the character not look good. But I have to admit that when I saw the wardrobe and that they were going to put grease in my hair, I wasn't overjoyed. I was like, "Really, guys? Actual grease?" It's a struggle sometimes.

In the acclaimed Hulu streaming series The Path, *Kathleen plays the mother of the leader of a controversial religious movement. The series stars Aaron Paul, Michelle Monaghan and Hugh Dancy, and has been running for three seasons.*

But at the end of the day, vanity just can't factor into it. I need to look like the character. If the character is meant to look fantastic, then I should look fantastic. But if the character is supposed to look dumpy or run down, then that's how I need to look.

D.M. You haven't done many glammed-up roles recently.

K.T. Tell me about it. "Ms. Turner, would you like to keep any of your wardrobe?" "Um, no thanks!"

D.M. It cracks me up when you see plays or movies where a big star is supposed to be playing, like, a crackhead or a hardened convict or something, and they look just beautiful and all made up, with perfect teeth and artfully disheveled hair.

K.T. I know, it's ridiculous. Many actors want to play unattractive characters, but they don't physically want to appear unattractive. It just doesn't work, because the moment you start worrying about how you look, you're not the character anymore, you're just you.

D.M. I imagine in many cases that it's not the actors' faults that they look as good as they do, but the producers or the studios. It doesn't surprise me, for example, that the people that made the film *Monster* had to go to a small studio to get it released. From the shallow, misguided point of view of a major studio sinking a fortune into marketing a movie, what's the point of buying a Charlize Theron movie if she's not going to look beautiful in it?

Monster *is the film for which Charlize Theron won a Best Actress Oscar. She played the notorious serial killer Aileen Wuoros.*

K.T. Of course. Can you imagine my character in *The Virgin Suicides* if I'd have been all glammed up? Or my character in *The Perfect Family*? Or my character in *The Path*? It's ludicrous. Hollywood has a very narrow view of its stars.

D.M. And there's a palpable sense of misogyny running through the film industry, which doesn't help.

K.T. That's the truth! The biggest problem with Los Angeles, even bigger than the sense of isolation one feels out there, or that element of people using each other that you referred to, is its attitude toward women. L.A. is anti-woman, plain and simple. There is an intense pressure that women there feel to conform to insane standards of beauty and body type. It's a very negative place for women, especially young women. I feel bad for young women raised in that environment.

D.M. I couldn't take that city because of that sense of isolation you mentioned. Everyone there lives in their cars. And no one you ever meet has a job outside the industry. It's impossible to meet anyone interesting.

K.T. And if you don't drive yourself to a party, or screening, or restaurant or whatever, you could get stranded there. You can't go home when you want. You can't just step out on the curb and expect a cab to come around the corner, and you can't walk to a subway.

D.M. I could never go back to living in a car culture. Like New York, Portland is a city of cyclists, walkers, and public transit riders. You just feel more engaged with the people around you in that kind of city.

K.T. One of the reasons I've always lived in New York City is that it's as close as I can come to the rest of the world. You can't live in L.A. and be a citizen of the world. You live in your car there, you're isolated and protected. In New York City, you are forced to interact with other people, to be a participant in the world and not just an observer of it.

D.M. You must have to think of yourself, to some degree, as a brand.

K.T. To a large degree. "Kathleen Turner" is a brand, a business. Theater is the industry, and I'm the brand. I could have accepted a lot of terrible roles over the years, and made a lot more money than I did, but it would have cheapened the brand. I have responsibilities to my family, to the people who work with me, to the charities I work for, and to myself, to guard that brand very carefully. It's all I have, I have to protect it.

D.M. It must be hard though. Even if you managed a Fortune 500 company, the product and the company are the brand, not you yourself. When *you* are the brand, it seems it'd be hard to make that separation.

K.T. It is. But you have to remember that I have been famous since 1981. I've had a lot of practice, and I've known for a long time now exactly what the "Kathleen Turner brand" is and what it means, and so it's not hard for me to decide what I will and will not do.

D.M. Since we're on the subject of fame and fandom—what actors are you a fan of? What actors do you really love to watch?

K.T. I'm not going to pick favorites, I don't want to leave anyone out and hurt somebody's feelings.

D.M. Okay. How about classic actors then? Ones that have expired?

K.T. I don't know. I'm not good at picking a favorite anything. I don't have a favorite play or movie or book or anything.

D.M. How about Lauren Bacall?

K.T. Why, because we have similar voices? Please. No, I guess I would go with Rosalind Russell. She kills me in *Auntie Mame*. I think I could do that character someday.

D.M. I would love to see "Kathleen Turner in *Auntie Mame*."

K.T. Well, cross your fingers then.

D.M. Are there specific theatergoing experiences where you can remember really connecting with an actor?

K.T. Oh, there are too many to count.

D.M. How about an early one?

K.T. When I was a teenager in London I somehow managed to get a front row seat for *Danton's Death* with Christopher Plummer, and at one point in the play he sort of laid down on the edge of the stage and our eyes met. I'm not sure he could really see me that well, because of the lights, but I felt this sort of electric jolt go through my body. It was like he was looking right into me. It was truly, literally, a jolt of recognition. He was amazing in that performance. It's stuck with me forever.

And Maggie Smith in *The Lady in the Van*, oh my god. Brilliant! I get such joy sometimes from watching actors prance around the stage and have fun.

D.M. I didn't realize that was also a play.

K.T. It was a play long before it became a film, and she was even better onstage than she was in the film. Maggie is an actor that always seems to be having the time of her life, relishing every moment on stage. She's a joy to behold.

In fact, that's one of the oft-overlooked great pleasures of going to the theater—watching the actors enjoy what they do. When they are having fun, the audience is swept up in that. Even if your character is crying and suffering and tortured and in a terrible place, there is glee inside at all times, at all stages, and the audience totally gets that. They're suffering right along with you and they're loving it! It's that love of the work that the best actors bring to the stage to share with the audience.

D.M. When I was young, you were certainly playing a lot of characters that were dealing with things that I couldn't understand. As a ten-year-old, I wasn't going to relate to the bereaved mother of *The Accidental Tourist*. And yet I could see the great joy you demonstrated in taking on these interesting parts. That's part of what got me so interested in filmmaking at a young age. The best character actors do that, you can see them relishing the opportunity to take a role and really run with it. The actor's joy at engaging with the material is infectious in the audience.

K.T. I have always thought of myself as a character actor, except I happen to be in the lead roles.

D.M. I would agree. I would say you're a lead actor with the methods and talents of a character actor. Which is a tough place to be in, because there are great responsibilities placed on both of those roles, and they are very different.

K.T. To some degree, I am jealous of the straight-up character actors. They get to come in and do their shtick, steal a scene or two from the leads, and leave. God bless them.

D.M. Is it frustrating, as a lead, to see that? Stanley Tucci all but walks away with your film *Undercover Blues*, and almost all the praise for the acting in the reviews for that film was reserved for him, but it's a very small role and you and Dennis Quaid also do some solid comic work in that movie.

K.T. It's really not frustrating, as anything that makes the project better is ultimately a good thing.

D.M. I just feel that sometimes—not always, but sometimes—the lead actors don't get the credit for what they do. If you watch *Rain Man*, Tom Cruise is terrific in that movie, but because he rendered an entirely plausible autistic character, Dustin Hoffman got all the attention and all the awards. But Tom Cruise carries every scene of that movie on his shoulders alone. Hoffman's character plays a specific role, but he doesn't propel the narrative forward, and he doesn't provide a character the audience can relate to, a point-of-entry for the moviegoer. Because Hoffman, for most of that movie, is the only actor Cruise has to play off of, Cruise has to do that work all on his own.

And some lead actors that are consistently good in every movie, especially in less-respected genres like action or sci-fi never seem to get much recognition for it. It's just taken for granted that they'll be solid. Tommy Lee Jones had the showier part in *The Fugitive*, and got all the recognition and awards, but Harrison Ford carries that whole film on his shoulders and he's awesome in it.

K.T. Part of it is that the thing that makes a lead actor a great lead actor is somewhat indefinable. It's certainly harder to pin that down than it is to identify what makes a great character actor. It takes a certain level of innate charisma to be a lead actor, a magnetism, and that's a hard thing to define. And it certainly isn't something that can be learned.

D.M. Yes, some actors just pop on the screen and others don't. Have you seen Maggie Smith in *Downton Abbey*?

K.T. Of course, she's wonderful in it. She's a good friend of mine, but I can say without bias that that's great, great acting.

D.M. And it's a good example of what you were talking about, letting the audience know that you are enjoying what you do. She seems to be having the time of her life with that part.

K.T. Totally. Even though she played this stern and forbidding and dis-approving character, she had this constant little twinkle in her eye. She does that well. So does Judi Dench. And so does Emma Thompson. When you watch Emma, I think you always get a sense of what a great time she is having. And that's essential to her likeability and success as an actor.

D.M. She's also a terrific writer, and a former stand-up comedian, and I think you can see that intelligence in her performances as an actor. Meryl Streep has that, too, a demonstration of intelligence that informs each role.

K.T. And they're both great at conveying their passion for the work.

D.M. Can that passion be faked?

K.T. It can, but if you have to fake it then what are you doing? Time to reevaluate. The hope is always that that joy you convey is authentic. You should really feel it. If you are not enjoying yourself, if you are not having the time of your life doing what you are doing, then why are you doing it? Are you literally wanting to suffer along with your character? And if so, what is your purpose? Is it some kind of therapy? Go to a shrink, for god's sake. There are better places to work out your personal demons than on a stage.

D.M. There have got to be easier ways to figure out your life than going into acting, that's for sure.

K.T. Yeah, and what fun is it for the audience if that's your M.O.? The audience doesn't care about your problems, leave them at home.

D.M. The only danger of that idea of letting the audience see you enjoy your work, it seems to me, might be that your real personality might begin to override that of your characters. Jack Nicholson always seems to be having a great time onscreen, and his joy is obviously infectious in the audience, but as we discussed a bit earlier, he often seems to be playing variations of Jack Nicholson.

K.T. I think some of that is Nicholson just not risking enough. It's almost as if he wants to wink at the camera and say, "You know, it's okay, it's just me, the Jack you know and love."

D.M. But especially when you look at some of his early roles, like *The Last Detail* and *Five Easy Pieces*, or a few later indie films like *The Pledge* and *About Schmidt*, it's clear he can disappear into a role when he wants to make the effort.

K.T. He's one of the greats, there's no question.

D.M. William Hurt is an actor that I could never tell was having any fun. He's obviously deeply gifted, but he sometimes seems joyless in his roles.

K.T. Well, he has changed and loosened up a lot over the years. I think he was really making himself suffer in the early days. He had some sense of having to, how do I put this, "expiate something."

D.M. Some inner demons?

K.T. Perhaps. But I think he has grown out of that. He's mellowed.

D.M. Do you ever have an outside-the-character experience when you are working opposite someone brilliant like Hurt or Nicholson, where they are really cooking, just doing something amazing in a scene, and you catch yourself for a moment stepping outside your character and thinking, "Wow, look at what they are doing!"

K.T. Not often, because when I am in a scene, I am in the character 100%. But on rare occasion, yes.

D.M. Example?

K.T. Fiona Shaw, who I worked with on *Undercover Blues*, is an actor that can just dazzle me. She is somebody I can watch over and over on stage or on film and just never cease to be floored by. I went out to see her in the play *Happy Days* out at the Brooklyn Academy of Music, and it was incredible. I went backstage and said, "Darn it, I have been planning on doing this play and now you have set me back at least ten years." There's just no way I can follow that anytime soon.

Shaw is an accomplished Irish actress and theater director. Although long prolific and successful in the theater, she is perhaps best known for her roles as Petunia in the Harry Potter *films and her recurring role as Marnie on the HBO series* True Blood.

D.M. She really is wonderful.

K.T. On *Undercover Blues*, she was so outrageous! We were doing this scene together and I got so caught up in watching her I think I went slack-jawed and silent. And then somebody says, "Um, your line, Kathleen." I was so mesmerized by her I think I forgot I was in the scene!

Undercover Blues *is a 1993 action-comedy in which Kathleen and Dennis Quaid play married superspies and parents of a new baby. Shaw plays the film's villain, a psychotic Czech arms dealer.*

D.M. As a huge fan of Irish cinema, I am naturally a big fan of hers as well. She was fantastic in *My Left Foot* and *The Butcher Boy*. I love her voice, it's really rich and resonant.

K.T. She has a very expressive voice, and she uses it very well.

D.M. Speaking of resonant and expressive voices...

K.T. I know, I know! Let's get into it.

USING THE VOICE

DUSTIN MORROW I won't lie, one of the small pleasures of having these long conversations has just been listening to your voice.

KATHLEEN TURNER Gee, I haven't heard that before!

D.M. If smoke had sound . . .

K.T. Okay, let's talk about it.

D.M. Has it always been deep?

K.T. Always. Always. When I was a child they made me sing with the boys section in choir at church!

D.M. I imagine that when many people hear your name, the first thing they think of is your voice. Do you think the voice is hard to think objectively about, especially for a developing actor, since your voice is something you have carried with you for every second of your life? Is it something that you really have to learn to listen to?

K.T. Oh yeah, definitely. The first realization you have to come to when you begin to work on your voice is that what you hear in your head is not what anyone else hears. All you really have to do to understand that is record yourself and listen to your playback. You realize very quickly that the difference between what you hear and what everyone else hears is significant, and you must take that into account in thinking about how you want to be heard. The way you think you sound, and the way you actually sound, are very, very different.

D.M. That's something we all forget about until we do hear ourselves in a recording. Many people, listening to a recording, can't stand the sound of their own voice. Me included.

K.T. What's wrong with your voice? You have a lovely voice.

D.M. Thanks. I guess the slightly nasal Midwestern flatness of it bothers me. But I don't hear it or notice it unless I'm listening to a recording of myself.

K.T. Of course. Nobody does. Imagine the hell of walking around and disliking the sound of your own voice all the time.

D.M. What else do actors need to think about with regard to the voice?

K.T. Secondly, you must realize that the entire oral cavity—the back of your mouth, the throat, up past the sinuses, is all muscle that is expandable and retractable. There are literally exercises that you can do to stretch the muscles in your mouth.

To begin with, a simple stretch anyone can do, is to take a really huge yawn, open up and you feel how the back of your mouth lifts up, widens, in both directions—up and down and side to side. Memorize how that stretch feels and work it, work it, work it. As you would build any muscle, you will work that stretch so that when you want it, you can just go to it without actually having to work up a genuine yawn. Warm ups are important, warming up your voice is essential.

D.M. What are the things that you will do to warm up?

K.T. Begin with the vowel sounds, place them in the very front of your mouth, place them in the middle of your mouth, then place them at the back of your mouth. Work the consonants, especially the T's, the D's, the F's, and work the softer letters like the M's, the S's, and the V's. You don't want to allow much air to escape as you work the letters, so you want to be sure, for example, that your teeth are well-done so that you don't have leakage through the teeth that you don't want. I found, at one point, during the onset of the rheumatoid arthritis that my jaw was so affected that I was losing air through my teeth. My teeth were no longer meeting and matching and I had to have some of my back teeth ground down because my bite had changed significantly.

D.M. I imagine most actors just want good matching teeth for cosmetic reasons.

K.T. Yes, but even more important than what they look like is what the teeth do to the voice. There are plenty of great actors with questionable looking teeth, but their teeth aren't messed up in such a way as they are letting air escape and screw up the voice. Also, if you have an underbite or an overbite, you need to learn how to compensate for it as your voice is concerned. You may need to do something with your jaw that most actors don't have to do.

You also want to treat all of your oral and nasal cavities well, and use saline solutions several times a day, whether you feel you need them or not. They hydrate all of the tissue around your nose and throat. When that tissue dries out, that's when you start to force a voice, force a sound, and you literally risk tearing or damaging some of the tissue around your throat. Ideally you should never, ever feel your voice in your throat unless you mean to scream or summon a really guttural sound because the tissues in the throat are so fragile. You can inflame or tear them very, very easily. One scream is not worth not being able to talk, so if for example in a play you have a scene where your character is in terror, say, or in anger, you have to be careful to place that scream well or decide how much it's going to cost you.

So some nights you might modulate it, or maybe on Sunday matinee you will give it your all because you've got a day to recover from it before the next performance. It's not that you want to pull back on your performance, but you do have to choose how much to use as it will affect how you do the play the next day.

It's the same thing in film in that you can easily blow out your voice there as well. Although film doesn't make the same demands on the voice because of all of the microphone placement possibilities, the potential is still there to mess up your voice.

D.M. Actors could probably learn a great deal from singers.

K.T. Yes, and vice versa. One interesting thing is that I have talked to so many singers who say that singing is a lot easier to do, to sing eight shows a week, than to speak in eight shows a week. That's because singing requires a very specific placement of the voice, and you have so many more choices in speech than you do in singing in terms of placement. There's much more variability. You tend to make more mistakes in speech so you have to learn exactly where to put the voice so that you protect it.

It's a true discipline and it should be absolutely studied, it should be practiced and practiced and practiced and practiced. You should never,

ever feel that you have it down and that you don't have to worry about it again. That's rubbish, because every time you go into eight shows a week you have got to protect that voice. Vocal rest is imperative, you have to think about exactly how much you talk on a working day. You don't sit around chattering all the time because you are using up your voice. You have to think of it as a resource, but a limited resource. It's not unending. There's no bottomless reservoir of voice. There really is a limit to how much one could or should talk in order to maintain the quality of the voice.

D.M. I know that food and beverages will affect a voice, too.

K.T. Absolutely. I avoid acids on performance days, so no citrus juices. I don't have orange juice or grapefruit juice or lemonade or anything like that. Those things can strip the membrane from your throat. Don't have too much coffee as that also carries a great amount of acidic influence. At the same time, on the other hand, you don't want to go too far toward a base. For example, you don't want dairy before a show because it coats the vocal chords and then you have to clear them before the show and that's no fun. You don't want chocolate because chocolate will clog up your chords. It really is that specific. Every actor should have a list of what they can and can't eat and drink before a performance.

D.M. Are there elements of a voice that you think are more important than others? When you start talking about things like tempo and rhythm, articulation, pronunciation, pitch . . .

K.T. Well, the important thing to remember is that all of those things are tied to each other. Each affects the other. And even more outwardly, the voice is connected to what you do with all of the muscles in your body. Many people think that they can "divy up" their bodily functions. Like, that they sit down and relax without putting pressure on their head, or on their breathing. Or that they can go for a ten-mile run and "rest their voice." You may not be using your voice while running, but you better believe that something is happening to it. You can't compartmentalize your system in that way. Your body, from head to toe, is like a pond—any disturbance, any action or inaction, is going to send out ripples of waves that are going to effect every other part of the system.

Now. Having said that, articulation will carry you through a lot because ideally the first thing you want as an actor is to be understood, to have the words understood. A lot of American actors struggle with that, actually. Maggie Smith saw *Virginia Woolf* and came backstage and said, in perfect Maggie Smith style, "Darling, I understood every word! That is so rare in America!"

So your first goal should be articulation, hitting your consonants. I, of course, much prefer to seek lower tones because that works for my voice. Because higher frequencies carry better than lower, more stretched frequencies, I have some additional work to do with my voice. Lower tones are a longer, lower frequency than higher, a soprano will have a much tighter sound wave than a base. So I may have to add volume to that base that a soprano will carry automatically because of the length of the sound wave.

So I have to think of that. It's all about learning the limitations and possibilities of your individual voice, and tracking how it changes. My voice has always been low, but now it's even lower than it was when I started out as an actor. It's a science. It's cool. Getting to know your voice and what you can do with it is one of the joys of acting.

D.M. How often do you take stock of, really reassess your voice?

K.T. With each new job. I do it again for each new role, because I have to do it in the context of what needs to be highlighted for every play and every film. One thing that's fun about film is that you can sink down into almost nothing, you can get very small and quiet with your voice and it will still be picked up. It allows you to do incredibly subtle things. It also allows you to experiment with changing your voice over the course of the storyline. In *Romancing the Stone*, I start the film with the voice up higher and let her voice gradually, subtly deepen as she becomes more confident. Her discovery of her personal freedom is mirrored in the change of her voice.

D.M. That had to be tricky, given that you shot that film out of sequence, to keep track of the pitch at which your voice was to be in each scene.

K.T. It wasn't that tough. The confidence she exudes in each scene naturally informs her voice. They were, in a sense, one and the same.

D.M. How deep is your voice, have you actually had it measured?

K.T. Not lately. But my voice has been registered to the bottom of the piano. I can go all the way down to that key on the far left. When I have a cold my voice just sits down there.

D.M. I can't imagine your voice with a cold. You could probably give seasoned blues singers a run for their money.

K.T. Indeed. It gets pretty deep.

D.M. Do other members of your family have low voices?

K.T. We all do to some degree. My mother had quite a low voice. My voice has changed quite a bit over the years. My voice in *Body Heat* is almost a full octave higher than it is now. That's just aging. And smoking—I used to smoke quite a bit. I've used my voice so much over the years—my career *is* the use of my voice—that it's naturally deepened over time. Which is great, because I've had a lot of fun going to that low register. The episode of *Nip/Tuck* that I did was basically an opportunity to have fun with my voice. I played a phone sex operator who went in for a vocal cord lift because my voice was getting too deep and I was starting to lose customers.

> *Nip/Tuck is a controversial comedy/drama series that ran on the FX network for seven seasons, about two plastic surgeons, their patients and their tumultuous personal lives.*

D.M. People always have trouble placing your accent.

K.T. Of course, because it developed while I grew up in so many different cultures.

D.M. The comedienne Janaene Garofalo used to do this bit in her act, an impression of "Someone Watching an Interview with Kathleen Turner on Television." It was something like, "What is that . . . is that . . . uh . . . is that . . . French?"

K.T. Ha! Yeah, it's tough to place. I just call it mid-ocean.

D.M. You seem to occasionally code-switch in your accent, too.

K.T. Yes, if I spend a protracted amount of time in London—say, if I'm there for several months doing a play—then those aspects of my accent might become pronounced for a time.

D.M. Do you think having had an international upbringing and developing that mid-ocean accent has actually helped you as an actor?

K.T. I think it definitely has. First of all, my whole upbringing has allowed me look at things differently than a lot of Americans. I won't have the same kind of reference and framework for a lot of ideas that somebody who has only lived in one country all their life might have, whether they realized it or not. Growing up overseas gave me the opportunity to hear different accents, different inflection patterns, different rhythms, and I think it has always been helpful because the cadences of language are incredibly different around the world. I don't care for German cadences at all but boy, if you want something said a certain way then they've got a rhythm that just works, you know? I don't like listening to it but it really works and I've used it.

People often say they can't place my accent, and that's a good thing. Growing up in multiple cultures was good for me, because I'm not marked as having a recognizable, easily identifiable accent. I think having an immediately identifiable homebase is probably not good for actors. How many actors have had to spend time, sometimes years even, getting rid of their accents? It is too limiting.

In addition to classical vocal training, I think it's also useful for young actors to study foreign languages, because different languages use your voice in different ways. It's great vocal exercise. I'm fully bilingual in Spanish and I can speak quite a bit of Italian and French.

D.M. Very cool.

K.T. My father used to say, "If you have only one language, you have only one way of thinking." He was a wise man.

D.M. It might be interesting to do a role in another language.

K.T. I've never done a role entirely in another language, but I have done roles where I had to use other languages in part. For awhile, I toyed with the idea of doing a Spanish language version of *Virginia Woolf*. Who knows, maybe one of these days I'll get around to it.

D.M. Wow, that would be an interesting challenge for you.

K.T. Wouldn't it, though? That's what attracts me to it.

D.M. Do you find it easy to do accents? Or is it something you really have to work at?

K.T. It comes pretty easily to me. But I do think you need to have a kind of an ear for it, like you might have for music.

D.M. That makes sense.

K.T. I think you need to be able to hear the rhythms and pitch, just like you might in music. If you naturally have great pitch, I think it is probably much easier to learn new accents. Accents can always be learned, but pitch is tougher. You can study it, but to some degree you may just have to be born with it.

D.M. That's true. Some people can take singing lessons their whole life and never find pitch.

K.T. Yes, it's tough. I have great pitch. And my daughter has excellent, flawless pitch, even better than mine. Mine is good but hers is astounding.

D.M. Well, she's a professional musician.

K.T. And when she was growing up, even as a little kid, whenever she heard an accent she could just do it, immediately. She'd absolutely nail it. It was great, just delightful.

D.M. Career-wise, do you think it's ever been hard for you to get past your voice because of its iconic properties? I could see how it could occasionally be a detriment.

K.T. It has only become iconic over the years. At first it was actually very much in my way. As I said, in my early twenties I looked like a total ingénue, I'm this beautiful young blondish thing, but as soon as I open my mouth I can't get cast as an ingénue. And most of the parts for women at that age were ingénue parts, so that was a real problem. Nobody wanted a Juliet who sounded like an adult, it just didn't work. So in the beginning that was actually frustrating for me because they simply didn't write many strong women characters at that age with deep, solid voices.

Luckily, *Body Heat* came along and the voice absolutely worked for that. It started to become an attraction and an asset where it had previously been something of a liability. But if you look at my early roles, I did play many women years older than myself. Up until *Virginia Woolf* I played women that were older than me, basically. Now I actually often play younger. Mrs. Robinson was thirty-seven, and I was forty-eight when I played her.

D.M. Do you often have to pitch your voice higher in a performance, since it is so naturally low?

K.T. Of course, when the role demands it. For example, I did try and keep my voice light in *Serial Mom*, at a higher pitch. And I guess I played my own age there, kind of. So there were exceptions to my not playing my age along the way.

But by this point in my career my voice is so recognizable that it also becomes a bit of a hurdle because you hear the voice and you go, "Oh, it's Kathleen Turner." So I have to work a little harder sometimes to make people forget it's me when I'm doing a character, because everyone knows the voice.

D.M. I think there are only a handful of famous actors in history that have probably had to deal with voice recognition on the level that you have had to deal with it.

K.T. Well, you know, if you pick up a phone, dial someone you haven't met, and you say, "Hello, may I speak to so and so" and they go, "Kathleen Turner?", you know you're in a little trouble. I will say this—one asset of the voice is that it will get me a seat at any restaurant in town. When I call someone up and say, "Hello, this is Kathleen Turner," they respond, "Why, yes it is!"

D.M. I think you, Morgan Freeman, James Earl Jones and Jack Nicholson should form a club of some kind.

K.T. James and I have actually talked about this.

D.M. Have you really?

K.T. Yes, but he says he doesn't have to worry about it because he's more or less retired.

D.M. And that voice is his bread and butter.

K.T. Of course it is, and it has been for forever.

D.M. CNN probably sends him a lot of checks.

K.T. Oh, right! "This is *CNN*."

D.M. My favorite thing that has been done with your voice was actually the episode of *Sesame Street* you did where the Count is goading you to read a screenplay he's written, and the entire script is just a list of numbers.

K.T. I remember that. He urges me to keep going because he likes listening to my voice read numbers.

D.M. It's hilarious, he gets really excited listening to you count. I'm not sure there's been a better sort of reflection of the iconic properties of your voice than that.

K.T. It's so funny when people say, you know, that silly old cliché, "She could read the phonebook and I'd listen to it." I've gotten that a lot. And that *Sesame Street* sketch was basically that, I was just reading a list of numbers. So there you go, folks!

D.M. That bit is actually a borderline subversive piece of comedy. It comedically tests the patience of the audience. It's about five minutes of you reading numbers and getting increasingly frustrated. As the Count urges you to keep counting and counting, there's this question of how long the show is going to let the sketch run. The comic timing and limit-pushing is really impressive.

K.T. It's a wonderful show and I was honored to be asked to appear on it.

D.M. That scene is on YouTube. If you haven't seen it recently, you should watch it, it's so funny.

K.T. I should check it out.

D.M. Do you find yourself having to approach a role differently when you are doing voiceover acting, like in *Monster House*, *Who Framed Roger Rabbit*, and *The Simpsons*?

On her episode of The Simpsons, *"Lisa vs. Malibu Stacy," Kathleen played the creator of Malibu Stacy, a doll that Lisa campaigned against because she felt it was a sexist representation of young women. In part for its positive political content, it is among the series' most critically acclaimed episodes.*

K.T. It's great fun, but yes, it's a different process with its own unique set of challenges. I used to do occasional radio dramas for the BBC, we did radio plays of a couple of the *V.I. Warshawski* novels. We did this passage at one point and the producer came on the headphones and said, "That was great, but I could see your smile but the audience can't."

So the challenge became, how do you *hear* a smile? That sort of thing is great fun to wrestle with for an actor.

Kathleen reprised the Warshawski role for the BBC radio productions of the books Deadlock *and* Killing Orders. Deadlock *was also the novel on which the film* V.I. Warshawski *was based.*

Doing voiceover is fun because the timing is so exact. No matter how you read it, the timing can't change. So within that parameter, you do it as many different ways as you can. You give them humorous reads, serious reads, somber reads, playful reads, sexy reads, but the running time on all of the reads is identical. It's really cool.

D.M. It must be frustrating for you, with those roles, since you are such a physical actor, to have only the vocal part of the performance be in your control.

K.T. I give a physical performance regardless. I move in the recording booth as much as I can without being away from the microphone. I can't seem to separate that—I start gesturing and doing the movement, I can't help myself.

D.M. And they videotape the actors during the recording sessions, for the animators.

K.T. Usually, but primarily for lip-matching. But I imagine that some of the physicality of an actor's performance in the booth must make it into the animator's renderings of the character. Anything you can give the animators can only help them.

D.M. When you are doing animated work do you have images of the character in front of you?

K.T. Sometimes. I usually know what the character is going to look like before I voice her. With Jessica Rabbit, they'd sent me drawings of the character, but also footage of Bob Hoskins performing the scene, where most of the time he's playing to this sort of metal rod that gives him an eyeline for the to-be-animated character. That was useful to have since my character was opposite him, in a way I was having to play the scene opposite him even though I couldn't physically be opposite him and get all the things from him that you would get if you were actually acting directly with another actor.

And then I would get the footage again, but with Jessica sketched over the metal rod, lightly in pencil, only without eyes and a face, just so I could get a sense of how she moved and adjust my breathing accordingly. It was great fun to see it all come together.

D.M. Jessica Rabbit might actually be your most iconic character.

K.T. Perhaps. I have gotten fan mail from grown men who were legitimately turned on by her. A cartoon character. They address the letters "Dear Jessica." It's a little alarming, to say the least!

D.M. Yikes!

K.T. Yeah! But she was great fun to do. One thing the animators did which cracked me up was that they listened for spots where I took a breath in my dialogue, and they seized those as opportunities to make Jessica's breasts heave up and down and bounce around. Hilarious.

And you know, I was huge and pregnant when I recorded her voice! In fact, I missed the last recording session because I was in labor. I called them from the hospital to tell them I wasn't coming in that day.

D.M. Wow. Now I'll never be able to watch *Roger Rabbit* again without thinking about Jessica Rabbit as a pregnant woman.

K.T. As an absolutely enormous, nine-months-pregnant woman, yes!

D.M. That was your first animated role.

K.T. I believe so.

D.M. Was it really trippy the first time you saw the film? It seems like it'd be completely surreal.

K.T. I loved it. The whole production was so fantastic. At the time, live action and animation had never been integrated that seamlessly, with that level of sophistication.

D.M. Even in this age of CGI, it holds up. It's still a dazzling-looking film.

K.T. I totally agree. And it was a privilege to work on. Few actors get the experience of hearing their voice come from an animated character. Oh, it made me laugh. I giggled my butt off the first time I saw it.

D.M. Jessica, like Dolores Benedict in *The Man With Two Brains*, was another comic take on the femme fatale for you.

K.T. Yes, except that, unlike Dolores, Jessica had a heart of gold. If she caused trouble, it wasn't her intent.

D.M. "I'm not bad, I'm just drawn that way."

K.T. Right. It's a funny line, but in some ways it's also the key to her character. She genuinely loves the rabbit. She and Roger, while an odd-looking match, are a great couple. They really love each other, and that's what I had to convince the audience of in my performance.

D.M. Robert Zemekis, like Lawrence Kasdan, is one of a small group of directors you've worked with multiple times. Was the experience of collaborating with him on *Roger Rabbit* different than on *Romancing the Stone*?

K.T. Well, the first time I worked with Bob, he had not done much. I think *Romancing* was only his second or third film.

D.M. It was his third, after *I Wanna Hold Your Hand* and *Used Cars*. I think he had tried to get *Back to the Future* set up before *Romancing*, but it didn't happen because his first two films underperformed at the box office. They're both cult classics now. *Used Cars* is especially good.

K.T. It was actually the success of *Romancing* that enabled him to get *Back to the Future* set up. On *Romancing*, he was a total camera and special effects nerd. Everything with him was about the camera, and you wouldn't believe some of the awkward positions Michael and I would have to get into in order to accommodate what he wanted to do with the camera. But by the time I did *Roger Rabbit* with him, even though that was actually a more effects-driven film than *Romancing*, he had become an excellent actor's director.

D.M. You can tell, watching films like *Cast Away* and *Flight*, that he knows how to direct an actor. Tom Hanks and Denzel Washington are incredible in those movies. It makes me wish Zemekis would make more live-action films.

K.T. I actually did another animated film with him, too.

D.M. Yes. He produced *Monster House*.

K.T. Right. Bob said to me, "You've played the sexiest animated character of all time, now you can play the ugliest." I've always known I was versatile, but I never dreamed I would play an actual house.

D.M. I liked that film.

K.T. I think it's scarier than it needs to be for a children's film, and I didn't love what they ultimately did with my character, but there are things about the film that I really admire.

D.M. Radio plays seem like such a relic from a bygone era. What was it like to do the ones you did for the BBC? I haven't heard them, were they very traditional radio dramas, a full two hours long?

K.T. Yes. They were great fun to do. You've got all the sound effects going on all around you, so it's not that hard to imagine the locations. For example, there was this scene where we were supposed to be in a car driving, so we sat on these chairs and they put up these plexiglass barriers around us so our voices would sound like they were coming off windows, like in the interior of a car. And the sound effects people would be doing all of this interesting stuff all the time to fill in the environment. That was just great fun.

D.M. And you did a similarly styled performance of *The Graduate* for National Public Radio.

K.T. Yes. We did that one before a live audience in an auditorium. That was interesting, because we had all these cues marked on the stage floor, so you always knew your depths of sound with regard to the placement of the microphone at the front of the stage. And we had a wonderful sound effects person pouring drinks, clinking glasses, lighting cigarettes, that sort of thing. It was so much fun, I loved it.

D.M. When I hear you talk about the physical things you do while you are doing the voice acting, even though no audience will ever see those things, it makes me think about how often people do that in their everyday life.

K.T. How do you mean?

D.M. Well, for example, thinking about how people speak on their cell phones while driving or walking down the street, they are always gesturing or making facial expressions. If you roll your eyes while talking on a cell phone, the person you're talking to can't see it.

K.T. But they can absolutely hear it, if they are paying attention. I'm sure it comes out through the voice.

D.M. Yeah, that's just it. It's hardwired, that relationship between the voice and gesture and expression.

K.T. Imagine trying to talk with absolutely no expression and no movement. Don't you think it would automatically have to make your voice almost monotone? Could you keep your face emotionless and convincingly express happiness, passion and enthusiasm? It would be tough.

D.M. There were radio actors long before there were television actors, and I wonder if they were really up and moving around in their performances or if was just a different style of acting that was based entirely in the voice. Can you do a performance where it is literally all in the voice?

K.T. I don't think you could entirely separate the voice from physical action. I know I couldn't.

D.M. A couple of weeks ago I watched the television remake of *Rear Window* that Christopher Reeve starred in.

K.T. I missed that.

D.M. The original is pretty close to the best-made film of all time for me—I go back and forth between it and *Taxi Driver*—so I was skeptical going into it. I watched it as a big fan of Reeve's, but I'm happy to report it's actually a pretty good remake. It's well-done.

K.T. I'll have to check it out.

D.M. Anyway, I mention it because I believe that Reeve did the film while he was still on his ventilator at least part-time, so not only did he only have his face and his voice as instruments in his performance, but his voice was limited by the strict rhythm of his ventilator. His speech patterns were restricted and they tried to edit around it the best they could, but ultimately what Reeve did with it was very interesting.

He uses his vocal rhythms to create a character that is significantly darker than the one Jimmy Stewart played in the original. He gives a weird-in-a-good-way performance where he ratchets up the edgy darkness of that voyeuristic character to the point where he comes across as quite a creepy guy. And yet, he also never loses your sympathy or his position in the narrative as the hero. And he does it all with his voice. It's actually quite a remarkable piece of acting. He deservedly won a Screen Actors Guild Award for it.

K.T. We did *Switching Channels* together. He was a sweetheart, a true gentleman.

D.M. I always thought he was underrated as an actor, unfairly typecast as Superman. He was incredible in this twisted little thriller he made with Morgan Freeman called *Street Smart*.

K.T. A sad loss.

D.M. Do you get asked to do a lot of voice-over narration work?

K.T. Less than you'd think. Just like with commercial voice-overs, if your voice is too recognizable, producers are actually a little hesitant because they fear that the audience will be thinking about the narrator, or trying to place the narrator's voice, and not thinking about the content of the show.

Kathleen actually received a Grammy nomination for a work of narration, as part of an ensemble of actors nominated in the Best Spoken Word category for The Complete Shakespeare Sonnets *album in 2000.*

So I don't do a lot of narration work. I'll do it when it's for a cause I really believe in. I was honored to provide the narration for the documentary *Answering the Call*, which was about New York's courageous response to the events of 9/11. Like many New Yorkers, I felt quite helpless after that day, and narrating that documentary was one of the ways I found that I could give back to the city I love so much, and to the brave firefighters, police officers, and EMTs who responded on that day.

D.M. So do you think that the recognizability of your voice has cost you many roles?

K.T. I don't think so, but that's hard for me to say. If they didn't want a woman character to stand out too much, then the voice definitely hurt me. But that's okay, I don't want parts that don't stand out anyway. I suspect the voice has gotten me many more roles than it's lost me.

D.M. Has anyone ever asked you to change your voice significantly?

K.T. Not really. Why would they? If you hire me, you hire my voice. I will change my voice sometimes to fit a character—for example, I had more middle-American inflections in *Peggy Sue*—but the basic quality of my voice, its timbre and resonance, is very communicative and that's something I want in all my roles. I've worked very hard on my voice over the years, to increase the resonance in it, and that's something I'm not willing to intentionally limit.

To change your voice is to change the way you communicate with people, on a fundamental level. It amazes me how few people think about that. Really, anyone could benefit from voice training, not just actors. I don't think most people realize how much the voice is a part of how they present themselves, how they come across to the people around them. It's the primary tool of communication in our lifetime. People spend all this time thinking about what to wear, what makeup to put on, how to present themselves visually, and so little time concentrating on what they can do with their voices. You can control a room with a good voice. Hearing is your strongest and most used sense. There's a great book, *Use and Training of the Human Voice*, by a voice teacher named Arthur Lessac, that everyone should read. He wrote brilliantly about how to effectively use one's voice.

D.M. That's great advice for young actors: get to know your voice and how to use it.

K.T. That would be near the top of the list. You can't be an actor, period, unless you've done that work. You have to know your voice, period.

ADVICE FOR DEVELOPING ACTORS

DUSTIN MORROW What are the questions that are asked of you most frequently by young actors?

KATHLEEN TURNER "How do I get started?" That's number one. I have to tell them, honestly, that it's been over thirty-five years since I started. So I imagine that a lot has changed and I'm not sure that my advice is entirely useful anymore. But one thing I do suggest to young actors is to try to get around to the major casting directors in town. Don't wait until you have representation before going after casting directors. Submit your photo and resume to all of them. If a casting director sees your face over and over again, they actually begin to believe they know your work because they know your face.

And ask casting directors if you can be a reader for them. Being a reader means that you're not being auditioned—you are off camera, off to the side. But every casting director needs someone there to read the characters opposite those being auditioned. And that's a lot of exposure to a casting director for an unknown actor. When we're casting a play that I'm doing, they will go through at least two sessions of general casting and narrow it down to three to five actors before I come in to read and work specifically with those last five choices. So that's a lot of time that a reader could be doing my role in front of a casting director.

D.M. That's a paying job.

K.T. The reader is usually a paying job, yeah. But more importantly, the casting director becomes very familiar with you and you get to meet different directors and producers and other actors. Even though your job is not necessarily to stand out, or even to interpret the character that you're reading, you're still there in front of the casting director. Back when I was starting out, agencies were required, I think once a month, to have an open auditioning process. And whoever came in, sort of like an open mic night at a nightclub or comedy club—whoever signed up first, got in.

That's actually how I got my first agent. I went to one of those things, did my four little audition pieces: a classic, a modern, a comedy, and something else. Each piece was about three minutes long. And at the end of my pieces, they asked me to sign. Which is somewhat unusual, of course. I'm not sure if the agencies still have those events on a monthly basis.

D.M. Was the idea just to give struggling actors an opportunity?

K.T. Yes, to give them a window where there wasn't one. It was so that it didn't seem like such a closed system, that discovery of new talent. I'm not sure, as I say, whether they do that or not anymore. But I think, obviously, getting to know casting directors is a very valuable thing to do.

D.M. What other resources allow you to network successfully?

K.T. Teachers with connections. Ask your teachers and professors to make recommendations of people in the industry you should know, especially agencies and casting directors.

D.M. Do you think, to that end, that there's more value in studying acting in New York as opposed to somewhere else?

K.T. Not necessarily. Chicago seems to be a great place to do theater now. They are open to auditioning and discovering new talent, and Chicgao has a wonderful improvisational theater scene.

D.M. I have actor friends in L.A. that do theater work, but I get the feeling that their work is not getting noticed in any significant way.

K.T. I haven't worked onstage there extensively, but my impression is that L.A. is not all that serious about theater. I don't think that there's much value placed in theater there. If a show comes through with the original Broadway cast, then you'll probably see full houses, but for a developing piece, an off-Broadway piece, it's tough. Tourists might go, but the industry people won't. The people you need to see you as an up-and-coming actor won't go out to the theater. It's definitely harder to get noticed in Los Angeles. Young actors there spend a lot of money assembling these reels, these DVDs, with one-second clips of them playing a background role on a TV show. God bless 'em, that's tough going.

D.M. "Police officer #7." "Man on Boat." "Friend #2."

K.T. Yeah, those kinds of roles. I think you should have at least one line before you put it on your reel. Don't put "extra" work on your reel.

Extras, or background talent, are the performers with no lines of dialogue, who fill out the background of a shot. For example, in a restaurant scene, all of the people at the tables in the background, pretending to have conversations, are extras.

D.M. The presence of formal training on an actor's resume is really valuable.

K.T. It can be of great value. It can open doors. Students who have on their resume that they took my class have an automatic entry into several casting directors here in New York. If the casting director sees my name, the actor will be seen. But that wouldn't necessarily work in Los Angeles.

D.M. Do your students ever ask you about balancing your professional life and your personal life?

K.T. Not so much the men, but the young female students ask me that question a lot. "You had a very long and successful marriage, you raised a kid who grew up well, you had a busy, marvelous career. How do you manage to have all of that at the same time?" And my answer is, and always will be, that either you or your husband will have to have enough money to hire a wife. Because you cannot do it all.

You cannot be the one who makes sure there's milk in the fridge everyday, who is always available to pick up the child from school or take her to an extracurricular activity. You cannot do it all. You have to be able to hire someone to fill in for all the roles that mothers and wives usually provide. That's a tough answer, but if you are going to go to the level of success I have found, it's the honest truth. There's simply no way around it.

It's really hard to do this job and raise a small child. It's a delicate balancing act. My schedule used to be that I would get up early in the morning to get Rachel up and off to school, then I would go back to bed for a couple hours. Then I would wake up again, eat, and be off to the theater by 5:00. By the time I got home after the show, Rachel was in bed. That's tough, only having that limited interaction with your child.

D.M. Many of my students tend to be wiser about the industry than those I used to see in my courses. Do you feel that, when you get new students, they're generally pretty savvy about what they're going to have to do to succeed and how they're going to do it?

K.T. Yes and no. I think most of them have some sense of how to plug into the system, go through the motions to get their career underway, but few of them understand that to really get ahead, sometimes you have to buck the system and do things your own way.

D.M. For example?

K.T. Well, this seems obvious, but sometimes, if you set your sights on a role, you have to approach the people who'll enable you to do it. I'm amazed at how many actors just won't do that. It doesn't even occur to them. But you have to be proactive. Go to the roles, don't wait for them to come to you. When I finally felt ready to do *Virginia Woolf*, I went after it. I couldn't wait for it to fall in my lap because it never would have on its own.

D.M. But do think that acting students generally have a firm understanding of what the profession entails now?

K.T. I think the students I encounter now think of it as more of a business than I did when I started out, and they think about how to manipulate it as a business. As opposed to focusing on it specifically as a passion or as a vocation like any other. For me, it was my passion, and it was my job, and that was it.

I was talking to a young actor about a week ago. He was outlining how he planned to compare and contrast and pit against each other managers, agents, and publicity representatives, and he was so analytical and dry that it came off as almost cold-blooded to me. But he's probably extremely sensible to do that, because the business is tougher than ever. I was always afraid to be that analytical about the process because I didn't want it to interfere with my willful naïveté about the work. The idea that I do a role because I *have* to do this role, not because this was a better offer than the other role, or has a chance to be a longer run, or will allow me to work with more important people. It was always because

I loved a role and had to do the role. Not because it was necessarily the best director or the best contacts that I would be gaining from it.

Things are different now than when I started out. There was a lot of competition when I started out, and a lot of money in Hollywood and on Broadway, but nothing like there is today. Perhaps I would have gone a different path if I were coming up today. I don't think I'd be happier, but perhaps I'd be wealthier.

D.M. If you had been that kind of actor, you probably would have just made nineteen versions of *Body Heat* . That's the kind of choice that that young actor you spoke with would make.

K.T. Believe me, I was offered nineteen versions of *Body Heat—Body Heat 2*, *Body Heat 3*, *Son of Body Heat*.

D.M. I like *Son of Body Heat!* I want to see that.

K.T. It was just never going to happen for me. I could never do it. But this isn't to say that that kind of actor doesn't have artistic integrity as well. It's just the way that they think of it as a manipulation of an industry, of a system, that I find rather chilling. That extends to most roles in the entertainment industry, it's not just actors.

D.M. But there's something so organic and pure about acting that it sort of feels stranger to hear it coming from an actor.

K.T. Yes. I've never taken a role because it might lead to another role. The role has always been the end itself. But I'm naïve. Willfully naïve.

D.M. Yeah, but I think that's a good thing, that naïvete.

K.T. So do I! But it may not be the most sensible thing in this market. Addressing the industry now may require a different mindset to reach the level of success I've experienced.

D.M. I don't know that careers built on manipulating the industry have the longevity that a career like yours has had, though. I think that if you're making choices that way then, inevitably, you're going to make some bad choices.

K.T. Well, as I said earlier, the worst choice I've made as a film actor was to do *Switching Channels*, a movie that I did for the money, so there you go. It was the only time I ever did that, and I've always regretted it.

The other problem with building a career on a manipulation or "playing" of the industry is that the turnover within the business side of the industry is so fast that your connections, the people you depend on to advance your career, may not be tomorrow the people that they are today.

D.M. Right. Someone who is the head of a studio today is unemployed tomorrow, and every project he was developing is gone with him.

K.T. It happens all the time, turnover in the entertainment industry is constant. So if your career is tied too closely to some of these specific personalities or positions within the industry, then you're always, to some degree, hanging by a thread.

D.M. Some of my best friends are actors and—

K.T. My condolences.

D.M. Oh now, I love my actor friends! They're so fun to hang out with and yet there's this feeling I get that no matter how close I get to them that they're speaking this language I'll never fully understand, or that there's this bond between them that there's no way I could ever have with them. There's a support system there that I see few other places in the arts.

K.T. It's a tough business, we actors have to stick together.

D.M. You mentioned earlier that you didn't have a familial support system for you regarding your decision to become an actor in your earlier career.

K.T. No, definitely not. My father was dead-set against my pursuing such an "impractical" profession. And my mother just tolerated it. But you have to understand the family I was coming from. When I was in college my older sister was getting her doctorate in urban sociology and city planning. My older brother was getting his doctorate in psychology and hospital administration. And my younger brother went on to get a doctorate in government administration. And here I was, the black sheep, getting my BFA in acting. At the time, my mother told me that my siblings were all working to do things that would benefit mankind, that would help people. And the implication was that what I was doing was somehow selfish.

And I would say to her that if I could manage to do the work that I hoped to do as an actor, then I could ultimately help more people than my siblings would ever meet in their careers. Years later she wrote me a letter and told me that I was right. And I returned it with a letter of apology, for being so bull-headed at the time. I felt that through much of my life I undervalued her, and if I have one great regret in life, that's it. She was an amazing person, a true heroine to me.

D.M. So if not from your family, where did you initially find that support? I guess you have to find it among a community of actors then.

K.T. You find it in the work. Each production, each job, be it a film or a play, creates a sort of false world, where you spend fourteen hours a day, everyday, with a small group of people. You spend more time with these people, the crew and cast, than you do with your friends and family, for months at a time. And it creates this kind of false intimacy. It doesn't feel false, it's just that when the job ends, it ends. So it's false in that sense. Maybe "artificial" is a better word.

Because the day you wrap that film, it's "see ya later." I'll never forget the day we wrapped *Romancing the Stone*, we wrapped it here in New York and we'd been together for at least four months, in New York, then Mexico, then a studio, then back in New York. I lived here in New York, but almost everyone in the entire crew and the rest of the cast, they all lived in Los Angeles. So I literally woke up the day after we wrapped and realized that ninety people that represented my most intimate relationships, for months on end, had vanished overnight. And I had barely talked to my outside friends for all of those months. To wake up that morning and realize all of those people were gone, I felt completely alone.

So you become so interdependent on each other, which is a very good thing, as long as you have good people around you. And the construction of it may be artificial, and you may not stay in touch after the film or the play wraps, but for the time that you're working, that interdependence creates a true friendship. I mean, I need that second camera operator and he needs me. And I need my dresser in the theater, and she needs me to do her job. We need each other, and that creates trust as well as a friendship. And it's very intimate, even though it's temporary.

D.M. I feel like if I went through that again and again that I would get kind of jaded.

K.T. No, you don't get hardened because, during the process, during the work, the needs don't change and the relationships don't change.

You have to get a little tough about losing everybody though—suddenly and all at once. It's too difficult otherwise. And you have to decide who, and how much of the relationship, to hang on to. It's harder for me to work in film because almost everyone in film is based in Los Angeles. In theater it's much easier for me to keep up with friendships, because most theater people live here. But when it comes to film, I won't see or talk to some of my closest collaborators for years.

D.M. It's important for actors to have friends outside show business.

K.T. Beyond important. It's absolutely necessary, to keep your sanity. First of all, I think it's extremely boring to listen to a bunch of actors sitting around together talking about acting. It's what you do all day, why the heck would you want to get together in your free time and rehash it? My best friend is an accountant. I have this women's poker game we do once a month, and I'm usually the only actor at the table. I don't have any really close actor friends. I have friends who are actors, but we're not that close.

It's boring. I would much rather hear what my friend the accountant did that day than what another actor did. Because I just did the same thing they did. I already know that world, I already live in it.

D.M. And having all those friends from outside your industry informs your life as an actor. You pull things from them.

K.T. Of course. I get a lot of information from them that I wouldn't necessarily get if I just stayed within the actor world.

D.M. The arts can be a cocoon that can become easy to get trapped inside of.

K.T. Indeed. That's where your family and your friends come in, to free you from that. And your other work, like the service and charity work and advocacy. All those interests take me outside and free me from my theater and film work for awhile. If I'm not working, I'm happier doing that stuff than following the latest theater or film. I'm willfully ignorant of who is doing what in the business. Someone will ask me to go to a huge new movie, and I'll say, "What's that? Never heard of it." I have to pause for a moment. But that's good. It's good to get away from your work world, because your work world can exhaust you.

STUDYING ACTING

DUSTIN MORROW As a professor, I think it's really important for a young actor to study at a university, even though many of them would rather skip it and go straight into the business.

KATHLEEN TURNER I think university is excellent because I think you need time to grow up. I think you need those years to simply mature. And you need the time to get some experience under your belt. This is why I don't think a conservatory—something like Julliard, say, or a school whose main purpose and curriculum is only one art form—I don't think that that is such a good thing. I think you need as broad an education as you can possibly get, because there is nothing an actor does not draw upon, or shouldn't be able to draw upon.

And you should go to a university where you can get a lot of time onstage. In a conservatory or an acting school, like some of the British schools like the Royal Academy of Dramatic Art or the London Academy of Music and Dramatic Art, you're often not even *allowed* onstage for two years. You have to study and learn their technique before they will let you participate in a production. I actually auditioned for the Royal Academy of Dramatic Art after I finished high school in London. And when they told me that I wouldn't be allowed onstage for two years, I thought, "What a waste of time." I also thought, "How will I learn what it is that makes my acting unique if I spend my whole education acquiring their defined set of skills?" If everyone were able to simply conquer the skills laid out by some school or some program, then in theory anyone could be an actor.

That's obviously not true, though. It is the unique outlook, the unique interpretation, and the ability to enact the thoughts and emotions of a character—to communicate—that makes an actor stand out. You don't stand out because you can replicate a specific style of acting as well as the thousands of other actors who studied that style. Don't waste two to four years learning someone else's technique, only to learn that their technique doesn't serve you and your unique quality as an actor. So I suggest that people go to a university where they have many disciplines and much greater opportunities to be onstage, because at those universities, acting is simply *doing*. The more you do it, the more you learn. And the less you do it, the less you learn. It is not something you can learn from a book, it is not something you can learn by talking to yourself in the mirror. You need to be out doing it in front of an audience.

D.M. How do you understand the different schools of acting to operate, and where would you put yourself in the spectrum, if you had to position yourself somewhere?

K.T. Well, granted I don't know a great deal about the traditional schools of acting, but my understanding of the spectrum is that it runs from a feeling of disconnection, an ability to reproduce the impression of an emotion, without actually feeling the emotion, over to feeling the emotion and having it be a very real thing.

D.M. The latter would be the Method school.

K.T. Right, it would be Stanislavsky, Strasberg, Hagen. And the other would be a more classically British, like Diderot.

D.M. I'm less familiar with that one.

K.T. Well, the idea is that as an actor you can create some verisimilitude in your performance—the appearance of truth in the performance, without there actually being genuine, truly felt real emotion behind the performance. It's all technique. For example, you could get really angry in a performance, but you wouldn't actually feel any anger inside you, where the method actor might tap into genuine anger.

At a base level, I think I have in a way combined the English and American stage acting traditions. In England there's more emphasis on the vocal and the spoken word than on the physical, and in America it's the other way around. I like to think that I've incorporated the best of both traditions into my practice.

287

D.M. Unlike most things you might study in college, there's no "acting test" at the end of the curriculum. So how does someone know when they are really, finally, an actor? It seems like there are a lot of self-proclaimed actors out there who never seem to do any acting.

K.T. Well, as you said, there's no test for someone as an actor. So anyone can say they are an actor, even if they have no skill for it and never book jobs doing it.

D.M. Because it's an art as well as a profession. If I make music, even if it's terrible music, then I can call myself a musician.

K.T. Yes, but I'm talking about acting as a career. If you aren't working as an actor, then you are not a professional actor. You are something else, and you act on occasion.

D.M. That's a tough truth that many actors can't deal with.

K.T. Every professional actor goes through periods where they aren't working, but if you are spending, overall, more time not working than you are working, then you're probably an aspiring actor, not a professional actor. I hope that doesn't sound discouraging, because that's not how I meant it. Lord knows I was an aspiring actor for some time.

D.M. I think the perception of your career is that you came out of nowhere, very young.

K.T. Well, I was fairly young when *Body Heat* happened, and *Body Heat* made me so big so fast. But I struggled. A lot of hard work and blood, sweat and tears led up to *Body Heat*.

It was just that I was lucky enough, once I found some success, to keep that ball rolling quickly. I got an off-Broadway show, then a soap opera, then a Broadway show, all during the first year I lived in New York. I was on the radar of a number of prominent casting agents. I found out after *Body Heat* happened that several casting agents were watching me carefully and had a private bet as to who would cast me in a film first.

I know I've been lucky as hell in my career, I've worked hard and I've been good. And at the end of the day, no matter what anyone tells you, that's the only formula that works. Simply being good is not enough, simply working hard isn't enough, and simply being lucky isn't enough.

But when you're lucky and you're good and you really keep at it, you're golden.

D.M. Graduate school can be valuable for actors. Many of my favorite actors have MFAs in the craft.

K.T. Of course it can be, but I suggest that young women, in particular, do not necessarily go on to graduate school, because for young women age is tremendously important to their careers. A man can wait until he's forty to start acting. A woman cannot. It's not fair, but women just need to get out there quicker. Many major actors, like Jack Nicholson and Morgan Freeman, didn't start acting with major exposure until they were well into their thirties or forties. That just doesn't happen for women.

D.M. Actresses also lose their commercial viability more quickly.

K.T. Not so much in theater, but definitely in film. To the small degree to which women have commercial viability in film, that is. Although we've made inroads, Hollywood is still largely run by men, and they don't really think women sell tickets, regardless of how successful their last film was. So the idea of seriously discussing rising or declining box office clout as it applies to actresses is kind of inherently ridiculous.

D.M. Why can't women start playing leads later in their careers?

K.T. I don't know. It's sad, but it's simply a fact of the business. By forty, if you're not yet playing leads, then in all likelihood you won't start. You may have a career as a good, solid supporting actor, but the leads will have passed you by. I'm only able to continue playing leads now because I established myself when I was young and was able to maintain career longevity.

Having said all that, playing leads isn't the end-all and be-all. The career of a supporting actor can be a wonderful one. Everyone knows that the supporting roles are juicier than the leading roles. And there are responsibilities that go with being a lead that have nothing to do with playing the part and carrying the narrative of the play or the film.

D.M. Like what?

K.T. When you are the lead actor in a play, it's your job, along with the director, to set the tone, the level of commitment, the level of courtesy and respect. You are the moral center not just of the play, but the production. You have to lead by example. If you don't respect the work of your collaborators, you can't expect the stagehands, or the grips, or anyone else to do so. You literally have to lead the production, but in a way that doesn't place you in a position of privilege.

That's especially true with travelling productions. When traveling with a play, it's important that the entire production work as a team, and that means that no one, not even the lead actors, gets preferential treatment. I shouldn't get better housing or more perks because I'm famous. That creates friction. Traveling with a production is such an intense, tiring experience for everyone involved, and it shouldn't be easier on me than anyone else, even if I might shoulder more responsibility for the success of the production. We have to function as one unit.

D.M. Obviously it's a different game in film, where stars have huge trailers and insane perks.

K.T. As with anything, Hollywood is always going to do things its own way.

D.M. It's great to hear you champion supporting actors. I think a lot of young actors only want to play leads, and they have some warped idea that if they don't end up with a career playing leads that somehow they've failed. The business is so tough, I would think that just being a working, regularly employed actor is enough.

K.T. Well, I understand the desire to play leads, but it's not necessary to feel rewarded and nurtured by your work as an actor. Many actors have made a great life as supporting players. You see these people over and over again on TV shows or in Broadway plays that are solid supporting actors, that have a good income and a career that will support them throughout their lives. But they're not the stars. They're not the leads, and they never will be. So if playing leads is what you truly want, then that has to happen earlier than later. Get out there as soon as you can, but after you've gone to university and had time to grow your confidence and get comfortable on stage.

D.M. There are many other specific disciplines or things that they can do at a university that would be really useful to a student studying acting.

K.T. Physical training. Totally. And I don't mean simply the study of movement, I mean take a sport. Become an athlete. One of the benefits I've had from growing up as an athlete is the ability I have to control my muscles. I can isolate and move independently any muscle in my body. I know the name of every muscle in my body, and I know how they interact with each other. I'm proud of that, it took a lot of work and practice to be able to do that. I have the kind of control over my body that a professional dancer has. And it hasn't come easy, I've worked at it.

D.M. And it's all about connecting that control of the body back to the mind.

K.T. That's absolutely what it's about. Simply working out, getting in shape, is pointless for an actor if they don't understand about how to link their physicality to their mental processes. As you think about the role, the body responds. When you warm up before a performance, getting your body loose and your mind clear at the same time, you are creating a neural pathway. Warm-ups are less about the actual preparation of the body's muscles—although that is important—than they are about strengthening and unifying the mind-body connection.

D.M. Are there specific sports that you think it's worthwhile for actors to get involved with?

K.T. Any sport is better than none, although some of them lend themselves to the training of an actor better than others. Gymnastics is a great sport for actors to take up. So is swimming. They would set you up for almost anything you could ever have to do as an actor. Work on your ability to say to your left quad, "Move," and find yourself halfway across the room. Learn to be hyper-aware of the individual parts of your body and how they interconnect. When my yoga instructor says to me, "Activate your left calf," I know what that means and I know how to do it.

I once took one of my Pilates instructors to the acting class I teach at New York University. And I had the students do a solid hour of core work, to think about where their breathing comes from, where their support system is. That was on a Tuesday. When I came in on Thursday, they were in such pain. Because they simply didn't understand what you need to do to truly support your body so that you can move in any direction, and sit, stand, kneel, fall, and do whatever you need to do as a performer. The poor dears were so sore! Three decades older than them, and I was in better shape than all of them. I have to admit, that felt good!

So I would recommend any type of core training. I would also recommend a sport that requires heavy hand-eye coordination—baseball, volleyball, fencing, badminton. Anything that has eye-hand coordination will prepare you to have a special relationship on stage with not only your fellow actors, but all the props and set dressing. It's very useful to be able to immediately assess and understand the exact distance and degree that you are from everything around you.

D.M. How about studying something like writing or psychology? Those seem like useful skills for an actor.

K.T. I can't see that they wouldn't be useful. I'd think any kind of good writer could give you insights into a character—why a character behaves the way they do. And psychoanalysis can be part of breaking down a character.

D.M. Put your character on the couch.

K.T. Yes, put her on the couch. As if you were trained to do it.

D.M. How about training in music?

K.T. Voice lessons can be very beneficial to a developing actor. I would suggest some basic singing as well, even if they have no interest in musical theater. Find out if you have pitch, if you have an ear that can hear pitch. Even if you have zero interest in ever doing a musical, studying pitch will make a difference in how you voice your characters.

D.M. What else?

K.T. History. Take tons of history. Learn about people, about civilizations, about the evolution of our society. Learn how we've evolved to where we are now and the basis of that evolution. Learn about how that evolution emerged from decisions that we made. In the same way that you'd think about the decisions of a character you were going to play, think about the decisions that we've made that have gotten us where we are.

D.M. How about travel?

K.T. I think it's very important to travel. If you have the opportunity and can afford it, study abroad while you are in college.

D.M. I agree 100%. People don't realize how important travel is, how important it is to expose yourself, especially at a young age, to different cultures and ways of life.

K.T. Americans in particular don't travel enough.

D.M. I agree. I have led several study abroad programs, where I teach young people how to navigate foreign cultures with grace, humility, and an open mind.

K.T. It's good that you do that. It's important work.

D.M. It's very rewarding for me. I've seen young people go through incredible changes in their character and their outlook on the world in short periods of time. My study abroad programs are culturally immersive, I want them to experience a location as the people who live there do. I teach them to be travellers and not tourists.

K.T. Where have you taken them?

D.M. I've led programs in London and Dublin, and taught for a program in Northern Ireland.

K.T. Wonderful. How long do you take them overseas for?

D.M. Usually four to six weeks. It's not long, but it doesn't take long to have your eyes opened when you're out of your comfort zone. I believe that travel is a political and moral act—there would be a lot less conflict in the world if more people got a passport.

K.T. Yes, when you travel, you realize that the world isn't such a big place after all, and that we have more in common with people around the world than we think we do. We all want the same basic things—friends, families, food and shelter, a rewarding job and a comfortable life.

D.M. There's a term, "Cultural Quotient," that I believe was coined by the Harvard Business School, that refers to an individual's capacity and willingness to understand and communicate with other cultures. There are exams you can take to measure your C.Q. I think it's used primarily in business schools, but as a professor I feel that it's something that could be extended to programs across universities. The internet and changes in modern communication have shrunk this planet. We need to know how to communicate with one another in all professions, and travel will be the most valuable tool in accomplishing that.

K.T. That's true. And I would encourage anyone who has the opportunity to actually live and work overseas, even if it's only for a short time, to take it. Much of what I have learned about how to interact with other cultures I learned while I was growing up and living in foreign countries.

D.M. And you continue to work overseas to this day.

K.T. Absolutely. I love doing plays in the West End. I did a new play called *Bakersfield Mist*, with the great English actor Ian McDiarmid, not too long ago.

D.M. What do you like about working in London?

K.T. Aside from the fact that I get to live in London for awhile?

D.M. Yeah, aside from that.

K.T. Well, for one thing, the audiences are different.

D.M. How so?

K.T. They're more educated about theater. Not more educated in general, mind you—just more knowledgeable about the traditions and the unspoken rules and behaviors that surround theater and theater-going. Of course, they just flat-out go to the theater more often, which is a huge part of it. Broadway tickets have gotten so expensive that they've gotten out of reach for many Americans. And many of the people who do go to Broadway plays can only afford to go one a year, so of course they're going to go to the sure thing, the blockbuster hit. If you only see one production a year, you're not going to go to something edgy or experimental. The audiences in London will take a chance.

D.M. Is the culture surrounding theater work different over there?

K.T. Tremendously. One thing that frustrates me about the theater scene in New York is the constant need to pigeonhole performers and technicians into limiting categories. You're either a Broadway actor or you're an Off-Broadway actor. You're an actor in plays or you're actor in musical theater. You're a stage actor or you're a TV and film actor. It makes no sense. If you like my work, if you think I'm good, then why do I have to stay in one category?

They just don't do that in London. Of course one of the reasons that they don't do that is that all of the work is so close together. You don't get labeled a TV actor or a stage actor because you can literally do both in the same day. Most of the film and television production in Britain happens in London, so you can act in a TV series during the day and then make it to the West End by evening to do a stage production. My friend Harriet Walter can shoot *The Crown* during the day and then run down to the West End to do *The Tempest* at night. I'm definitely jealous of that.

D.M. How old were you when you moved to London as a kid?

K.T. It was in 1968, so I was fourteen. I was there for all of high school.

D.M. Did your parents just set you loose or were you chaperoned everywhere?

K.T. Oh, my siblings and I were absolutely set loose. This was long before this idea that we need to watch our kids like hawks. Back then you left the house in the morning and your parents didn't want to see you until the end of the day. My brother and I used to jump on the London Underground everyday and just travel around and explore the city. We went everywhere, it was an incredible kind of freedom that most young people today don't experience. I think we must have scared the heck out of our mother to some degree because we probably checked out a lot of neighborhoods we really had no business being in. But that freedom was important in teaching us confidence and independence.

And this is an important reason that I brought my daughter up in New York City. When you're twelve, you get the metro card and you get that sense of being able to take yourself places by yourself. That is an important part of finding a sense of who you are and what you are capable of. My daughter is a very strong, independent woman, and I am sure that the freedom I gave her when she was young is part of that.

D.M. I can't believe your parents let you just run all over London like that.

K.T. They didn't have much choice in the end. We were pretty adventurous, precocious kids. And if you think that's bad, we also used to take the train out of the country on our own.

D.M. To where?

K.T. My older brother and I would often jump on a train and shoot over to Amsterdam. My father had this sort of an honorary aunt who lived there, and we'd show up on her doorstep occasionally and crash for the night. We'd also train over to Paris occasionally, and just walk around. It was great to have all that freedom.

D.M. It sounds amazing. We had very different upbringings. I grew up on a lake out in the country, near a bunch of small towns. My high school graduating class was about forty kids.

K.T. I'm sure that in its own way that was just as lovely.

D.M. I wouldn't trade it for anything, I had an awesome childhood. I spent every summer swimming and skating on a beautiful lake, grilling out in the evening and taking it easy. And the winters were all ice skating and sledding. It was quite idyllic.

K.T. It sounds wonderful.

D.M. We've really digressed.

K.T. Well, we do that.

D.M. We do. Getting back to the study of acting—do you think that it's something you really have to have a natural affinity for? Or do you think you could take somebody who exhibits no skill at it and actually mold them into a good actor, or even a great actor?

K.T. No, at the end of the day, I don't think you can. I think there is an essential element that I've been trying, over the years, to identify. At this point in my life, I think of it as a kind of "communicable compassion." There has to be an inherent compassion in a good actor. A compassion that isn't so much learned as just *there*.

For example, some of the things that human beings are capable of can be pretty awful, or just seem appalling, but if you can ask why the person did this terrible thing they did, and actually begin to understand them, then with that understanding comes compassion. And an actor really has to have that.

And I'm just not convinced that you can teach someone to be compassionate. I think you can be made aware of whether or not you have it, but you can't learn it, so to speak. And I certainly have known people who were born without it and never found it.

D.M. There aren't schools of acting that you respond to positively, that you've liked.

K.T. I never really took any of them too seriously, no.

D.M. Because you didn't get the opportunity? Or just because of that idea you mentioned of not wanting someone else's system to frame how you approach what you do?

K.T. The latter. I don't want to identify with anyone else's system. When I was young, when I was in college, I read many books on acting. And there were some very useful things in those texts. I liked Chekhov's book that focuses on the personal gesture. That the repetition of the personal gesture would help to lead you into a character—I thought that was useful. I can't think of many other ones that I have actually used.

Kathleen is referring to the 1912 book On the Technique of Acting *by Michael Chekhov, the well-regarded Russian-American stage actor and director who was considered by Stanislavski to be his finest student. His techniques have been notably employed by actors such as Jack Nicholson, Marilyn Monroe, and Clint Eastwood.*

D.M. Are there any that made you think the opposite, that "this is not doing it the right way"?

K.T. In a sense, most of them. I usually avoid reading about the theory of acting. I truly believe that one has to find the way one acts, that each individual actor has to find their own unique path. Of course there are tools that can help you, and maybe some of those tools will come from a teacher, or a book, or a fellow actor, but in the end it's up to each actor to build her own unique toolkit. Did I just kill this book?

D.M. No, not at all!

K.T. I have taught acting at NYU and at Studio One on One, so obviously I think there's much you can get from a teacher, from studying acting seriously in an academic setting. I just think that the best thing a teacher can ultimately do is not to say, "This is the way to do it," but to help the growing actor find their own way of doing it well.

D.M. I find Method acting really interesting.

K.T. Oh, brother. Give me a break.

D.M. Not a fan?

K.T. Most Method actors are young and foolish. It's too earnest. Don't take life so seriously, you will enjoy it more.

D.M. Did you ever have any mentors who were actors?

K.T. Not really. To be honest, I think I've gotten more from the great directors I've worked with—Coppola, Huston, Kasdan—than I have from other actors. And then, the learning came out of the rehearsal, the delving and the digging that those directors gave me the room to do. It wasn't so much that they told me what to do, but they helped me find my way of doing it. And that's what I try to help my students with. I don't want them to do things "the Kathleen Turner way," I want to assist them in finding their own ways to do it.

THE PROCESS OF AUDITIONING

DUSTIN MORROW You've mentioned going to open calls, and becoming a reader for casting directors. But there are other ways for a young, unknown actor to get access to agents and casting directors.

KATHLEEN TURNER I'll tell you what some of my students have done, which is really quite exciting to me. About six of them paired up with six young playwrights. They created six new scenes, and together they rented a theatrical space for one night. I think they told me it was about four hundred and fifty dollars, so amongst the twelve of them, this is extremely affordable for one night. They sent out flyers and notices to all the major agencies. What really worked for that workshop in particular, because it was very well-attended, was the fact that it coupled new actors *and* new playwrights. The audience was experiencing new writing as well as getting to see some exciting new actors.

D.M. The skills required of auditioning are different from the skills required of a good actor.

K.T. Oh, they're completely different. You can be a brilliant actor and a lousy auditioner. Auditioning effectively is something every young actor needs to work on. The most important aspect of auditioning, from the actor's perspective, is the ability to do a cold reading well. You have to be extremely good at cold reading.

D.M. Cold reading seems like a somewhat terrifying prospect.

K.T. To you, because you're not an actor. We're used to it. It's basically picking up a script or a side that you've never seen before and being able to make choices right away. They may be the wrong choices, but at least the director or casting director will see that you make firm choices.

A side is a portion of a script, selected by the producer or casting director to use in the audition; often, actors aren't given the sides until they arrive at the audition.

Often at an audition the director or casting director may offer you a little direction, and they may be looking less at your capacity to actually perform as they've requested and more at your willingness to take direction. You would be surprised how many actors cannot take direction and put it to use straight away. They will say, "Yes, I understand," and they will do it exactly the same way they just did it. Those actors don't get the role.

D.M. Is it okay to ask for that direction or do you just have to wait for them to volunteer it?

K.T. It's okay to ask for a little direction, politely. Something along the lines of, "Thank you for having me in today, is there anything else I can show you, or any other way you'd like to see me do this piece?" Just don't be aggressive about it. If they say no, then thank them again and make your exit.

D.M. Are there any errors you see young actors repeatedly making in auditions?

K.T. I've found in all the auditions that I've held for my classes at NYU and Studio One on One, almost universally these young actors have been taught to look just over the head of the person they were auditioning for, into this sort of vague middle distance. That drives me absolutely nuts. I felt like turning around and looking up, and saying, "What the hell are you looking at?" I cannot understand why they were coached not to meet anyone's eyes in an audition. Perhaps they think it's confrontational, perhaps they think that it would make the people auditioning them uncomfortable. I don't know. If they're there as a director, as a reader, as a casting director, or as a writer/producer, they should be able to handle your eye contact.

D.M. Perhaps they're shifting their eyes around a projected, imagined audience.

K.T. I don't think so, unless the imagined audience is one guy in the back, because they focus on a fixed point. It's maddening.

D.M. So what are the other little things that you can do in an audition to give you an edge? You said asking for some direction at the end of the audition can be a good thing. I'd imagine that demonstrates that you can take direction and that you'd be interested in being directed, and that might work to your advantage.

K.T. It's also a little bit of an assumption, a way to demonstrate some confidence without being pushy.

D.M. There's also a social aspect to auditioning.

K.T. Of course. Always be incredibly polite, obviously. Introduce yourself to everyone there, including the reader. Offer your hand. Even if there's some kind of barricade between you, go around it and say, "I'm glad to meet you." The few moments it takes to meet everyone also gives you time to assess the room and time to settle down. That way, you don't just walk in the door and start performing.

D.M. I know it's been a long time since you had to audition for anything, but do you remember specific auditions?

K.T. Oh yeah! Every actor can recall some auditions. I remember the *Body Heat* auditions like they were last week. They went on for some time, it was quite a process. First they were casting it here in New York with two male casting directors, and they refused to allow me to audition because I had no film credits and they felt it would be a waste of their time. I couldn't get in the door. But three months later, I went out to L.A. to audition for a different film, and while I was there, I met a woman casting director named Wallis Nicita, who had heard of me through colleagues in New York. She was handling the *Body Heat* casting in L.A. and asked me to read. I did so, and she ran down the hall and pulled the director and producer into the room and asked me to replicate the audition I'd given moments earlier. They were polite but noncommittal, and I went back to my hotel to start packing. Then I got a call telling me to stick around for another audition the next day, where I'd have to do a scene I'd not seen before.

For that first audition I had dressed up like a total femme fatale—I had on a tight dress, high heels, full makeup, whatever I could do to look mature. I was twenty-five, so I was trying to look older than my years. But the next day I wore blue jeans and a white t-shirt and sneakers, with minimal makeup and glamour. Because there was more to Matty Walker than just the noirish femme fatale aspect. Larry Kasdan handed me a scene to read, and I had a couple minutes to read it over and figure out how I wanted to do it. I decided to make myself comfortable, to just stretch out on the couch in his office. I did the scene laying on his couch, it was very cheeky of me! But it demonstrated Matty's confident sexuality perfectly. Larry said, "I never thought I'd hear that the exact way I heard it in my head when I was writing it." It was a fantastic compliment.

So Larry wanted me, but the studio didn't. I'd been on Broadway and I'd been on *The Doctors*, but I had no film credits and they weren't thrilled about giving me the lead role. So I had to meet all of these studio executives and charm their pants off. You asked about the social aspect of auditioning? Well honey, this was it. I charmed them! I worked that room like you wouldn't believe!

D.M. How did you do it?

K.T. We were in this white-on-white-on-white room—white carpet, white chairs, white everything, and on the middle of this table was this ashtray filled with cigarette butts. And all these executives, reeking of smoke, say, "Can you make us laugh?" As if the role required comedy! So I went into a sort of drunk routine and I threw the script down on the table and it hit this ashtray and sent it flying all over this white rug. I thought, "Okay, that's it . . . it's over," and I'm down on my knees, picking up the cigarette butts. And then they started laughing! Somehow it worked.

D.M. That's crazy! Was that actually what clinched the part for you?

K.T. Not quite. Then we went onto the next step of the process, which was to do a film test with Bill Hurt. That took two full days. We did two scenes from the film and then did makeup tests and color tests and wardrobe tests. Then I went home . . . and nothing. I heard not a peep from anybody. I was going out of my mind. Finally, after about two weeks, the call came that the role was officially mine.

Years later, I found out that George Lucas was the one who ultimately sealed my casting, so I owe him for that. Larry, who wrote *Empire Strikes Back* for George, called him in to weigh in on the final casting because he was having trouble finalizing a decision. And based on those film tests that I did with Bill, George stood up for me and told Larry that he had to cast me.

D.M. So you owe a great deal to a legendary filmmaker you've never actually worked with.

K.T. Indeed. Then my next audition was for the film *The Man With Two Brains*. The director, Carl Reiner, says, "Okay, so you're gorgeous, you're sexy, but can you be funny?" Hollywood thinks that if you do one thing very well, it must be the only thing you can do. That's how people get typecast—they're just not offered anything else.

D.M. "Everyone knows a pretty girl can't be funny, too."

K.T. Exactly. It's such nonsense. So I went into Carl's office to audition opposite Steve Martin, and I end up throwing myself across his desk, crawling up Steve Martin's leg and making a spectacle of myself.

D.M. From what I know of how shy Steve Martin is offscreen, that was probably terrifying for him.

K.T. He hated it! He was so uncomfortable, he couldn't wait to get me off of him! Anyway, it worked, because I got the part and there was never again any question of whether I could do comedy.

And then came *Romancing the Stone*. I was coming off *Body Heat* and *The Man With Two Brains*, both of which were hits and in both of which I played very confident, strong women. And so there was this question of, "Can she look plain? Can she lack confidence? Can she do the early part of the film, before Joan Wilder finds her confidence?" As if I'm not an actress. So frustrating. So I got some sweat clothes, cut them up, didn't put on any makeup or wash my hair, and I went in to the audition and just kind of bumped into furniture and was totally uncomfortable in my skin. And that got me the part. I had to prove myself over and over and over again, for years and years. Because people lack the capacity to see you in more than one way, so you have to show them.

D.M. When you went in for *Romancing* in sweat clothes or for *Body Heat* dressed as a femme fatale, were you ever worried that you were going too far for an audition, that it might be read as desperation or overkill or something?

K.T. Absolutely, but those risks paid off. It is something to be conscious of, though.

D.M. It seems like it'd be easy to overdo it.

K.T. Definitely. I mean, don't go rent a costume or anything. I auditioned this guy for the role of the priest in *High* and he came in with the white collar and the full clerical outfit. I was like, "Come on, give me a break. Don't tell me you're a priest, show me you're a priest. Act it."

D.M. On-camera auditions differ from those that are not on-camera.

K.T. They're much different now than they were when I was starting out, because back then we did auditions on film. That was a big deal, because film is so expensive, so they'd want to get it narrowed down to the smallest number of people they could before actually shooting the auditions. Rarely did more than three or four actors get auditioned for a part on camera in those days. Now that they shoot screen tests on video, a much larger number of actors get screen-tested.

D.M. And those screen tests are showing up as bonus features on DVDs.

K.T. Yes, with the rough, unflattering lighting. Yeesh.

D.M. Would you like to revisit some of your old auditions from back in the day?

K.T. God, no. No thank you!

D.M. Choosing an audition piece must be a stressful decision.

K.T. One common mistake I see is actors choosing to do monologues from films. In films, you are being served by the cinematography and the editing and the score and the location. When you strip all of that away, all you have is the script, and the average film script is not going to stand up to a theatrical script.

D.M. I don't like it because it makes me think about the actor from the film. I was casting something recently and an actor came in and did a very recognizable monologue from *Good Will Hunting*. And all I could think about was Matt Damon, because he's so linked to that part, he's been my only experience of that part, and even though the guy may not have been that bad, I felt like there was no way for me to give him a fair shot because I was so distracted. It just seemed like he was doing a sad knockoff of Damon's performance. It was very awkward.

K.T. Yeah, the cinematic image is very powerful. That's another good reason not to use a monologue from film, because the image is already imprinted in our memories. Plays don't usually work that way. It's more than likely that the person hasn't seen it, or that they saw it a long time ago, or that they don't remember it well enough that it's imprinted on their brain like a moment from a film they've seen a dozen times.

D.M. What else should an actor think about when selecting an audition piece?

K.T. Obviously, choose something age-appropriate. You'd be surprised how many actors don't do something that simple. Also, look for a character that has a few eccentricities. If you're unknown, think about your type—if you're a young, pretty woman with a light voice, choose an ingénue role. But choose one that has some self-determination to it, so the character isn't just this vacant doll without a will. That's not the easiest thing to find. But go to *Born Yesterday* or something similar—there are possibilities out there.

D.M. Do you remember what you used when you first started auditioning?

K.T. I do, actually. As a classic I used Shakespeare's *Taming of the Shrew*, the role of Kate. For a drama I used part of Jean Cocteau's *The Human Voice*. I'm not sure what my comedy was—it was more than thirty-five years ago.

D.M. How prepared should a monologue be? Should the actor leave room for discovery and impulse?

K.T. Not really. Your monologue should be mastered. Which isn't to say that its performance should be rote and robotic, but you should have it down.

One mistake that a lot of young actors make is that they believe that a monologue is just about one thing, since it's a short piece of text. When the reality is that there are layers of meaning in every single line, let alone every monologue. They'll think, "This is a monologue about sorrow." And they'll work and work on playing that sorrow, and they'll nail that one note, but they will leave no room for anything else and they end up delivering the entire monologue at one emotional pitch. There'll be no up and down, no variation. When I see my students doing that, I tell them to extract completely that one emotion they are playing. I'd tell that actor to perform the monologue with no sorrow whatsoever. And then as she develops it, I'd have her slowly, with each additional performance, start to put small amounts of sorrow back in, until the right note is eventually found and the performance isn't so one-note because it's shaded by all the stuff she did to replace the sorrow when she took it out completely.

D.M. The callback is the subsequent round of auditioning, after the producers have narrowed the field from the initial audition. Should it be handled differently than the initial audition?

K.T. Yes. Don't presume anything. I see that's a mistake that many young actors make. When they come into a callback, they come in with a kind of swagger, as though they're presuming that because they've been called back that it's in their pocket. Nothing puts me off more. It makes me want to go, "Oh yeah? I don't think so." So be as respectful and unassuming as you were in the original audition. That's important.

D.M. What's the big difference between a first audition and a callback?

K.T. The major difference with a callback is that you will have had much more time to work on the material and you will probably have an indication of what the director is looking for. In a callback, the director will almost always give you some direction, whereas in a first audition they might just sit and observe. So the important thing becomes using that direction right away, immediately adjusting your own thinking and manifesting physically and mentally the choice that they've indicated. Again, cold reading cannot be overemphasized. The ability to take something and instantly make use of it is probably the most important skill you can have in an audition.

D.M. Is it ever fair to request more information or ask questions of the director at the callback? Or is that considered a big faux pas?

K.T. You shouldn't do it before you've done the piece at least once. If you've gone through the scene once, then I think you have the right to say, "I don't quite understand why the character says this," which is a legitimate inquiry. And if the director takes the time to discuss your question with you, that's a good sign.

D.M. Is there anything else actors should know about callbacks?

K.T. Yes, have your lines memorized! Be 100% off-book! There's no legitimate reason to have that piece of paper in your hand inhibiting you, because it gets in your way. If you've been called back, then you've had the time to learn your lines. Nobody expects it in a first audition, but it's bad form not to be off-book for a callback. Plus, it will improve your performance and thus your chance of getting the role, because it will free you physically to do whatever you want, rather than having to be restrained by this paper you keep referring to. Your body language, your eye contact, your gestures—these things are such an enormous part of your performance, so why would you want to inhibit them with a script in your hand?

DEALING WITH REJECTION

DUSTIN MORROW Many actors feel beaten-down by constant rejection. It's important for young actors to learn to think about rejection in a specific way in order to survive such a tough industry.

KATHLEEN TURNER Absolutely. The amount of rejection in this industry is overwhelming. It's important to know, from the outset, that it is the job of most of the people in this industry to say no to you. That is what they do. Period. They "protect" the people in power, and that means that they reject you, no matter what.

When I started out, I made the mistake of telling my mother, when I'd call home, about what I'd auditioned for that week. So the next week, she'd say, "Did you get it, did you get it, did you get it?" And of course I never did. Just getting the audition at that point in my un-established career was the accomplishment, but there was no way to explain that to her that would sound reasonable.

So, first of all, don't talk about it with a lot of people who don't understand how it works. Don't set yourself up to have to explain anything. When non-actor friends say, "Did you get some auditions this week?" you can respond in the affirmative without having to be specific. Otherwise they're later going to inevitably ask, "Did you get it?" And it hurts to say you didn't.

D.M. It's like a false sense of failure. Plus, inevitably, they'll have to comment later on who did get the role and patronize you with "But you're so much more talented than her . . ."

K.T. Yeah! And who needs that stuff? Nobody. So that's rule number one. You will be continually rejected, it's part of the process. And it's going to hurt. I've heard many actors say, "They thought I was too tall" or

"Too short," or "They wanted a blonde," or "I was too old," or "I was too young," blah blah blah. Some of those things may be true, but it doesn't protect you personally from the feeling that they didn't want *you*. And that is the hard part. Whether you were too tall or too short, too young or too old, they didn't want *you*. And that will always hurt, there's no way around it.

D.M. And that sense that it's you that's being rejected, and not your work, is what seems to separate rejection in acting from rejection in other artistic disciplines, let alone rejection in other careers. If you are a photographer and you submit photos to a gallery, and the gallery rejects them, it's the photos that are rejected. When you lose a part in acting, it's you that's rejected. I mean, it isn't really, because as we discussed before, there's a difference between the actor and the performance—the performance is the work.

K.T. Right, but the problem is that it *feels* like it's you that's being rejected, not the work.

But the thing that truly separates acting from almost any other art form, which you hinted at earlier, is the lack of "the test." A classical musician must be able to read the score—if you can't read a score, you can't play in a symphony, it's that simple. A painter truly has to understand the brushes, the consistency of the paint, and he has to be able to draw. That is a specific skill. These are certifiable, demonstrable skills that everyone understands. There is no such skill that you can demonstrate when acting. There is no almighty test you can pass that says, "Yes, you can act."

It's all extremely vague and it's very much an individual, personal ability. An ability to effectively communicate. There's a shapeless, gauzy qualification for acting, as it were, which makes it extremely difficult not only to know how to go about it, which is why I emphasize that you must find your own unique sense of acting, but also makes it very hard to feel legitimate and to be regarded as legitimate by others. It took me many years to say, "Yes, I am an artist." For years I'd say, "I am an actor," but not necessarily an "artist," and I did not feel that I had reached a point where my work could be labeled art. I did reach that point eventually, where I believe that what I do is art, but that was after years of hard work.

It undermines the actor as well, because you doubt yourself, and you doubt whether what you're doing is really worthy. I think sometimes, "Look, if I turn off my phone for a few hours, nobody is going to die, right? I'm not a brain surgeon, or something like that, where someone's life depends on whether or not I get on that stage right now." Nobody's life depends on what I do. And of course it doesn't have to for me to feel like what I do makes a difference in the world. But I want to make a difference in the world. I have always wanted that. That's part of why I do the political work and charity work that I do. I want my work to matter.

And I do believe that I matter, but a lot of that belief has come along with success. The ability to focus attention and support on, or make use of my fame in the aid of certain causes or actions is important to me.

D.M. But that ability comes not from being an actress, but from being a celebrity.

K.T. Absolutely. It's hard, as an actor, to feel inherently worthwhile sometimes, and I don't think this is just my own insecurity, I think it belongs to the profession as well. And men suffer from this more than women, because acting is not considered a very masculine profession in this country. It's quite legitimate in England and many other countries, of course, but not here in the U.S.

So if we had some structure, some kind of "test," that we could measure ourselves against, it would be easier to believe in ourselves, but we do not and I don't see any way that we can.

D.M. One of the things that seems inherently cruel to me about the profession it is that some of the personality traits or skills that you need as an actor, like empathy and sensitivity and compassion, are the very things that would make feeling rejected so painful.

K.T. That's true. Those things make a person *feel* deeper, experience things personally, and rejection is one of those things every actor has to feel at some point.

D.M. Tell me about the social game of networking in getting cast. Much of the casting process depends on being adept at social interaction.

K.T. Oh boy. I'm probably not the best person to ask about that. I've never been very good at the social game, I'm afraid. I think I've actually consciously, or maybe subconsciously avoided that because I never wanted to feel that I was socially manipulating someone or was being manipulated by someone. However, I know that's naive. Certainly social networking is an important part of the business. Most of my friends are not in the entertainment industry, so it doesn't usually occur to me to call in professional favors based on personal friendships.

But obviously, that kind of thing happens all the time in entertainment industries. If I'd settled in Los Angeles and stayed in the strata of movie stardom that I was in throughout the eighties, then I imagine playing that social game in order to maintain that level of stardom would have become a necessity. It was about a choice of lifestyle. I just don't care to live that way or to live out in L.A. because of the way one has to live there. That sacrifice isn't worth it to me.

D.M. Do you think people will forgive poor behavior in the service of talent? Phrased another way—if you're a genuinely enjoyable person to work with, can that be more important than a demonstration of talent?

K.T. Well, you certainly don't get to be unpleasant unless you've got a hell of a lot of talent. Don't push that button, baby, unless you can really back it up! It's amazing how many people that's lost on.

Obviously I would think that a basic level of respect and courtesy toward anyone and everyone, no matter what their job is, should be standard practice. I worked with a director once who was notorious for being a bit abusive and contemptuous. Of course, we all knew this going in to start the film. And one of the first days of the shoot, he beckoned to one of the crew members and said, "You! Green shirt! Come here!" And I pointedly said, "Do you want *John*? The gaffer, whose name is *John*?" And he responded very sheepishly, "Yes, I want John." I said, "That's what I thought." I make a point of putting a name in front of every single person I work with, and I don't tolerate that kind of dehumanizing behavior from my collaborators, even the producers and directors. And I heard from people who worked on that director's next film that he was like a changed man, that he'd never been so respectful and amicable on a shoot. I'd like to think I had something to do with that!

The truth is, being pleasant to work with only helps you as an actor in the end. All of the work of the other people on a production serves to help your performance. And, crucially, most of that work is done *before* you give your performance. All of the design, both on stage and on film, all of the crew work, all of the preparation, comes before your opportunity to actually act. And you won't be there and in a place where you can do good work unless they're doing their job and they're doing it well. So you should not ever take for granted anyone you work with, from the director all the way down to the production assistant or stagehand.

That respect also pays off in people's commitment and their loyalty—they will work a little harder, go ten minutes overtime without charging the show, to live up to your belief in them. It's very good practice.

And of course, it pays to be courteous and responsive to agents, casting directors, and any directors and producers you may meet because they could prove to be a valuable contact. No one likes attitude. Exhibit attitude and you may have lost the job before you've even auditioned for it. That's basic good business practice.

D.M. Many acting students grapple with some degree of stage fright or nervousness or stress about actually getting up on the stage.

K.T. There are a lot of great stories about this, of course. And certainly I have nerves also, at times.

D.M. Still, even?

K.T. Oh sure. But unlike many actors, my solution to being nervous is to get on stage.

D.M. As the title of the NYU course you teach states, "Shut up and do it," right?

The full title of the course Kathleen occasionally teaches at NYU is "Practical Acting: Shut Up and Do It!"

K.T. Indeed! Just shut up and do it! Just let me get out there and fix it! There's a great story that the brilliant Elaine Stritch told me about her days as a heavy drinker. This was years ago when it was much more accepted that actors might not always be stone cold sober. She was off stage, with her drink in hand, waiting for her cue and standing next to a fellow actor who was always there with his own drink, also waiting for his entrance. And he didn't have a drink that night. And she said, "What are you doing?" And he said, "Um, I've decided that I'm not going to have a drink before I go on." She responds, "You mean you're going out there alone?"

Because to her, I guess, it was a liquid courage, in a way. That would terrify me, to go on stage having had some drinks. I'm scared of anything that might have an influence on my performance. Now *that* would make me crazy. That would scare the hell out of me. I was a heavy drinker at one point, using it to cope with the pain of my rheumatoid arthritis, but I never let it influence my work. For some actors, it works, but not for me.

D.M. If you use a substance, be it alcohol or something else, while you work, then you don't really know who's doing the work.

K.T. Exactly. I saw this actor once who was on some kind of drug and gave a spectacular performance. Absolutely amazing. He was just flying. And after the show everyone was commenting on how extraordinary he was that night and he said, "I'm scared to death. Does this mean I have to do this every night I want that performance?" He didn't know whether it came from him, or whether it came from the use of the drug. That road is a real dead end. That's something I know I never want. I don't ever want to have to doubt that my work was my doing. And that way I'll always know that if I want to, I can do it again.

D.M. I can see how a stiff drink could help with stage fright, though.

K.T. Trust me, there are better ways! But dealing with stage fright, and dealing with audition fright, is tough, and to some degree it never goes away.

D.M. But nor should it, probably. A certain level of nervous energy is useful.

K.T. Yes, there should always be some small level of nerves. Otherwise you've gotten overconfident, and that's as bad as being scared. There are some basic things an actor can do to fight stage fright. Breathing exercises, relaxation exercises, taking a moment to center yourself.

I think one of the biggest mistakes I see these days is young actors trying to distract themselves—listening to music, or playing with their phones, or texting or fiddling with a laptop. They feel they have to keep their mind off the fact that they're going to walk in that door and have to try and audition for this job. *Really* bad mistake. If you can't live in the quiet of yourself, then you're in deep trouble. They should be doing the exact opposite, closing down outside distractions and focusing on what they need to do. If you're sitting in a chair outside the door of the audition, waiting your turn, then relax your feet, relax your ankles, relax your knees, relax your thighs, relax your hips—go up your body, from toes to head, with a basic relaxation exercise.

And then start to work on your breath, take your breath to the bottom of your lungs, take your breath to the middle of your lungs, take your breath to the top of your lungs. Stretch your neck, loosen your mouth, loosen your jaw, let your eyes relax, let your forehead relax. Loosen up as much as you can because the first thing that will happen to you when you go into an audition is that you will tighten up. You will step through that door and your body will automatically seize up. So the looser you can be before you walk in that door, the better shot you've got at not tightening up fatally. It's real simple, but necessary stuff.

D.M. Meditation would be useful.

K.T. Sure. For me, not strict meditation, but meditative practices, especially breathing exercises. There are some basic things any actor can take from mediation and yoga practices, like simply making the exhalation longer than the inhalation. Inhaling is part of the body's seizure, the automatic tightening-up process that you want to avoid when performing. So inhaling and doing a deliberately over-long exhale will fight that.

D.M. I found a quote by you, where you once said that "the big gap between the ability of actors is confidence." Do you think that's really what separates one actor from another? Confidence in the self?

K.T. To a degree. But I've certainly known actors who claim to not be particularly confident in themselves but who still turn in interesting and intricate performances. But I don't believe that they are not confident, because clearly they've made choices in their performances. And making solid choices means you believe in your performance. Otherwise, you'd just be an amoeba, you'd be all over the place, kind of formless and directionless.

A lack of confidence is foolish. I'm not a big believer in suffering. Suffering for your art is a waste of time. If you can avoid it, do. You can't always avoid it, but if you can, do. This angst, this self-terror, or doubt, this "Oh God, will I be able to do it tonight?"—that level of fear and nervousness will only hurt you. It's better to start from the position of, "Yes, I can do this." Have that base of confidence, that belief in yourself.

Just dive in and skip that step of soul-tearing self-doubt. Not only will doing so help you, it will help your collaborators. Even if it's just a subliminal thing, a director will pick up on that note of self-confidence. And it kind of eases his burden a little, it frees him to do his work better. You're telling him, "I know that I can do this, you don't have to worry about me." And it's a relief for a director, it frees him to focus on the hundred other things he has to focus on.

D.M. Some directors rely on that, and they cast actors they aren't going to have to worry about. Woody Allen, notoriously, never gives his actors any direction on the set. He hands them the script and turns them loose.

K.T. Well, it certainly makes his life easier, and he casts so carefully that he gets the results he wants without having to overdirect his actors.

D.M. On the flipside, he's also famous for replacing actors, even well into a shoot. Kubrick would do that too.

K.T. Well, that would certainly keep you on your toes. It wouldn't exactly create an environment in which you felt protected by your director, which is one of the things your director should be doing.

D.M. How about confidence in auditions?

K.T. It's really important at the audition stage. Rather than going in and saying, "Oh I hope I can do this," and proceeding to give a decent performance, walk in and say, "I'm so glad I'm doing this, I'm so glad these people will get to see me do this," and absolutely nail it. It's subtle, but it can be the difference between getting the job and not. From the perspective of the people evaluating your audition. Who needs the person who has to be continually supported, approved, coddled, and cradled? They don't want that actor. They want the actor who's going to be confident in her choices.

D.M. But there's a danger in going too far, of seeming so confident in your choices that you're not going to be able to take input from the director.

K.T. Yeah, then you'll just seem close-minded. If you're cocky, if you project an aura of, "I know this part like the back of my hand even though this is only the audition," then that's inherently a put-down to the director and probably the writer. You have no right to claim to totally know a character because you haven't lived with it yet. After a few months, any good writer or director will acknowledge that the actor knows that character better than they ever will. But to walk in to an audition and pretend you already know best is just disrespectful.

D.M. I can pick those people out in an audition easily. It's easy to spot.

K.T. Absolutely. And in most cases, they're just faking it. They come in with this little swagger, this appalling cockiness, because they're scared out of their minds, or because they want it so badly that it's all they can do to get through the audition. It's not a very good idea. It's self-defeating.

D.M. So the whole idea behind the name of your memoir, *Send Yourself Roses*, is to give yourself something nice, like flowers, when you're not working or not getting the accolades that you got when you first began working.

K.T. Right. Don't wait for someone else to do it for you. Treat yourself well. Even if it's a small thing—eat out instead of cooking at home, or take a cab instead of riding the bus or the subway. Treat yourself to something small.

D.M. How do you reward yourself now?

K.T. Primarily with alone-time. Solitude. Time to be quiet, to spend with myself. I can get so busy that finding a moment alone, or at least a moment where I'm not actively working on something, can actually become a great challenge.

D.M. There are other things you can do as an actor when you're not working to feel like you're a part of the artistic community.

K.T. I find myself, when I'm not working, going to at least one show a week, sometimes two. It's actually lovely to have the chance to see so many plays that, if I were working, I'd never have a chance to see.

But really, my best advice to actors on this issue is to make sure that you have a life outside your art. I would hope that every actor would have to have more to their lives than just what they do in their work, because they won't be working every week. Or even every month. A lot of actors start families, once they get to a certain point where they aren't having to scrounge for work. And believe me, that can take up *every* second of your time.

D.M. Now that your daughter is grown, how do you like to use your time?

K.T. Activism. I can fill a lot of my time by getting out to work for the organizations I believe in.

D.M. Political advocacy is a huge part of your life.

K.T. It always has been. I believe strongly in civic duty and responsibility, my father instilled that in me at a young age. I've been on the Board of Advocates of Planned Parenthood for 28 years, and I've served on the Board of People for the American Way for 32 years.

D.M. Those two organizations are more important than ever before, given the current political administration.

K.T. Absolutely. The People for the American Way fights to protect the First Amendment and serves as the watchdog of right-wing extremists. And Planned Parenthood is the leading provider of health services for women in the United States.

D.M. And a profoundly misunderstood organization, thanks to smear campaigns by right-wing politicians.

K.T. Well, they're always trying paint Planned Parenthood as some kind of abortion factory, when the truth is that abortion services make up only 3% of what Planned Parenthood covers. What it really does is offer health services like cancer screening, STD testing and treatment, and contraception and educational programs to low-income women who may not have any other option for health care available to them.

D.M. And despite what many Republicans would have us believe, not a single tax dollar can go to abortion services. Planned Parenthood uses not one dime from the government for abortion services.

K.T. That's correct.

D.M. And you're also still active with City Meals-on-Wheels, right?

K.T. I'm on their advisory board, and I help deliver the meals to seniors when I can. On Christmas morning my sister and I will be in a soup kitchen on East 74th street cooking meals for homebound elderly.

D.M. That's fabulous.

K.T. The organization provides more than a million-and-a-half meals to more than 18,000 people a year.

D.M. It's an amazing program.

K.T. That kind of work fulfills me and satisfies me tremendously. You get back way more than you give, trust me.

D.M. Have you ever thought about running for a political office?

K.T. People ask me to run quite often. Seriously, it comes up a lot. But I actually think I do more good as a working actor who also holds all of these offices in these important organizations. I travel a great deal, speaking out for and fundraising for these organizations, and I believe that that's how I can best use my celebrity for the public good.

The only hiccup with service is that you have to be careful, as an actor, not to make very long-term commitments because you might get a job—acting jobs can come up very quickly and unexpectedly. So you have to say, "With the time I've got, this is realistically what I can do." Don't make promises you can't keep.

I tell my students to schedule their community service as they would a class, for example. "All right, every Thursday at four o'clock, I'm in the soup kitchen, and every Friday I'm volunteering at the clinic." Just schedule it as you might, "Okay, I've got Literature 205 on Tuesday mornings at ten, and on Thursdays at ten, I have Advanced Acting." Don't do service on a whim, do it on a schedule.

D.M. And there are things you do that are extremely artistic and creative that help you to burn off creative energy when you're not working.

K.T. All kinds of things. There's a group here in New York that I do lunchtime readings with. Usually it's down in Gramercy Park, and I just give a day to it. A bunch of us actors meet at nine or ten in the morning and read through the script once, and then around ten-thirty, our small audience, mostly seniors, starts arriving, and at one o'clock we do a staged reading of the play, for free, to an incredibly appreciative audience. We call it Lunchtime Theater, it's a lot of fun. Our audiences tend to be well-educated, so we can do something like a Cocteau piece, and they have enough of a background in literature that they can appreciate the work and understand its context. It's very satisfying.

D.M. It sounds lovely.

K.T. And I would imagine there are groups like that all over the place.

D.M. It's a great idea. I've had friends who are actors and they'll go for long stretches between gigs, and they'll work jobs as paralegals or as waiters, and I think that at a certain point they stop feeling like they're actors.

K.T. Right. They don't feel like their gifts are being used.

D.M. I've had more than one of them say separately to me that they wonder at what point they stop being an actor who waits tables and start being a waiter who wants to act. It's that tough question of how to maintain that sense that you're an artist, that acting is what you do.

K.T. Yeah, that's haunting. That's really haunting. If you're still working as a waiter, the odds are you haven't made enough money or created enough of a reputation. But you do what you have to do. *Body Heat* didn't pay me enough to leave my waitressing job. In that six-month lag between when the movie was shot and when it was released, I had to go back to waitressing.

D.M. That must have been a jarring transition.

K.T. Yeah, it was tough. I went from a starring role on the set of a big Hollywood movie to waiting on a lot of New Yorkers with a lot of bad attitudes! But there's no shame in waiting tables, and it's a great job for actors, because of the flexibility it provides. And waitressing *is* acting, to some degree. It's a grueling job, but you have to stay cheerful and positive no matter how bad your day is going. You have to act as if your clients are guests in your home, no matter how terrible they may behave.

D.M. And you can't work a regular nine-to-five job and get to auditions.

K.T. Exactly. But there's no reason to worry about not being involved creatively. Get together a group of like-minded young people, with the same sort of desires and situation, to once or twice a month pick a play and do a reading. Whether it's just for yourselves, or whether it's for a nursing home, or a church, or a school, it doesn't matter. Just get together and exercise your creative muscles. It will keep you sharp and keep your skills developing.

D.M. And one thing I like about that idea, which I think is an important thing for young, struggling actors, is it doesn't cost anything.

K.T. A definite plus.

319

D.M. I once dated an actor who was always taking acting classes, but never booking gigs. And while I respect that acting classes serve a purpose and they sharpen your skills, they're also very expensive. And it wasn't like she didn't have a college degree in theater with years of training as an actor.

K.T. Many of those classes are a sham.

D.M. I'd never tell someone to stop training and stop learning, but there are a lot of these classes that seem to exist solely so that actors who aren't being paid to act can find a place where they can go act—but it costs them money! That drives me crazy. These acting instructors are profiting off of the tough marketplace for actors.

K.T. I'm even more suspicious. I think it has a lot to do with the teacher's ego. But I'm more cynical about it, probably.

D.M. It's just something that's always bothered me.

K.T. It bothers the heck out of me, and I think it's absurd. If my own daughter came to me and said, "If I wanted to take an acting class, where would I go?" I would say, "Use me." Not all, but *many* private, for-profit acting teachers are opportunists who aren't booking jobs themselves.

D.M. Could you really see your daughter taking acting lessons from you?

K.T. Ha! If you knew Rachel, you'd know how funny that question was. Let's put it this way: it's unlikely to happen.

WORKING IN THE INDUSTRY

Dustin Morrow There's a lot to consider for the young, inexperienced actor in searching for an agent.

Kathleen Turner Probably most importantly, the size of the agency. The smaller agencies are the ones that will develop talent. They will help you develop your strengths and work on your weaknesses. They'll work tirelessly to broaden your appeal. The bigger agencies, and this is more and more true every year, have absolutely no interest in developing talent. There's no money in developing new talent. ICM, CAA, William Morris—they all have big overheads, big offices, and a *lot* of goddamn agents. They need money desperately, and they need to have it continually flowing. They would probably turn down a perfect project for an actor, based solely on the percentage that they would get.

It's the actor who gets hurt at these big agencies. You really have to be careful to make sure that they understand that they're there to work for you, and that no decisions are made without your knowledge, none whatsoever. Big agencies are like vultures—they wait for the smaller agencies to develop talent into something bankable, then they swoop in and steal the talent away.

D.M. Pretty ugly.

K.T. Well, that's their job, that's their business, that's what they do. They're able to do it because it also means that they inflate the actor's salary, usually, which is pleasing to the actor. But for a young, unknown actor, do *not* go to a big agency. It's a waste of your time and it will ultimately hurt your feelings, because you'll be essentially ignored.

D.M. Have all of your agents also been your friends? My agent and I are friendly, I like him a lot, but we don't hang out or anything.

K.T. It doesn't have to be a friendship, per se, but mutual respect and a common vision, and common goals, are a must. That's why I ultimately left ICM—our values had become so different. They didn't care about theater and they didn't care about contracts worth less than five million dollars.

My agent for many years, until he got too old to continue the work, was Sam Cohn. He was a legend, the most respected theatrical agent in the business, period. And he came to me one day and said he wanted to represent me, which was a great honor. It was really quite thrilling. And I grew to really, really love Sam. He was a great man, with a great ability to appreciate talent, and words, and he was a bit of a philosopher. A true gentleman.

And he was a fighter. You want an agent who will fight for you. Hollywood has always been run on this archaic model in which all actresses make less money than actors, and that's going to have to change.

D.M. Many young actresses have admirably become more vocal in their opposition of that difference in pay. Jennifer Lawrence was very critical of the studio for paying the supporting actors, all of them male, more than she made for her lead role in the *Hunger Games* films.

K.T. And I was behind her 100%. This kind of salary inequity has been going on forever. When I look back on some of my biggest hits—Romancing, *Body Heat*, *Prizzi's Honor*—I estimate that I made about half as much as my male co-leads made on those films. Up until the last fifteen or twenty years, Hollywood has felt that the majority of money in U.S. households was controlled and spent by men and so films targeted at men were the way to go. But it's not true anymore—in more than 40% of households, it's the woman who is the major breadwinner. She controls the money. Hollywood's going to have to adjust to this if they want to remain as profitable as they have been.

D.M. Back to agencies—when you find representation, are you repped by just one agent or by the entire company?

K.T. It varies. I've worked with agencies where I've really liked one agent, but usually have more than one representing me. You'll have one for theater, one for film, one for commercials—it's usually a kind of a committee.

D.M. At different agencies or all under one roof?

K.T. All under one roof. If you're with a New York agency and they don't have a Los Angeles branch, you may be able to split representation, if the two agencies agreed, but most agencies cover both coasts and most aspects of the industry. Some agencies specialize—they might not have commercial departments, for example, in which case you're free to go find a commercial agent. But if they do have a commercial department in-house, then it's usually expected or even required as part of your contract that you just work with them.

D.M. Seems like there'd be a danger of a competitive element—if you've got a commercial agent who is trying to book you on such-and-such a date and your theatrical agent is trying to book you at the same time, that could take some finessing.

K.T. That's where it becomes useful if they're under the same roof, because you can say, "Work it out, you two." They can negotiate the schedule so I can do both projects. Not that I like to do commercials, that's one thing that I don't understand at all, why all of these huge stars are doing tons of commercials.

D.M. You've never done one?

K.T. I have, but I don't make a habit of it. They take no time to do, and they pay very, very well.

D.M. That's for sure. When I was editing, I'd be paid four times as much as I would on almost any other job. And if I was getting paid so well, I can't imagine what you got paid.

K.T. They pay well, but that's the only reward in them.

D.M. It seems like a lot of actors who say they're against doing commercials just won't do them here, but you go to Japan and all of a sudden there's Jack Nicholson selling toilet paper or something.

K.T. Yeah, and he gets a couple easy millions out of it. I'd like to think I'm done with commercials, but I don't know, maybe I'd think twice if the money were that insane. I'm a working actor, I have to make a living like every other working actor.

D.M. I can only imagine what you've been offered to use your voice in commercials. I mean, how many voices are out there that are more famous—Morgan Freeman, James Earl Jones, Jack Nicholson, maybe Alec Baldwin . . . it's hard to think of too many others.

K.T. Well, it works for me and it works against me. Because the voice is so recognizable, commercial agencies will say, "Do we want this product to immediately be identified with Kathleen Turner?" Or, "Will Kathleen Turner overshadow the product?"

D.M. Yeah, that's why I wonder just how successful celebrity voiceovers actually are, especially given the short duration of the average commercial. If you're only spending thirty seconds with a commercial, and you spend the whole thirty seconds thinking, "Is that Morgan Freeman?" then you're not thinking about the product.

Besides the salary, what are some of the things an agent is negotiating for you on a job? And do you need your own attorney to finalize a job contract?

K.T. No, most agencies will have an in-house lawyer, who specializes in entertainment law. And the basic union contracts protect you from being exploited. That's inherent in the unions. However, there are so many things that an agent may negotiate, depending on the level at which you're operating, by which I basically mean, are you a lead or a supporting player? There are dozens and dozens of things, really. For example, if you're on the road, what kind of per diem do you make? Because it isn't enough to have a salary on the road, since you know you'll spend money that you wouldn't spend at home.

That negotiation process is very important, because once you sign the contract, you are basically at the mercy of the production. Hopefully you will have the privilege of working in a collaborative relationship with your director and other actors, but at the end of the day the only real right you have as an actor is the right to say no to the role. Once you take a role and sign the contract, you must fulfill it according to the director's wishes. You are fulfilling someone else's creative vision. A play, or a film, is not all about the actor.

D.M. There is some regulation of that negotiating process.

K.T. There is a bottom line, provided by our unions, by Equity, by SAG-AFTRA. But you have to have an agent and be a SAG member to have a binding union contract. And your agent will take 10% of your fee, although that's tax deductible. When you have a union contract, you can't be paid under a certain amount, you can't be worked over a certain number of hours, things like that. Basic health care coverage is guaranteed if you've worked enough under any one of the unions or all of them to qualify for it. And then there's always workman's comp and a million other details.

> *The stage actors' union is the Actors Equity Association, or AEA. It has more than 50,000 members is often referred to as Actors Equity or simply Equity. The Screen Actors Guild/American Federation of Television and Radio Artists, or SAG-AFTRA, is the film actors' union. It represents approximately 160,000 people. Both unions are among the most powerful in the entertainment industries.*

But every actor's contract is negotiated individually. If it's a Favored Nations contract, then you will all be paid the same. And everyone knows that they'll be receiving the same pay, the same deal. But if it's not Favored Nations, then your agent is free to negotiate the best deal he can. So how much you make, if you get a percentage of the house, how much time you'll be willing to give to press or promotional work and what your recompense will be for that, what kind of living accommodations you will have while traveling, what kind of access you will have to a car, etc. The list goes on and on.

D.M. "Will the production pay my speeding tickets?"

K.T. I hadn't thought about that one.

D.M. I lived in Iowa at the time they were shooting *The Bridges of Madison County,* and I remember hearing that a certain big star was getting pulled over for speeding a lot. I always wondered if Clint Eastwood was footing the bill for those tickets.

K.T. Maybe SAG should put something in the contract.

D.M. Yes—the speeding ticket clause! How do you feel about the unions? The SAG card really seems to be the golden ticket to every young actor.

K.T. Well, SAG has the very best health care and the best support system available within the profession. So it's very good for that. You can only do so many jobs within a union, and have a union contract, without being a full-paid member of the union. For example, in Equity, I believe you get to do two shows that are Equity-level shows, within a certain amount of time, but you can't do a third without having to join the union. Now, you can't join the union *unless* you've got an Equity job or qualified for Equity points in another job. The producer can't hire you for that third job, unless you have joined the union. This is true of all of the unions. You get one or two SAG jobs free, without having to join the union, but then you must join, if you want to continue working on SAG productions. It's all a bit complicated.

On the whole, I think the unions are a good thing, but I've certainly had issues with them. Particularly with Equity—we have something like ninety percent unemployment in Equity. So about ten percent of the actors in Equity are basically carrying the entire union. Because we're the ones paying, not only dues, but a percentage of our salaries, membership is assessed on salary level. So many years ago, I tried to pass something in Equity where if you had not worked an Equity contract for ten years, then your voting rights would be suspended. As soon as you got another Equity job, you'd be re-instituted—you'd be a voting member again. The idea was that the union couldn't then be controlled by this ninety percent who simply weren't working.

Well, you can imagine how wildly that was defeated. That idea did not go anywhere! But I still think that way. There's a lot of dead weight in the unions, and working actors are the ones that pay for most of it.

D.M. The actors' unions, I must say, are among the toughest unions I've ever worked with. Which is good because so many actors are taken advantage of, I think, before they join.

K.T. Definitely. Many actors are exploited in terms of wages and hours.

D.M. It's not uncommon in both theater and film for actors to be asked to work for free, or to take a stipend that's really borderline insulting, or work for the mythical "deferred payment." And it's just because there's this culture around acting that is like, "Well, it's so tough to get work that you're lucky to be acting at all."

K.T. "Who knows, somebody might see this, you might get discovered. Work for free."

D.M. Right! "Your pay is your exposure from the project!" So that's one great thing about the unions, they legitimize the profession in the eyes of many who'd otherwise try to exploit it.

K.T. They acknowledge it as one worthy of compensation and therefore respect and consideration. There's enough exploitation of talent in this industry as it is, I can only imagine how bad it would be without the unions. They are a great resource and I'm happy to be a member and support them.

TEACHING ACTING

DUSTIN MORROW I want to talk about the classes you've taught at NYU and Studio One on One. Since you don't endorse any of the traditional schools of acting, you are just basically using your own methods there.

KATHLEEN TURNER Yes, I don't teach the traditional schools at all. But I wouldn't say that I outright don't endorse them, I just have very mixed feelings about them. I think they can help a developing actor who has already largely found their own voice to continue to work on that voice. That voice that is distinctly theirs. It can be colored and influenced, and grow as a result of studying Strasberg, Adler, any of the classic schools of acting. But I think that subscribing to a specific school *before* an actor has had a chance to develop their own voice can be very dangerous and more harmful than good.

I mean, why do it the way a bunch of other people have done it? Why limit yourself to acting in the same way that a million other actors before you have? How does that distinguish you? How does that make you unique? How is that going to help you stand out from the million other actors with whom you are competing for a role? And how are you going to feel about your talent knowing that, basically, you developed it from someone else's voice?

Be unique. Find your own way, then study the masters and think about how what they did can fit into what you already do well.

D.M. Did you feel like that even when you were studying them as an undergraduate or is this something you figured out later?

K.T. I never really studied them.

D.M. At all?

K.T. Not really.

D.M. But they did that level of theoretical exploration when you were an undergrad.

K.T. Of course they did, and I read it when they assigned it to me, but I didn't let it influence my acting at all. It didn't sink in, and I didn't give it much thought at the time. I was too busy on stage, just doing it, finding my own voice. I figured out once that I had only 14 nights in a school year when I wasn't on stage or in rehearsal. That was my training ground—the stage itself. The idea of taking what I learned sitting in a classroom, or reading a bunch of theory, and putting it to work on stage didn't really connect for me. Vocal exercises, physical exercises, yes, but some kind of theory, no.

No one was going to tell me how to approach a role, I was going to figure that out myself, just through doing it. Through experimenting, through making mistakes, through working with the text up on the stage. I loved the study of theatrical history, the study of movement, the vocal training, but when it came to finding the inner life of a character, I knew I had to find it on my own. It wasn't magically going to come to me because I applied someone else's theory.

D.M. For the record, I think that's one of the ideas behind this book we're doing. All of the literature that's out there about acting tends to subscribe to a specific school of the craft.

K.T. Well, this one will too, to some degree. The school of Turner!

D.M. Yes, but the school of Turner seems to be, "Do it for yourself. Find your own voice." Which I think is a good message for young, developing actors. It's no coincidence that the master class you teach is called "Practical Acting: Shut Up and Do It."

K.T. Right. Put down the books, stop theorizing it, get your ass on the stage and start doing it. It's always been my way of working, but it goes against even what they do at NYU, and that's a great university. I think many faculty and administration over there think I'm downright subversive.

D.M. You boat-rocker.

K.T. That's me! Ever the troublemaker.

Look, there's nothing wrong with studying theory, but what surprises me about many acting curricula is how little work they do in preparing young actors to transition from the college setting to the real-world, professional setting. They just never seem to discuss or teach what happens when you graduate. They don't teach the practical side. That's why I decided to call my course "Practical Acting." The "Shut Up and Do It" part came later, when I got into the classroom and realized that the students preferred sitting around and talking about acting to actually getting up on their feet and doing it.

D.M. You seem to really love teaching.

K.T. I love it! It's really become a passion for me over the last decade or so. It's so much fun to see young actors just starting out, all passionate and excited and naïve.

D.M. Not yet totally jaded by the industry.

K.T. Right, not yet!

D.M. What is it you like about teaching?

K.T. I like working on details within a performance, really taking a performance apart, examining its smallest components, and then putting it back together. And I get to do that as a teacher. I also really appreciate the enthusiasm and the work ethic of the young actors I have instructed. I'm proud of them and the work I've done with them.

D.M. What does your class consist of?

K.T. In the "Practical Acting" course I teach for about four hours a week. I take juniors and seniors, students who've demonstrated a commitment to pursuing acting as a profession. I audition them for the course. I get them up on their feet performing in the very first class. Everyone performs in every class, that's a rule. We spend the first half of the semester working on stage acting. I take them into these enormous Broadway theaters, like the Neaderlander, and put them onstage to test their vocal projection and their ability to work with the sound systems in these huge spaces.

I like to have them do three and four person scenes, to work on shifting the focus around the stage and on working together. You'd be amazed how many young actors don't understand how to work with their fellow actors in service of the story. It takes some of them awhile to realize that it's not about them, it's about the story. They'll be showboating all over the stage, and the focus of the narrative will get totally lost because the audience will have no idea where they are supposed to be looking. In film, the camera and the editing can do most of that work, but onstage it's the actor's responsibility.

Then in the second half of the semester, we work on camera acting. I teach them about lenses and about the subtleties of film acting. Most of the students come across way too big on camera at first, because of their stage background.

I also like to bring in guests from the industry to visit with the students. I've had some big-name playwrights come in. Even Albee came in once.

Kathleen has always been supportive of young actors, even before she began teaching. According to the producer of Who's Afraid of Virginia Woolf, *Kathleen exerted her pull only once during the production, to insure that the young supporting actors, then-unknowns David Harbour and Mireille Enos, be billed in the show's advertisements alongside Kathleen and her co-star Bill Irwin. The production was not contractually obligated to do this, but Kathleen made it happen.*

D.M. It sounds like a fun class.
K.T. I also teach at Studio One on One, which is a great organization that offers classes, private coaching, workshops, and opportunities to interact with the industry. In the class I do there, I work on monologues with the students, then I give them sides from both theater and film and television, and we go through them as a class in a mock audition format. One on One is different from most networking-centered studios in that it auditions its members, so by the time they get to my class, the students have been pre-screened, in a way. So the caliber of talent in those classes tends to be pretty high, which is great.
D.M. The mock auditioning aspect seems like it would be especially useful.
K.T. I think so. The bottom line in all of my classes is "Get the damn job." I want them to work professionally as actors, and get paid for their talent.
D.M. It sounds like a rigorous learning experience.

K.T. It really is—I definitely put them through their paces. The other thing I do, in all of my classes, which I think is very helpful, is attempt to pass on a professional code or ethics, a way of behaving in the workplace, that will hopefully benefit them throughout their career. It's easy for actors to get so wrapped up in their own private processes that they forget about their relationships to everyone else on the production. But the actor is usually the last piece of the puzzle, the last person who gets to come in and do their job, and without that lighting technician, that construction foreman, that box office worker, that stagehand, there is no job for the actor to do. Forget the above-the-line and below-the-line nonsense. Without every piece of the puzzle, no one has a job, including the actor. Actors need to remain humble, grateful, and always remember that they are part of a team.

But it's all great fun. My students and I laugh a lot, and I really care about them and feel vested in their success. We have a good time and we learn a lot.

D.M. Do you see in these young actors the conviction that you had as a young actor?

K.T. Absolutely. They are serious about it. And some of them are phenomenally gifted. I think many of them will be among the next great generation of actors. They should have rewarding careers and rewarding lives.

D.M. So you are hopeful for the future of the craft.

K.T. Oh, definitely! There are so many talented young actors coming up right now, in both theater and film. We're going to be in good hands.

ACTING AND DAILY LIFE

DUSTIN MORROW Let's talk about the many ways in which acting can be rewarding offstage. That is, all the ways that it can enrich your everyday life.

KATHLEEN TURNER There's a lot to talk about there.

D.M. For starters, I would imagine that acting makes you more understanding of people in general, especially the people around you.

K.T. Yeah, it does. I think it helps to create a tolerance. I've spent much of my life examining the actions of characters in plays, or films, or books, or whatever, asking, "Why did they do that? Why would they make that choice?" That process forces you to look at life from other viewpoints. It doesn't mean you agree, but it does mean you understand. It's easy get into the habit of doing the opposite of that—of not putting yourself in someone else's shoes. Acting trains you to do it naturally, so it's almost second nature. It's a kind of automatic exploration. It doesn't mean that you won't continue to hate what they say, but it will give you that pause. That pause to be able to determine your response, without intolerance or automatic knee-jerk reaction.

D.M. It seems then that two actors in a relationship should be a dream marriage, but it so rarely works out!

K.T. Oh, I don't think so! I think when two actors get married, one of them is inevitably always working more than the other, and that starts to create a bit of friction—there's an inherent competitiveness that has to build if one is getting much more work than the other one. One level of fame and success is rising and the other isn't. That signals bad things ahead. And if they're both working their butts off, then there's barely a home life. And the odds are, they're spending very little time together. So, no, my advice would be to not marry another actor if you're an actor.

D.M. So acting can teach you tolerance and can teach you patience, just maybe not for a spouse who's also an actor!

K.T. Tolerance, definitely, but I wouldn't say patience. I would say it teaches you the ability to step back a bit, which creates that breathing space that leads to empathy and understanding. As an actor you have this viewpoint on yourself that's almost like a third eye, like a tape recorder. A way to see yourself from outside yourself.

D.M. Like a higher level of self-awareness.

K.T. Kind of. But it's not judgmental. It's just this device that you can play back to review your own work. It gives you this sense of detachment, where part of you is able to observe yourself as a working performer all the time. It's valuable in the work and in life.

D.M. And your skills as an actor have helped you to be able to read people.

K.T. Oh, definitely.

D.M. To assess motivations and things like that?

K.T. Absolutely. And also how to communicate with them better. How to appeal to people, how to approach them—for example, when I go to Washington to speak on behalf of Planned Parenthood, or for the rights of women and children, or one of my other causes, being able to read the room and to know which approach is probably going to be most effective is invaluable. Especially when I'm dealing with a room of close-minded right-wing jerks!

I can read the body language. Just by how they're sitting, I can tell what they're thinking and adjust my rhetoric to that. If they're sitting toward you or leaning away from you, if they make eye contact or avert their eyes, if they're tense or if they're relaxed, if they're respectful or disrespectful, I can read them like books. And if I start to lose their attention, I can tell, and I can get it back just like I can command the attention of an audience in a theater.

D.M. That's interesting. You would therefore think that actors are more socially adept than other people because of these abilities.

K.T. You would think they would be, wouldn't you?

D.M. Absolutely, based on what you're saying.

K.T. And yet I've known so many who aren't. No, I think I am an exception in many ways to this sort of thing. I find it intriguing and fun to read people and make use of that knowledge. But I have met a lot of actors who are not socially very savvy. Not very swift on their feet, as it were. I think part of that comes from the fact that a lot of actors, a lot of very "intense" actors, say—put some quote marks around that, please—aren't very social, period.

First of all, if you're working, you see the people in your company and crew day after day after day. You probably see them more than your own family. That's true for both film and for theater. We spend more time with a very small group of people, and we're not out there meeting a lot of people or attending many social events. You're doing eight shows a week. You don't have dinners out, you don't go to the movies, you don't do anything but go home, go to the gym, and go to work! You're just at the theater, all the time. You're in a cocoon, a bubble.

So you get rusty. You can get out of practice, in terms of dealing with other people. I've had times in my life when I've just thought that going out to deal with a bunch of people that I don't know is just overwhelming. Just too much to handle. I just want to withdraw, be a turtle and pull my head back into my shell.

But on the other hand, I recognize when I'm doing that and I am able to understand the reasons that I feel that way, and it's okay. When you reach a certain level of fame, you become a bit of a trophy. And you know that that's how many people see you, and it's dehumanizing. It means that sometimes people ask you to do things for their own reputation, and it has nothing to do with you personally. They just want to say to the people they know, "Look, I can produce Kathleen Turner." Or, "You want her here? I can get her here." And in fact, I would never allow a charity event, or a service organization-aimed event, to use my name unless I was actually going to be there. That's a hard and fast rule for me, and people know that. People know that if my name is on that invitation, it means I will be there and they will meet me.

But there are a great many people who will want to exploit that. And it becomes almost like a competition. One group will say, "Damn, we couldn't get Kathleen Turner," and another one will say, "Well, we did." And you feel like you're this trophy, that you're being used. And you have to decide if the use of your name is worth it or not. It does make you a little cynical and it makes you a little withdrawn, I think. It makes you feel exploited and anxious. And it can make you resentful and reluctant to go out at all sometimes. I think a little anti-social feeling emerges, understandably.

D.M. Does being an actor help with your memory? Are you good with names and faces?

K.T. I never forget a face. Faces, excellent. Names, awful.

D.M. Why is that?

K.T. Are you kidding? Can you imagine how many people I meet in a week?

D.M. I didn't think about that.

K.T. But I'm fabulous with remembering faces. I mean, I will run into someone I haven't seen for ten years and say, "I met you ten years ago at the City Meals-on-Wheels benefit!" I never forget a face. But names—forget it. I don't even try anymore.

D.M. I wonder if that's relatable in any way to how you use your memory as an actor? Do you think you have a visual memory?

K.T. I believe I do. If I see a name written down, I'll retain it much longer than if I just hear it.

D.M. You mentioned that you have a virtually photographic memory when it comes to learning and retaining a script.

K.T. I do. I can learn a long script in no time flat, and I pretty rarely forget a line. It happens, but not often.

D.M. I just find it so strange then that you'll forget all your lines within a week of finishing a show. That's so odd.

K.T. Well, why would I retain them? What am I going to do with them? They'd just be taking up space in my memory that I could use for something else.

D.M. I think our brains work very differently.

K.T. That's why I'm an actor, Dustin.

D.M. And that's what's going to give our book some spice.

K.T. You are looking for trouble, mister.

D.M. Here's a fun question for you: do you think actors make good liars?

K.T. Oh, you're definitely trying to get me in trouble here! Yes, I do. I think they probably make excellent liars.

D.M. That's the source of a little bit of a paranoia I feel around my actor friends.

K.T. Really?

D.M. Yeah, especially the ones I know to be very good. There's occasionally this element of, "Am I being performed for here?" Like they might be pulling my leg. I'll bet there are situations in your everyday life where you feel performative.

K.T. Definitely. On a daily basis, even. When I walk to the gym, I run into people on the street, total strangers, who'll go, "Kathleen Turner! I love your work!" Which is swell, but I don't know these people at all. I'll thank them profusely, and tell them that what they've said means a lot to me, but that bright response is an automatic act. It's not that I don't mean it, because I do—I am very happy when someone tells me I'm looking good or that they just saw me in a play and liked what I did, but it happens so often that my response has become automated and performative, if you will.

D.M. Which makes sense on another level, if you think about it. Because they don't see Kathleen, the person, they see Kathleen Turner, the celebrity. So it *is* a role you are playing for them.

K.T. That's true.

D.M. Have any of your good friends ever called you out on anything?

K.T. You mean a lie?

D.M. Yeah.

K.T. Yeah, it happens. I've had some good friends say, "Okay, cut the crap, Turner!" But that's usually just when I'm lying about my own feelings, telling everyone I'm not in any pain when I am, or lying about not feeling down in the dumps when I am. I'm not really trying to put anything over on them, I'm just being self-protective. But I have good friends who can see right through it. Which is nice, really.

And frankly, I'm a terrible liar. I'm sure many actors are great liars, but I'm not one of them.

D.M. Really?

K.T. Yeah! In fact, I suspect that the older I get and the better actor I become, the worse a liar I also become. Unfortunately.

D.M. Why unfortunately?

K.T. Well, sometimes you want to protect people's feelings, don't you? I'm pretty incapable of giving a dishonest review of something, and sometimes that gets me in trouble. But heck, I suppose it's not helpful to someone if you lie to them and tell them their work is great when it isn't.

D.M. Is family a different story?

K.T. Oh, I'm always completely honest with my family. My daughter is very creative, and I always give her honest, constructive criticism. Thankfully I love her music. I was a little nervous to listen to her album, precisely because I am so candid and honest, but it turned out to be amazing. Not that I ever really doubted her.

D.M. Thanks for giving me a copy—she's a terrific songwriter.

K.T. She's so talented, I'm very proud of her. She even wrote a song for me, called "Strong Like You." She played it at the opening of *Mother Courage*, and every mom there started crying. It was great.

D.M. I can hear echoes of your voice in hers—it's raw and smoky, but really lovely. With that voice and the strong jazz influence in her work, she reminds me in many ways of Adele and Amy Winehouse.

K.T. She gets that a lot.

D.M. So acting doesn't help you lie to people, but it does help you to see where they are coming from. The great thing about acting, in everyday life, seems like it would be the empathy that you feel for the people around you.

K.T. And to communicate well with them, yes.

D.M. Are there any ways that being an actor can hinder you as you move through your everyday life? Or has it only ever been a good thing?

K.T. I don't feel it interrupts or takes away from any situation. I can't see any place where it wouldn't be helpful, except perhaps in a life-or-death situation of some kind, where a decision had to be made on a moment's notice. We actors like to ruminate on things, you know!

D.M. A friend of mine studied as an actor, but his day job is that of a motivational speaker. And he goes into these big corporations and teaches them basic acting skills, as well as skills in improvisation. He teaches them to apply the skills of an actor to the corporate environment.

K.T. Well, since so much of acting is about empathy, who wouldn't benefit from that, in any environment? Heaven knows the corporate world could use a little more empathy.

One of the best things about acting is that it's a career based on the study of human behavior. So every year I am alive I learn more, and how I change reflects in the work. There's no cap to how much you can learn and grow in this profession, because the art of it is rooted in human interaction and there are no limits to the observation of human behavior.

D.M. I'll bet your skills as an actor help you cope with change easier. That is, I can see it helping you adapt to a new situation with more finesse.

K.T. It's not that it helps you negotiate a major change in your life with any ease, so much as it makes you more open to the idea of change. As an actor, you go from job to job, role to role, city to city, and from one set of co-workers to another. There's a level of almost constant change. It's not a stable, consistent way to live.

D.M. And acting has affected your attitude toward change.

K.T. I live for it now. Change isn't always easy, but it's always, in the end, a good thing. Change is good. Why would you want to live your entire life the same way? Change, take a chance, risk something, live for an adventure. Change is good. We actors are good at that—any actor worth their salt is not afraid of making a fool of herself on a semi-regular basis. Everytime we go onstage we're ready on some level to potentially fall on our faces. We get up and dust ourselves off. Life without risk isn't worth living, honey.

D.M. What's the most important thing that acting has taught you about life?

K.T. Humility. I am less self-involved now than I was at the beginning of my career, and that's come in large part from my experiences as an actress. I'm also much more interesting as a person now than when I began my acting career. I've relaxed a bit, and I have more mature, evolved perspectives now.

But at the same time I am less idealistic. I still believe, deep down, that good will win, that good will prevail over evil, and I won't ever stop believing that, but I am perhaps more cynical about how that's going to happen. The greatest quality in life is compassion, and that covers just about anything. But where I used to think that all people were capable of some compassion, after my decades of working on behalf of the political causes that I advocate for, I'm no longer so sure that's true. And that's sad, because idealism is a virtue, and I miss feeling so idealistic.

D.M. I've found that, too. That's just aging, and exposure to the changing world.

K.T. Yes. All we can do is continue to be hopeful.

LOOKING AHEAD AND
MOVING FORWARD

DUSTIN MORROW All these decades into your career, what do you feel like you are still developing, still working on as an actor?

KATHLEEN TURNER That's tough to answer, because each new project brings new challenges and new things to work on. So it's hard for me to say until I start the next project. But I will only ever choose projects that challenge me, that teach me new things. I will always continue to develop as an actress, to get better and better, until the day I'm done.

D.M. You never fear running out of great material, of not being able to find something to interest you.

K.T. I don't know why I should. There are so many great plays I haven't done, and so many new playwrights doing interesting work. I have come to love developing new plays—both *High* and *Red Hot Patriot* were new plays that I had a hand in guiding.

And the thing to remember about opportunity is that it changes as actors change. As I age, some roles slip away from me, but many more great roles become available to me. Less so on film, of course, but there are so many great roles for a woman my age on the stage. And while some of my physical abilities may have lessened with age and with the rheumatoid arthritis, I continue to see great growth in other capacities, like my vocal abilities, which have grown tremendously and opened new opportunities to me.

Somebody asked me the other day if I was ever going to retire and I said, "Why on earth would I?" It just never occurred to me that I would ever retire. What would I do if I retire? I'd prefer to be Helen Hayes and just keep going forever. I'll do *Airport 17*. Sign me up!

D.M. As long as you keep getting these great roles, there's no reason to stop.

K.T. Exactly. I have no reason to retire because my job, luckily, opens up new opportunities as I age. Actors always bemoan getting older, but it's really a gift. Not only are your skills better, but the roles you can play, onstage anyway, get richer as you get older. Age is an ally, not an enemy.

D.M. That's true. To use your friend as an example, Maggie Smith is eighty-two, and between *Harry Potter* and *Downton Abbey* and some other projects, she's gotten some of the best roles of her career in the last ten years.

K.T. Exactly. Of course, I may not always be able to perform as often as I do now, there are not many women Maggie's age who can do eight shows a week. There are a couple now, but not many.

But there are so many venues in which to stay active and successful as an actor. Maggie is proof of that. Who would have thought fifteen years ago that she'd have a huge role in the most successful film franchise of all time?

And there's really no chance that I'm ever going to run out of great roles. Williams's *Sweet Bird of Youth*, Beckett's *Happy Days* . . . I'd love to do another Shakespeare, maybe Lady MacBeth, or some George Bernard Shaw. I want to play Lear.

D.M. A female Lear—that's fantastic.

K.T. Hell yes. I love love love subverting gender expectations and sexual politics.

D.M. Indeed, you even played Scrooge.

K.T. I was the first female Scrooge in the history of WNYC's annual radio performance of *A Christmas Carol*.

D.M. That must have been incredibly fun.

K.T. So much fun! The only issue I had was that they brought back the brilliant Fred Newman from *A Prairie Home Companion* to do all the sound effects for the production, and beholding his creativity and timing was sometimes so awe-inducing that I'd lose my place in the script.

D.M. Are there other roles you'd like to do that are usually reserved for male actors?

K.T. I'm sure there are. There are a lot of great roles for men out there that I would love to get my hands on.

D.M. Gender role subversion in the American Theater is important politically, perhaps now more than ever.

K.T. Absolutely! Theater has always been political. It's a great forum for addressing issues of gender politics. That's one of the reasons I took on directing *Would You Still Love Me If* . . . It was the kind of bold, important work that could only be mounted in the American theater.

D.M. Who else would you like to play?

K.T. I want to keep working on new plays, developing plays that will be added to the American theatrical canon of great works. I did a new play by Stephen Sachs in the West End of London, called *Bakersfield Mist* and it was so much fun to originate a role, to play a character no one had ever played before.

D.M. Your reviews for that were some of the best you've ever gotten.

K.T. Yes, the critics were very kind. It's a marvelous little play that tackles big ideas—questions of authenticity, class warfare, education and privilege, and the transformative power of art. And it does it with a lightness and wit that never gets too self-important.

Bakersfield Mist, by Stephen Sachs, was inspired by the true story of California long-haul trucker Teri Horton, who purchased a splattered painting for three dollars at a junk shop only to discover later that it was a Jackson Pollack worth millions. In the play, Kathleen plays Maude, a blue collar, trailer park resident who buys what she believes to be a Pollack for a few bucks. The great British actor Ian McDiarmid (best-known to audiences around the world as the Emperor in the Star Wars *movies) plays opposite Kathleen as Lionel, a snobby art historian and critic who is sent to validate the authenticity of Maude's painting. Fireworks ensue as the two engage in a vicious battle of wits, fueled by issues of social class, education, privilege, and the question "What is Art?".*

It's great fun to do a new play, and to know that I'm bringing to life a character that no actress has ever before played. There are more great plays out there than I will ever be able to get to—I'm not concerned about finding material.

D.M. After *Cat on a Hot Tin Roof* and *Virginia Woolf*, you seem have a history of correcting the roles of Elizabeth Taylor, so maybe *Cleopatra's* in your future . . .

K.T. I think I've managed to evade that one, thankfully!

D.M. There must be a lot of actors that you are still really itching to work with.

K.T. Oh, dozens.

D.M. Give me one.

K.T. Frances McDormand would be fun to collaborate with. She was amazing in *Good People*. And I would have loved to have gotten onstage with Alan Rickman. It would have been a beautiful blend of our voices and our humor. I admired him greatly, and I think he and I would have worked very well together.

D.M. So as you age, does your method for choosing parts change? Do you apply different criteria now than you did closer to the beginning of your career?

K.T. Not really. It's still about taking creative risks, doing parts I can learn from, that challenge me, that are unlike things I've done in the past. I am pleased with myself, that I still take huge risks at this stage in my career. That I still say, "I haven't done that before, let's see if I can" as opposed to only doing things that I know I can do well.

Where's the fun in repeating yourself, anyway? And as scary as it is to take risks, isn't it scarier on some level not to? If you repeat the same work year after year, *then* what do you do? Do you hope that you did it as well as you did it last year? Isn't that kind of sad? If you're a high jumper and you become expert at clearing fourteen feet, do you spend the rest of your career easily clearing fourteen feet and going out of your mind with boredom, or do you go for fifteen feet?

In the end, I think that I would miss the vitality in the work if I began to only do parts I know I can do easily. To do something you are not sure you're going to be able to pull off is so much more interesting and exciting, and results in much better work. The risk *is* the work. I hope that doesn't sound pompous. It is truly how I feel.

D.M. I don't think it does. In fact, it sounds even more like a sincere life philosophy than a work philosophy.

K.T. I suppose it is, in some ways.

D.M. Do you have a mantra?

K.T. Hmmm. I suppose it would be "Be brave, be strong, be true." In the end, that's all you need to know as an actor, and as a person who strives to live a fulfilling life—be brave, be strong, be true. If you can do those three things, you're good as gold.

D.M. And take risks.

K.T. And take risks. If you never take any risks, then nothing special is ever going to happen to you.

D.M. This book is proof of that. I was scared about approaching you to do it, but I took the leap and it's worked out well. I've learned a lot, it's been a great experience for me.

K.T. Why were you scared?

D.M. Well, I knew from reading previous interviews you've done that you weren't one to sit down and talk about process. After all, your class, "Practical Acting: Shut Up and Do It," has the phrase "Shut Up" in it!

But I sold you on it.

K.T. Yes, you sold me on it.

D.M. Plus, you have a reputation for being very tough. Not difficult, but definitely no-nonsense.

K.T. Who, little ol' me?

D.M. Maybe it's the voice.

K.T. Ha! Yes, the voice can be scary. I was doing *Red Hot Patriot* in Philadelphia and I overheard a whispering conversation in the wings while I was onstage. After the performance I went over to the guy, and *very* calmly and in as nice a way as I could say it, said, "Please don't do that again" and he burst into tears. So maybe I sometimes come across a little strong!

D.M. On the DVD commentary track for *Serial Mom*, John Waters has perhaps my favorite quote about your reputation.

K.T. Oh dear. I'm afraid to ask, but what's that?

D.M. He says something to the effect that working with you is like "working with a lion—show no fear and you'll be just fine."

K.T. That sounds like something he would say! A guy once told me that my epitaph would be, "More woman than you'll ever get, more man than you'll ever be." I like that one.

D.M. That's pretty great. And sitting down to chat with you has been a real treat.

K.T. For me as well. I spend so much time "just doing it" that I don't often slow down to think about process and history, about what's behind it. About what makes it all work. This was good for me, too.

D.M. I learned a lot.

K.T. As did I.

D.M. Thank you, Kathleen.

K.T. Thanks, Dustin.

D.M. But really, no chance of getting you to do the *Serial Mom* bird call for my ringtone? "Who-wee, who-wee!"

K.T. Go home and record it off your television, kid.

A CLOSER LOOK AT THE FILM PERFORMANCES

As I noted in the Foreword of this book, the following series of mini-essays and observations is provided to guide you deeper into Kathleen's cinematic work, so you may more carefully examine the nuances of her performances by studying the individual choices she makes in each selected scene. This is an exercise I do in my film production courses when I'm teaching my students how to direct actors for the camera. My hope is that reading through these pieces and watching the associated scenes will help you develop a critical eye for film acting. Like all great actors, Kathleen makes her work seem effortless. If you are watching her and observing her work as a performance outside the boundaries of the film's narrative, then she hasn't done her job. She is there to serve the character and the story. So it's easy to forget that what you're watching is actually something that's been carefully considered and intricately constructed.

Anyone who has seen her in person in the theater will tell you that Kathleen is an even better stage actress than she is a film actress. But unfortunately, when a stage performance is rendered, it's gone forever. This is, of course, part of the beauty and excitement of live theater, as Kathleen explained to us earlier in this book. But it's great to have a record of the film performances, and through DVD and streaming media, we can rewind them over and over again, pause them, slow them down, study them up close. That's a great gift to educators and students of acting and directing, and to anyone interested in closely examining the performing arts. It's fun to peek behind the curtain on occasion.

It should be noted that all of these observations were written entirely from my perspective, without the consultation of Kathleen. These are merely my interpretations of her performances, and may or may not accurately reflect the actual motivations in the choices she makes in each selected scene. I hope that you enjoy these short think-pieces, and that they inspire you to look closer at the work of other actors you admire.

A SCENE FROM *BODY HEAT*

Body Heat is, of course, the film that put Kathleen on the map, and in it she breathes new life into the stock femme fatale archetype just as writer/director Lawrence Kasdan brilliantly twists and updates the entire genre of film noir. In *Body Heat*, Kathleen plays Matty Walker, a mysterious young woman who seduces sleazy lawyer Ned Racine (played with an oily, unlikeable deliciousness by William Hurt) into murdering her wealthy husband so she can abscond with his fortune. The film is quite aware of its relationship to classic noirs (particularly *Double Indemnity*, to which it obviously owes most of its narrative), and launched a mini-genre of less-compelling postmodern noir films that continued through the eighties into the early nineties. The film is still frequently recognized as among the sexiest ever made, with multiple publications citing the scene where Ned breaks Matty's door down to embrace her as the single sexiest scene in film history. With its frank, graphic sexuality and nudity, the film was a huge risk for the then-unknown actress, but it paid off in spades, marking one of the splashiest film debuts by an actress in all of cinema history.

At the twelve-minute mark, Ned picks up Matty in a bar. Or so he thinks—the entire meeting, of course, has been orchestrated by Matty. She's setting her trap. It's the second time he's seen her, and he's hooked. What is remarkable about Kathleen's work in this scene, and the subsequent scene at the house, in which she has invited Ned home to look at her collection of wind chimes (yeah, right) is the amount of complete sincerity with which she plays the character. That sincerity is couched in a careful combination of sexual daring, in the sense that Matty is encouraging Ned to make his lascivious advances, and delicate vulnerability, in that Matty is presenting Ned a version of herself in which she is the neglected housewife and an easy target for a "master seducer" like himself. She's so good at seeming genuine and sincere that you might be forgiven for thinking that this neo-noir's real raison d'etre is to reverse the femme fatale cliché at the end (it doesn't, but that's a good thing). And of course, there's the other layer she's simultaneously acting, the layer of play-acting within the acting, that Kathleen and I discussed in her interview. Kathleen's performance in this scene, and in the entire film, is effective on two levels—Matty the oppressed young trophy wife, a creation she's playing to ensnare Ned, and the "real" Matty, a lonely gold-digger and deceitful murderer. In the scene I've cited, it's a performance within a performance within a performance, and through all its complex layers it's great fun to watch.

A SCENE FROM *THE MAN WITH TWO BRAINS*

The title character of *The Man with Two Brains* is Steve Martin's Dr. Michael Hfuhruhurr ("It's pronounced just like it's spelled," he says at one point). He's a widowed brain surgeon who has perfected a new form of "screw-top surgery" (it's exactly what you're picturing). Kathleen is Dolores Benedict, a treacherous femme fatale who marries Dr. Hfuhruhurr but refuses to consummate their relationship. On their honeymoon, the good doctor meets a mad scientist and finds that he can telepathically communicate with one of the scientist's brains-in-a-jar (voiced by Sissy Spacek). A love triangle between Dolores, Dr. Hfuhruhurr and the brain ensues. Would you believe it's a gritty, realist drama? No?

The Man with Two Brains was directed by Carl Reiner and written by Reiner, Martin, and George Gipe. It was the third in a series of deeply silly comedy collaborations between Martin and Reiner, beginning with *The Jerk* and *Dead Men Don't Wear Plaid* and followed by *All of Me*. While not the absurdist masterpiece that is *The Jerk*, *The Man with Two Brains* is a very, very funny movie that provided Kathleen with the opportunity to do some truly broad physical comedy. After *Body Heat*, she was offered a million cookie-cutter femme fatale roles in lesser movies. So in typical Kathleen style, she decided to do a movie that gave her the opportunity to spoof those parts, to have some fun with the image she'd earned from making such a notable debut with *Body Heat*.

At the one hour, two-minute mark begins a scene that opens, appropriately for the madness that is to immediately follow, with Kathleen asking Martin, "Michael, were you out on the lake today kissing your brain?" What follows is a riotous sequence of sustained hilarity, a real coming together of three talented artists—Martin, Reiner, and Kathleen—to wring every drop of comedy out of a broadly comical setup. In the scene, Dolores has discovered the affair Michael has been carrying on with the brain, and seeks revenge. At first she plays the victim, flinging herself, melodramatically and with convulsing sobs, face first onto a sofa. Then Martin receives a phone call, alerting him to Dolores's duplicitous plans to clean out his bank account. He declares a "citizen's divorce" and she responds by trying to melt the brain in the stove. Martin frantically saves the brain and Kathleen attacks him with a butcher knife. Really, you've got to see this stuff to believe it.

They struggle over the knife and then he flings her off his front porch into a ridiculously large puddle of thick dirty muck while screaming, "Into the mud, scum queen!" I'd be lying if I didn't tell you that this is one of my favorite comedic moments in all of film. Covered head to toe in dripping brown mud, Kathleen affects a positively demonic, guttural voice and swears her revenge. The comic rhythms and the interplay between the two actors is very sharp, considering the broad tone of the sequence. Martin was well-established in this type of role, and it's his film. He goes way over the top. Interestingly, what Kathleen has to do, which is most evident in this scene, is come close to matching the heightened, absurdist tenor of Martin's performance while remaining just grounded enough to provide the bulk of the story's progression in the scene and pitched just low enough to make the delivery of his line after he flings her into the mud read as triumphant in tone as well as narrative intent. It's unfortunate that comedic performances are not as often recognized, especially by awards like the Oscars, as dramatic acting. Especially broad comic acting like this, which can flirt so finely with crossing from ridiculously funny to just plain ridiculous. It's misleadingly delicate, and it's an art of its own.

A SCENE FROM *ROMANCING THE STONE*

The blockbuster hit *Romancing the Stone* tells the story of Joan Wilder, a pulp romance novelist living a lonely, meek and sheltered life in New York. She's forced way out of her comfort zone (to put it mildly) when her sister is kidnapped by two gangsters who want a treasure map that her murdered brother-in-law sent to her just before being murdered. Joan is forced to travel to the jungles of South America to deliver the map and save her sister, where she's pursued by local mercenaries and the kidnappers, and romanced by a soldier of fortune (played by Michael Douglas) who she hires to guide her out of the jungle in one piece.

If *Body Heat* put Kathleen on the map, then *Romancing the Stone* cemented her place as the top actress in the industry in the 1980s. Directed by a young Robert Zemekis (who had no prior hits to his name; *Back to the Future* wasn't to come until the following year), *Romancing* was a monster critical and commercial success, and won Kathleen her first Golden Globe award. The film was written by the late Diane Thomas, who was a waitress when she scripted the film, and produced by Michael Douglas, who originally sought only to produce the film but ended up stepping into the lead role after failing to secure an appropriate actor. It was a shrewd move, as the film solidified him as a leading man (while his career as a producer was well established—he'd won an Oscar for *One Flew Over the Cuckoo's Nest*—as an actor, he'd been largely limited to supporting roles; his most noteworthy work as an actor to that point had been his role as the sidekick to Karl Malden on the cop show *Streets of San Francisco*). While a few critics unfairly held that the film was derivative of *Raiders of the Lost Ark* (the screenplay for *Romancing* long-predated the release of *Raiders*), the movie has since been recognized as a contemporary classic, and among the first films of its era to successfully genre-mash, combining romance with flip comedy, light suspense and high adventure.

I love this movie. A lot. It's my favorite movie, so it's hard for me to choose one scene to spotlight. The arc of the character of romance novelist Joan Wilder is enormous, and Kathleen conveys it not only through the film's swashbuckling action, but through an ever-subtly evolving discovery of her physicality, her sexuality, and her inner confidence and strength of character. Joan appears mousy and weak at the open of the film, but no one could write the novels she writes without a true inner strength, and a capacity to dream. People often forget that the world's most enduring superheroes, from Superman to Spiderman, were all created by young people who were once bullied, who didn't fit in, who were oppressed by their peers. That's the case here—as demonstrated in the early scene in which Joan walks down a Manhattan avenue, getting pushed around by street vendors, as if all of New York is beating her down.

But deep inside Joan is Angelina, the beautiful and brave heroine of her pulp novels. In the film's final action sequence, Zemekis has Joan mirror the actions of Angelina from the opening book-within-a-film vignette, as though Joan were applying pieces of her imagination to extricate herself from a real-life dangerous situation. When the dream becomes a reality, Joan is up to the challenge. Even the story of *Romancing*'s creation fits this fairytale: screenwriter Diane Thomas was a struggling waitress with a dream—to be a Hollywood screenwriter—and this film was her real-life happy ending. *Romancing*, above all other things, is a film about dreaming, about discovering and believing in your true self. The film's optimism, heart and spirit are surely no small part of its enduring popularity.

If you twist my arm and force me to cite one scene as the best of Kathleen's work here, then I would go with the climactic moment of the film's romantic storyline. Having survived all manner of danger, from fleeing gunmen to shooting mudslides to swinging over cavernous gorges, Joan and Jack find themselves in the midst of a small Colombian village's evening carnival. Lights are strewn everywhere, and people dance, drink and make merry. It's an incredibly lush setting. Jack and Joan discuss her writing, and she tells him, "I suppose it's my way of living in another age." He gives her a lovely pendant with the inscription "El Corazon," the name of the treasure they're seeking. After she puts it on, Kathleen does something remarkable—she looks up at Douglas with an expression of innocent surprise, as though the pendant and the carnival setting awakened something within her that she did not know was there. It's a magical moment—something that only the medium of cinema could provide, with the use of the closeup and the penlight the cinematographer employs to provide Kathleen's eyes with the canvas she needs to convey what she subtly conveys in that moment.

Joan resists at first, because she doesn't know how, but Jack convinces her to join him on the dance floor. This is where the sequence really soars, and where you can see the mastery of Kathleen's physical performance, so evident in the action sequences in the movie, and in the seductive moments and physical comedy sequences of her two earlier films (*Body Heat* and *The Man with Two Brains*, respectively). As Joan learns how to dance, to let herself go, you can see Kathleen open up the character's movement, and slowly change the way she carries herself and responds to Douglas's flirting. She is discovering the pleasure of being swept off her feet, and the moment is intoxicating. The audience can feel it, too. The rhythmic editing of the sequence, by Donn Cambern and Frank Morriss, who received well-deserved Oscar nominations for the film, lends an able assist. The scene unfolds as a summary of Joan's journey through the entire film—as the dance progresses, you can see her grow more confident with each step. Her wide eyes and surprised but delighted expressions give way to expressions of assuredness, confidence and joy.

The dance sequence is played without dialogue, and what Kathleen achieves is deadly crucial to the narrative, for in the next scene it is Joan who suggests that she and Jack go after the treasure themselves before handing the map over to her sister's kidnappers. It's a plot point that would absolutely not have worked had filmmakers not been able to convey what they did during the dialogue-free dance scene. And the carnival scene ends with fireworks exploding in the background, a lushly soaring piece of Alan Silvestri's terrific score, a camera that pulls up to show the entirety of the festive town square, and for my money the most romantic kiss in all of filmdom. Who could ask for more than that out of the cinema?

A SCENE FROM *CRIMES OF PASSION*

Legendary British film director Ken Russell's career spanned four decades and dozens of films, all of them challenging and dark. Among his uncompromising, love-'em-or-hate-'em works were *Women in Love* (1969), *The Music Lovers* (1970), *The Devils* (1971), *Lisztomania* (1975), *Altered States* (1980), and *Crimes of Passion*, his collaboration with Kathleen, made in 1984 right after she finished *Romancing the Stone*. In this twisted but compelling (and oddly, ultimately moving) melodrama, Kathleen plays Joanna Crane, a deeply unhappy fashion designer who by night becomes a bold, confident prostitute named China Blue. In the midst of her identity crisis, Joanna/China is pursued by two men, an amateur detective (John Laughlin) and a psychotic street preacher (Anthony Perkins in a truly frightening performance).

But describing the plot of this psychosexual comic thriller gives you little sense of it—to actually see it is to be consumed by its surreal set pieces, its outlandish costumes and sets, its hallucinatory photography and stream-of-consciousness dialogue, and its blaring synth score, which is mostly composed of variations on Dvorak's "New World Symphony." To call it the edgiest, most out-there film Kathleen ever made is to undersell it—it might be the most unusual role ever undertaken by a prominent mainstream Hollywood actress. That she did it in the same year that she made a populist Hollywood entertainment like *Romancing* further underscores how truly different this film is. While response to the film was understandably mixed, Kathleen's performance garnered her rave reviews and solidified her reputation as an actress willing to take incredible risks.

At the forty-three minute mark in the film, there's a long scene in which China Blue entertains the young client (Laughlin) who will ultimately fall in love with her. She evades his attempts to get to know her on even the shallowest level, and then seduces him in a seamy, neon-drenched hotel room while dressed as a Sixties-style Pan Am stewardess. They make love, an act Russell shoots with great style entirely in silhouette, while the psychotic preacher played by Perkins spies on them through a peephole. Twisted stuff, to say the least.

During the latter half of this scene, Kathleen does some of her best work in the film. After they've had sex, a fragility and deep hurt enters her voice that was not present in the pre-coital seduction. It's as if the will to masquerade has been driven out of her, and she's a shadow of a

354

person by the end of the scene. Her transformation from the beginning of the sequence to the end is startling. When I teach screenwriting I spend a great deal of time talking to my students about the three-act structure, a writing model that says that every solid narrative needs a beginning, a middle, and an end. Each of these acts performs a specific purpose—we introduce the characters, reveal the exposition, and establish the central conflict in the first act, play out the struggle within the conflict over the course of the second act (which constitutes the majority of most feature films), and resolve the conflict in the third act. Although not every scene in a film has one, many truly great scenes in cinema contain a three act arc of their own. This is one of them, and it's driven by Kathleen's character and her performance. She begins the scene as China Blue, the powerful call girl, and ends the scene as Joanna, the fragile, damaged designer. The sexual act generates a catharsis for the character, forcing her to reckon with her inability to find confidence through anything but play-acting at it. Watch the scene and note how Kathleen leads you through it less with dialogue than with the tenor of her voice and the physicality in her body language.

For all of its decadence and seediness, *Crimes of Passion* is ultimately not a film about sex and perversion but about love, our capacity to accept it and our willingness to look for it when we feel we don't deserve it. The great surprise of this crazy movie is just how pure and traditional its core values end up being. Not many movies can be described as truly one of a kind, but this is one of them.

A SCENE FROM *PRIZZI'S HONOR*

It was John Huston's final big Hollywood movie—he would do only one more film, the tiny indie drama *The Dead* (1987), before passing away. *Prizzi's Honor* is a rich, delicious black comedy about two professional killers, Charlie and Irene, who fall in love, but find that their chosen professions, and his deep ties to the fierce mafia family the Prizzis, will ultimately tear them apart. By the end of the film, they've both taken contracts on each other's lives. One of the best-regarded comedies of the eighties, the film revels in its dark humor (at one point, Jack

Nicholson's Charlie exasperatedly frets to himself, "Do I ice her? Do I marry her? Which one?"). Its freewheeling mix of crime-thriller tropes with comedic family dysfunction led to a healthy box office take and a massive number of award nominations, including seven at the Oscars, and multiple Golden Globe wins, including Best Picture (Comedy/Musical), Best Director, Best Actor for Nicholson, and Best Actress for Kathleen.

At the one-hour, fifty-seven minute mark in the film, near the conclusion, is the scene in which Irene realizes that she's going to be whacked. It's not a long moment, it reveals itself quickly and subtly. But it might be my favorite scene of Kathleen's in the film, because the speed at which the character is forced to realize what's about to happen, process that information, weigh her options, and make a decision about how best to survive, is dizzyingly quick. It's played almost entirely as a reaction shot on Kathleen, and she has very little dialogue, but she makes the most of it.

This scene, like the rest in the film, is framed from Charlie/Nicholson's point-of-view. Just as Irene is an outsider in the Prizzi clan, so is the character in the film. Kathleen plays the character with an interesting mix of confidence and insecurity. One doesn't get to where she has in her profession without self-assurance, but she's also smart enough, and cautious enough, to know that the Prizzis could flip on her at any moment. Part of the fun of the film, as with Matty in *Body Heat*, comes in trying to figure out when she's being sincere and when she's playing Charlie for a fool. The shades of gray in the performance, the idea that she's capable of doing both at the same time, is part of what makes Kathleen's work fun to look at closely. It's actually relatively uncommon for a character to be presented with such heavy information and have to make a life-and-death decision so quickly in a film, because screenwriters and directors understandably want to milk moments like this for every ounce of drama. Huston was not afraid to overplay the moment (see the famous ending of *Chinatown*), so it's interesting to see the challenge he puts to Kathleen at the conclusion of *Prizzi's Honor*. It's a lot of narrative for an actress to play in a very brief moment.

A SCENE FROM *PEGGY SUE GOT MARRIED*

In Francis Ford Coppola's magical, lyrical comedy, Kathleen plays the title character, a woman who gets a second chance at creating the life she always wanted when she's knocked unconscious at her 25-year high school reunion and time travels back to her senior year of high school. Eschewing most of the easy gags found in time travel comedies (even the great ones, like *Back to the Future*), Coppola goes for something deeper here, a questioning of the big decisions that can be made for the best of reasons, but can lead to a lifetime of regret and compromised dreams. The film was a box office hit, restored Coppola's reputation after a string of disappointments, and earned Kathleen a mountain of award nominations, including ones from the Golden Globes and the Oscars.

The film is full of some of Kathleen's finest moments as a comedienne, like her over-singing of "My Country Tis of Thee" in her high school classroom, and the jaded inflection in her one-liners (she dryly informs her math teacher that she will never need algebra—"I speak from experience"). But it's the darker, dramatic moments that really resonate. Every scene set in the past, no matter how wispy or humorous, is laced with deep melancholy, which makes the final scene, beginning at the one hour, thirty-six minute mark, particularly tricky.

In the scene, Peggy Sue wakes up in a hospital bed in the present, and dances around a discussion of their future with her husband, who has disappointed her for many years, and whether they'll even have a future together. The challenge put to Kathleen in this scene lies in her needing to convince us that, in spite of all he's put her through, and her experience of going back to high school and seeing the disappointment that lies ahead, she still believes that she could find love with this man. It's a resonant and poignant ending (screenwriter Charlie Kaufman employed a similarly effective version of it later at the end of 2004's *Eternal Sunshine of the Spotless Mind*), delicately played, as it finds two people choosing to love each other, even though they know that with that love will come a mountain of pain. And it's all there in Kathleen's face, as she smiles through welling tears, that embrace of a hope that things will be better and an acceptance of the fact that's there is no good in life without the bad to make it mean something. It is the rare thing that an actor gets to play in modern Hollywood filmmaking—emotional maturity—and you can see the actress relishing the opportunity to make the most of it.

A SCENE FROM *SWITCHING CHANNELS*

Switching Channels is Kathleen's least-favorite of her movies, a role she took for the paycheck since she was about to have a child and knew she would not work for awhile. While not a great film by any stretch of the imagination, I've always enjoyed its manic, frenetic energy, and I think there's much to admire in it, including a sly, funny supporting turn from Christopher Reeve that lampoons his blue blood, Superman image, and some clever updating of the source material to the dawn of the 24-hour cable news setting. That source material is Ben Hecht's and Charles MacArthur's classic Broadway comedy *The Front Page*, which was made into the equally classic screwball film *His Girl Friday*, starring Cary Grant and Rosalind Russell.

In this update, Kathleen plays Christie Colleran, a successful cable television news reporter whose conniving ex-husband, Sully (played by Burt Reynolds, with whom Kathleen famously clashed on the set), attempts to prevent her retirement from reporting and her impending marriage to a wealthy, handsome corporate mogul (Reeve). The film was not a commercial or critical success, and it would perhaps have been a sharper work with its original lead, Michael Caine, but I hold that it has its pleasures, not the least of which is Kathleen's breezy, funny performance.

Early in the film, at the eleven-minute mark, is the scene in which Christie informs Sully that she's met someone and that she's retiring from reporting the news. Still in love with her but not wanting to show it, he's understandably shocked, but attempts to play it cool. She sees right through him, and his exasperated response amuses her to no end. In a film where the upper hand shifts between the two characters ten or twenty times in every scene, she's clearly calling the shots in this moment and enjoying every second of it. Kathleen somehow makes her character's smugness likable and cute—an acting challenge that requires walking a highwire where you have insufferableness on one side and sentimentality on the other. It's classic, seemingly effortless "romantic comedy acting." She delivers the entire scene as a one big "na-na, I told you so," and yet the audience is right there with her. Kathleen bites into the film's rapid-fire verbal sparring with gusto, and despite the fact that she and Reynolds did not get along, they're well matched as this kind of quick-fire comedy plays to his strengths, too. As battle-of-the-sexes comedies go, it's no *War of the Roses*, but it's also much better than its reputation might indicate. Acting in romantic comedies has to feel effortless for the films to work, and so the intricacies of the performances often go overlooked. Watch Meg Ryan's work in *When Harry Met Sally*—the character is in many ways an annoying prude, and yet you not only root for her but fall for her. There's more to it than just being innately likable as an actor. It's hard work, and that Kathleen pulls it off when the film that surrounds her is not that strong is interesting.

A SCENE FROM *THE ACCIDENTAL TOURIST*

Based on Anne Tyler's enormous bestselling novel of the same name, *The Accidental Tourist* is the story of a travel writer (William Hurt) who has become disconnected from the world around him following the tragic death of his young son. His marriage has disintegrated and he's left by his wife (Kathleen), who can no longer handle his emotional distance. Through a burgeoning relationship with a loopy dog trainer (Geena Davis, in an Oscar-winning performance), the depressed travel writer begins to reengage with life again. The film was directed by Lawrence Kasdan, who also adapted (with Frank Galati) the book into the screenplay. Kasdan has become an important, influential filmmaker whose body of work includes *The Big Chill*, *Silverado*, *Grand Canyon*, and as a screenwriter, *Raiders of the Lost Ark* and *The Empire Strikes Back*. *Body Heat* was his debut as a director, as well as his first teaming with William Hurt and Kathleen.

Kathleen took the more understated and far less showy of the two female leads in the film. It is Davis's character who acts as the lively free spirit to Hurt's dour writer. As the depressed and grieving wife, Kathleen has the far quieter part. Not to demean Davis's tremendous performance, but Kathleen actually has the tougher job here. Her character must undergo an enormous journey, much of it offscreen and therefore implied subtly through the limited screen time she does have, in which she reaches for and fails to find some kind of healing without her husband. When she risks losing him to this new woman in his life, she makes a last-ditch effort to make the marriage work. Better to have little than to have nothing at all. Like the mother she played in *The Virgin Suicides*, who also lost a child, this is a profoundly sad character, adrift in pain, confusion and grief, unsure of the degree to which she may ever be able to rebuild her life.

And as in *The Virgin Suicides*, Kathleen has no big moment of catharsis in *The Accidental Tourist*. There is no scene in which she gets to break down, cry and scream and throw things about the room. Her character's grief is of the worst kind—inert, building up inside her, dragging her down like a weight about her neck. More than she even realizes.

While there are certainly bigger scenes for Kathleen in the film, I think her most elegant moment comes during a quiet scene at the one hour, seventeen-minute mark. The spouses have not seen each other for some time, since she left him, when they run into one another at a wedding in which he is a groomsman and she is a bridesmaid. It's a furiously awkward and painful encounter, with each seeking information about the other, and trying to gauge the other's emotional health, without saying anything too confrontational. After a deadly pause, Kathleen says, "I know you're living with someone." The way she says it, with tears and a forced smile waging war in her expression, will break your heart into a thousand pieces. It is among the film's most powerful moments. The scene concludes with the two of them gazing at each other from across the altar as their friends get married. They don't speak, but we can feel the lifetime of shared experience and sadness between them. It's a truly lovely piece of nonverbal acting. A look can say everything. An actor's eyes and voice are perhaps their most valuable tools. Watch this scene while giving careful consideration to how both William Hurt and Kathleen use their eyes. When do they make eye contact and when do they avert their gazes? How do they look at each other? How do those looks change over the course of the scene?

Kathleen has said that, despite its healthy box office, rave reviews, and the slew of awards that it won, the film still feels underrated. I think I agree—it's surprising that the movie isn't remembered and cited more often today. While less showy, it is a film every bit the equal of the principals' earlier collaboration, *Body Heat*, and Kasdan's work on the film as both writer and director proves a textbook example of how to effectively translate a complex novel to the screen.

A SCENE FROM *THE WAR OF THE ROSES*

The War of the Roses, based on the novel of the same name by Warren Adler, is a very dark comedy about the bitter divorce between upper-class WASPs Barbara and Oliver Rose. The movie chronicles the escalating battle between the couple, as both refuse to move out of their beautiful home. The film was the third monster box office hit for Kathleen, Michael Douglas, and Danny DeVito (who directed as well as played a supporting role), and was a great critical success. Michael Douglas and Kathleen both received Golden Globe acting nominations, and the film was nominated for Best Film (Musical/Comedy). The movie's shocking-but-inevitable ending is distinctly anti-Hollywood, and was hard-won in a battle between the three stars and the studio executives, who wanted a more conventional happy resolution.

At the twenty-seven-minute mark of this razor-sharp black comedy, Kathleen has a brief monologue that demonstrates her ability to turn even words of frustration and anger into music. The speech centers on Kathleen's character, Barbara Rose, interviewing a live-in caretaker for her large home, at the insistence of her husband Oliver (played by Douglas, in one of his richest and most underrated performances). As Kathleen begins to speak, all of the frustrations felt by her character focus themselves in a hurricane of verbiage, a borderline stream-of-consciousness outpouring of emotional release.

The words are searing and painful, and a lesser actor might have played them with straightforward anger, but Kathleen manages to convey Barbara's stifled dissatisfaction without losing the humor inherent in the scene. On the page, the monologue reads with hard, clipped sounds, and a staccato stopping-and-starting pattern as the character struggles to organize her thoughts. But Kathleen instead infuses the language with a rhythm of fluidity, allowing the words to pour out of her as if she's speaking faster than she can formulate ideas. This delivery serves the movie's central stroke of genius—it makes Barbara Rose *every* woman who has ever felt confined by the potentially restricting roles of Mother, Housewife, Homemaker, and Caretaker. As delivered by Kathleen, the words come from someplace deep inside. From the gut.

Kathleen's rhythms are distinctly comic, punctuated by sharp moments of deeper pathos. The humor in her performance is assisted by DeVito's intermittent cutting to reactions of disbelief from the caretaker she is interviewing (played by the wonderful German actress Marianne Sagebrecht). But the darkness in this otherwise very funny scene is entirely Kathleen's creation. Listen to how she punches the word "crammed" when she says, "I have a wonderful house, *crammed* with beautiful things." She nearly chokes on the last word in the line, "I suppose some people would find my life *disgusting*." And there is an incredible flash of sorrow and doubt in the word "proud," when she states, "I am *proud* of what I have accomplished." In concert with the tone and intent of the film, Kathleen plays the scene with a mixture of sadness, regret, and exasperation, without losing sight of the biting comedy that drives the narrative.

A SCENE FROM *V.I. WARSHAWSKI*

V.I. Warshawski was meant to be the first in a franchise of films based on author Sara Paretsky's gutsy Chicago detective, but its lukewarm critical reception and poor box office performance led the Disney studio to cancel the planned sequels. Based on the Paretsky novel *Deadlock*, the film teams the tough-talking Warshawski with the daughter of an ex-professional hockey player as they attempt to solve the murder of the girl's father. Paretsky and critics praised Kathleen's performance (she later reprised the role in a series of BBC radio plays), but didn't care for the narrative, out of which the studio reportedly cut all the grit and guts. The film needed more edge, and is a frustrating watch because so much about it is so good. Kathleen is indeed fantastic in the part, the Chicago setting is shot beautifully, the musical score is tremendously fun, and the film is full of delightful supporting characters (inhabited by great character actors like Stephen Root and the late Charles Durning), but it strands them with little to do. With a sharper script and a different studio behind the wheel (Paretsky's novels have too much substance and attitude to withstand being Disney-fied), perhaps audiences would have followed this no-nonsense detective into as many films as Kathleen would have wanted to make.

The character may be the closest in many ways to the real Kathleen— she's witty but steely, tough but warm, accommodating but no-nonsense. The film doesn't provide a lot of opportunity for acting pyrotechnics, relying instead on Kathleen's natural charm and charisma. Her standout scene might be the one near the open of the film (at the seven-minute mark) in which V.I. visits a classic Chicago tavern and decides to pick up the hockey player who will later become the murder victim at the mystery's center. With warm humor, Kathleen flips a number of gender stereotypes as she spots him, decides to make her move, preps herself, and goes in for the kill. The delicate line that Kathleen so effectively walks in her performance is that of keeping it on the side of gender-political satire and away from what might easily have become cheap male-bashing. She does this by nearly winking at the camera, inviting the audience in as partners on the jokes. This was something her co-star on *Prizzi's Honor* was famous for, this acting style in which he played the scenes while also kind of commenting on them through the affected quality of his performances. It's a controversial choice—Nicholson has often been criticized for playing versions of his own public persona instead of new characters. *V.I. Warshawski* is perhaps the closest Kathleen gets to that, but it's hard not to be amused by the musicality in her line readings in this film, especially when she's saying stuff like "Never underestimate a man's ability to underestimate a woman" moments before she flattens a hoodlum by socking him square in the nose.

A SCENE FROM *SERIAL MOM*

John Waters is the legendary Baltimore-based King of Bad Taste. His early films starred an equally legendary three-hundred pound transvestite actor named Divine, who in the most infamous moment of Waters's most notorious film, *Pink Flamingos*, consumes a pile of just-excreted dog feces. Waters later went semi-mainstream with movies like *Polyester* and *Cry-Baby* (starring a young Johnny Depp), and fully mainstream with the hit Broadway adaptation of his film *Hairspray*. But pre-Broadway, during that pseudo-Hollywood period, he made the hilarious *Serial Mom*, in which Kathleen plays Beverly Sutphin, a suburban housewife who is a terrific homemaker and responsible member of her community. She also happens to be a ruthless serial killer, happy to dispatch her victims for the smallest of infractions, such as the failure to recycle as assiduously as she does. Way ahead of its time, the film brilliantly skewers our morbid fascination with things like true crime stories, celebrity culture, and reality television.

At the time she took the part, it was considered a huge career risk for an actress of Kathleen's stature to work with a maverick like Waters. But the proof is in the pudding, as *Serial Mom* has since become a cult classic and is regarded by many (including Waters himself) as the director's best film. The movie's comedy is often very broad, but Kathleen's work, when carefully examined, is incredibly nuanced. No actor will ever win an Oscar for a John Waters movie, which is a shame, because this may have been the best performance by an actor of either sex in 1994.

Choosing one scene to write about is tough, because Kathleen does something joyful whenever she's onscreen here, which is most of the movie. In nearly every scene, Kathleen plays a psychotic act, whether it's a profane prank call or chasing someone down the street with a butcher knife, as a natural extension of her similarly exaggerated but non-criminal behavior as a wholesome wife and mother. Just witness the wacked-out enthusiasm with which she belts out Barry Manilow's "Day Break" while she recycles her bottles and cans (at the twenty-five-minute mark). It's a scene played as insanely as the one in which she murders an old woman with a turkey leg. Waters constantly equates the two types of behavior, asking the questions he's asked in all of his offbeat films about loveable weirdos: who gets to decide what is normal, and what does normal mean anyway? The tone in Kathleen's performance, despite the insanely varied content of the individual scenes, is somehow wholly consistent throughout the film.

At the thirty-three minute mark, watch an hysterical scene in which Beverly follows her daughter's philandering boyfriend into a public bathroom at a swap meet and plants a fireplace poker in his back. While exhibiting no second thoughts or remorse over her murderous action, when she extracts the poker it comes with his liver, and she's disgusted as she tries to remove it. And then, in true John Waters style, she slips on it. Throughout the entire sequence, despite her actions, Beverly just seems so quintessentially loving and maternal. The tone of the scene, and the entire film, is so incredibly specific that the danger in underplaying it or overplaying it is enormous. And indeed, there are many actors who haven't fared well in Waters's films. While actors must recalibrate performances based on genre, they also have to attune their work to match the tonal vision of the filmmaker, which is not an easy endeavor (of course, it's the job of the director to convey that tone, so more often than not, when it doesn't work, it's not the actor's fault). In Kathleen's filmography, the earlier *Crimes of Passion* is another great example of this—the film is thoroughly surreal, and the actors in it have to work in concert with the tone director Ken Russell is pursuing or the narrative would fall apart.

A SCENE FROM *THE VIRGIN SUICIDES*

The Virgin Suicides was Sofia Coppola's first feature film as a writer/director. At a time when most people knew her only from her stilted, much-maligned performance in *The Godfather Part III*, Kathleen and Francis Ford Coppola, Sofia's father and a producer on *Virgin Suicides*, believed in her vision for this cinematic adaptation of Jeffrey Eugenides's haunting novel of the same name. Their confidence in her was well-founded, because the film has gone onto become something of a modern classic, and launched Coppola's career as a filmmaker. With its Seventies light-rock soundtrack, hazy cinematography, florid art direction, elliptical editing, and melancholy score by the French electronic duo Air,

The Virgin Suicides is unique in its narcotic tone. It tells the story of a family with five young girls, all of whom are beautiful, mysterious and obsessed over by the young boys in the neighborhood. As intimated by the title, the film chronicles the short period of time in which each girl decided to end her life.

While the film features strong performances from then-newcomers Kirsten Dunst and Josh Hartnett, it is James Woods and Kathleen who ground the film, as the parents of the girls. Both actors give sad, haunting performances, and it is their pain that prevents the film from becoming too dreamy to fail to evoke a profound sense of loss. It's no accident that Coppola's camera lingers on a silent, stressed Kathleen and strongly registers her valid concern after the girls go off to prom (a delicate moment well-played, seen at the fifty-one minute mark).

At the forty-two minute mark is a lovely, understated scene full of interesting little choices by Kathleen. Hartnett's character, high school dreamboat Trip, has been invited by Dunst's Lux to watch TV with the family. Kathleen sits between them, rigid as a board, looking thoroughly worried. When Lux offers Trip more soda, Kathleen looks at the beverage as though it's a dangerous love potion. And when he props his foot on the coffee table, her offence at the action is palpable. As he departs for the evening, he offers Kathleen his hand and she stares at it as though it's carrying the plague. Her eyes bore into his back as he walks out of the room. If looks could kill . . .

And yet nowhere in the scene, or in the entire film, does she register the emotions that I thought upon first viewing were to be the natural destination for this character: rage and anger. The audience maintains a deep sympathy for Kathleen's character even as we hold her partly responsible for the smothering actions that played a role in her daughters' sad decisions. The Virgin Suicides contains some of Kathleen's quietest and most finely-tuned work.

A SCENE FROM *THE PERFECT FAMILY*

In Anne Renton's indie comedy The Perfect Family, Kathleen plays Eileen Cleary, a devoutly Catholic woman who believes her chance at winning the "Catholic Woman of the Year" award will be jeopardized by her family, which includes a husband with a drinking problem, a son whose marriage is breaking up, and a daughter who is pregnant and about to marry her girlfriend. After a long time away from lead roles in film, Kathleen received a warm reception from critics, who universally praised her performance, but expressed a general desire that the film had been a bit edgier and taken more of a stand in its politics.

At the one hour, seven-minute mark comes perhaps the film's most powerful scene, and one of its only purely dramatic moments. In the scene, Eileen seeks to comfort her daughter Shannon (played by Emily Deschanel), who's just suffered a miscarriage. At first her attempts to console her daughter are rooted entirely in her own reliance on the church. "It just wasn't in God's plan right now," she tells her daughter. Shannon's understandable anger at this source of solace, so rooted in everything that her mother has used in the past to keep her at arm's length, turns almost immediately personal. Her assumption, that her mother's life has been relatively free of this kind of grief and loss, is then exploded by a heartbreaking confession by Eileen that she sought an abortion many years earlier, a troubling experience that changed her in profound ways.

It's the kind of monologue that only an actress with the right amount of life experience could play. All of the world-weariness and the regret of the character's life, lived quietly and alone despite being surroundsed by the family and the structure of the Catholic Church, comes out in Kathleen's performance. As a character, Eileen gains several new dimensions in this scene, and the tricky work Kathleen does here is to make you understand and sympathize with Eileen, even if you don't necessarily agree with her view of the world. Specifically, Kathleen uses the fast-changing rhythms of her breathing as the scene unfolds to convey Eileen's exasperation and feelings of hopelessness. In this scene, Eileen finds doubt, and with it, humility. The knowledge that Kathleen's own moral and political views are so completely different from Eileen's serves to make this performance even more interesting.

SELECTED STAGE CREDITS

MR. T (1977)
By Michael Zettler
Directed by Bob Zuckerman
Starring Kathleen Turner

GEMINI (1978)
By Albert Innaurato
Directed by Peter Mark Schifter
Starring Anne DiSalvo, Danny Aiello, Kathleen Turner

TRAVESTIES (1980)
By Tom Stoppard
Directed by Edward Gilbert
Starring Kathleen Turner

THE SEAGULL (1980)
By Anton Chekhov
Directed by Arif Hasnain
Starring Tom Hulce, Kathleen Turner, Linda Thorson

TOYER (1985)
By Gardner McKay
Directed by Tony Richardson
Starring Kathleen Turner, Brad Davis

A MIDSUMMER NIGHT'S DREAM (1985)
By William Shakespeare

Directed by David Chambers
Starring Kathleen Turner, Avery Brooks

CAMILLE (1987)

By Alexandre Dumas
Directed by Ron Daniel
Starring Kathleen Turner

LOVE LETTERS (1989)

By A. R. Gurney
Directed by John Tillinger
Starring Kathleen Turner, John Rubinstein

CAT ON A HOT TIN ROOF (1990)

By Tennessee Williams
Directed by Howard Davies
Starring Kathleen Turner, Charles Durning, Polly Holliday, Daniel Hugh Kelly
Awards for Kathleen: Tony Award for Best Actress in a Play (Nominated)

INDISCRETIONS (1995)

By Jean Cocteau (translation by Jeremy Sams)
Directed by Sean Mathias
Starring Kathleen Turner, Jude Law, Eileen Atkins, Roger Rees, Cynthia Nixon

OUR BETTERS (1997)

By W. Somerset Maugham
Directed by Michael Rudman
Starring Kathleen Turner, Rula Lenska, Nigel Davenport

TALLULAH (1997 – Great Britain; 2000 – U.S.)

By Sandra Ryan Heyward
Directed by Michael Lessac
Starring Kathleen Turner

THE GRADUATE (2000 – Great Britain; 2001 – Canada; 2002 – U.S.)
By Terry Johnson (adaptation of Buck Henry's screenplay)
Directed by Terry Johnson
Starring Kathleen Turner, Jason Biggs, Alicia Silverstone

THE EXONERATED (2003)
By Jessica Blank, Erik Jensen
Directed by Bob Balaban
Starring Kathleen Turner

WHO'S AFRAID OF VIRGINIA WOOLF?
   (2005 – U.S.; 2006 – Great Britain; 2007 – U.S. Tour)
By Edward Albee
Directed by Anthony Page
Starring Kathleen Turner, Bill Irwin
Awards for Kathleen: Tony Award for Best Actress in a Play (Nominated), Drama
   Desk Award Best Actress in a Play (Nominated)

CRIMES OF THE HEART (2007-08)
By Beth Henley
Directed by Kathleen Turner
Starring Jennifer Dundas, Sarah Paulson, Lily Rabe

THE THIRD STORY (2009)
By Charles Busch
Directed by Carl Andress
Starring Charles Busch, Kathleen Turner

RED HOT PATRIOT: THE KICK-ASS WIT OF MOLLY IVINS
   (2010 – Philadelphia; 2012 – Washington DC; 2014 – Berkeley)
By Margaret Engel and Allison Engel
Directed by David Esbjornson
Starring Kathleen Turner

HIGH (2011 – Broadway; 2012 – U.S. Tour)

By Matthew Lombardo

Directed by Rob Ruggiero

Starring Kathleen Turner, Evan Jonigkeit, Stephen Kunken

Awards for Kathleen: Drama League Award for Distinguished Performance
  (Nominated)

THE KILLING OF SISTER GEORGE (2012)

By Frank Marcus

Adapted by Jeffrey Hatcher

Directed by Kathleen Turner

Starring Kathleen Turner, Clea Alsip, Betsy Aidem, Olga Merediz

MOTHER COURAGE AND HER CHILDREN (2014)

By Bertolt Brecht

Translated by David Hare

Directed by Molly Smith

Starring Kathleen Turner, Nicholas Rodriguez, Nehal Johsi, Meg Gillentine, Rick
  Foucheux, and Erin Weaver

BAKERSFIELD MIST (2014)

By Stephen Sachs

Directed by Polly Teale

Starring Kathleen Turner and Ian McDiarmid

WOULD YOU STILL LOVE ME IF . . . (2015)

By John S. Anastasi

Directed by Kathleen Turner

Starring Kathleen Turner, Roya Shanks, Rebecca Brooksher and Sofia Jean
  Gomez

THE YEAR OF MAGICAL THINKING (2016)

By Joan Didion

Directed by Gaye Taylor Upchurch

Starring Kathleen Turner

SELECTED FILM CREDITS

Body Heat (Released August 28, 1981)

Directed by Lawrence Kasdan

Produced by Fred T. Gallo, Robert Grand

    Written by Lawrence Kasdan

Starring William Hurt, Kathleen Turner, Richard Crenna, Ted Danson, Mickey
    Rourke

Running time 113 minutes

Awards for Kathleen: BAFTA Award for Best Newcomer (Nominated), Golden
    Globe Award for New Star of the Year (Nominated)

The Man with Two Brains (Released June 3, 1983)

Directed by Carl Reiner

Produced by William E. McEuen, David V. Picker

Written by Steve Martin, Carl Reiner, George Gipe

Starring Steve Martin, Kathleen Turner

Running time 93 minutes

Romancing the Stone (Released March 30, 1984)

Directed by Robert Zemeckis

Produced by Michael Douglas

Written by Diane Thomas

Starring Michael Douglas, Kathleen Turner, Danny DeVito

Running time 106 minutes

Awards for Kathleen: Golden Globe Award for Best Actress—Motion Picture
    Musical or Comedy (Won), Los Angeles Film Critics Association Award for
    Best Actress (also for Crimes of Passion) (Won), National Society of Film Crit-
    ics Award for Best Actress (First Runner-Up)

A BREED APART (Released June 1, 1984)

Directed by Philippe Mora

Produced by John Daly, Derek Gibson

Written by Paul Wheeler

Starring Rutger Hauer, Powers Boothe, Kathleen Turner

Running time 95 minutes

CRIMES OF PASSION (Released October 19, 1984)

Directed by Ken Russell

Produced by Barry Sandler, Larry A. Thompson

Written by Barry Sandler

Starring Kathleen Turner, Anthony Perkins, John Laughlin, Annie Potts

Running time 107 minutes

Awards for Kathleen: Los Angeles Film Critics Association Award for Best
Actress (also for Romancing the Stone) (Won), Sant Jordi Best Foreign Actress
Award (Won)

PRIZZI'S HONOR (Released June 13, 1985)

Directed by John Huston

Produced by John Foreman

Written by Richard Condon, Janet Roach

Starring Jack Nicholson, Kathleen Turner, Robert Loggia, Anjelica Huston, William
Hickey

Running time 130 minutes

Awards for Kathleen: Golden Globe Award for Best Actress—Motion Picture
Musical or Comedy (Won), People's Choice Award Favorite Actress in a
Motion Picture (Nominated), Sant Jordi Best Foreign Actress Award (Won)

THE JEWEL OF THE NILE (Released December 11, 1985)

Directed by Lewis Teague

Produced by Michael Douglas

Written by Mark Rosenthal, Lawrence Konner
Starring Michael Douglas, Kathleen Turner, Danny DeVito

Running time 107 mins

PEGGY SUE GOT MARRIED (Released October 10, 1986)

Directed by Francis Ford Coppola

Produced by Paul R. Gurian

Written by Jerry Leichtling, Arlene Sarner

Starring Kathleen Turner, Nicolas Cage, Don Murray, Barbara Harris, Joan Allen, Jim Carrey, Maureen O'Sullivan, Sofia Coppola

Running time 104 min

Awards for Kathleen: National Board of Review Award for Best Actress (Won), National Society of Film Critics Award for Best Actress (Runner-Up), New York Film Critics Circle Award for Best Actress (Runner-Up), Academy Award for Best Actress (Nominated), Golden Globe Award for Best Actress—Motion Picture Musical or Comedy (Nominated), Saturn Award for Best Actress (Nominated), People's Choice Award Favorite Actress in a Motion Picture (Nominated), Sant Jordi Best Foreign Actress Award (Nominated)

JULIA AND JULIA (Released February 5, 1988)

Directed by Peter Del Monte

Produced by Radiotelevisione Italiana

Written by Peter Del Monte, Silvia Napolitano, Sandro Petraglia

Starring Kathleen Turner, Gabriel Byrne, Sting

Running time 97 minutes

Awards for Kathleen: Sant Jordi Best Foreign Actress Award (Nominated)

SWITCHING CHANNELS (Released March 4, 1988)

Directed by Ted Kotcheff

Produced by Martin Ransohoff

Written by Jonathan Reynolds

Based on the play The Front Page by Ben Hecht and Charles MacArthur

Starring Kathleen Turner, Burt Reynolds, Christopher Reeve

Running time 105 minutes

WHO FRAMED ROGER RABBIT (Released June 22, 1988)

Directed by Robert Zemeckis

Produced by Frank Marshall, Robert Watts

Written by Jeffrey Price, Peter S. Seaman

Based on the novel Who Censored Roger Rabbit? By Gary K. Wolf

Starring Bob Hoskins, Christopher Lloyd, Charles Fleischer, Kathleen Turner, Joanna Cassidy

Running time 104 minutes

THE ACCIDENTAL TOURIST (Released December 23, 1988)

Directed by Lawrence Kasdan

Written by Frank Galati, Lawrence Kasdan

Based on the novel The Accidental Tourist by Anne Tyler

Starring William Hurt, Kathleen Turner, Geena Davis, Amy Wright, Bill Pullman, David Ogden Stiers, Ed Begley, Jr.

Running time 121 minutes

THE WAR OF THE ROSES (Released December 8, 1989)

Directed by Danny DeVito

Produced by James L. Brooks, Arnon Milchan

Screenplay by Michael J. Leeson

Based on the novel The War of the Roses by Warren Adler

Starring Michael Douglas, Kathleen Turner, Danny DeVito

Running time 116 minutes

Awards for Kathleen: Golden Globe Award for Best Actress—Motion Picture Musical or Comedy (Nominated), David di Donatello Award for Best Foreign Actress (Nominated), Hasty Pudding Theatricals Woman of the Year Award (Won), People's Choice Award Favorite Actress in a Motion Picture (Nominated)

V.I. WARSHAWSKI (Released July 26, 1991)

Directed by Jeff Kanew

Produced by Penney Finkelman Cox, Jeffrey Lurie

Written by Edward Taylor, David Aaron Cohen, Nick Thiel

Based on the novel Deadlock by Sara Paretsky

Starring Kathleen Turner, Jay O. Sanders, Charles Durning

Running time 89 minutes

NAKED IN NEW YORK (Released April 13, 1994)

Directed by Daniel Algrant

Produced by Frederick Zollo, Martin Scorsese

Written by Daniel Algrant, John Warren

Starring Eric Stoltz, Mary-Louise Parker, Kathleen Turner, Ralph Macchio, Jill Clayburgh, Tony Curtis, Timothy Dalton

Running time 91 minutes

UNDERCOVER BLUES (Released September 10, 1993)

Directed by Herbert Ross

Produced by Mike Lobell

Written by Ian Abrams

Starring Kathleen Turner, Dennis Quaid, Stanley Tucci, Viola Davis

Running time 89 minutes

HOUSE OF CARDS (Released June 25, 1993)

Directed by Michael Lessac

Produced by Lianne Halfon, Wolfgang Glattes, Dale Pollock

Written by Michael Lessac, Robert Jay Litz

Starring Kathleen Turner, Tommy Lee Jones

Running time 109 minutes

Awards for Kathleen: WorldFest Houston Gold Award (Won)

SERIAL MOM (Released April 13, 1994)

Directed by John Waters

Produced by John Fiedler, Mark Tarlov

Written by John Waters

Starring Kathleen Turner, Sam Waterston, Ricki Lake, Matthew Lillard

Running time 95 minutes

Awards for Kathleen: Chlotrudis Award for Best Actress (Nominated)

MOONLIGHT AND VALENTINO (Released September 29, 1995)

Directed by David Anspaugh

Produced by Tim Bevan, Eric Fellner, Alison Owen

Written by Ellen Simon

Starring Elizabeth Perkins, Gwyneth Paltrow, Jon Bon Jovi, Kathleen Turner,
  Peter Coyote, Jeremy Sisto, Whoopi Goldberg
Running time 105 minutes

A SIMPLE WISH (Released July 11, 1997)
Directed by Michael Ritchie
Produced by Michael S. Glick, Jeff Rothberg
Written by Jeff Rothberg
Starring Martin Short, Mara Wilson, Kathleen Turner, Amanda Plummer, Ruby
  Dee, Teri Garr
Running time 89 minutes

THE REAL BLONDE (Released February 27, 1998)
Directed by Tom DiCillo
Produced by Terry McKay, Tom Rosenberg, Sigurjon Sighvatsson, Ted Tanne-
  baum, Marcus Viscidi, Meredith Zamsky, Richard S. Wright
Written by Tom DiCillo
Starring Matthew Modine, Catherine Keener, Maxwell Caulfield, Daryl Hannah,
  Bridgette Wilson, Marlo Thomas, Kathleen Turner, Elizabeth Berkley, Denis
  Leary, Steve Buscemi, Dave Chappelle, Christopher Lloyd
Running time 105 minutes

BABY GENIUSES (Released March 12, 1999)
Directed by Bob Clark
Produced by Steven Paul
Written by Steven Paul, Francisca Matos, Robert Grasmere
Starring Kathleen Turner, Peter MacNicol, Kim Cattrall, Christopher Lloyd, Ruby
  Dee, Kyle Howard
Running time 95 minutes

LOVE AND ACTION IN CHICAGO (Released May 1, 1999)
Directed by Dwayne Johnson-Cochran
Produced by David Forrest, Beau Rogers, Betsey Chasse, Danny Gold
Written by Dwayne Johnson-Cochran
Starring Courtney B. Vance, Regina King, Kathleen Turner

Running time 95 minutes

Awards for Kathleen: Video Premiere Award for Best Supporting Actress
   (Nominated)

THE VIRGIN SUICIDES (Released May 12, 2000)

Directed by Sofia Coppola

Produced by Francis Ford Coppola, Julie Costanzo, Dan Halsted, Chris Hanley
   Written by Sofia Coppola
   Based on the novel The Virgin Suicides by Jeffrey Eugenides

Starring Kathleen Turner, James Woods, Kirsten Dunst, Josh Hartnett

Running time 97 minutes

BEAUTIFUL (Released September 29, 2000)

Directed by Sally Field

Produced by John Bertolli, B.J. Rack

Written by John Bernstein

Starring Minnie Driver, Joey Lauren Adams, Kathleen Turner

Running time 112 minutes

PRINCE OF CENTRAL PARK (Released September 22, 2000)

Directed by John Leekley

Produced by Julius R. Nasso, Steven Seagal, John P. Gulino

Written by John Leekley

Based on the novel The Prince of Central Park by Evan Rhodes

Starring Kathleen Turner, Danny Aiello, Harvey Keitel, Cathy Moriarty

Running time 109 minutes

MONSTER HOUSE (Released July 21, 2006)

Directed by Gil Kenan

Produced by Jack Rapke, Steve Starkey
   Written by Dan Harmon, Rob Schrab, Pamela Pettler

Starring Kathleen Turner, Steve Buscemi, Maggie Gyllenhaal

Running time 101 minutes

MARLEY AND ME (Released December 25, 2008)

Directed by David Frankel

Produced by Gil Netter, Karen Rosenfelt

Screenplay by Scott Frank, Don Roos

Based on the book Marley & Me by John Grogan

Starring Owen Wilson, Jennifer Aniston, Eric Dane, Kathleen Turner, and Alan Arkin

Running time 121 minutes

THE PERFECT FAMILY (Released April 24, 2011)

Directed by Anne Renton

Produced by Jennifer Dubin, Cora Olson

Written by Paula Goldberg, Claire V. Riley

Starring Kathleen Turner, Emily Deschanel, Jason Ritter, and Richard
Chamberlain

Running time 84 minutes

NURSE (Released February 7, 2014)

Directed by Douglas Aarniokoski

Produced by Mark Bienstock

Written by Douglas Aarniokoski and David Loughery

Starring Paz de la Huerta, Katrina Bowden, Corbin Bleu, Martin Donovan,
Kathleen Turner and Judd Nelson

Running time 84 minutes

DUMB AND DUMBER TO (Released November 14, 2014)

Directed by Bobby Farrelly and Peter Farrelly

Produced by Charles B. Wessler, Riza Aziz, Joey McFarland, and Bradley Thomas

Written by Peter Farrelly, Bobby Farrelly, Sean Anders, John Morris, Bennett Yel-
lin, and Mike Cerrone

Starring Jim Carrey, Jeff Daniels, Laurie Holden, and Kathleen Turner

Running time 109 minutes

EMILY AND TIM (Released August 29, 2015)

Directed by Eric Weber

Produced by Josh Sugarman and Eric Weber

Written by Eric Weber

Starring Olympia Dukakis, Andre Braugher, Kal Penn

Narrated by Kathleen Turner

Running time 87 minutes

ANOTHER KIND OF WEDDING (Released 2017)

Directed by Pat Kiely

Produced by Pat Kiely, Philip Svoboda, Robert Vroom, and Arnie Zipursky

Written by Pat Kiely

Starring Kathleen Turner, Jessica Pare, Frances Fisher, and Wallace Shawn

Running time 90 minutes

LIFETIME ACHIEVEMENT AWARDS

Savannah Film and Video Festival (2004)

Provincetown International Film Festival (2007)

International Antalya Film Festival (2015)

Montclair Film Festival (2016)

SELECTED TELEVISION AND RADIO CREDITS

THE DOCTORS (1978–1979)

NBC

Created by Orvin Tovrov

Starring David O'Brien, Larry Weber, and Nancy Pinkerton, Kathleen Turner as
Nola Aldrich

SATURDAY NIGHT LIVE

NBC

Created by Lorne Michaels

Guest Host Kathleen Turner with musical guest John Waite (January 12, 1985)

Guest Host Kathleen Turner with musical guest Billy Joel (October 21, 1989)

SESAME STREET (1989)

PBS

Created by Joan Ganz Cooney, Lloyd Morrisett

Guest star Kathleen Turner

Episode: "06504"

DEADLOCK (1991)

BBC Radio

By Sara Paretsky

Adapted by Michelene Wandor

Directed by Janet Whitaker

Kathleen Turner as VI Warshawski

KILLING ORDERS (1991)
BBC Radio
By Sara Paretsky
Adapted by Michelene Wandor
Directed by Janet Whitaker
Kathleen Turner as VI Warshawski

THE SIMPSONS (1994)
FOX
Created by Matt Groening
Developed by James L. Brooks
Kathleen Turner as Stacy Lavelle
episode: "Lisa vs. Malibu Stacy"

LESLIE'S FOLLY (1994)
Showtime
Directed by Kathleen Turner
Written by Lynn Mamet
Starring Anne Archer, Charles Durning, and Mary Kay Place
(Made-for-television movie)

FRIENDS AT LAST (1995)
CBS
Directed by John David Coles
Written by Susan Sandler
Starring Kathleen Turner, Colm Feore, and Julie Khaner
(Made-for-television movie)

LEGALESE (1998)
TNT
Directed by Glenn Jordan
Written by Billy Ray
Starring Kathleen Turner, James Garner, Edward Kerr, and Gina Gershon
(Made-for-television movie)

CINDERELLA (2000)

Channel 4

Directed by Beeban Kidron

Written by Nick Dear

Starring Kathleen Turner, Jane Birkin, and David Warner

(Made-for-television movie)

KING OF THE HILL (2000)

FOX

Created by Mike Judge, Greg Daniels

Kathleen Turner as Miss Liz Strickland (3 episodes)

Episodes: "Rodeo Days," "Hanky Panky," "High Anxiety"

FRIENDS (2001)

NBC

Created by David Crane, Marta Kauffman

Kathleen Turner as Charles Bing

Episodes: "The One with Chandler's Dad," "The One with Monica and Chandler's
    Wedding" Parts 1 & 2

LAW AND ORDER (2006)

NBC

Created by Dick Wolf

Kathleen Turner as Rebecca Shane

Episode: "Magnet"

NIP/TUCK (2006)

FX

Created by Ryan Murphy

Kathleen Turner as Cindy Plumb

Episode: "Cindy Plumb"

CALIFORNICATION (2009)

Showtime

Created by Tom Kapinos

Kathleen Turner as Sue Collini

Episodes: "Wish You Were Here," "The Land of Rape and Honey," "Verities & Balderdash," "Zoso," "Slow Happy Boys," "Glass Houses," "So Here's the Thing. . . . ," "Mr. Bad Example," "Dogtown," "Mia Culpa"

HOLLYWOOD ENDINGS (2014)
BBC Radio

Written by Ron Hutchinson

Directed by Eoin O'Callaghan

Starring Kathleen Turner, Nathan Osgood, and Laurel Lefkow

A CHRISTMAS CAROL (2015)
WNYC Radio

By Charles Dickens

Adapted by Arthur Yorinks

Starring Kathleen Turner, John Schaefer, Jeff Spurgeon, and Julian Fleisher

Directed by Elliott Forrest

THE PATH (2016–2017)
Hulu

Created by Jessica Goldberg

Kathleen Turner as Brenda Roberts

Episodes: "A Homecoming," "Return"

ABOUT THE AUTHORS

DUSTIN MORROW

Dustin Morrow is an award-winning filmmaker, author, programmer and educator. As a media artist, his works frequently explore the intersections of music and the moving image; the actor-director relationship; genre filmmaking; and issues of and relationships between landscape/space and personal, communal and cultural identities. He was born and raised in western Illinois, and received his MFA in Cinema from the University of Iowa. He taught media production at Temple University in Philadelphia for seven years, and is currently a professor at Portland State University in Portland, Oregon, where he teaches courses in digital cinema production and film studies.

Professor Morrow's short and feature films have won numerous awards and been shown in major film festivals and other venues in more than thirty countries around the world. He has written extensively about film and pop culture for a host of online and print publications. Before re-entering academia, Morrow was an editor and director of short-form projects and series television in Los Angeles, working with such clients as MTV and the Discovery Channel, and such filmmakers as Spike Jonze, Michael Apted, Kathy Bates, Denzel Washington and Steven Soderbergh. He continues to operate his own independent production company, Little Swan Pictures, for which recent projects have taken him as far away as the Aleutian Sea.

Morrow's projects cross many media platforms. Among his recent works are a contemporary musical feature film; a feature film thriller about the conflict in Northern Ireland; an anthology of short international documentary videos; a television production of a classic opera; a photo essay that's been exhibited in both group and solo gallery shows; several short films exploring psychogeography; and a cinema discussion forum produced as both a web series and a television series. Focal Press, the nation's largest imprint for media-related texts, published his textbook *Producing for TV and New Media*. Professor Morrow has received grants for his work totaling more than half a million dollars.

Professor Morrow was the Director of the Greenfield Youth Film Festival, one of the largest youth-centered film education programs in the country, for three years. Presently he is the founding Director of the Portland Music Video Festival, one of the only festivals in the world dedicated exclusively to the art and craft of music videos. He often programs for independent movie theaters, and is an in-demand speaker at conferences and workshops nationwide about issues related to film, music and new media production. In 2013 he was a TED speaker.

A passionate advocate of study abroad and study away education, Professor Morrow has during his summers run programs in London, Dublin, and New York, as well as taught documentary filmmaking in Northern Ireland. At Temple University, he co-created a new degree program in Globalization and Intercultural Communication. Morrow is also an active promoter of art therapy programs, and sat on the Board of Directors of the Arts and the Quality of Life Research Center, the internationally prominent Philadelphia-based art therapy advocacy organization. Learn more about Professor Morrow at his website, www. dustinmorrow.com.

KACEY MORROW (ILLUSTRATIONS)

Kacey Morrow is an award-winning designer and professor in the Department of Design at Western Washington University in Bellingham, Washington. She teaches courses in motion graphics, digital video, and web and interaction design. Her acclaimed video work has appeared in numerous film festivals and exhibitions nationwide, including the Atlanta Film Festival and the Seattle International Film Festival. She is the co-author of the Focal Press textbook *Producing for TV and New Media*. Prior to her career as an educator, Professor Morrow was a professional motion, print, and multimedia designer at several production houses in Chicago. Learn more about Professor Morrow at her website, www.kaceymorrow.com.

SOURCES

Body Heat

Screenplay by Lawrence Kasdan

The Man with Two Brains

Screenplay by Carl Reiner, Steve Martin and George Gipe

Prizzi's Honor

Screenplay by Richard Condon and Janet Roach

Romancing the Stone

Screenplay by Diane Thomas

Serial Mom

Screenplay by John Waters

The War of the Roses

Screenplay by Michael Leeson

Who Framed Roger Rabbit

Screenplay by Jeffrey Price and Peter S. Seaman

Based on the novel *Who Censored Roger Rabbit?* by Gary K. Wolf

ACKNOWLEDGMENTS

There are a number of people I should acknowledge who assisted in the creation of this book. I owe a great debt to all of them.

Thank you to my best girl, Lisa Molinelli, for acting as a sounding board during the long construction of this book, and for loaning me her peerless editorial talents when I reworked it and reworked it, and then reworked it some more. I couldn't have completed this project without her.

Thank you to my sister Kacey for contributing her illustrations to this text. She is an astonishing talent and an inspiration to me creatively and in every other aspect of my life.

It's not easy to grow up as a film buff in rural western Illinois, where the nearest movie theater and the nearest Blockbuster Video were half an hour away from my childhood home. But my parents used to take their little cinephile to the movies nearly every single weekend. Thank you to Robert and Sandra Morrow, for supporting my love of film and the arts in a community where few kids express such interests, and for supporting every other endeavor I've since undertaken. If I've gotten anywhere in life, it's because of them.

Thank you to Kathleen's management team for helping me connect with Kathleen and for sharing my ideas.

Thank you to my research assistants and transcribers, Donna Ferretti and Emily Diego, for all of their hard work and commitment to the project.

Thank you to my agent Sam Fleishman and to my editor Mark Gompertz for their ideas, their support, and their unwavering dedication to bringing this book to the masses.

This book was supported in part by a grant from Portland State University. Thank you to all of my colleagues, past and present, for their support.

And finally, thank you to Kathleen, for telling the stories she tells, and sharing the gifts of her talents. I've seen *Romancing the Stone* well over a hundred times, and I will watch it a hundred more. Thank you to Kathleen for the memories she's given to me, and for the ones still to come.

"Joanie, you're now a world-class hopeless romantic."

"No, hope*ful*. A hope*ful* romantic."

Romancing the Stone, by Diane Thomas

The Abusing Family

Revised
Edition